Factional Politics in Post-Khomeini Iran

Modern Intellectual and Political History of the Middle East

Mehrzad Boroujerdi, *Series Editor*

Other titles in Modern Intellectual and Political History of the Middle East

Cultural Schizophrenia: Islamic Societies Confronting the West
Daryush Shayegan; John Howe, trans.

Freedom, Modernity, and Islam: Toward a Creative Synthesis
Richard K. Khuri

Iranian Intellectuals and the West: The Tormented Triumph of Nativism
Mehrzad Boroujerdi

The Story of the Daughters of Quchan: Gender and National Memory in Iranian History
Afsaneh Najmabadi

God and Juggernaut: Iran's Intellectual Encounter with Modernity
Farzin Vahdat

FACTIONAL POLITICS
IN POST-KHOMEINI
IRAN

 Mehdi Moslem

SYRACUSE UNIVERSITY PRESS

First Edition 2002
02 03 04 05 06 07   6 5 4 3 2 1

The paper used in this publication meets the minimum requirements of
American National Standard for Information Sciences—Permanence of
Paper for Printed Library Materials, ANSI Z39.48–1984.∞™

Library of Congress Cataloging-in-Publication Data

Moslem, Mehdi.
Factional politics in post-Khomeini Iran / Mehdi Moslem.—1st ed.
p. cm.—(Modern intellectual and political history of the
Middle East
Includes bibliographical references and index.
ISBN 0-8156-2978-8
1. Iran—Politics and government—1979–1997. 2. Iran—Politics and
government—1997– 3. Islam and politics—Iran. I. Title. II. Series.
DS318.825.M67 2002
320.955—dc21
2002008073

Manufactured in the United States of America

To the memory of my father and
the love of my mother

Mehdi Moslem has a B.A. in politics from Portland State University, an M.A. in Middle East Studies from the Jackson School of International Studies of the University of Washington, and a Ph.D. in politics from Oxford University's Oriental Institute. He is Research Associate at Oxford University's Oriental Institute and has written numerous journal articles on postrevolutionary Iran.

Contents

Acknowledgments

The insights and comments of many individuals and scholars both in England and Iran, who read parts or all of this work and commented on different aspects of the book, proved invaluable. Among them were: James Piscatori, Homa Katouzian, Moncef Khadder, Derek Hopwood, Hadi Semati, Majid Tafreshi, Naser Hadian, Venessa Martin, Jackline Ismael, Eric Knudsen, Mohsen Milani, and Mehrzad Boroujerdi.

◆　　◆　　◆

Four people, however, deserve special recognition. The intelligent observations of Reza Sheikholeslami on the nature of politics of Islam helped me to put together the puzzle of Iranian state. I will be indebted to Eric Hooglund and Ali Rahnema indefinitely. Eric read the entire manuscript—some chapters more than once!—devotedly and patiently. His invaluable and studious suggestions about the content of each chapter, illustrated both his exceptional knowledge of Iran and his love for its people. Ali remained, diligently and generously, my mental springboard for more than two years when I was trying to make sense of the perplexing nature of Iranian factions. Ali's own work on post-revolutionary Iran was undoubtedly a major impetus for me to take up the writing of this book. Finally, the patience and understanding of my wife Jahan-Dokht Nikoopour when I was struggling with this book was exemplary. She was a tower of strength and support to me.

Abbreviations

Abbreviation	Full	Factional Affiliation
Ansar	Ansar-e Hizbollah (The Patrons of Hizbollah)	Neo-Fundamentalists
IRP	Islamic Republic Party	Left and Conservative Right
IRCG	Islamic Republic Guards Corps	Conservative Right
Kargozaran	Kargozaran-e Sazandegi (The Servers of Constructiveness)	Modern Right
KII	Komiteh-ye Inqelab-e Islami (The Committee of the Islamic Revolution)	Left
JMHEQ	Jame'eh-ye Modarresin-e Howzeh-ye Elmiyeh Qom (The Society of Qom Seminary Teachers)	Conservative Right
JRM	Jame'eh-ye Rouhaniyat-e Mobarez (The Society of Combatant Clergy)	Conservative Right
Hamsu	Tashakkolha-ye Hamsu (JRM's associated organizations)	Conservative Right
JI	Jumhuri-ye Islami (*The Islamic Republic* daily newspaper)	Conservative
MII	Mojahedin-e Inqelab-e Islami (The Crusaders of the Islamic Revolution)	Left
Mo'talefeh	Jam'iyat-e Mo'talefeh-ye Islami (The Allied Islamic Society)	Conservative Right
MRM	Majma'-e Rouhaniyun-e Mobarez (The Association of Combatant Clergy)	Left
Sepah	Sepah e Pasdaran (IRGC)	Conservative Right
PVPV	Propagation of Virtue and Prohibition of Vice (Amr-e be Ma'ruf va Nahy-e az Monkar)	
Tahkim	Daftar-e Tahkim-e Vahdat (The Office of Strengthening of Unity)	Left

Abbreviation	Full	Factional Affiliation
Motlaqeh	Velayat-e Motlaqeh-ye Faqih (The Absolute Rule of the Jurisconsult)	
MM	Mozakerat-e Majlis (Majlis Debates)	
Khobregan	Majlis-e Khobregan (The Assembly of the Experts)	Conservative Right
Nehad(s)	Nehadha-ye Inqelabi (Revolutionary Bodies)	
JAM	Jame'eh-ye Islami-ye Mohandesin (Society of Islamic Engineers)	Conservative Right

Factional Politics in Post-Khomeini Iran

Introduction

For the outside world, perhaps the most intriguing aspect of Iranian politics since the landslide victory of President Mohammad Khatami in May 1997 have been the conflicting official statements emanating from the Islamic Republic of Iran. One line, best exemplified by Khatami and his followers, preaches pragmatism, toleration, and temperance. Khatami has expressed regret for Iran's past extremism and declared Iran's readiness to comply with international norms based on mutual respect for member states, regardless of their ideologies. Gone is the traditional rhetoric of depicting international affairs as being dictated by hegemonic powers such as the "Great Satan," the United States. Significantly, Khatami has announced Iran's readiness to gradually normalize ties with the American government. Instead of loathing the amoral, secular West, the president praised the ideological foundations of Western democracies. Above all, Khatami implicitly challenged the "Clash of Civilizations" scenario[1] when he declared that Islam and modernity were not diametrically opposed to each other but that "true" Islam in fact embraced Western liberal-democratic sentiments such as human rights, individual freedom, civil society, and freedom of expression.[2] In the same spirit, the Iranian foreign ministry has declared that the government would not carry out Ayatollah Ruhollah Khomeini's February 1988 death *fatwa* (religious ruling) sanctioning the killing of British author Salman Rushdie, whose novel *Satanic Verses* contained passages about the Prophet Mohammad and his wives that pious Muslims considered obscene and offensive.

Another line coming out of Iran is less compromising, more zealous, and indeed more familiar. Ayatollah Ali Khamenehi, Khomeini's successor, has maintained that Iran's struggle against the world's "number one despot" must continue, as the country's animosity towards the American government was

1

eternal.[3] Other influential figures have opposed Khatami's brand of "liberalism," arguing that it undermines the morality of the Iranian state and threatens its Islamic virtue. According to the former head of the Iranian judiciary, Ayatollah Mohammad Yazdi, "Islam does not accept absolute freedom, and the activities of both the private and public spheres therefore must conform to the limits set by Islamic principles."[4] To make matters more perplexing, there are a host of interpretations besides these of the various policies of the regime. These contrasting positions highlight the predicament facing the Islamic Republic of Iran today: more than twenty years after the revolution, the very essence, objectives, and the modus operandi of the regime are still being contested and debated by the leadership.

Such ideological divisions among the Iranian elite date back to the early days of the revolution, when Khomeini's disciples disagreed on some key issues and policies. While Khomeini was alive, any ideological tension resulting from these differences was, by and large, successfully diffused through his timely and commanding interventions. Since the ayatollah's death in June 1989, however, these differences have both solidified and intensified to the extent that ideological discord among the governing elite has become the most salient feature of politics in the Islamic Republic. As a result, the Iranian polity is composed of ideological blocs with each bloc sharing and advancing its own particular interpretation of issues and policies. Today, these blocs are known as "factions" who are engaged in a struggle for more power and influence recognized as factional politics or factionalism. Factions in Iran comprise groups, organizations, and classes, clergy as well as nonclergy, who supported Khomeini, the revolution of 1979, and the idea of Islamic state, but who disagree on the nature of the theocracy's political system and its policies in different spheres. Factional politics signify the ongoing "politicking" among various factions, where each group strives to promote and advance its own interpretation of policies.

This book is a systematic study of the nature of factional politics in the Islamic Republic since the death of Khomeini. At the heart of this work are the following questions: in their effort to gain and exercise more influence, how do factions push through their views regarding various policies of the regime? What are the roots of these ideological disputes? And, finally, how has factionalism affected politics and the political process of the postrevolutionary regime as a whole?

Factional Politics in Postrevolutionary Iran:
Preliminary Observations

Lenin said in the midst of the Russian Revolution of 1917, "The basic question of every revolution is that of state power."[5] This remark foreshadows a phenomenon present in most modern revolutions: the power struggle that takes place among revolutionaries after the victory of the revolution. For instance, what united various revolutionary forces in the Russian and Chinese revolutions was their common desire to topple the *ancien régime*. Once this goal was accomplished, however, they disagreed on the nature, principles, and direction of the postrevolutionary regime.[6] In the case of Iran, too, the anti-shah forces, which included secularists, religious nationalists, Marxists, and Islamic Marxists, all wished for the downfall of the Pahlavi monarchy.[7] However, each group envisioned a particular form of postrevolutionary regime. These ideological differences ultimately led to open conflict, with the proponents of Khomeini's brand of Islamic theocracy, the *velayat-e faqih* (the rule of the jurisconsult), eventually subduing and pacifying all other contenders by 1981.

While the struggle for power among revolutionary forces during and immediately following the Iranian revolution was comparable to the intragroup conflicts that took place in Russia and China, the Iranian case has been different in one important aspect. Although there were some differences of opinion with regard to policies of the nascent postrevolutionary regimes within the leadership in the Soviet Union and China,[8] these differences remained by and large minor in both Russia's and China's postrevolutionary regimes. Once the Bolsheviks in Russia and the Communists in China had consolidated power, their leaderships were successful in creating a powerful, centralized, and, most importantly, ideologically coherent states.[9] This has not been the case in Iran. In contrast to the Russian and the Chinese experiences, the ideological differences and bickering among pro-Khomeini forces have progressively increased rather than abating throughout the postrevolutionary years. Pivotal to Iranian factional politics has been "doctrinarism." Each faction claims its own interpretation of a religiously sanctioned Islamic state is an authentic and genuine model. Support for one reading or another of the Islamic state serves many purposes: it distinguishes one faction from another, provides an opportunity to discredit other factions' views while justifying one's own often abstract and ideological positions on issues, and it clouds the real political motives of each faction.

Here it must be asked why the factions propose such divergent views of the principle features of the Islamic Republic. Is there not a guideline or a specific model of an Islamic state and its governing principles? The answer is no. Although Khomeini's concept of the Islamic government emphasized the Islamicity of the postrevolutionary regime, he did not provide specific guidelines about what this Islamicity meant in terms of governing principles or particular policies in different spheres of government. Moreover, by repeatedly oscillating and changing his views on major issues during the ten years of his leadership, Khomeini offered differing and at times conflicting readings on what constituted a "true" Islamic republic. As one MP observed, these maneuvers were aimed at overcoming ideological tensions, maintaining the factional balance of power and preserving the Islamic system as a whole:

> In all stages and through different means the Imam tried to keep the wings [factions] in balance and use the executive, ideological, populist or political power and efficacy of each wing for the benefit of the state. He tried to preserve this balance in order to keep one wing from becoming too powerful, and every time he felt that one was aiming to monopolize power he would put his weight behind others to keep the [balance of] power intact.[10]

Although he had brought together the republic in times of crisis, Khomeini's interventions also helped to fuel the competitive nature of Iranian politics by allowing diverse interpretations of his decrees and views, thus crystallizing ideological orientation among the factions in the country. Consequently, Khomeini not only failed to sketch a clear portrait of the government of God, but his changing pronouncements created additional confusion. Capitalizing on this ambiguity, his supporters since 1989 have been constructing their own rendition of the Islamic state and its policies in the political, economic, sociocultural, and foreign policy spheres. Each faction has been able to refer to enough of Khomeini's views and declarations to justify its own model of an Islamic state. Because Khomeini's words and actions don't provide a blueprint, the factions have resorted to other sources such as the Iranian constitution, the *fiqh* (Islamic jurisprudence), and the views of other Islamic ideologues and/or activists to justify their version of the genuine prototype of an Islamic republic. Consequently, although rhetorically united under the mantle of Islam, factions in post-Khomeini Iran are ideologically quite distinct.[11]

One faction adheres to principles espoused by most Third World leftist revolutionary forces: anti-imperialism, the export of revolution, and state-sponsored redistributive-egalitarian[12] economic policies. This faction, essentially for lack of a better word, is called the "left" or the "radicals" in Iran.[13] Another faction holds "conservative"[14] and nonrevolutionary views. This faction believes in the sanctity of private property, a minimalist state, a free market economy, and the strict implementation of Shari'a (Islamic law) in sociocultural life. Because of its adherence to a highly orthodox interpretation of the Shari'a and its conservative views on economic and sociocultural questions, this faction is recognized as the "traditional right." The "modern right" faction is made up mostly of state technocrats whose main objective is politico-economic modernization of the Islamic Republic along the path of developing countries such as the East Asian Tigers as well as maintaining liberal sociocultural views. They are labeled "modern" because of their views in the economic sphere and "right" because of their belief in a free market economy. Finally, the neo-fundamentalist faction is comprised of young, highly religious, zealous individuals whose self-proclaimed "holy duty" is to prevent the infiltration of Western cultural norms into the country as well as fighting immorality in the Islamic Republic.

This lack of ideological cohesion and clear direction has adversely affected Iran in all areas of policy making. For instance, divergent views of the necessary characteristics of an Islamic economy have prevented the regime from constructing or pursuing a specific economic policy. Notwithstanding the fact that the regime has helped the needy and the poor to some extent, the creation of an Islamic economic system, designed to fulfill the constitutional aim of "laying the foundations of a correct and just economy on the basis of Islamic rules" (preamble), still remains illusive. In reality, economic policies and programs are often based on ad hoc policies, annual budget constraints, and spontaneous and improvisational efforts. The result, by the admission of the leadership itself, is that no specific model of Islamic economy has been established.[15] Sociocultural policies under the Islamic Republic are no more ordered and are another casualty of factional dispute. Factions aligned with the traditional right and the neo-fundamentalists advocate strict implementation of the words of the Qoran and the Prophet in this sphere while the left and modern right believe in more tolerant policies that take into consideration the realities of contemporary life. As a result, policy making is by-product of extended maneuvering and politicking, and the final version of any particular policy depends largely upon which faction controls the responsible organization or ministry. In short, for most of its postrevolutionary era, Iran has experienced systemic and ideological disarray as there are multiple centers of power and numerous sources of authority.[16]

Understanding Factional Politics in Iran: The Need to Bring the State In[17]

Although the notion of factionalism is embedded in most substantial works on post-Khomeini Iran, the subject has yet to receive the attention it deserves. Except for one book, works that focus on factional politics in post-Khomeini Iran are limited to a handful of articles in journals. The articles are generally descriptive accounts of the views of the factions, discussing who among the elite belongs to what faction. Susan Siavoshi's "Factionalism and Iranian Politics: The Post-Khomeini Experience," for example, is a description of the ideological inclination of various factions, their positions vis-à-vis the centers of power, and the growing conflict between the traditionalists and the modern right after the death of Khomeini.[18] Nader Entessar's "Factional Politics in Post-Khomeini Iran: Domestic and Foreign Policy Implications" also offers an overall view of the factions and deals with how the existence of factions prevents the Islamic Republic from forming coherent domestic and foreign policies.[19] The only major work that discusses factionalism beyond describing the positions held by the individual groups was published in 1996 under the title of *Parliamentary Politics in Revolutionary Iran; the Institutionalization of Factional Politics,* by Bahman Baktiari.[20] Baktiari illustrates how various factions challenge each other's views and push through their interpretations of various policies in the parliament (the Majlis). As the title indicates, however, this book does not place factionalism at the center of its analysis. Rather, it is an analysis of parliamentary politics in postrevolutionary Iran and examines the dynamics of politics on different levels, treating factional politics as one of its dimensions.

Although informative, the first drawback of the literature on Iranian factional politics is its descriptive and nonanalytical nature. In spite of this focus, the conventional literature lacks a clear and systematic definition of factions, and none of the cited publications provides a working definition of factions: they are simply categorized as different groups within the elite who share similar views on issues. The historical roots, makeup, and reasons for the emergence of factions are largely ignored. Moreover, the existing literature on factionalism deals with this topic only until 1994. Factional politics, and indeed the entire political landscape in Iran, have witnessed many changes since 1994, including shifts and rifts in factional alliances and in the balance of power: changes that often challenged previous assumptions about factionalism and factions' views. An important contribution of this work is the its coverage of factional politics after 1994.

The third limitation, which is related to the second, is that the conventional literature on factionalism neglects the role, influence, and impact of Iranian society in the ideological controversy among the elite. Contrary to what the existing works implicitly suggest, factional politics in Iran are not restricted only to the elite; ideological discord at the top has permeated Iranian society as well. Various segments of Iranian society have taken sides in the ongoing dispute among the clerical elite and are inclined to support, in a variety of ways, one faction or another. The traditional Iranian bourgeoisie, the powerful merchants of bazaars, ultra-conservative ulama, and the religiously orthodox segments of the population are believed to support the traditional right faction. University students and Islamic intellectuals supported Rafsanjani when he was president (1989–97) and now are backing the left and Khatami. A prime example of how society in Iran has had an impact on factionalism was the election of the reform-minded Khatami to the presidency despite the wishes of the conservative "establishment." It emphasized that the role of society in Iranian politics is indeed quite significant because, although the regime has installed systemic filters to prevent "unfit" elements from running for office,[21] all of the officials of the regime, including the leader himself, are either directly or indirectly elected by popular vote for those who survive the institutional filters. To overlook the views, interests, and participation of Iranian society is to ignore an important component of both the political process and, through this, factional politics in Iran. Finally and most critically of all, the standard accounts of factionalism lack theoretical and analytical rigor, leaving unanswered fundamental questions about politics, the political system, and the political process of the Islamic Republic.

Regarding this last point, there are two interrelated theoretical questions that can be raised within the current mode of analysis of factional politics in Iran. First, the existing literature neglects to explain clearly how and why various factions are able to force through their preferences and promote their views within the regime despite the existence of other factions who want to do the same thing. Such capabilities require a tremendous amount of sociopolitical power, authority, and legitimacy. Indeed, except for Khomeini, whose power, authority, legitimacy, and most importantly charisma transcended all convictions, institutions, and laws, no one person or group in postrevolutionary Iran has possessed enough power and popularity to determine the course of events in Iran with total disregard for formal procedures.[22] My second "theoretical" critique of the conventional literature, which relates to the main premise of this work, is that current publications fail to link factional politics to the Iranian political system as a whole. Such linkage is imperative for one simple yet fundamental reason. If factionalism entails the act of politicking by various factions, then the term must be placed in a wider political context.[23] The point here is that if political power in all contemporary societies is chiefly exercised through the institutions of the most cardinal of all actors in society, the state, then what is the role of the Iranian state in the midst of these factional disputes and power struggles? In other words, if one were to pose one question that would entail putting factional politics into a proper theoretical and systematic perspective, hoping to shed some light on the current political embolism of the Islamic Republic, it would be: what role does the state play in factionalism?

To sum up, the current literature on factional politics oversimplifies the puzzle of factionalism and the maze of politics and the political process in the Islamic Republic. By themselves, the existing narratives on factionalism serve only as a starting point for a more critical analysis of factional politics and the nature of the political system of the Islamic Republic of Iran. As narratives, these studies investigate factionalism in a vacuum, neglecting the institutional boundaries of the (political) power of each faction. A major shortcoming of the literature is its neglect of the institutional imperatives of the political system of the Islamic Republic, the environment within which factions jockey for more power and influence and where factionalism takes place. Therefore, for a more systematic, comprehensive, and critical analysis of the dynamics of factional politics in Iran, we must examine the arena where the struggle for power takes place, the state.

That said, the main theoretical premise of this work will be that there is a causal relationship between the nature and attributes of the Iranian state and how factions compete with each other. The Iranian state is composed of three ideological elements (dimensions), the religious, the populist, and the revolutionary. These elements are used by the factions in the construction of various political, economic, and sociocultural discourses. Each faction is able to draw upon these differing discourses to varying degrees, stressing one or another aspect of the three elements in forming its version of the "true" Islamic regime and its policies. On the other hand, the peculiar properties of the state and the manner in which power is allocated among its institutions allow for factions to challenge the predominance of each other. As a regime based on religious values, populist principles, and revolutionary doctrine, the state in the Islamic Republic is comprised of institutions that both embody and fulfil all three principles. However, political power in the Islamic Republic is distributed unequally in a hierarchical and preferential way among state institutions, so some institutions have more authority. By ignoring the principles of separation of power and equality before the law, the Iranian constitution enables the more powerful institutions to legally override the decisions and policies of what it considers to be institutions of secondary importance within the state hierarchy. Consequently, the various factions in the political system in Iran can manipulate this uneven distribution of power among state institutions to compete for stronger position.

In other words, while factions express their differences and challenge each other's views on an ideological plane, the struggle for power among them is conducted through institutional battles. To support this claim, the focus of this book is the illustration of a common "mode" of factional contest, the use and manipulation of state institutions and their unique properties. By discussing numerous incidents of factionalism in various realms (political, sociocultural, economic, and foreign policy making), a theme will emerge: regardless of their ideological inclinations, factions rely on the same methods to compete and promote their interests and views. Focusing on these incidents will bring out the recurring patterns of factionalism in the Islamic Republic and show that rather than being an ad hoc phenomenon, factional politics in Iran is, by and large, patterned and predictable.

Although the views and ideological dispositions of factions are discussed at length, the primary focus of the discussion that follows is not on the factions themselves but their "politicking." Additionally, because most cases of factionalism in one sphere are related to incidents in another sphere, a comprehensive analysis of factional politics in Iran can only be constructed by discussing the power struggle among factions across contexts rather than limiting the discussion to any particular area of conflict. Individual policies will not be examined independently of others but will be cited as evidence of how factions use their institutional power to challenge one another.

Sources

As the secondary literature on post–1989 factionalism is insubstantial, this work has used primary Persian sources such as daily newspapers, books, Iranian journals, and Majlis debates in addition to personal interviews with government officials in Iran, including members of various factions. Most of these officials, however, requested anonymity. The Persian periodicals are *Abrar, Akhbar, Arzeshha, Asr-e Ma, Azad, Bahar, Bahman, Bayan, Ettela'at, Hamshahri, Iran, Iran-e Farda, Jahan-e Islam, JAM, Jahan-e Islam, Jomhuri-ye Islami (JI), Kar va Kargar, Keyhan, Keyhan-e Havai, Kian, Khordad, Komiteh, Mobin, Neshat, Neyestan, Payam-e Daneshju, Payam-e Imruz, Payame Inqelab, Rah-e No, Resalat, Salam, Shalamche, Shoma, Sobh, Sobh-e Imruz, Tehran Times,* and *Tus.* Data hitherto either unpublished or not readily available to the general public is also used. This includes manuscripts, pamphlets, memoirs, and confidential newsletters of various factions.

CHAPTER I

The Islamic State in Iran

From Theory to Reality

Two factors were influential in the creation of the Iranian state and its unique composition: Khomeini's vision of the nature of the postrevolutionary regime and the immediate sociopolitical realities of the country after the revolution. It took nearly three years for pro-Khomeini forces to successfully implement the notion of *velayat-e faqih,* subduing in the process other competing revolutionary forces.

By 1981, Khomeini's concept of the Islamic state, captured in his book *Hokumat-e Islami* (Islamic Government), had gone through five stages, during which Khomeini altered the principle ideas behind his notion of Islamic government in order to fit the realities of the times. Rather than dismantling the institutional legacies of the previous regime, the formation of the Islamic Republic following the victory of the revolution meant erecting and institutionalizing new religious and revolutionary organizations parallel to those of the central government. These bodies were trusted both to safeguard the Islamicity of the regime and to fulfil its revolutionary objectives. However, the preferential status given by the Iranian constitution to these postrevolutionary bodies allows them to challenge, undermine, and override the decisions made by the central government. The diffused nature of the Iranian polity has provided the institutional basis for factional infighting in post–Khomeini Iran.

◆   ◆   ◆

Stage One: The Nonrevolutionary Khomeini 1920–1964

Khomeini's idea of direct clerical rule was nearly fifty years in the making. The ayatollah began formulating his ideas on religious and political matters at the age of nineteen. As a young theology student at the Arak Religious Seminary, Khomeini was under the tutelage and influence of the conservative ayatollah Abdolkarim Haeri who refrained from directly challenging the modernizing Reza Shah. Later, Khomeini accompanied Haeri to the Qom seminary, the most powerful—but certainly nonrevolutionary—religious seminary in the country.[1] With the death of Haeri, Khomeini's radicalism was still overshadowed by the conservatism of Ayatollah Hossein Boroujerdi, the most prominent religious figure in Iran at that time.[2]

The first time Khomeini advanced an idea of a government role for the clergy was in 1942 when he wrote *Kashf-e Asrar* (Secrets Revealed) in which he contemplated a supervisory (*nezarat*) role for the clergy, a position provided for in the Iranian Constitution of 1905–6. This constitution positioned the ulama to ensure that Islamic tenets were observed in the government and that the interests of Islam were not imperiled.[3] It took some time for Khomeini to expand his earlier concept to *velayat-e faqih,* or direct rule by the clergy. He eventually added to his original writing with the notion that Islam was far more than just religious codes of worship and that in fact the *Qoran* dealt with socioeconomic and political issues as well.[4]

Early in his career, in other words, Khomeini's pronouncements were more or less in line with the apolitical and nonrevolutionary stance of the Shii clerical establishment. Though at times critical of the kings and their policies, the Iranian clergy never desired the total destruction of the state, nor did they wish to rule directly.[5] This fact was reiterated by Khomeini in *Kashf-e Asrar,* where he maintained that "the mojtahids never have and never will oppose kings and temporal powers even if they pursued un-Islamic policies."[6] Indeed, Khomeini at first was not only conciliatory toward the shah but in fact recognized his rule as legitimate.[7] It was after 1963 and only after many letters and requests that Khomeini instigated nationwide condemnation of the shah and the Pahlavi regime.[8] Before then, Khomeini's reference to *velayat-e faqih* and Islamic government was minimal at best.

Stage Two: The Revolutionary Ayatollah Khomeini 1964–1978

It was in the 1971 book *Hokumat-e Islami* that Khomeini broached the idea of direct rule by the clergy and offered his rationale: "It is now more than one thousand years since the lesser occultation [*gheybat*]. What if the *Hazrat* [the Mahdi: last Imam of shii Islam who is in occultation] sees it fit not to come for another one hundred thousand years? Should the rulings of Islam remain laid down and not carried out? . . . There is a need to implement Islamic laws, and anyone who claims the contrary is against Islam and its eternal nature."[9] By referring to the time of the Prophet Mohammad when he not only conveyed but administered the words of God, Khomeini maintained that "similar to the choosing of a caliph by the Prophet, we believe in the need for a caliph who would carry out Islamic laws."[10] Because there is no one in modern times to appoint such a person, Khomeini argued the caliph should be chosen from those who are well versed in Islamic law, the *foqaha,* or legal experts: "Just as the Prophet was charged by God to execute holy decrees and establish Islamic order, and obedience to him was indispensable, the just *foqaha* must be both leaders and governors [*hakem*], executing decrees and establishing the Islamic social order [regime]."[11] Islamic society, he argued, should be governed by a *faqih* who is a role model (*marja'-e taqlid*) and who rules according to the precepts of the Qoran. This *faqih* must possess two qualifications for a legitimate leadership: knowledge of the shari'a and justice.[12]

Khomeini provided extensive rationale for the legitimacy of the leadership of the ulama by citing the Qoran and the sayings of the Prophet (the Hadith). The logic behind the legitimacy of clerical rule is as follows. Divine guardianship of the Islamic community is delegated directly first to the Prophet, then to the imams, and finally during the occultation to the just *foqaha*. The *vali-ye faqih* would in turn rule according to the interests (*maslahat*) of the community as he saw them. Given this succession, it is the religious duty of all Muslims to accept the reign of their religious guardians, the ulama. One observer has categorized such a regime as direct divine legitimacy (*mashruiyat-e bela vaseteh-ye ilahi*). In such a system, Muslims willingly give up their sovereignty and rights and relegate them to the *foqaha*. In other words, with the explicit consent of the public, the sovereignty and authority of clerical rule take precedence over that of the people.[13] Thus the unquestioning support and compliance of the population at large was assumed in *Hokumat-e Islami*.

The granting of such extensive religious and political powers to the clergy and delegating such immense authority to the *vali-ye faqih* by Khomeini was unprecedented in the history of Shiism in Iran. Aside from being generally apolitical, prominent maraje' had perceived the role of the clergy to be merely the custodians of the community.[14] For Khomeini, however, the clergy were clearly much more than custodians. In his view, the *foqaha* were perceived as "not simply benign dispensers of advice and consent, but as real wielders of power,"[15] and the *vali-ye faqih* was the sole person qualified to be the ultimate arbiter and ruler of the Islamic political order.

Such an extensive mandate of the *faqih* over the lives of the people, sanctioned in the 1979 constitution, was further augmented in 1988 when, in a decree, Khomeini stopped short of providing the *faqih* with powers more than those of the Prophet and the imams.[16] Such omnipotence bestowed on the religious leader became known as the "absolute rule of the *faqih*" or *velayat-e motlaqeh-ye faqih*. The first prime minister after the revolution, Mehdi Bazargan, claimed that such a reading of the power of the *faqih* was tantamount to "religious despotism": a head of state with this much power nullified the rights and powers of the people, making empty symbols out of expressions of the popular will such as the constitution.[17]

Khomeini's vision of the Islamic state was to replace the secular regime of a monarchy that he viewed as corrupt and a by-product of colonial influence in Iran. But perhaps with an eye to his own future ambitions, in *Hokumat-e Islami* Khomeini noted, "If a person who has these two qualifications [knowledge of the shari'a and justice] rose and established such a government, it would be the duty of people [Muslims] to obey him."[18]

Hokumat-e Islami: In Search of a State

In *Hokumat-e Islami,* Khomeini dealt extensively with two facets of his theory of Islamic government: why there was a need for an Islamic government and who should rule according to what religious justification. Although Khomeini was clear as to the sovereignty and legitimacy of his proposed government, the specific makeup of an Islamic government—or the question of how and through what institutional mechanism the *foqaha* should govern—was left largely unanswered.[19] Although he made passing reference to concepts such as ministries and offices of the government,[20] Khomeini did not describe in any detail the state that would set in operation his concept of an Islamic government. His vision remained an ambiguous, idealized, and historically limited political order.

> The Islamic government is unlike any other contemporary one. It is neither despotic nor totalitarian but constitutional. This constitutionalism differs from the conventional [Western] version in that rulers abide by and must execute the words of God and the Prophet Mohammad and not the will of the people. Unlike constitutional monarchy or republicanism, where representatives of the people or the Shah legislate, in an Islamic government legislative power belongs solely to God. . . . No one has the right to legislate except the shari'a. . . . Sovereignty belongs to God and laws are his commands.[21]

Although in *Hokumat-e Islami* the structure of the Islamic state is not clearly stated by Khomeini, certain inferences can be made from the bits and pieces of information provided by the ayatollah. For instance, the most prevalent theme expressed in *Hokumat-e Islami* is that the Islamic government is modeled after rule under the Prophet Mohammad. Such a prototype does not provide a concrete example to follow. Most experts believe that what is normally conceptualized as the state in its legal/institutional form did not exist during the dawn of Islam. Rather, there existed a tribal political community devoid of the complexities of statehood, in either its traditional or modern forms, headed by the Prophet himself.[22]

Furthermore, Khomeini's argument runs, the actions of the Prophet were not politically motivated but were aimed at spreading the word of God. "Mohammad was no more than a messenger of a purely religious calling, that is, not colored by any inclination to govern or by any claim for a state. The Prophet had no rule or government, nor did he establish a kingdom in the political sense of the word. He was only a messenger, not a king or a builder of a state or a proponent of monarchy."[23] By referring to the government of the Prophet as a model government where the words of God are both conveyed and implemented by the Prophet himself, Khomeini implicitly hinted that one characteristic of the Islamic government was that the just *foqaha* constitute both the legislators and executors:

> The prophet was at the pinnacle of the executive and administrative power of Islamic society. . . . He would not only pronounce the religious decrees [*ahkam*] but would also execute them himself. . . . The prophet did not choose the caliph only to utter ideas and religious decrees, but also expected him to implement them. . . . [Thus] in the same way that Islam has enacted laws, it has also established executive power. The *vali-ye amr* [the leader] is in charge of the executive power as well.[24]

Passages like this lead one to assume that in the *Hokumat-e Islami,* by the term "government" Khomeini referred to both government officials and the state. Such supposition on the part of the ayatollah is problematic. Although it is tempting and indeed common to use the terms "state" and "government" interchangeably, they signify different concepts. While the term "government" refers to the person or persons who possess the highest political authority within a country, "state" is defined as a "set of autonomous, centralized, and formally coordinated political institutions and organizations within a given territory."[25] In other words, "government" indicates those who rule or "steer" the country, and the state is the institutional arrangement through which they accomplish the act of steering. As Andrew Vincent notes, the need for separation of the two terms is a critical one:

> One important value in distinguishing the state from the government is that it allows the structured changes and removal of governments to proceed while still maintaining the continuity and legitimacy of the social order. If governments were totally identified with the state, then each removal of government would entail a crisis in the state. This point should also make us very wary of linking up all the practices of government with the state.[26]

Khomeini's injudicious use of the two terms lies within this dichotomy, which makes the conceptualization of an Islamic government more obscure. One reason for the imprecision of the ayatollah may be the shortcoming of the Persian language itself and/or our own reading of his writings. In Persian, the terms "state" and "government" are both interchangeably defined as *hokumat* or *dowlat,* with *hokumat* also interpreted as "rule" or more specifically "political rule." When Khomeini spoke of *Hokumat-e Islami,* he most likely meant an Islamic rule or regime rather than a specific type of government or state. Given his double usage of the term "government," it is difficult to know whether Khomeini was conscious of the difference between the two terms or in which context he used them.

A further possibility may have been the fact that Khomeini saw no need to separate the two. Khomeini envisioned a political system that enjoyed universal and eternal legitimacy—as the political order of the time of the Prophet did—not a government that required a mechanism for change. There would be no need for the autonomous institutions of the state to ensure the future stability of *Hokumat-e Islami.* Moreover, because the government is an Islamic one, the division between state and (civil) society is unnecessary; in the time of the Prophet, the two were closely intertwined and perceived to have a holistic relationship. In short, the need for some sort of administrative apparatus, for whatever reason, was either not recognized as necessary or simply ignored by Khomeini. One can suggest that a shortcoming in Khomeini's theory is that even the clergy would require some sort of administration to execute the word of God.

Although Khomeini provides no detail in 1971 about what kind of state apparatus would enact his Islamic regime, one can nevertheless reach some conclusions as to what he opposed. A close look at *Hokumat-e Islami* shows that Khomeini assailed the legitimacy of the godless secular Pahlavi state not only on ideological and moral grounds but also because of its institutional features, function, and role in society. In Khomeini's view, Pahlavi bureaucracy was not only a symbol of the state's oppression of the masses but a useless societal burden: "Administrative and organizational excesses [of the state] are alien to Islam. Paper pushing and useless administrative formalities within the system lead to nothing but unnecessary financial burden to the society, which is religiously forbidden [*haram*]. This type of administrative system is foreign to the Islamic system."[27] The Iranian army and universal conscription, introduced by the founder of the Pahlavi dynasty, Reza Shah, was viewed by Khomeini as a means of "coercing Iranian youth and exposing them to further corruption and prostitution and ultimately training them in the art of thuggery and robbery."[28] In the place of the professional army of the shah, Khomeini proposed an Islamic army that drew its legitimacy and power from religious principles. Khomeini was also against modern forms of taxation, which he considered to be one more avenue through which the state imposed its will on society. In his view, taxes should be in the form of traditional religious taxes, *khoms* and *zakat*, rather than paid directly to the state.[29]

Khomeini's idea of Islamic constitutionalism also differed from its conventional modern connotation. Rather than being a contractual agreement between the state and society, according to Khomeini constitutional government is "the condition that those who govern must pursue and implement the words of the Qoran." In short, Khomeini disapproved of the secular monarchical state and contravened nearly all aspects of its behavior and function in society.

By the time he wrote *Hokumat-e Islami,* Khomeini had in mind an Islamic political system. The Islamicity came from the rule or governance of the *foqaha* and the implementation of the shari'a as the sole law of the land. But the institutional features of this political system—hence the nature of the state—were not clearly defined by Khomeini. Finally, it should be borne in mind that when he wrote *Hokumat-e Islami,* Khomeini spoke only of an "Islamic regime" and not an Islamic republic. As we shall see next, when he introduced the term *jomhuri* (republican) on the eve of the revolution, Khomeini's concept of Islamic government would undergo a dramatic alteration both in theory and in application.

Stage Three: From Islamic Government to Islamic Republic—The Obliteration of *Velayat-e Faqih,* Paris 1978

The nature of the state in Khomeini's Islamic political system became clearer after his exile from Iraq to Paris in 1978. In response to numerous questions about the nature of the future Iranian regime, the ayatollah announced: "We have declared an Islamic Republic, and the people through their numerous marches have voted for it. It is a regime [*hokumat*] based both on the will of the people and Islamic principles."[30] He provided further details on the nature of the future regime when he said, "We strive for the establishment of a regime based on the will of the people where its ultimate configuration will be determined by our society based on the prevailing circumstances."[31] As to the compatibility of his notion of an Islamic republic with that of the government of the Prophet, Khomeini said, "Our regime in an Islamic Republic will take its inspiration from that of the Prophet and Imam Ali and will be based on public opinion." [32]

Although in Paris Khomeini clarified some of the ambiguities of his early formulation of an Islamic political system, he also developed a set of conflicting ideas with regards to the nature of an Islamic republic. The most significant development was Khomeini's abandonment of the theory of *velayat-e faqih* when he announced that neither he nor other clerics would be directly involved in the administrative matters of the next regime. "In the future [after the victory of the revolution], I shall have the same role as I do now, that of guiding and directing. If there is a need, I will intervene. If there is treachery I shall fight it, but I shall not have any role in the *dowlat* [government or state]." [33]

By placing the term "Republican" next to the term Islamic, a remarkable transformation took place in Khomeini's doctrine. His remarks in Paris show an attempt on his part to establish some sort of theocracy, a government inspired by divine principles, by combining aspects of a modern republicanism with what he called the government of the Prophet Mohammad. Khomeini was trying to apply his notion of an Islamic political order within the structure of contemporary forms of government. His "mixed theory," however, aside from altering his earlier ideas in *Hokumat-e Islami,* resulted in inherent contradictions and incompatibilities both theoretically and empirically. Theoretically, by supporting republicanism, Khomeini placed the task of carrying out the words of God in the hands of precisely the kind of state and institutional arrangement he had persuasively negated. Because the most successful contemporary republican parliamentary systems are based on states with well-developed infrastructures, Khomeini's previous staunch opposition to such an institutional setup therefore needed some alteration. Empirically, by choosing republicanism, Khomeini ignored the fact that modern republicanism and contemporary representative parliamentary systems are based on secular principles and not on religious ones. Sovereignty in such systems belongs not to God but to the people. A related complication that introducing republicanism posed for the concept of an Islamic state is the issue of the role of the public. The problem was that by insisting that the people (*mardom*) determined the legitimacy of the regime, the regime was no longer direct divine legitimacy but divine-populace *(ilahi-mardomi)* legitimacy.[34] Thus, the Islamic republic would be based on dual or shared legitimacy. In essence, Khomeini altered his earlier doctrine by choosing a republican system for an Islamically inspired regime.

Granting a "partial" role to the people by the ayatollah, a role denied earlier in *Hokumat-e Islami,* was at least politically necessary if not a genuine change of heart. Faced with tremendous grassroots participation in the revolution, Khomeini could not afford to appear undemocratic. What need had the public of another regime that did not need its mandate? But what need was there for a regime to resort to public opinion in enacting the governing laws of the country if it was already known that the regime was going to implement strictly Islamic rulings?

In other words, Khomeini's revised theory still contained contradictions. For instance, if the clergy were to have a minimal role in the affairs of the republic (one of either guidance or consultation), who or what institution(s) would decide if the affairs of the government or the actions of the population at large were in line with Islamic tenets? Does the assumption of minimal intervention by the clergy imply the nation and all the institutions in the Islamic Republic develop naturally and act along lines consistent with the doctrines of Islam? Who will determine which of the sources of legitimacy will take precedence and in what circumstances? Through what institutional mechanism or through what kinds of arbitration would future conflicts of this dual legitimacy be settled?

This duality was formalized following the victory of the revolution. The task of safeguarding the Islamic character of the regime fell to postrevolutionary religious supervisory bodies and revolutionary organizations within the government. At the same time, a separate conventional state apparatus dealing with day-to-day management of the country also developed.

Stage Four: The Making of the (Revolutionary) Islamic Republic

Although all the revolutionary forces joined hands to confront the monarchy, there was no shared understanding of the nature of an Islamic republic. It became apparent after the victory of the revolution that neither Khomeini and his revolutionary clerics, nor Mehdi Bazargan, a trusted aid of Khomeini and the Islamic Republic's first prime minister, had any notion of what, in practice, constituted a religious republic or how to go about creating it.[35] The sudden and somewhat unexpected fall of the ancient regime of the shah in February 1979 made the task of introducing the new regime to the public a more urgent matter for the clergy.

The general consensus in Iran was that Bazargan would form a provisional government and run the affairs of the country until the general election, at which time the people would state their preference as to the nature of the next regime. In addition, it was expected that the clergy would indeed have at best a minimal role in the next regime, just as it had been declared by Khomeini in Paris. In reality, by the summer of 1981, the Islamic Republic had been transformed into a monopoly of power by the pro-Khomeini forces and the institutionalization of clerical rule, the rule of *velayat-e faqih*. This was achieved through the successful mobilization of the masses in Iran and the construction of a distinct revolutionary Islamic political order alongside the central government.[36]

While Bazargan gradually tried to put things in order, from the outset he and the Western-educated members of the provisional government were at a disadvantage. As the inheritors of the delegitimized institutions and apparatus of the old regime, Bazargan and his supporters in the central government confronted nationwide resistance to their efforts to instill the rule of law and run the country in an organized, controlled manner rather than by revolutionary action.[37] Bazargan noted that it was, more than anything, the nature of the institutions of the state and their modus operandi rather than the persons occupying them that people resented: "Any government in power would have confronted such treatment by the people. The problem lies in the fact that state institutions [*dastgah-ha-ye dowlati*] are the creation of the old regime and 2500 years of despotism. . . . Because [all the] atrocities were committed by state institutions, the people have developed an inborn hatred, fear, and disinclination towards both the state and the government."[38]

The clergy capitalized on the universal hostility and antistatist disposition of the masses towards the central government, and, led by Khomeini, they slowly began to pursue their tacit goal of monopolizing power in the new regime. Although the clergy lacked a clear blueprint of how they were going to rule, they were keenly aware of the need to consolidate power and institutionalize their new authority. To do that, they needed either to destroy or weaken the institutional legacies of the old regime, now controlled and occupied by Bazargan and his followers in the government, or create their own institutions. They chose the latter route as they directed, coordinated, and took over the leadership of the newly created revolutionary and religious organizations that soon became the "instruments of statehood" of another parallel state, coalescing the pro-Khomeini forces in Iran and representing their religious and revolutionary aspirations.[39] Assembled through the orders of Khomeini in Paris, the Islamic Revolutionary Council was the super-government overseeing and providing general guidelines and direction for the revolutionary movement. Three other important bodies were set up to ensure clerical rule: the Guardian Council (*Showra-ye Negahban*), the Islamic Republic Party (the IRP dissolved in 1986), and the revolutionary courts. Composed of six theologians and six civilian jurists, the Guardian Council was to review all laws passed by the parliament to make sure they were in line with shari'a. The IRP became the political party of supporters of Khomeini, those known in the conventional literature as the Shii fundamentalists.[40] It united pro-Khomeini supporters and served as a powerful political institution to challenge other well-organized pro-revolutionary forces in Iran.

A second group of spontaneously created postrevolutionary bodies were the revolutionary organizations (*Nehadha-ye Inqelabi,* hereafter *Nehads*). They were created both to safeguard the religious and revolutionary principles of the regime and to realize the egalitarian and redistributive rhetoric of the revolution expressed by Khomeini. The Corps of the Islamic Revolutionary Guards (IRGC), better known as the *Pasdaran* (the Guardians), was established in May 1979 and recruited members from the poor sections of the population. They soon became a loyal alternative option to the unreliable imperial army.[41] The Committee of the Islamic Revolution (*Komiteh-ye Inqelab-e Islami,* hereafter KII) directed and coordinated by various clergies in mosques, became responsible for keeping law and order and safeguarding local neighborhoods from antirevolutionary forces until the provisional government was well established.[42] The creation of the *Nehads* opened up the revolutionary dimension of the Iranian revolution (the other two being the religious and the populist). Both in Paris and immediately after the revolution, the discourse used by Khomeini and the leadership as whole was highly egalitarian.[43] They spoke about the historical struggle of the haves (*mostakbarin)* and the have-nots (*Mostaz'afin).*[44] It was understood, therefore, that a top priority of the new regime in Iran would be attending to the plight of the poor, hitherto marginalized economically and socially by the old regime. Thus from the outset the *Nehads* were trusted to enact another distinguishing aspect of the new regime in Iran. The Foundation of the Disinherited *(Bonyad-e Mostaz'afin)*, founded in March 1979, was entrusted with "the task of taking over the financial and industrial properties of the Pahlavis and using the income to attend to the needs of the *Mostaz'afin*."[45] Imam Khomeini's Relief Committee *(Komiteh-e ye Imdad-e Imam Khomeini)* was established in March 1979 to provide material and spiritual assistance to the rural areas in Iran.[46] The Reconstruction Crusade *(Jihad-e Sazandegi)* aimed to mobilize Iranian youth to rebuild the country, especially the disadvantaged areas, while similar tasks were delegated to other organizations such as the Fifteenth of Khordad Foundation *(Bonyad-e Panzdah-e Khordad)* and the Martyr Foundation *(Bonyad-e Shahid)*. Headed by prominent clergy, the *Nehads* increased the institutional and ideological influence of the pro-Khomeini forces throughout the country. Through their Islamic and revolutionary credentials, these bodies accelerated the process of indoctrination and the Islamization of society.

The process of creating the Islamic Republic of Iran also set certain political precedents. For one thing, the clergy both implicitly and explicitly encouraged hostility toward the central government's authority and institutions. Members of the revolutionary organizations, which were headed by the clergy, ignored the law and acted independently of the central government. Khomeini's supporters, the party of God or the Hizbollah, organized and orchestrated by Hadi Ghaffari, took it upon themselves to implement the word of God in the streets.[47] Ignoring the government's pleas, they attacked opponents of *velayat-e faqih,* disrupting their public gatherings and forcing the closure of opposition newspapers.[48] Thus, a prevailing feature of the postrevolutionary regime soon became the implementation of law not by officials of the central government but by the revolutionary organizations and the Hizbollahis. Bazargan frequently complained about the Hizbollahis' unrestrained purges of the bureaucracy, calling them "those Islamic bearded people who under the pretext of purification accuse everyone of being a spy and antirevolutionary."[49] Following the US embassy takeover on November 4, 1979, Bazargan described the situation in Iran as a city with one hundred sheriffs and resigned the next day.

The newly created revolutionary bodies were indispensable to the success of *velayat-e faqih* for three reasons. First, the clergy and their supporters relied heavily on popular revolutionary organizations to further their goals. These bodies were effectively coordinated and mobilized by the various clergy to confront both foreign and domestic opposition. Therefore, although there were growing fears among the clerical leadership that they would get dangerously out of hand (and indeed after 1981 efforts were made to establish more control over them), pro-Khomeini forces relied heavily on the revolutionary organizations to insure institutionalization of their rule. Hossein Musavi (prime minister from 1982 to 1988) once said, "if we lose these bodies we lose the revolution." [50] Secondly, the revolutionary milieu and the war with Iraq also came to assist pro-Khomeini groups. In the first years of the revolution, supporting so-called revolutionary measures was fashionable, and upholding principles such as law and order or professionalism or expertise in fields other than religion were deemed antirevolutionary. As with most modern revolutions, advocates of "Permanent Revolution" in Iran favored strict implementation of Islamic ideas of the revolution not by experts but by the faithful. As a result, statist tendencies in the central government were presented by the revolutionaries as antirevolutionary, hence un-Islamic. The active role played by the revolutionary organizations in the war with Iraq increased their prestige, support, and usefulness for the new regime in Iran. Thirdly, Khomeini's public support contributed to the success of the supporters of *velayat-e faqih* in the revolutionary bodies because it legitimized their discourse regarding various socioeconomic and political issues in Iran. His opposition to "Big Brother" demonstrated from early in his career provided a useful pretext for the supporters of *velayat-e faqih* to not only challenge the central government, but to present themselves as the vanguards of the Islamic revolution, thus shouldering the responsibility for bringing it to fruition.

The revolutionary bodies maintained that without them the revolution would never have taken place:

> It was the *Komiteh* who captured the shah's agents and handed them over to the revolutionary tribunal. It was the *Komiteh* who protected government property from counter-revolutionaries and profiteers. It was the Komiteh

who took care of people and safeguarded their honor and property. . . . The structure of corrupt military bureaucracy (of the shah) . . . could not be of any service to the revolution let alone adopt itself to the requirements and necessities of the revolution. The most basic and immediate requirement of postrevolutionary Iran was organizations that could answer the various needs of the people.[51]

[handwritten annotation: loyalty through presence]

This kind of observation was prophetic as the revolutionary years gradually saw such claims become the basis for more and more autonomous action in Iran by both the revolutionary organizations and the factions controlling them. Both Bazargan and later the first president of the Islamic Republic, Abolhasan Bani-Sadr faced difficulties in performing their duties for a variety of reasons. They had both opposed clerical domination of the affairs of the country and believed in bestowing the task of running the government not on the faithful but on largely (Western) educated experts and professionals.[52] Therefore, their methods were deemed by the revolutionary masses as elitist, antirevolutionary, a return to the modus operandi of the old regime, and—most damaging of all—anti-Islamic.[53] Subsequently, with the endorsement of Khomeini, all the legislative, executive, and judicial powers of the central government were undermined, duplicated, and treated as superfluous by the postrevolutionary institutions. The flustered Bazargan cried, "Unless this [duality of power] is rectified and resolved, the mere election of a president and election of [parliamentary] representatives will not be enough."[54]

The revolutionary courts, again with the blessing of Khomeini, acted independently of the justice ministry and disregarded the appeals of Bazargan to halt summary executions. In response, Khomeini reiterated, "Those in detention are not charged but guilty. They must be killed. Nevertheless we provide them with a trial."[55] Members of postrevolutionary bodies were interfering in the activities of the central government nationwide and not just in Teheran. Daily newspapers were filled with the news of local governors who resigned while complaining of "unofficial personnel" paralyzing the executive branch.[56] The activities of the religio-revolutionary bodies were supported by Khomeini, who repeatedly criticized Bazargan and his government for being conservative and not acting in a revolutionary manner. Worse still, Khomeini compared the ideological tendencies of those in the government and the actions of governmental institutions to those of the shah's.[57] In short, as the following words of Bazargan indicate, just a few months into the revolution the dual authority system was well in place:

> At the top there is the leader [Khomeini], in the absence of the Majlis we have the Council of the Revolution acting as a Majlis: so far two sources power. Next there is the government hence the executive where authority should lie. . . . It is true that those sources (Nehads) stem from these three poles and that they have been created by the imperatives of the revolution. Nevertheless they cut corners outside the government and go over the head of the government. This is done by institutions such as the Imam's Committee, the IRGC, the Revolutionary Courts, and many other such institutions. . . . Moreover, these committees assume for themselves a certain internal independence. . . . They follow local religious leaders.[58]

Stage Five: The November 1979 Constitution, the Return of Velayat-e Faqih

In May 1979, the Assembly of Experts for the Drafting of the Constitution, a six-hundred-member body made up of clergy and lay members, was elected to draw up the new Iranian constitution. Until the summer of 1979, no one spoke about the concept of velayat-e faqih. Despite this, Khomeini's supporters had virtually silenced all opponents, and their views on the topic were quite distinct from other revolutionary groups. Gradually, pro-Khomeini forces imposed the idea of rule by the clergy. Khomeini made public his disapproval of omitting the clergy from the political scene in May 1979.[59] The first person who implicitly referred to velayat-e faqih was Ayatollah Hossein Ali Montazeri who, on the eve of the drafting of the constitution, remarked, "If people voted for an Islamic state, then the faqih must be at the pinnacle to ensure that the regime is indeed Islamic."[60] Khamenehi said that "the velayat-e faqih must be an essential component of the new constitution."[61] In his speech to the Assembly of Experts for the Drafting of the Constitution, Khomeini publicized his preference for the nature of the constitution in commanding fashion and set the parameters for the coming debates in the assembly:

The constitution and all other laws in this republic must be one hundred percent Islamic, and if one article is contrary to Islamic laws it will be tantamount to opposing the people's majority vote. Therefore, any proposed opinion or scheme by members [of the assembly] that is against Islam is flawed and contrary to the path of the people. . . . The discernment of whether articles are in line or opposed to Islamic decrees belongs solely to the esteemed *foqaha*.[62]

Although by seeking an "Islamic" constitution Khomeini emphasized the significance of the Islamicity of the regime, the constitution of the Islamic "Republic" was also to include the populist as well as the religious aspects of the regime. Thus the enterprise of framing the constitution entailed resolving the conundrum of the shared rulership that emerged in the last phase of Khomeini's theory of Islamic state: the sovereignty, authority, and power of the clergy on the one hand, and of the population at large on the other. After much heated debate, the assembly, which included fifty-five clerics, most of whom were supporters of *velayat-e faqih*,[63] provided the clergy and the religious dimension with a level of authority above and beyond of that of the people and placed the *vali-ye faqih* at the pinnacle of the regime.

The debates in the assembly were also significant in that the postrevolutionary regime witnessed its first incident of ideological dispute among the supporters of Khomeini. While in principle all members of the assembly endeavored to put together an Islamic Republic, its exact nature was hotly contested. Over time such disputes crystallized and not only formed the basis for the formation of factions but shaped the factional discourse over doctrinarism. As would be true in the future, the different views over the two authorities of the regime (the people and the clergy) became the distinguishing ideological positions of the members of the assembly. At one end of the spectrum was the view expressed by nonclergy members such as Bani-Sadr, Ezzatollah Sahabi, Rahmatollah Moqaddam-Maraghehi, and Mohammad Ali Musavi-Jazayeri as well as clergymen like Ayatollah Mahmud Taleqani and Mohammad Javad Hojjati-Kermani: the republicanism of the regime was of equal if not more significance than its religious dimension. Consequently, they opposed clerical domination of major centers of power and pleaded for a supervisory role only for the *faqih*. On the other end of the spectrum, the likes of Mohammad Beheshti, Hossein Ali Montazeri, Ali Khamenehi, Ayatollah Mohammad Mehdi

Rabbani-Amlashi, Hasan Ayat, Jalaloddin Farsi, and Mohammad Kiavosh argued that the regime first and foremost must be Islamic and thus advocated direct clerical rule and an all-encompassing role for the *faqih*.

From the third session onward, during the debate over an article of the constitution designed to sanction the principle of *velayat-e faqih* and make the *faqih* the ultimate source of authority and power, members who favored religious control began invoking Khomeini's public wishes and provided various justifications for their vision for the Islamic Republic. MP Kiavosh, for instance, declared that "no article or principle should be accepted in the constitution unless it is based on the Qoran and the Prophet's *Sonna*. . . . Anywhere the word 'law' is used, it must refer to God's laws and commands."[64] The person who most staunchly advocated the notion of *velayat-e faqih* was MP Beheshti, the founder and secretary of the IRP, who stated, "The people have voted for an Islamic Republic; it is not enough for the regime to remain Islamic by name only." He further argued, "The inclusion of *velayat-e faqih* is the only way to make certain that in the future the country does not become Communist or Socialist."[65] In line with stage two of Khomeini's theory of *velayat-e faqih*, Khamenehi criticized Western models of democracy that uphold the supremacy of the rights and sovereignty of the people and argued that "sovereignty based on Islamic principles belongs to God, who delegates such rights to people and they in turn choose us [the clergy] as the *faqih* and their representatives."[66] Abdolrahman Heydari also argued for the supremacy of the religiousness of the regime over its republicanism and said, "*Vali-ye faqih* must have the responsibility of the three branches of government. It is his right."[67] Rabbani-Amlashi remarked, "If the constitution of the Islamic Republic is not imbued with *velayat-e faqih*, how can we call it an Islamic constitution?"[68]

The republicans in the assembly maintained that the notion of *velayat-e faqih* and the role envisioned by its supporters would ultimately lead to total disregard for the population and their rights. According to MP Moqaddam-Maraghei, for instance, "We cannot change or transform the will of the people to that of the *faqih*'s."[69] Ezzatollah Sahabi believed, "Such measures in the constitution would be betraying the people whose main aim in the revolution was freedom."[70] And this is how Mohammad Ali Musavi-Jazayeri expressed why *velayat-e faqih* was undemocratic: "The regime, as its name indicates, is made up of the Republic and the Islamic. Republican means that it belongs to the people. If everything is made and decided [for them by the *faqih*] then how is it populist? What role do the people play in this system? What is the sum result of these two terms? Yes, we can claim that this system is both holy and populist, but how can we say that the regime is a republic?"[71] The conflict between the two groups became particularly heated over article 110, which dealt with the "duties and authorities of the leader." The proposed article stated the power of the *faqih* would include "appointing the *foqaha* of the Council of Guardian in addition to the highest judicial figure, declaring war and peace, appointing the commander of the armed forces, and having the power to dismiss the president in cases of treason and dereliction of duty after a majority vote by the Majlis."[72] Arguments over the last two items of the article, which contained a potential conflict between the president—the head of the republic—and the *faqih,* created the most controversy. Opponents of the article such as Ayatollah Hojjati-Kermani warned the assembly that sanctioning this article and such an "authoritarian" reading of *velayat-e faqih* would damage the reputation of both the clergy and the regime and create a negative reaction in the population at large.[73] Ayatollah Naser Makarem-Shirazi argued that because the president is elected by popular mandate, as the head of the republic he should be the supreme commander of the armed forces. He noted that with the existence of screening bodies such as the Guardian Council, there is no need for the watchful eyes of the *faqih* over the president. He also pointed out the adverse publicity that the article would cause: "The outside world will call us despotic. . . . They will say that we [the clergy] framed the constitution in order to award ourselves absolute power. We should not render sovereignty of the people empty. They [the people] may be silent and accept this article today, but later they will abolish the constitution."[74] Supporters of the article provided various justifications for inserting in the constitution the supreme power of the *vali-ye faqih* and how the crucial post of the head of the republic could not be granted to a fallible president without the holy supervision of the *faqih*. According to Montazeri, "By definition, Islamic Republic entails the implementation of Islamic decrees. . . . Only an expert in Islamic laws [a *faqih*] and not a Western-educated person can discern the Islamicity of laws." Moreover, he suggested that the *faqih* should announce his choices for the presidency, and the people choose among those approved candidates. "This process," Montazeri argued, "means that people have [democratically] elected their president."[75] In the same vein, Farsi believed that "a non-*faqih* who is elected because of his managerial expertise and is responsible to the people and not to God cannot be trusted to head the armed forces."[76] For Khamenehi, it was only logical for the *faqih* to have dominion over the executive "because he already enjoys such powers over the judiciary."[77]

To help the passage of this article, some members of the assembly, such as Farsi and Ayatollah Abdolhossein Dastghayb, emphasized the religious significance and meaning of the position of imam (leader of Islamic community and Friday prayer, and in shiism one of twelve descendants of Prophet) and how this entitles him to untrammeled authority. "Imam means leadership and guidance of the community, the one who looks after the people and takes charge of all affairs and does not allow those with satanic tendencies to seize power," maintained Dastghayb.[78] According to Bani-Sadr, however, "any decision made outside the jurisdiction and parallel to the government is tantamount to despotism." He utterly opposed the *faqih* having the power to dismiss the president, saying, "This is the job of the justice ministry or the Majlis."[79] He also criticized Montazeri's idea of preselected candidates for president: "What kind of election is it if the leader can decide who should run for the presidency and what the president should do? This is tantamount to saying you can elect anyone but elect the one I choose; this is neither freedom nor republicanism."[80]

The constitution that was passed in November 1979 laid the foundation of a theocracy and made the *faqih* the central figure in the Iranian polity and the shari'a the basis for the country's legal system. According to article 5 of the constitution, "During the occultation of *Hazrat-e Vali-ye Asr* [the twelfth imam], the leadership of the nation in the Islamic Republic of Iran shall be the responsibility of a *faqih*."[81] In addition, other religious institutions would have their share of "supervision" over public activities. Based on articles 91 through 99, the Guardian Council "reviews all laws passed by the Majlis to check their Islamic credentials, and has a right of veto in interpreting the Constitution and supervising the elections of the Assembly of Experts, the president, the Majlis and referendums."[82] In December 1982, an all-clergy eighty-three-member body called the Assembly of Experts (*Majlis-e Khobregan,* hereafter referred to as Khobregan) was created and entrusted with the task of selecting the next *faqih*. Gradually, a plethora of other bodies was created to safeguard the Islamicity of the regime and ensure the continuation of the rule of the *faqih*. However, as the debates over the drafting of the constitution vividly displayed, the absence of a clear vision and consensus among the leadership in Iran on the nature of the Islamic Republic was conspicuous from the outset. Moreover, while the Islamicity of the regime became the rallying cry, its successful fusion with republicanism has haunted Khomeini's supporters ever since the victory of the revolution, and the elite has yet to successfully fuse the two dimensions of the regime. Consequently, although the framers of the first Iranian Constitution (the constitution was revised in 1989) had "unity of words and unity of action" in mind, they designed the Islamic state in such a way that left the door open for institutional conflict and factional rivalry.

The State in the Islamic Republic of Iran: Modern, Traditional, and Revolutionary

As the name of the Iranian state indicates, the political system in Iran mirrors the contemporary form of a modern republican state; it has a constitution and three branches of government. Indeed, a cursory reading of the Iranian constitution suggests that the governing principles and the political system of the Islamic Republic share more features with the contemporary Western European model of modern states than with its proclaimed theocracy. However, a closer look reveals that although modern in name, republicanism is only one side of the complex character of the Iranian state. For in the Islamic Republic, unlike other modern states, the republican institutions of the central government are not the sole source of initiating, making, and implementing laws and policies in the country; neither do they have the exclusive right of rule-adjudication and the maintenance of law and order. Rather, a host of institutions with religious authority are legally empowered to duplicate, constrain, and ultimately challenge the function and activities of the central government. This point may best be illuminated by putting forward some fundamental questions about the Iranian regime.

The first question that might be asked is: who and what institutions make and unmake the governing laws in Iran? The answer for a republican regime would be the parliament. However, although the Iranian parliament is the main governmental body engaged in the enactment of laws, the Majlis must share its decisions, hence power, with another twelve-member body, the Guardian

Council. In fact, the constitution clearly states that without the existence of the Guardian Council, the Majlis is devoid of sovereignty. In addition to the parliament and the Guardian Council, there is another body that has the authority to make laws in the Islamic Republic, the Expediency Council (*Majam'-e Tashkhise Maslahat-e Nezam,* literately the assembly of determining what is in the best interests of the regime). Established in 1988, this is an arbitration body that settles disputes over laws between the parliament and the Guardian Council and makes the final binding decision.

Another question that might be asked about a republican regime is: who is the highest official in the country? In a republican system it would be the president. Not so in Iran, because according to the constitution of the Islamic Republic (article 112), the highest religious figure, the leader, is the ultimate source of authority and power in the country. Among the vague but all-encompassing constitutional powers of the leader are "the power to determine the general policies of the system of the Islamic Republic of Iran; supervise the effective performance of the regime's general policies; supreme command of the armed forces; declaring war or peace" (article 110). If the hierarchy is still unclear, article 113 states that "after the leader, the president is the highest official in the country."

The challenge to the authority of the judiciary is more subtle. For instance, article 8 of the constitution states, "Inviting good deeds, directing [the people] to do what is lawful or good and enjoining [them] to commit what is unlawful or bad [*amr-e be ma'ruf va nah-ye az monkar,* propagation of virtue and prohibition of vice, or PVPV] should be a public and reciprocal duty of all people vis-à-vis each other in the Islamic Republic of Iran, of the government vis-à-vis people and vice versa." Consequently, it has frequently been the case that influential individuals not only challenge policies of the government by labeling them as un-Islamic, antirevolutionary, or improper but, with authority based on this article of the constitution, declare their own "proper" version on these policies. What is more, contradictory rulings on issues can be delivered by any influential *foqaha* that could pose a challenge to the decisions of the Iranian judiciary. As Ayatollah Mohammad Yazdi noted:

> The fatwa of one scholar says state punishment, the fatwa of another says religious punishment. If it is religious punishment it is unpardonable, if it is state

punishment it is pardonable. Well, let me ask who should the judicial branch emulate? If we emulate anyone other than the ruler, will there be any rule left? . . . In Shiraz there will be one decree, in Isfahan another, [another] in Kaman and Tehran. In the leadership, too, one scholar says we can have relations with that country; another says we cannot. One scholar says collect taxes; the other says do not. This is not administration.[83]

Due to their institutional-functional disposition, the *Nehads* can and have ultimately shared or challenged the independence and autonomy the central government. Initially, the aim of most of these bodies was to work alongside the government to deal with the socioeconomic and spiritual needs of the population at large, and safeguard the religious and revolutionary principles of the new regime. However, as these organizations are not accountable to the government, postrevolutionary bodies such as the Foundation of the Dispossessed have gradually mustered so much socioeconomic and political power that today they act quite autonomously within the political system of the Islamic Republic.

According to the Iranian constitution, in the hierarchy of political institutions,[84] the highest-ranking set of institutions is comprised of what are referred to here as the "religious supervisory bodies." They are under the authority of the *faqih,* as it is he who appoints and removes the heads of these bodies. Put simply, these bodies are constitutionally empowered to make certain that all public activities in the Islamic Republic are in line with Islamic precepts. They have overriding authority that supersedes all other decisions made within the political system, and over and above the three branches of the government. Rather than enacting the principles of separation of power and equality before the law, the constitution provides more power to institutions such as the supervisory bodies, allowing them not only to interfere in the working of the central government but in fact to override its decisions without being contested. Based on their political significance and authority, the supervisory bodies can be divided into two groups. The first group of "religious super-bodies" include the Guardians Council, the Assembly of Experts, and the Expediency Council. The second group of religious supervisory bodies, the "extension" or "the extended arms" of the *faqih,*[85] is not mentioned in the constitution and theoretically is devoid of legal status. They are entrusted to ensure that the religiousness of the regime remains intact. This group includes the representatives of the *vali-ye faqih,* the Association of Friday Prayer Leaders, ideological–political organizations (*sazmanha-ye aqidati-siyasi),* the Special Court for the Clergy (*Dadgah-he Vizheh-ye Rouhaniyat),* which deals with offences committed by the clergy, and the Islamic associations (*anjomanha-ye Islami).* These organizations provide a wide variety of services for the regime. For instance, the offices of the representatives of the *faqih,* created in 1983, safeguards the Islamization of higher education in Iran. Their job has been to introduce and enforce the teaching of Islamic curriculum, preventing the spread of deviationist ideas, and to help with the spiritual needs of the students.[86] Another example is the Islamic associations. According to the former Prime Minister Mir-Hossein Musavi, "The associations are self-governed independent bodies made up of doctrinaire believers in *velayat-e faqih* and given the task of ensuring that proper Islamic behavior is observed in various government offices."[87]

In the hierarchy of state institutions in the Islamic Republic, the second set of institutions is the republican, namely the three branches of government Westerners are familiar with: the executive, the legislative, and the judiciary. Again, the central government is classified as second in importance because, according to the constitution, the president and the three branches of government are to follow the religious leader. The third and final set of state institutions in Iran are the *Nehads.* Some of the most powerful of these organizations include the Foundation of the Dispossessed, the Fifteenth of Khordad Foundation, Imam Khomeini's Relief Committee, and the Martyr Foundation. The *Nehads* have a unique position in the regime in that nearly all have legal status (they are defined in the constitution), and most are considered to be governmental bodies. In practice, however, the central government exercises little or no control over them. Although they receive a considerable amount of their funding from the annual budget, as a rule they are not accountable to the government as their staffs are appointed by the leader rather than the president. Thus the *faqih* has influence over the activities of these powerful bodies as well.

In other words, within the Iranian polity there are numerous institutions, foundations, and organizations that have the legal authority to interfere, directly or indirectly, in the operation of the central government and who exercise political power alongside or even above the three branches of government. What provides the substructure for factional conflict is the hierarchical manner in which power is distributed among state institutions. The state in the Islamic Republic is unique in its institutional arrangements and distribution of power, and the exercise of political power in Iran is complex and multifaceted.

While it is institutionally modern, the Islamic Republic cannot be easily characterized as such; the general will, represented through republican institutions, is curtailed and challenged through other personal or informal institutional mechanisms. As a populist-revolutionary regime, the function and role of the central government and the revolutionary bodies are clear. But how should the powers of the leader and the religious supervisory bodies be understood? To make "political" sense of these unique features of Iran's political system, they must be placed in some sort of theoretical perspective. The overarching powers of the leader and the religious supervisory bodies can be seen as examples of what one scholar calls the "Despotic Power" of states. Such power, found in traditional states, is defined by him in the following manner:

> Despotic Power refers to the distributive power of state elite over civil society. It derives from the range of actions that state elite can undertake without routine negotiation with civil society groups. . . . Actors located primarily within states have a certain space and privacy in which to operate—the degree varying according to the ability of civil society actors to organize themselves centrally through representative assemblies, formal political parties, court factions, and so forth. They can alternatively withhold powers from central politics. A state with despotic power becomes either an autonomous actor, as emphasized in true elitism, or multiple but perhaps confused autonomous actors, according to its internal homogeneity.[88]

The Iranian state can be seen as a combination of both the modern and the traditional—thus in theory democratic as well as despotic—because of the unique set of institutions and interplay among them.

So the state in Iran is not easily defined; it does not easily fit into existing categories of traditional or modern, democratic or despotic state. An appropriate theoretical framework for the study of the Iranian state must consider its three ideological dimensions—republican, religious, and revolutionary—and the hierarchical distribution of power to the corresponding institutions.

The reasons behind the multilayered and institutionally diffused nature of the state in the Islamic Republic are understandable given Khomeini's theory of an Islamic state and its religious, populist, and revolutionary objectives. Events that immediately followed the revolution also complicated the development of the new regime. Early on, the regime had to reflect all three ideologies in order to be considered a legitimate revolutionary Islamic republic. Meeting these requirements meant keeping the republican institutions of the old regime and erecting two other sets of institutions, the religious and the revolutionary.

In the final analysis, one can assume that power and authority are distributed among the three groups based on their significance. As a political system with the primary task of conveying and implementing the word of God, the religious dimension would naturally have the most significance. Thus the religious supervisory bodies were given powers above and beyond the republican institutions or the modern institutions of the Iranian state. In the allocation of state powers, the republican institutions and the revolutionary bodies were to follow the religious lead.

Factionalism and the Inherent Paradoxes of the State in the Islamic Republic

In theory and according to the constitution, all three groups of state institutions work together to achieve the goals of the regime and function in harmony as part of a unitary state under the mantle of the leader. In practice, however, because of the unequal distribution of power among the branches of government, the Iranian polity is riddled with inefficiencies and systemic paradoxes. In the first place, the institutional clutter and the numerous decision-making centers overlap, leading to inefficiency and thus institutional inertia. More detrimental for the regime, however, is that due to its hierarchical institutional arrangements, the state becomes prone to factional rivalries on many levels and in many forms. In a faction-ridden political system, factionalism could commence from the lowest levels of the regime up through the *faqih* himself. With the absolute power that the *faqih* holds, a partisan leader can play a deciding role in factional power struggles. For instance, by publicly supporting the views of the conservative right and appointing conservatives to influential bodies such as the Guardian Council, ministry of radio and television, and various *Nehads,* Khamenehi has fortified the ideological and institutional predominance of this faction, particularly after 1994 (see chapters 4 and 5). Ironically, a partisan *faqih* throws into question a fundamental ideological premise of the Islamic Republic, as the *faqih* is held to be above mundane (factional) politics, and is presumed to be virtuous and infallible.[89] When it comes to the *faqih,* the constitution and the regime make strong assumptions and demand unblemished righteousness.

This assumption is challenged by factions that read the constitution in a way that attributes less significance to the religious dimension. One of the main ideological tenets of the left, including the current president Khatami, is that the populist (republican) dimension should be considered just as significant as the religious dimension and its associated institutions. As a result, this faction in post-Khomeini Iran has opposed the existing power structure and the idea of an unassailable *faqih.* Conversely, members of the conservative right have strongly upheld the supremacy of the religious dimension of the regime over its republicanism, supporting therefore the current institutional arrangements in Iran and espousing an absolutist reading of the *velayat-e faqih.*

Support for one dimension or another by factions, however, is often politically motivated and depends on what institution(s) a given faction controls. Whether motivated by the desire to gain political position or by sincere ideological beliefs, factions can make political capital out of the inherent institutional rivalry to serve their own interests. In post-Khomeini Iran, the conservative right has enjoyed the support of the leader and its members have occupied powerful super-bodies such as the Guardian Council and the Assembly of Experts. The left saw their presidential candidate elected in 1997, who is currently in office and dominated the third Majlis, had a tangible showing in the fifth, and the majority in the sixth Majlis. However, during the first decade of the revolution, this faction was staunchly supportive of an all-encompassing *faqih*—perhaps because of Khomeini's support for the left—while it was the conservative right who opposed a powerful leader (see further chapters 2 and 3). The coexistence of the two in theory fundamental pillars of the regime provides factions with a great deal of ideological maneuverability at any given period of time.

Another way that factions compete for more influence in Iran is through control of the revolutionary institutions. With regard to the religious and populist dimensions of the regime, the constitution is clear about which has more power. However, the coexistence and therefore potential rivalry between the revolutionary and populist dimensions of the regime has not been clearly addressed by the constitution. As a result, based on their religio-revolutionary credentials and the fact that they are under the authority of the *faqih* and therefore unaccountable to the central government, the *Nehads* have frequently challenged the dominance and policies of the republican institutions as they have independent sources of legitimacy, sovereignty, and authority outside of the central government. In addition, aside from their designated tasks, the *Nehads* are entrusted with safeguarding the regime's ideological doctrine and are considered instrumental in the preservation of Islamic and revolutionary principles in Iran. By frequently citing Khomeini's statements regarding the independence, authority, and legitimacy of the *Nehads,* these organizations claim to be the legitimate institutions of the Islamic Republic as they are representatives of the revolutionary aspirations of the masses and act on their behalf. For instance, the duties of Revolutionary Guard were not only to safeguard the revolution from internal threats but to ensure the Islamic purity of all the affairs in the government.[90] The IRGC can always claim independence from other state institutions such as cabinet ministries and the army.[91]

The *Nehads'* protected position enables them to be another arena for factionalism. During the fifth parliamentary election campaign in 1996, when it appeared that the more liberal and reform-minded members of the left and the modern right could enter the Majlis, the arch-conservative head of the IRGC at the time, Mohsen Rezai, warned that "the Guards will knock down the 'liberals' and prevent them from entering the Majlis even if they were elected."[92] The recent head of IRGC, Rahim Safavi, has also made similar comments against Khatami and his ministers, claiming that the words and actions of the more liberal elements surrounding the new president are undermining the principle of *velayat-e faqih* and thus are threatening the main pillar of the regime and the revolution: "We do not interfere in politics but if we see that the foundations of our system of government and our revolution are threatened . . . we get involved. When I see that a [political] current has hatched a cultural plot, I consider it my right to defend the revolution against this current. My commander is the exalted leader and he has not banned me [from doing so]."[93] The saga of Salman Rushdie is perhaps the most famous example of how, by claiming independence and rightfulness for their actions, the *Nehads* can play into factional politics. In 1996, in an effort to resolve the Rushdie affair, the Iranian foreign ministry announced that the government of Iran would not carry out the fatwa issued by Khomeini. However, Ayatollah Hasan Sane'i, the head of the Fifteenth of Khordad Foundation, maintained that the late Imam's fatwa was irreversible, and he doubled the price on Rushdie's head.[94] The foreign ministry and the Foundation at that time were in the hands of two competing factions, the conservative right and the left, respectively. Thus, by pronouncing the fatwa still valid, the left undermined the power of the conservatives. The reason Sane'i could challenge the official policy of the central government was that he could claim legitimacy for his view equivalent to that of the officials in the foreign ministry. In addition, by claiming that he is upholding the views of the Imam, he buttressed his claim politically, making his position practically unassailable.

The inherent dimensional-institutional rivalry of the Iranian state provides another arena for factionalism. Here, the basis on which decisions are made becomes the tool for factional power struggle. The power of each category of institution rests on different and sometimes contradictory bases. Consequently, their decisions are also made on differing principles. These differences are particularly pointed when comparing policy formation by the republican institutions and the religious supervisory bodies. As inherently modern secular institutions, republican institutions draw their sources of legitimacy, authority, and hence power from secular principles. Therefore, the Iranian parliament should enact laws on formal/rational principles, because lawmaking by modern parliaments is based on positivist notions and not on a particular ideology or belief. The outcomes are determined through votes, and in the belief that modern state is about the rule of law rather than the rule of men. One aspect of this positivism of modern parliaments, as Poggi points out, is that laws made by such parliaments differ from laws made based on natural or religious principles:

In the modern state the relation between the state and the law is particularly close. The law is no longer conceived as an assemblage of immemorially evolved, customary jural rulers, or of corporatively held, traditional prerogatives and immunities; nor is it conceived as the expression of principles of justice resting on the will of God or the dictates of "Nature" to which the state is simply expected to lend the sanction of its powers of enforcement. Modern law is instead a body of enacted laws; it is positive law, willed, made, and given validity by the state itself in the exercise of its sovereignty, mostly through public, documented, generally recent decisions.[95]

In contrast to this positivist decision-making mode of the republican institutions, judgments made by the leader, his extended-arm institutions and the supervisory bodies, and indeed all the decisions of all individuals and institutions responsible for ascertaining the Islamicity of various policies and activities in the regime are based on personal interpretation and thus subjective: in one form or another the decision maker is engaged in *ijtihad,* or the use of independent judgment and original thinking in arriving at new decrees. In Shii *fiqh,* the clergy issue Islamic rulings on different issues based on four sources: the Qoran, the Prophet's tradition (the *Sonna*), consensus of the community (or *ijma*), and reason *(aql).* The first two sources constitute the primary sources of the *fiqh,* and as divinely inspired sources they are eternal and indisputable. "Consensus" in Shii *fiqh* refers to how the ulama as a group deduce new laws based on the notion that such laws are in line with the general opinion of the Muslim community.[96] In producing Islamic rulings, the mojtahid uses reason and personal inference through syllogism of the Qoran and the *Sonna* to arrive at new rulings. Consequently, when issuing new injunctions, the mojtahids have historically looked for the "literal" meaning of the primary sources in addition to their own discretionary inferences. Ali Rahnema summarizes the process in the article "Islamic Jurisprudence and Public Policy:"

> Based on their individual assessment of the spirit of shari'a, jurists singled out criteria or standards they believed to be the quintessential attribute and object of law, on which legal judgments could be based. The sources of the law were expanded from the unalterable letter of the law to include the highly speculative and therefore maneuverable domain of the spirit of the law. Those single standards, which became accepted as sources of Islamic law, constitute the elements of the tertiary sources. Imams from different schools [of Islam], to the extent that they came to accept the use of such standards, identified different quintessential attributes of the spirit of Islam. Each, however, justified their newly articulated yardstick on the grounds that it furthered the public welfare of Muslims and facilitated their everyday life. Tertiary sources or standards

provide Islamic law with a considerable degree of freedom, leverage, and flexibility to deal with modern problems and issues.[97]

This independent, discretion-prone decision-making allows for all engaged in discerning the "Islamicity" of the regime to make factionally based judgments. Coupled with the fact that the religious institutions enjoy total autonomy, this has meant that nearly all the consequential incidents of factionalism have involved the religious dimension or its institutions. For example, since its inception in 1980, the Guardian Council has been dominated by the conservative right faction. The council on numerous occasions has vetoed bills proposed by leftist members in the parliament, arguing that they are incompatible with Islamic tenets. Other super-bodies such as the Assembly of Experts have experienced their share of factionalism. As the institution entrusted with the crucial task of selecting the leader, members of the assembly are able to rely on their "own" judgment as to who is fit to become the *faqih* in Iran. This means that whichever faction dominates the assembly can select a "fit" leader based on its own interests.[98]

Finally, mention should be made of how the historical practice of independent *ijtihad* in Shiism can be both conducive to factionalism and create further systemic confusion. There are many qualified jurists within the Shii establishment, potentially a destabilizing factor for the regime and particularly for the leader. If the religious credentials of the *faqih* are not superior to others, or if his rule is not sanctioned by any powerful members of the clerical establishment (as was the case with Khamenehi), the rulings of the leader and indeed his mandate could be contested by other *foqaha*. Khamenehi's legitimacy was questioned by Ahmad Azari-Qomi and Hossein-Ali Montazeri in 1997 when both of these senior ayatollahs questioned the leader's partisan politics and his qualifications as a source of emulation.[99]

To sum up, the new Islamic state that would develop out of the rubble of the shah's old regime was dependent on the politico-religious views of Khomeini and the social realities and political necessities faced by the postrevolutionary regime. The interactions of three dimensions—the religious, the populist, and the revolutionary—resulted in a political system based on multiple centers of power, a diffused polity where ultimate power and authority lay with the religious and revolutionary institutions and not with the central government. This political system espoused by the clergy not only served the immediate interests of the clerical elite but in many ways resembled the Islamic government spoken of by Khomeini prior to the revolution in *Hokumat-e Islami*. Yet the formation of an Islamic republic and the structural delineation of the three ideological dimensions of the postrevolutionary regime resulted in institutional contradictions and incompatibilities. In fact, if one uses Tilly's definition of a state (differentiation from other organizations in society, autonomy, centralization, and formal coordination of its parts) as a yardstick in Iran, one could argue that a state in its true sense does not exist in the Islamic Republic. Rather, one sees a collection of incoherent power structures that dispense power; enact, arbitrate, and execute rules; and allocate resources and values in society. For the factions, this unique polity becomes a tool for pursuing factional interests clothed in ideological terms.

The major focus of this work will be factionalism that takes place through the institutions of the religious and republican dimensions since, although the regime in Iran still upholds its revolutionary rhetoric, this dimension has withered away and is effectively approaching nonexistence. For example, the Revolutionary Courts have been integrated into the ministry of justice,[100] and the KII was merged with the gendarmerie and the police in 1991 to create the Law Enforcement Forces (*Niruha-ye Intezami*). The Martyr Foundation still claims to look after the needs of the families of the war martyrs, but they have not been successful in achieving their intended goals due to adverse economic conditions in Iran.[101] In fact, rather than serving their original noble causes, some *Nehads* such as the Foundation of Dispossessed have amassed great wealth and today resemble a business enterprise rather than a revolutionary body, as elaborated in the following case study.

Case Study: *Bonyad-e Mostaz'afin*, the *Nehads*, and Factionalism

The most powerful and influential of all revolutionary bodies today is the *Bonyad-e Mostaz'afin*. At its inception, the *Bonyad* was asked to assume control of the Pahlavi Foundation and employ its resources in charitable causes. From the very beginning, the *Bonyad* was essentially an independent organization, and it often made a point of stating that it only took orders from the *faqih* and the Revolutionary Council.[102] According to articles 4 and 9 of the *Bonyad*'s constitution, the *Bonyad* "is a financially and legally independent body, and only the Imam has total power over its activities."[103] Such claims were reinforced by the elite. Prime Minister Musavi, the Imam's representative to the *Bonyad* during the first decade of the revolution, reaffirmed its independence: "because the *Bonyad* is a revolutionary body, it is free from restrictive governmental and bureaucratic red tape."[104] The second director of the *Bonyad,* Sadeq Tabatabai, rebuffed accusations that the government should investigate the *Bonyad* and request an accounting of their management of the extensive property and wealth:"Only the Imam can ascertain what should happen to the confiscated things."[105] In accordance with Musavi's statement, Tabatabai agreed that:

> Revolutionary *Nehads* belong to the people and should be administered by them rather than by inflexible bureaucratic rules and regulations. Therefore, if there is misuse and irregularity [in the *Bonyad*] it is the people's. We are against the *Bonyad* becoming governmental, because this will strip its revolutionary spirit. The difference between this revolutionary body and other similar organizations is that, based on the Imam's rulings, the assets of the *Bonyad* belong to the people and are under the supervision of the *vali-ye faqih*. Thus, the holdings of *Bonyad* differ from [other] public possessions."[106]

This rhetoric was supported by Prime Minister Musavi, who on more than one occasion defended the *Bonyad* and its activities against accusations of corruption and accumulated wealth, and spoke against the fact that some people called the *Bonyad* the Foundation of the Affluent (*Bonyad-e Mostakbarin*).[107] All prominent figures supported the *Bonyad* and its actions, including Ali Akbar Rafsanjani, Speaker of the Majlis, who believed that "the *Bonyad* is another helpful arm for the government."[108] With such support, the *Bonyad* gradually became more and more wealthy, and its increasing wealth was accompanied by power. In October 1983, the *Bonyad* announced that, in order to lower the price of traveling by sea, it had created its own shipping line.[109] The same year, the *Bonyad* made an "official" statement of its assets: 50 billion rials in agricultural land, real estate worth about 20 billion rials, and ownership of eight hundred and fifty companies, of which five hundred were confiscated from the previous regime.[110] Not surprisingly, four months later *Tabatabai* was able to announce that the *Bonyad* "is not only the biggest economic enterprise in Iran, but one of the largest in the world."[111]

In 1984, the *Bonyad* announced that its total assets were worth 227 billion rials.[112] But instead of paying taxes, the *Bonyad* received many governmental benefits and concessions because its business activities were designed to help the poor. For example, in 1982 the government allowed *Bonyad* to release 85 thousand tons of goods from custom houses throughout Iran,[113] and in 1985 it was allowed to import 30 thousand tons of cotton.[114] The new head of the *Bonyad*, Tahmasb Mazaheri (appointed in 1984), announced in 1986 that the *Bonyad's* assets exceeded 53 billion tomans,[115] but curiously, a year later he stated that the *Bonyad* had spent only 70 million rials for the disinherited.[116] (A toman is worth 100 rials.) In 1989, the leadership of *Bonyad* changed hands twice. In February of that year, Mazaheri was replaced by Baqerian, and in September of the same year, the new leader, Khamenehi, elected Mohsen Rafiqdust to lead the *Bonyad*, a post which he has held until recently.[117]

The *Bonyad* was factionally plagued from the start. Its first director, Ali Naqi Khamushi, and its supervisor, Mehdi Araqi, were powerful members of the conservative right faction. However, as the regime became more radical, the influence of the left increased, and in fact the three directors after Khamushi were sympathizers of the left. Not surprisingly, the left strongly supported the *Bonyad*, and when in 1984 some MPs suggested more government control, leftist members of the Majlis strongly opposed such measures.[118] By the time Rafiqdust, a well-known member of the conservatives, was elected, things had changed. The political landscape of Iran had changed as well: Khamenehi had replaced Khomeini and the radicals were losing power (see chapter 3). This alteration directly affected the *Bonyad* when pro-conservative Khamenehi replaced Baqerian with Mohsen Rafiqdust before Baqerian's term had expired (leadership of the *Bonyad* is for two years). When control of the *Bonyad* was turned over to Rafiqdust, the power of conservative bazaaris was also strengthened.

In order to ward off possible challenges to his authority from the left, Rafiqdust immediately announced that no one except the *faqih*, Khamenehi, had power over him,[119] and Khamenehi reciprocated by further empowering the *Bonyad*. Before Rafiqdust came to power, there had been discussion that some of what *Bonyad* controlled should be turned directly over to the people or the government,[120] but instead, in March 1990 Khamenehi gave *Bonyad* total control over everything that was currently under its possession.[121] Once the conservatives had a man in the powerful *Bonyad*, they strongly supported Rafiqdust in order to strengthen him and their own position. The *Bonyad* controlled half of Iran's biggest sock company, Asia, and the other half was owned by a powerful, pro-conservative bazaari foundation called Al-Hoda. In November 1990, the foundation announced that it was giving up its share so that the *Bonyad* could have total control over the company.[122] Although this appeared to be a charitable contribution, it meant the company could take full advantage of the *Bonyad's* tax-free commerce status and customs duties exemption and enabled both the *Bonyad* and the bazaaris to reap increased financial benefits.

In addition to the money it was making from its businesses, the fortunes of the *Bonyad* increased because of governmental assistance. The *Bonyad's* budget for 1990 was 80 billion rials, of which nearly half was contributed by the government, and the 1991 budget was expected to be 210 billion rials, with the government providing 20 billion.[123] Rafiqdust consistently maintained a free market, pro-bazaari line: "We believe that the Iranian economy should be based on supply and demand where the government is only a supervisor."[124] In a two-part interview with the daily *Ettela'at*, Rafiqdust defended his free market philosophy by pointing out figures that indicated that *Bonyad's* unencumbered import of goods was indeed helping prices to fall, and he went so far as to claim that the profit made through the sale of cars imported by the *Bonyad* at reduced government prices was being spent on the *mostaz'afin*.[125]

Rafiqdust gave his support to other revolutionary organizations such as Imam Khomeini's Relief Committee, which was controlled by another famous bazaari, Habibollah Asgar-Owladi. In 1990, for example, the *Bonyad* "donated" 6 billion rials to the Committee, thus further binding the conservatives together.[126] By 1991, the *Bonyad* was doing business in tourism, clothing, plastics, fruit juice, and even chewing gum, all in the name of helping the poor. Rafiqdust continued to claim that the business he was conducting was religiously sanctioned (*shari'*),[127] and in spite of the objections that might have been raised, in 1992 Khamenehi reappointed Rafiqdust for another two years.[128]

Gradually the inconsistencies became too great to ignore, and the conservative-dominated fourth Majlis was forced to investigate the activities of Rafiqdust and the *Bonyad*. In 1993, the Majlis special committee investigating *Bonyad* found numerous instances of embezzlement and wrongdoing. The most important revelation was that the *Bonyad* would import goods as a shielded organization at government rates that were only a third of the open market prices, but would sell its goods at free market prices, thus making a huge profit.[129]

In spite of the special committee's findings, Khamenehi's support of Rafiqdust made him untouchable. In fact, Rafiqdust became aggressive and claimed that the *Bonyad* was a "private enterprise" and should not be classified as a public body.[130] Moreover, he even called on the government to break its monopoly on such sensitive enterprises as banking, and the *Bonyad* has in fact opened it own financial and credit institution.[131] In the face of this controversy, Rafiqdust has continued to be reappointed by Khamenehi every two years.

In the winter of 1995, the weekly *Payam-e Daneshju* uncovered perhaps the biggest financial scandal within the Islamic Republic thus far. The paper revealed embezzlement by Rafiqdust and his brother amounting to 123 billion tomans in one of Iran's biggest banks. Allegedly, the brother of the head of the *Bonyad,* along with his friend Fazel Khodadad, used Rafiqdust's influence to obtain this money from the bank.[132] In response to accusations of his involvement, Rafiqdust defended his position, stating that he had nothing to do with it but his brother should be punished if he was involved.[133] Ultimately, Khodadad was sentenced to death and Rafiqdust's brother received a sentence of life in prison, although he has reportedly been seen outside. As for Rafiqdust himself, he was reappointed by Khamenehi six months later for another two-year term as head of the *Bonyad.*[134]

CHAPTER 2

Factional Politics in Khomeini's Era

1981–89

With the dismissal of President Abolhasan Bani-Sadr in the summer of 1981, supporters of Khomeini had discouraged other political contenders and enjoyed a near monopoly of power in Iran. By the second parliamentary election in 1983, the process of eliminating opponents to *velayat-e faqih* was completed when the remaining opposition, namely members of the pro-Bazargan Freedom Movement, were not reelected to the Majlis.[1] The institutional arrangement of the religious and revolutionary organizations—the structure of the *velayat-e faqih* state—was now successfully established.

But Khomeini's simple emphasis on the Islamicity of the regime did not provide sufficient guidelines to determine the specific policies of the state, that is, its sociocultural policies, the nature of its economic system, and its foreign policy orientation. Disagreements over these choices led to the differentiation of factions and the upsurge of factional politics in the Islamic Republic of Iran. More importantly than the new government's policies, though, it was over the characteristics of the government of *velayat-e faqih* that the followers of Khomeini began exhibiting sharp ideological divisions. To the dismay of the leadership and their Islamist followers, the disagreement from the start among pro-Khomeini forces revolved, ironically, around the soul of the state, its Islamicity.

In September 1984, both the speaker of Majlis, Ali-Akbar Hashemi Rafsanjani, and the president, Khamenehi, conceded that two overarching ideological positions existed within the Iranian polity among the groups and individuals loyal to Khomeini: one conservative and the other radical.[2] The first position—which after some shifts in its views and membership gradually became known as the conservative or traditional right—maintained a conservative and nonrevolutionary stance on the nature of the postrevolutionary regime. Rightists believed in the sanctity of private property and opposed state taxation of the private sector, wanted strict implementation of shari'a in the sociocultural sphere, and opposed the export of the revolution to other Islamic countries. This faction enjoyed the backing of the traditional Iranian bourgeoisie, the merchants of bazaar, as well as of the ultra-orthodox clergy and the highly religious segments of Iranian society. Influential clerical members of this camp, the majority of whom were powerful members of the Qom Seminary (howzeh), included Ayatollahs Mohammad Reza Mahdavi-Kani, Ahmad Jannati, Mohammad Imami-Kashani, Ahmad Azari-Qomi, Lotfollah Safi, and Abolqasem Khazali, as well as hojjatol-Islam Ali Akbar Nateq-Nuri.

The other position, the radicals or the left, advocated the cause of the poor, believed in the export of the revolution, maintained a more tolerant view on sociocultural policies, and supported state-sponsored redistributive and egalitarian policies. Prominent figures from this camp included Prime Minister Mir-Hossien Musavi, Behzad Nabavi, hojajol-Islam Mohammad Musavi Khoeiniha, Mehdi Karrubi, Ali-Akbar Mohtashami, and Ayatollah Mir-Karim Musavi Ardabili.[3] The views of Ayatollahs Mohammad Beheshti and Hossien Ali Montazeri were also in line with the views of the left.

Aside from these two dominant ideological tendencies, another political bloc that gradually emerged is worth noting: those who supported the views of the speaker of the Majlis, or who I shall refer to as "Rafsanjanites." Unlike the conservatives, who believed in essentially a free market economy, Rafsanjani adhered to a mixed economy. Thus he supported, along with the left, statist measures such as the nationalization of domestic industries and high taxation, in addition to maintaining progressive views in the cultural sphere.

The current post-Khomeini factions mentioned in the introduction were eventually formed out of these ideological positions. To make sense of the maze of factions during this period, a few points need to be made. As a rule, despite Rafsanjani's occasional support for statist measures, the conservatives and the Rafsanjanites were considered as one camp while Khomeini was alive, due mainly to their stance on economic issues and a pragmatic foreign policy. Indeed they formed an alliance after Khomeini's death and until 1992 (when Rafsanjani became at odds with the conservatives and formed his own faction, the modern right), he was closer to the conservatives than the left. Consequently, the two camps were often regarded as one political bloc and called the right or the pragmatics during the first decade of the revolution. In this chapter, the distinction between the two camps will be maintained with regards to particular policies. Generally, both camps can correctly be referred to as the right and/or the two rights.

The different political, economic, or foreign policy positions held by the factions are perhaps the easiest for outsiders to perceive. The primary issue among factions in Iran, however, the one that they use as a differentiating principle, has been their views on political Islam and the interpretation of *fiqh,* or religious jurisprudence. The two ends of the spectrum are the traditional (interpretation of) *fiqh* or *fiqh-e sonnati,* and dynamic *fiqh* or *fiqh-e puya.* Put simply, those who follow traditional interpretation believe that primary ordinances (*ahkam-e avvaliyeh*) based on the two pillars of Shii Islam (the Qoran and the *Sonna*) provide sufficient means to govern an Islamic society. Jurists should deviate from this tradition and issue new religious decrees, or secondary ordinances (*ahkam-e sanaviyeh),* only in special circumstances and only when there is an "overriding necessity" in the society for the enactment of such decrees. The idea is that because the Islamic regime has (or should have) in mind a political order that resembles that of Prophet Mohammed's, reliance on the existing ordinances is sufficient to govern Muslims.

Supporters of dynamic *fiqh* believe that, although primary Islamic ordinances provide a solid foundation for the governing laws of the country, Muslims live in a different era and are faced with problems that did not exist during the time of the Prophet. As such, the shari'a must be constantly changing, adapting, and producing new decrees (hence the word dynamic) as new issues arise in society. Thus there is a greater need to create secondary ordinances.

In the context of factional politics in Iran, support for one *fiqh* or another becomes quite significant. Those who uphold a more "radical" (left) or "modernist" (Rafsanjani and the modern right) interpretation of the Islamic revolution support dynamic *fiqh.* Proponents of dynamic *fiqh* emphasize the significance of the populist and/or the revolutionary dimensions of the regime, and in that capacity they support a more deep-seated socioeconomic transformation of Iranian society, which entails tackling contemporary issues not discussed in the Qoran or addressed by the Prophet. Consequently, supporters of this *fiqh* place a particular emphasis on secondary ordinances.[4] Defenders of the traditional *fiqh,* on the other hand, maintain that the primary goal of the revolution should be no more than the implementation of Islamic tenets as they are stated in the Qoran and explained further by the Prophet's *Hadith.* New issues therefore must be dealt with in the context of the traditional *fiqh.* Such views are held by the conservatives in the regime.[5] As a rule, those who adhere to the traditional *fiqh* maintain that it is the revolution, the society, and the governing principles of the Islamic Republic that must adapt to the orthodox, historical Shii jurisprudence. Proponents of the dynamic *fiqh* believe that Islam and the Shii *fiqh* should be adapted to the needs of the revolution.[6]

The Conservatives

Organizationally, the backbone of the conservatives since the victory of the revolution is the Society of Combatant Clergy (*Jame'eh-e ye Rouhaniyat-e Mobarez,* hereafter JRM) and its associated organizations (*tashakkolha-ye hamsu),* the Allied Islamic Society (*Jamiyat-e Mo'talefeh ye Islami,* hereafter *Mo'talefeh),* and the Society of Qom Seminary Teachers (*Jame'eh-e ye Modarresin-e Howzeh-ye Elmiyeh-ye Qom,* hereafter JMHEQ). Since the victory of the revolution, the triangle of JRM, the *Mo'talefeh,* and the JMHEQ have maintained a close relationship and acted in the Iranian polity as a distinct faction with the JRM acting as its nucleus.[7]

The JRM and Its Satellite Organizations

Until the presidential election of 1997,[8] the JRM was considered to be the most powerful religio-political organization in the Islamic Republic.[9] Members of the JRM, which originally included both conservatives and radicals, have occupied the most prominent positions in the postrevolutionary regime. The society has provided the regime with two presidents (Khamenehi, Rafsanjani), two prime ministers (Javad Bahonar, Ayatollah Mohammad Reza Mahdavi-Kani), one leader (Khamenehi), three heads of the Iranian judiciary (Ayatollahs Mohammad Hossein Beheshti, Mohammad Yazdi, Mir-Karim Musavi-Ardabili), two speakers of parliament (Rafsanjani, Akbar Nateq-Nuri), and two ministers of State (Mahdavi-Kani, Nateq-Nuri), as well as a number of other senior posts. Clearly, JRM has played a key role in the institutionalization of the Islamic Republic and holds the lion's share of responsibility for its successful establishment.

The JRM and its political activities before and immediately after the revolution were crucial for the victory of the pro-Khomeini forces. Established in Teheran in 1977, members of the JRM had the goal of gathering all pro-Khomeini clergymen, rallying the dissatisfied masses, and organizing a nation-wide struggle against the monarchy in Iran. At the time of its inception, the central figures of the JRM were Beheshti and Ayatollah Morteza Motahari. The former was the coordinator of the movement, and Motahari, a respected and well-known scholar of theology at Teheran University, joined Khomeini as the other major theorist of the Islamic state. These two figures, along with other JRM members including Bahonar, Mahdavi-Kani, Rafsanjani, Khamenehi, Nateq-Nuri, hojajol-Islam Mehdi Karrubi, and Hadi Ghaffari, began spreading the word of Khomeini in mosques, universities, and bazaars in addition to organizing pro-Khomeini and anti-shah demonstrations throughout the country that ultimately led to the downfall of the monarchy.[10]

Having been such an influential player in the revolution and the establishment of the Islamic state, the JRM considered itself—perhaps rightly—entitled to an primary role in the postrevolutionary regime. Such an attitude is enshrined in the JRM's constitution, which states that the aim of the society is to embody and enforce the religious needs and aspirations of the Iranian Islamic community. The core objectives of the JRM are to guard the Islamic revolution and its ideological achievements; to prevent aberrations in the revolutionary path; to propagate Islamic learning; to oversee all organs and institutions serving the Islamic Republic of Iran (IRI); and to strengthen the mosques as the true bastions of Islam, in addition to increasing the role of all Islamic preparatory centers.[11]

In its original form, the central council of the JRM was composed of seventy clergy from Teheran who, apart from having religious credentials, had all been politically active in the toppling of the monarchy. Among the original twenty-eight members of the central council were: Motahari, Beheshti, Mohammad Mofatteh, Khamenehi, Rafsanjani, Bahonar, Ayatollah Fazlollah Mahalati, Yazdi, Nateq-Nuri, Ayatollah Mohammad Ali Movahhedi-Kermani, Ayatollah Abbas Ali Amid-Zanjani, Hasan Rouhani, Reza Taqavi, Ayatollah Mohammad Imami-Kashani, Abol-Hossein Moezzi, Mehdi Karrubi, and Muhammad Doai.[12]

Membership of the JRM has greatly changed since its inception. Of its original members, the more left-leaning individuals split off from the JRM in 1988, and, together with hojjajol-Islam Ali Akbar Mohtashami, Mohammad Musavi Khoeiniha, Khatami, and Mohammad Tavassoli, among others, established the Association of the Combatant Clergymen (*Majma'-e Rouhaniyun-e Mobarez*). Ayatollahs Motahari and Mofatteh were both assassinated in 1979, and Beheshti and Bahonar were killed along with more than seventy members of the IRP in the June 1981 bombing of the IRP's headquarters. Khamenehi resigned his membership of the JRM after replacing Khomeini as the leader but maintained close links to the society. Although officially still a member of the JRM, Rafsanjani gradually formed the modern right faction. A glance at the positions held by JRM members—all the rest are conservatives—in the Islamic Republic shows that, although somewhat weakened after the presidential election in 1997, the JRM still enjoys a great deal of prominence in the Islamic Republic. Following is a list of influential members of the JRM who are still active members of the society and some of the positions they have held since the victory of the revolution.

• Ayatollah Mohammad Yazdi: MP, member of the Guardian Council and the former head of the judicial branch

• Ayatollah Mohammed Reza Mahdavi-Kani: member of the Revolutionary Council, prime minister, supervisor of the Revolutionary Committees, chancellor of Imam Sadeq University, and currently the secretary of the JRM

• Ayatollah Mohammad Imami-Kashani: member of the Guardian Council, leader of Friday prayer of Qom

• hojjatol-Islam Ali Akbar Nateq-Nuri: MP, speaker of the fourth and the fifth Majlis, minister of the state, member of the Expediency Council, and member of the National Security Council

• Ayatollah Mohammed Ali Movahhedi-Kermani: member of the Council of the Experts, MP, representative of the *vali-ye faqih* in the Revolutionary Guard

• Ayatollah Mohyeddin Anvari: MP and currently deputy director for mosque affairs

• Hasan Rouhani: MP, representative of *vali-ye faqih* in the National Security Council, and head of the Center for Strategic Studies overseen by the president

• Reza Taqavi: MP, deputy director of the Islamic Propagation Organization, and the current speaker of the JRM

• Abdol-Hossein Moezzi: deputy for cultural affairs of Khamenehi until 1997[13]

The JRM's *Tashakkol-ha-ye Hamsu* (hereafter *Hamsu*) encompasses its satellite organizations and bodies, hence the word *hamsu* or "in line (with)." According to Mohammad Reza Bahonar, a powerful member of one these organizations, the reason for their creation was to give cohesion to individuals and groups within Iranian society who share similar views to the JRM's and believe that such views can be pursued more effectively under the guidance and the leadership of the JRM.[14] Some of the most important organizations of the *Hamsu* include the Zeynab Society, the Society of Islamic Engineers (*Jame'eh-e ye Islami-ye Mohandesin,* hereafter JIM), and the Islamic Society of Culturists (*Jame'eh-e ye Islami-ye Farhangian).*

The Allied Islamic Society (*Jamiyat-e Mo'talefeh-ye Islami).* The most powerful and influential of all of *Hamsu* organizations, however, has been the Allied Islamic Society or the *Mo'talefeh.* The society gained fame in the 1960s when Khomeini began his activities against the shah. In 1963, recently risen to the title of Ayatollah Ozma (Grand Ayatollah), Khomeini strongly objected to the shah's White Revolution, which included reforms such as land distribution programs, voting rights for women, and the omission of Islamic tenets from local election bills. Khomeini's opposition led to the famous uprising of June 5 (*Panzdah-e Khordad),* during which he was arrested and put under house arrest for ten months.[15] In February 1964 Khomeini was once again arrested, but this time he was exiled to Turkey for his opposition to a law that provided diplomatic immunity for American military personnel in Iran. Throughout the uprising, the bazaars and major mosques in Iran were turned into centers for mobilization of the traditional-religious segment of Iranian society who supported Khomeini against the state. The bulk of resistance against the shah came from all strata of the bazaaris, whose members were killed by the hundreds during clashes with security police. The organizers of the anti-shah forces in the bazaars were the Allied Islamic Religious Congregations (*Heyat-ha-ye Mo'talefeh-ye Islami*).[16]

The *Mo'talefeh* began its activity in April 1963 with the blessing of Khomeini. In the words of one of its original members, Habibollah Asgar-Owladi, "The *Mo'talefeh* answered the call of Imam in forming the Hizbollah."[17] The organization was made up of three separate groups headed by powerful bazaar merchants such as Mehdi Araqi and Sadeq and Hashem Amani, and reputedly enjoyed the support of five thousand highly religious bazaaris and their clients.[18] Following Khomeini's exile, the *Mo'talefeh* began an underground armed struggle against the shah and made history in 1964 when they assassinated the person whom they believed was responsible for Ayatollah Khomeini's exile, Prime Minister Ali Mansur. Hashem Amani and three young followers of *Mo'talefeh,* Mohammad Bokharai, and Morteza Niknejhad, were arrested and later executed for Mansur's assassination. Other prominent members of the *Mo'talefeh* included Asadollah Lajevardi and Asadollah Badamchian.

While Khomeini was in exile, the activities of *Mo'talefeh* were guided by Khomeini through Mohyeddin Anvari and Ayatollah Motahari.[19] Following the revolution, the organization renamed itself *Jamiyat-e Mo'talefeh-ye Islami.* The *Mo'talefeh* publishes a weekly paper entitled *Shoma (Shohada-ye Mo'talefeh-e Islami,* or the Martyrs of the *Mo'talefeh),* and receives the backing of the Society of Islamic Engineers (JIM), which expresses its views through its own monthly journal. Influential JIM members after the revolution are: Morteza Nabavi, Mohammad Reza Bahonar, Hasan Ghafuri-Fard, brothers Ali and Mohammad Javad Larijani, Mostafa Mir-Salim, Mohsen Rafiqdust, and Ali Naqi Khamushi.[20]

Since the victory of the revolution, the bastion of high-ranking ulama in Iran has been the Society of Qom Seminary Teachers, the JMHEQ. Members of this society include many powerful sources of emulation, *maraje',* such as Ayatollahs Mohammad Fazel Lankarani, Naser Makarem-Shirazi, Mohammad Taqi Behjat, Vahid Khorasani, and Javad Tabrizi, in addition to other powerful ayatollahs such as Ahmad Jannati, Hossein Rasti-Kashani, Mohammad Mohammadi-Gilani, Mohammad Yazdi, Ahmad Azari-Qomi, Mohyeddin Fazel-Harandi, Yusef Sane'i, Lotfollah Safi, Mohammad Mo'men, Abolqasem Khazali, Mohammad Imami-Kashani, Ibrahim Amini, and Ibrahim Jenati. In the Iranian polity, members of JMHEQ have been the theologians of the powerful Guardian Council (the present secretary Ayatollah Ahmad Jannati, Yazdi, Sane'i, Mohammadi-Gilani, Safi, Khazali, Imami-Kashani, Mo'men). In addition, the clergy of JMHEQ have been influential in the Council of Experts, as all are members of the Council.

The Historical Alliance of Clergy-Bazaar: The Fortitude of the Traditional Right

"The bazaar and the mosque are inseparable twins," noted Ahmad Ashraf, an observer of Iranian social history, "having served, for many centuries, as the primary area of public life in urban Iran."[21] Aside from the central government, "the alliance" has been the focus of socioeconomic power in Iran as it has been an effective political bloc in modern Iranian history. As the bastion of social movements, this alliance has been the major force behind three important political events in Iran: the tobacco incident of 1891 and the Constitutional Revolution of 1905–1906 in addition to the 1979 revolution.

In 1891, Naser-el Din Shah of the Qajar dynasty (1789–1925) granted a British subject the monopoly of the production, distribution, sale, and export of tobacco in Iran. The tobacco industry employed over 200,000 people at that time. The merchants in bazaars across Iran and the ulama, who also had a financial interest in the industry, began a nationwide campaign against the British monopoly. Ayatollah Hasan Shirazi, the most prominent clergyman at that time, issued a fatwa against the use of tobacco, and the merchants shut down the main bazaars throughout Iran. Unable to placate the protesters, the shah abrogated the concession in 1892.[22]

Thirteen years later, this scenario was to repeat itself during the Constitutional Revolution. The first Iranian constitution, hastily drafted by the European-educated Iranian intelligentsia on the model of the Belgian constitution, was meant to limit the power of the shah and empower the parliament to conduct the affairs of the country. The main forces behind the constitutional movement were the merchants, the ulama, and the intelligentsia. The merchants financed the revolution, the ulama gave its religious blessing, and the intelligentsia formulated the revolutionary ideology. All three groups either resented the despotism of the Qajars or had been adversely affected by the monarch's foreign and domestic politics as well as by the presence of imperial powers in Iran.[23]

To understand such sociopolitical power on the part of the ulama and the bazaar, one must trace its historical roots. The rise of the Safavid dynasty in the sixteenth century, the first dynasty in Iran to make Shiism the official religion, greatly enhanced the position of the ulama and created fundamental changes in the relationship between the ulama and the state. According to the Shii doctrine of government, the state was a transient form of political power, and in order to be considered as legitimate it needed the religious sanctioning of the ulama.[24] Lacking an independent source of legitimacy, the Safavids and later the Qajars became dependent on the clergy for religious legitimization of their rule. As such, powerful ulama in Iran could openly condemn the government and its policies, for example, during the tobacco incident. The ability to question and undermine the state's dominion has prompted many historians to suggest that dual authority existed in nineteenth-century Iran.[25] The ulama's monopoly of the interpretation of the *fiqh* and the financial might accumulated through collection of religious taxes and ownership of state-donated, religiously endowed land (*waqf*) provided them with considerable economic power and financial autonomy.[26] Moreover, as the spiritual leaders of the people, and as a group whose participation was needed to manage everyday matters, the ulama enjoyed an intimate relationship with the Iranian population. Ordinary Iranians looked to the ulama to mediate their grievances with the state and to protect them against the often despotic actions of the state, particularly during the Qajar dynasty.[27]

Among all the segments of Iranian society, the ulama had a special relationship with the merchants. Due to their religious sentiments, the bazaaris needed the services of the ulama to bless their day-to-day commerce in addition to needing the good will of the clergy, who had close ties with the state and with the population at large. In return, the merchants paid religious taxes and other funds to the ulama to conduct religious ceremonies and create religious schools. By themselves the bazaaris could not exercise enough sociopolitical power; however, in this alliance, through affiliation with the ulama, they became a powerful social force that the state had to reckon with.[28] The mosques in Iran traditionally are located at the center of bazaars made up of prosperous merchants *(tojjar)*, the heads of guild-like associations *(asanaf)*, foot-boys, small shopkeepers, and peddlers. The relationship between these groups created a closely knit socioeconomic and religious system.[29] One way of bringing the members of this system together were *heyats* or religious congregations:

> The major social instruments for sustaining cohesion among bazaaris as well as maintaining their networks for protest mobilization were *heyats* (primary religious groups), sermons of preachers, and the late-afternoon/early-evening congregational prayers. Prominent merchants and guild leaders were expected to gather in the major mosque of the bazaar, using the occasion to discuss matters of mutual interest in business and occasionally political realms. The religious groups are multifaceted and interpenetrate many levels of civic life through informal face-to-face groups which serve as occupational, neighborhood, religious, interpersonal, friendship, cooperative, self-help, or political networks in various sections of the bazaars and neighborhoods of different communities.[30]

During the reign of the Pahlavis, the nature of this alliance remained largely intact.[31] In fact, the June 1964 uprising solidified the alliance. Mohammad Reza Shah generally perceived the bazaaris as "fanatic" and resistant to his modernization efforts.[32] Although the bazaaris increased their material gain during the reign of the shah,[33] they once again, together with the clergy, formed an alliance against the state. As during the Constitutional Revolution of 1905–1906, the bazaaris were the main financial contributors to the revolutionary movement and were indispensable in forming anti-shah groups that radiated from the mosques in urban areas throughout Iran.[34]

One reason for the bazaaris' hostility towards the shah was his economic policies. The industrialization policies of the shah favored a modern, dependent industrial bourgeois over the traditional Iranian bourgeois, the bazaaris. The bazaaris, who during the 1970s "controlled most of the national imports, including more than two-thirds of the nation's domestic wholesale trade and more than 30 percent of all imports,"[35] saw their livelihood endangered through the state's interventionist policies such as increased taxation, import restrictions, price monitoring measures, and an antiprofiteering campaign. Moreover, the shah's support for the creation and expansion of cooperatives created further economic competition for the bazaaris on yet another front. Ever since 1963, the creation of these cooperatives had been deeply resented and disapproved of by the mosque-bazaar alliance, including Khomeini himself.[36] So the agitated bazaaris once again joined hands with the clergy to instigate another rebellion against the state:

> The bazaaris' conflicts with the government resulted from growing state intervention in capital allocation and accumulation and the increasing limitations and regulations of the market system. The state's development policies systematically favored the industrial and modern sectors of the economy. Government capital-allocation policies and lack of protection for small, traditional industries jeopardized artisans, while government intervention in the commercial sector adversely affected the bazaaris. These policies replaced the market mechanism and violated the rights of merchants, shopkeepers, and artisans, forcing them to engage in collective actions in order to defend their socioeconomic and political interests.[37]

The hostility toward the shah on the part of the alliance during the 1979 revolution thus was not a historically isolated phenomenon. In fact, there has been a pattern in the modern history of Iran whereby members of the alliance have become revolutionaries whenever policies of the central government had adversely affected their economic welfare. A case in point was the tobacco incident. Although the clergy appeared to be the main agitators of the revolt, in reality they were compelled by their constituents, the merchants, to issue a fatwa forbidding the use and sale of tobacco in Iran.[38] The same was true with the Constitutional Revolution, wherein the central government's economic policies of higher taxation, tighter control over imports, and imposition of customs duties infuriated the bazaaris and the ulama, thus sparking the revolution. Although some ulama supported the revolution, the bazaaris, hurt by the economic policies of the central government, further incited some of the hitherto nonrevolutionary clergy to participate in the movement.[39] In short, the bazaaris were politicized when their pockets were hit or when their ability to engage in import activities were impinged upon.[40]

It is useful to be mindful of the alliance's historical views, because its position after the revolution remained largely intact. This alliance eventually manifested itself as the traditional right faction after the 1979 revolution. From early on in the revolution, the majority of powerful pro-Khomeini conservative ulama such as Ahmad Azari-Qomi, Mohammad Reza Mahdavi-Kani, Ali Akbar Nateq-Nuri, Abolqasem Khazali, Mohammad Imami-Kashani, Ali Meshkini (the secretary of Council of Experts), and even Khamenehi remained closely connected to or sympathetic with the bazaaris and the *Mo'talefeh*. Scattered throughout the Iranian polity and in major political institutions such as the IRP, the Revolutionary Council, the Majlis, the Assembly of Experts, and the Guardian Council, this camp has championed the views set out above. Their twin goals have been maintaining the all-encompassing power of the clergy in all walks of life and defending an economic system conducive to the interests of the bazaaris.

Soon after the revolution, it became apparent that many prominent members of this faction, such as Mohammad Taqi Falsafi, Azari-Qomi, Akbar Parvaresh, Mahdavi-Kani, Khazali, and Nateq-Nuri, either belonged to or were sympathetic to a religious society called the *Hojjatiyeh* who upheld a entirely different perspective of the Islamic state and the religious leadership of the Muslim community during the occultation. Based on the views of its leader, Ayatollah Mahmud Halabi, who was staunchly anti-Baha'i in addition to having anti-Communist sentiments, the *Hojjatiyeh* was of the opinion that in the absence of the twelve imams, no government, Islamic or otherwise, could be truly legitimate and just. Moreover, the *Hojjatiyeh* believed in collective rather than individual leadership of the religious community. Finally, the society opposed direct clerical involvement in politics, supporting a more supervisory role for the clergy. Such intervention, argued the *Hojjatiyeh,* was in contrast to the historical status and function of the clergy as well as endangering Islam.[41] The original founders of the *Hojjatiyeh* were powerful merchants of the bazaar in addition to ultra-conservative clergy with close ties to the bazaaris.[42] Although none of the above-named individuals publicly admitted their association with the society, it was not difficult to detect that most of them were either members of the society or closely tied to it.[43] Naturally, such views placed Khomeini at odds with the *Hojjatiyeh* sympathizers as well as with the revolutionary mood of the population of the country. The conservative sympathizers of this society supported a free market economy (that favored bazaaris) and were against what they called radical government policies such as nationalization of trade and industry and land distribution, arguing instead for the sanctity of private property. After various attacks by Khomeini and the radicals in the Majlis, the society ultimately pledged loyalty to the Imam, announcing that it had ceased its activities in September 1983.[44]

The Radicals

The most organized radical-revolutionary voice among the pro-Khomeini forces after the victory of the revolution was that of the Crusaders of the Islamic Revolution (*Mojahedin-e Inqelab-e Islami,* hereafter MII). The MII came into existence in April 1979 through the union of six armed Islamic militia groups: *Ommat-e Vahedeh, Tohidi Badr, Tohidi Saaf, Falq, Mansorun,* and *Mohedin.*[45] Members of the new organization were devotees of Khomeini, and prior to the revolution they believed in armed struggle against the shah both inside and outside Iran. One of the first proclamations of the MII described the Imam as being "a supporter of the downtrodden and barefooted masses [*khlaq*] and against all kinds of economic exploitation." As with most pro-Khomeini Islamic groups in Iran, the MII claimed to have the goal of "guarding and spreading the principles of the Islamic revolution."[46]

Aside from the MII, more radical followers of Khomeini were some members of the IRP. The original members of the party, including its main founder Ayatollah Beheshti, were Khamenehi, Rafsanjani, Mohammad Javad Bahonar, and Ayatollah Mir-Karim Musavi-Ardabili. However, the IRP's central committee was made up of members of both the right and the left. The conservatives were Asadollah Badamchian, Abdollah Jasbi, Reza Zavarei, Habibollah Asgar-Owladi, Hasan Ghafuri-Fard, Jalalodin Farsi, Mostafa Mir-Salim, and Mehdi Araqi; the leftist members were Hasan Ayat, Abolqasem Sarhadizadeh, Mehdi Hashemi, Mir-Hossein Musavi, and Hadi Ghaffari. Although the conservatives within the IRP were further strengthened when, during the party's first congress in April 1983, more *Mo'talefeh* members were admitted to its central committee,[47] the IRP from the outset upheld a radical discourse, largely due to the influence of Beheshti and Musavi. The publication of IRP's book, *Mavaze-e Ma* (Our Positions), not only provided a more specific set of guidelines for the new regime and its supporters in the face of other contending revolutionary forces but indicated the broadly leftist position of the IRP. The IRP explicitly favored the dynamic *fiqh* as it "provided new solutions for new occurrences [*havades-e vaqe-eh*] and pondered issues [*masael-e mostahde-se*] in society."[48] According to the IRP, the populace willingly accepts the rule of the *faqih* but has a crucial role in the affairs of the country. But unlike other so-called democracies, this participation takes place through "Islamic channels." For the supporters of *velayat-e faqih,* the IRP's greatest success was that it weakened the nationalist and secularist opposition groups, and it resolved the Islamicity-republican dualism in favor of the former. According to the book *Mavaze-e Ma,* for example:

> In cases where the wishes of the people run counter to Islamic values, officials must not heed these desires. If they do so out of respect for people's wishes, the people later can reprimand the officials and tell them that it was your duty to make us aware not to follow our transient urges out of respect for people's views.[49]

In foreign policy, too, the IRP maintained a revolutionary position and believed that the "activities of the foreign ministry should be based on revolutionary principles and that the ministry must work for the export of the revolution and help all freedom movements [of the Third World]."[50] Economically, the party held a radical position. By emphasizing article 49 of the constitution, the IRP believed that personal ownership comes from individual work. In an Islamic economic system all exploitation by the capitalists (*saheban-e sarmaye*) must be destroyed, and no ground should be left for the rule of capital. Moreover, "taxes should be based on direct taxation and government should be directly involved in foreign trade and commerce," argued the IRP.[51] In order to be distinguished from other groups within the Iranian polity, particularly in the Majlis, radicals described themselves as *maktabi* (followers of the school of Islam), a designation that carried with it this particular doctrine of the left after the revolution. The other reason for members of the left calling themselves *maktabi* was to challenge the conservatives' claim to a religious–revolutionary position. To fulfill the revolutionary aspirations of the masses, the IRP believed that the new regime must be run by *maktabis.*[52]

Factional Politics in the Majlis and the Guardian Council

Factional conflict during the first decade of the revolution was most visible and heated between the conservatives and the radicals over the economic orientation of the regime and the role of the state in the economy. These battles were fought in the Majlis and the Guardian Council. From 1980 until 1988, the campaign was waged like this: the *maktabis* in the Majlis would propose radical solutions for the economy aimed at increasing the redistributive and regulative role of the state, and the conservatives would try to block the passage of such bills. If the conservatives failed to stop the bills from becoming law, they could rely on the conservative-dominated Guardian Council to reject most of the bills damaging to the interests of the bazaaris-clergy alliance. The first members of the Guardian Council, appointed by Khomeini in July 1980, were all conservatives from the JMHEQ: Ayatollahs Ahmad Jannati, Abdolrahim Rabbani-Shirazi, Morteza Rezvani, Lotfollah Safi, Yusef Sane'i, and Abolqasem Khazali.[53] When Shirazi died in March 1981, he was replaced by the JRM deputy, Mohammad Reza Mahdavi-Kani.[54] These members raised objections to 102 out of 370 bills proposed by the first Majlis and 118 out of 316 bills passed by the second Majlis, on the pretext of being un-Islamic or unconstitutional.[55] The leaders of the two camps in the Majlis were Prime Minister Mir-Hossein Musavi for the left, and Ayatollah Ahmad Azari-Qomi for the conservatives. This period also revealed the factional inclinations of Rafsanjani and Khamenehi. As the speaker of the Majlis, Rafsanjani moved shrewdly between the two ideological standpoints and presented himself as being above mundane factional politics. Khamenehi, as the president, was more partisan. By the end of 1988 and through his unrelenting confrontations with Musavi, he clearly displayed his affinity to the conservatives.

In the first Majlis (1980–1984), the IRP, MII, and JRM formed an alliance to undermine the position of the opponents of *velayat-e faqih* in the parliament, rejecting their credentials and using information provided by the students occupying the US embassy to taint their revolutionary reputation.[56] According to Bahman Baktiari, 120 of the 268 MPs in the first Majlis were *maktabis*. Prominent figures of this camp were Mohammad Musavi Khoeiniha, Asadollah Bayat, Morteza Alviri, Morteza Katirai, Hadi Ghaffari, Hadi Khamenehi, and Majid Ansari. The conservatives, which included *Hojjatiyeh* supporters, numbered sixty MPs, and included Mohammad Reza Bahonar, Mahdavi-Kani, Ali Akbar Velayati (foreign minister 1981–1997), Ahmad Tavakkoli, Ayatollah Mohammad Imami-Kashani, and Habibollah Asgar-Owladi. Sixty-three members followed the views of Rafsanjani; prominent among them were Mahmud Doai, Hasan Habibi, and Ayatollah Mohammad Yazdi.[57] To recapitulate, what set the Rafsanjanites apart from other pro-Khomeini supporters was the fact that while they supported a free market economy, they also advocated certain statist measures introduced by the left in the Majlis such as land reform, nationalization of foreign trade, and price controls.[58]

One of the first notable incidents of factionalism took place in the fall of 1981 when the *maktabi*-dominated Majlis refused Khamenehi's choice for prime minister, the conservative Ali Akbar Velayati. The left questioned both his competence and conservative ideological inclination.[59] This led to Khamenehi reluctantly introducing Mir Hossein Musavi to the Majlis, who comfortably secured the parliament's vote of confidence.[60] Khamenehi's support for the known conservative Velayati was another indication of the president's ideological leaning and the beginning of the personal struggle between Musavi and the president. On the second anniversary of its creation, and while stressing its support for policies such as nationalization of trade and commerce and land reform, the MII's most prominent figure, Behzad Nabavi, announced that the organization was experiencing serious differences on issues and policies with the conservative members of JMHEQ and the JRM, in addition to some members of the IRP.[61] These initial conflicts gradually evolved into harsh criticism of the conservatives. Nabavi laid the blame for food shortages in the country at the feet of the profit-hungry bazaaris, who monopolized import and distribution centers, and called for more government control over the economy.[62] Musavi followed suit and criticized the immoral bazaaris for making huge profits by creating black markets and hoarding goods.[63] Ayatollah Hossein Ali Montazeri gave his support to the radicals by calling on the government to exercise more control over the economy to prevent such abuses.[64] The anger in these attacks was perhaps fueled by the Guardian Council's rejections of many Majlis bills the radicals believed essential in creating a strong centralized economy and looking after the needs of the *mostazafin*. The left's arguments were based on and further buttressed by Khomeini's call to the first Majlis to act swiftly and work for the welfare of the dispossessed.[65]

The words of Khomeini, however, did not deter the Guardian Council from issuing conservative rulings and opposing radical measures almost immediately after its establishment. The most controversial of the bills passed by the Majlis, which created a nationwide debate, was the land reform law of 1981. In April 1980, the Revolutionary Council enacted the Islamic Republic's first version of this law, which aimed at distributing land among landless peasants. Such measures were quite controversial because land reform was one of the main objections raised by Khomeini against the shah during the 1963 uprising.[66] In August 1981, the Majlis, after extensive maneuvering by the factions, passed a revised land reform law. Ten days later, the Guardian Council announced its rejection of the bill on the grounds of its anti-Islamic content, claiming that it contradicted the Qoranic verse that states, "Muslims have mandate over their possessions."[67] In response, Rafsanjani, who had supported the bill in the Majlis, asked Khomeini to intervene. He remarked, "As the esteemed ayatollah is aware, due to the Majlis's need to enact laws that are of great urgency for the country but are outside of its Islamic juridical path [share'-e Islam] and thus beyond the authority of the Majlis, we ask for your assistance and guidance in this matter." Two weeks later, Khomeini responded, "The enactment and execution of those laws on which the survival of the regime depends are permissible on a temporary basis and so long as there is an overriding need."[68] After the bill was amended twice by the Majlis, the Council approved the Islamicity of the bill.[69]

Khomeini's ruling on land reform was significant for a number of reasons. It was his first secondary ordinance (hokm-e sanavi), paving the way for future rulings. It also boosted the radicals and clearly undermined the power of the conservatives and the institution they dominated, the Guardian Council. And finally, it was an indication that the realities of day-to-day politics would force Khomeini to lean toward dynamic fiqh, to issue injunctions that were unprecedented in orthodox Shii fiqh, which he did a number of times during the last two years of his life.

Despite this blow to their authority, Khomeini's ruling did not alter the Council's conservative attitude. In April 1982, the Majlis passed a bill for the nationalization of foreign trade. The bill, based on article 44 of the constitution that calls for a state-run economy, provided tremendous power to the government and particularly to the ministry of commerce. It allowed the government to essentially monopolize "the purchasing and import of all the essential commodities of the country, and establish various purchasing centers to supervise all other private and public purchases." [70] Undoubtedly, the bill aimed to curtail the economic power of the bazaaris by putting in place more control over their trade and distribution centers. The response of the Guardian Council was that "although the bill does not contradict the constitution, such government control over trade is unnecessary and un-Islamic." [71] Over two years the Majlis produced three new versions of the bill, but the Council rejected all of them on various grounds. The response of the Council to the Majlis's second attempt at the bill, for example, was, "The bill still does not prove an overriding urgency and the Imam has not said so." In addition, "By specifying complete nationalization, the bill disregarded the rights of privately financed imports altogether, something contrary to Islamic tenets that hold private trading sacrosanct." [72] In July 1984, the Majlis presented yet another modified version of the bill to the Council, but the Council maintained that the bill still provided too much monopolistic power for the government and rejected it again. [73]

Factional politics extended to the second Majlis and the second term of President Khamenehi. In their new newspaper *Resalat,* the conservatives insisted that in order for the regime to become more Islamic, the next government "must be less statist, support popular participation in economic affairs, and streamline the government institutions." [74] In the struggle between the left and the conservatives, manifested in the battle between the Majlis and the Guardian Council, Khomeini shrewdly pursued his unique policy of "dual containment." In December 1983, for example, he rebuffed criticism directed at the government's inability to solve the economic problems of the country and address the plight of the poor, strongly endorsed the "Islamic" nature of the Majlis, and stated that the prime minister was doing an "excellent" job. Rafsanjani, speaker of the Majlis, also supported Prime Minister Musavi by praising the "Imam's clinical understanding of events." [75]

With the remaining opponents of *velayat-e faqih* (known as liberals) in the first Majlis disqualified by the Guardian Council from running for the second Majlis, [76] the left increased its representation after the parliamentary elections of 1984. [77] Having the Imam's blessing and the speaker's support, Musavi felt assured that he would have a comfortable mandate for his next term. Surprisingly, and apparently counter to the wishes of the Imam, Azari-Qomi and others from the conservative camp opposed a vote of confidence for Musavi. Moreover, after gaining the majority in the Majlis (163), some MPs from the conservative camp refused to support five of Musavi's cabinet nominees. While the Majlis approved Musavi's replacement nominations, this was clearly a setback for the prime minister.[78] To make matters worse, Khomeini harshly criticized the prime minister and the government for turning against the private sector and blocking its economic activities.[79]

It is difficult to know why Khomeini suddenly turned against Musavi. David Menasheri and Bahman Baktiari both believe that Khomeini once again was trying to establish his neutrality in the fight between the radicals and the conservatives, particularly when disagreements between the two camps within the IRP had reached a peak. Menasheri adds the possibility that Khomeini was trying to appease the bazaaris in light of the government policies against the private sector.[80] Such assumptions about the "dual containment" policy of Khomeini at that point seem valid, given that a week later the Imam told the Guardian Council to ease its confrontational stand against the Majlis.[81]

Khamenehi was comfortably reelected as president in August 1985. This year witnessed an important outburst of factionalism in the form of a personal rivalry between the reelected president and the prime minister when the former moved to use his mandate to remove Musavi. Aside from belonging to opposing factional affiliations, the two men had pushed to strengthen their respective offices, both, of course, claiming to follow the Imam's doctrine.[82] Once inaugurated (September 1985), Khamenehi tried to remove Musavi by exploiting an ambiguity in article 136 of the constitution over precisely who has the power to appoint and dismiss a new government. Khamenehi believed that "nominating the prime minister should be the duty of the president."[83] When after nearly a month Khamenehi did not make the nomination for prime minister, 135 MPs wrote to the Imam asking for advice. Khomeini responded in his usual two-handed way by calling Musavi a "faithful and loyal servant" and adding that he did not consider change necessary at this time.[84] In October 1985, Khamenehi nominated Musavi to the Majlis for prime minister.[85] However, 26 MPs abstained and 73 opposed his nomination.[86] The 99 votes that Musavi did not receive were most likely from the Azari-Qomi camp.[87] Clearly sensing that factional conflict was reaching dangerous levels,

Khomeini admonished all MPs for their attacks on each other and once again reminded them of the need for unity.[88]

Another important arena for factionalism during this period was in the foreign policy of the Islamic Republic. The arms-for-hostages affair (the secret arms deal between Iran and the United States in return for Iran's efforts to release the hostages in Lebanon) was one such incident. When the news of the arms deal became public in November 1986, MPs from both the right and the left tried to make political capital of it and harshly criticized the foreign minister, Ali Akbar Velayati, demanding an explanation.[89] However, it was commonly believed that the criticism was really directed at the key player in the affair, Rafsanjani. The speaker of the Majlis in turn quietly made it known that the Imam was also aware of the arms deal.[90] Knowing very well that the incident could cost Rafsanjani dearly, Khomeini came to the support of the speaker of Majlis and expressed complete satisfaction with his performance.[91] In addition to what became known as "Iran-gate," factions were already divided on the issue of the US hostages. In an interview with *Iran-e Farda,* Abbas Abdi, the leading figure among the students who stormed the US embassy in 1979, revealed that while the Imam was staunchly supportive of the takeover, members of the conservative camp in the Revolutionary Council had been against it from the very beginning.[92]

Dissolution of the IRP and the MII, and the Formation of the Association of the Combatant Clergy

Following the death of Mohammad Beheshti, the conflict between the radicals and the conservatives heightened. In September 1983, Khamenehi, who replaced Beheshti as the secretary general of the IRP, admitted publicly for the first time the existence of ideological conflicts within the IRP:

> Many people are trying to say that this party belongs to a certain group. At times they say it is the party of *akhund* [derogatory name for the clergy] because there are five clergy on the top. Other times they say it is the party of bazaaris [because there are four distinguished revolutionary members in the central committee]. Some believe that this is the party of the President

[Khamenehi], the prime minister [Musavi], and Majlis speaker [Rafsanjani].
. . . There are differences of opinion among the members of the central committee but both [camps] follow the [doctrine] of Imam and agree on most issues. . . . It is OK for the two camps to think differently on issues related to
fiqh or the economy. . . . No one should speak badly about Mr. Musavi or Mr.
Asghar-Owladi, as they are both distinguished revolutionaries.[93]

It is worth mentioning that the rift within the IRP further revealed the ideological inclination of Khamenehi, who at times found fault with the left by implicitly criticizing Musavi and those "who use revolutionary rhetoric for
political purposes."[94] These divisions within the IRP, coupled with factional
contention in the Majlis, ultimately paralyzed the IRP and arguably put the entire regime in danger. In 1987 Rafsanjani and Khamenehi therefore asked
Khomeini to give permission to dissolve the party. The two men argued that
the IRP had served its original purpose of defeating challengers to the rule of
velayat-e faqih and its services were no longer needed. Khomeini agreed, and the
IRP ceased its activities in May 1987.[95]

At its inception in 1979, the Crusaders of the Islamic Revolution (*Mojahedin-e Inqelab-e Islami,* or MII) asked Khomeini to select a leader for the new
organization. Khomeini appointed an ultra-conservative member of JMHEQ,
Ayatollah Hossein Rasti-Kashani, to provide the MII with its necessary spiritual guidance. The ideological differences that emerged in the Iranian polity
after the revolution permeated the MII, and the organization was soon to split
into conservatives and radicals. The more radical members of the MII, headed
by the likes of Behzad Nabavi and Mohammad Salamati, had difficulties with
the conservatism of Rasti-Kashani and split from the organization in 1982.[96]
These ideological differences gradually peaked and in October 1986, Rasti-
Kashani asked the Imam for permission to dissolve the MII, and Khomeini endorsed that course of action.[97]

In a last effort to mend the ongoing factionalism before intervening,
Khomeini in February 1987 called on factions one more time to settle their
dispute:"We must all be together and support the Majlis and the government as
it is our religious duty. We must make sure that foreign press do not remark that
there is contention in Iran. If we see that, God forbid, disagreement is going to

occur, it is our religious duty to prevent this at all costs, even if it means sacrificing one person or one group for the people."[98]

Khomeini's plea fell on deaf ears. Just before the election of the third Majlis in April 1988, a group of JRM (Society of Combatant Clergy) members, Mehdi Karrubi, Mohammad Musavi-Khoeiniha, Mahmud Doai, Mohammad Tavassoli, Khatami, and Mohammad Jamarani, and Ayatollahs Hasan Sane'i and Sadeq Khalkhali announced the creation of the MRM.[99] In a letter to Khomeini asking his permission to form the party, members of the new association maintained that they had struggled with other respected clergymen in the JRM to reach a consensus but to no avail. Consequently, in order to serve the Imam and the people better, they had decided to create another organization.[100] Khomeini responded by giving his blessing to the new organization and stating that "splitting from the JRM to express your views freely is not tantamount to conflict."[101] In addition, Khomeini tried to present the split as indicative of pluralism within the Islamic polity and not a power struggle: "The clergy are united and there are not two fronts. Of course, there are two groups and two views, it must be [like that]. A society that does not have differences of opinion is imperfect. If difference of opinion does not exist in the Majlis, this Majlis [is also] imperfect."[102] Others from the left followed suit in their remarks. Mohammad Musavi-Khoeiniha, for example, said, "Although the guidelines for both camps are Islamic tenets and Islamic action, disagreement on interpretation and rendition are inevitable."[103] However, although the split was portrayed by the regime as amicable, the rift in the JRM was in reality the culmination of the power struggle between the left and the traditional right that began in mid-1981. Thus, some members of the new association such as Khatami revealed that the split was not due to mere brotherly disagreements over the interpretation of the *fiqh,* but rather that the two camps had been engaged in a power struggle from the beginning. In fact the differences between the clergy had been quite significant:

> Members of the JRM were split [along ideological lines] from the very beginning of the revolution. Now, we [the MRM] have no choice but to pronounce our opinions as the MRM of Teheran, because some [of our] views [in the JRM] are being ignored. . . . There have been differences of opinion

among the membership of the JRM regarding at least seventeen points. . . .
We must close the door on those who do not believe in the eternal war between the rich and the poor and who exploit Islam for their own political and
material well being. . . . [This] American brand of Islam must be eradicated.[104]

The words of Khatami were indicative of the differences that existed between the two prominent camps in Iran after the revolution: the conservatism
and elitism of the traditional right versus the populist-revolutionary aspirations
of the left. The labeling of conservatives as practicing an "American brand of
Islam," used for the first time in 1988 by Khomeini to discredit them,[105] became
the prototype of the anticonservative discourse of the left after the death of the
ayatollah, when the left accused the conservatives of betraying the revolutionary aspirations of the masses. In sum, factionalism was reaching new heights by
1988, and the political maneuvering was reducing the government's ability to
function due to divisions and embolism (Guardian Council vs. the Majlis). The
Imam was able to muddle through by constantly maneuvering and refusing to
show a preference in the factions' struggle for power. But he was forced to
change this policy to ensure a more solid and predictable course after his death,
provide a clearer understanding of what his legacy was for his followers, and
above all to avert a major crisis in the regime.

Crisis and Reforms

Ten years after the victory of the revolution, the Islamic Republic was facing
tremendous pressures and confronting difficult issues on both the domestic and
international fronts. It had been involved in a bloody war with Iraq from September 1980 until August 1988 and faced (partially self-imposed) international
isolation. Domestically, the fate of the regime appeared even more precarious.
The failure to deliver on earlier promises of economic prosperity, social justice,
and fair government raised serious doubt about the leadership of the Islamic
Republic and its ability to govern. Early signs of societal alienation and erosion
of confidence on the part of the masses had appeared by 1986 when the leadership was at pains to find volunteers for the *karbala*-7 offensive against Iraq. This
situation was particularly alarming to the leadership in Teheran because the

bulk of volunteers for the war had come from the poor masses or the *mustazafin,* the backbone of support for the regime.

This diminishing public support was clear from the remarks made by various leaders. In April 1986, for instance, Khomeini proclaimed that "filling the [war] front is among the most important holy duties."[106] Two months later, and in contrast to the early days of the revolution when martyrdom was considered a religious honor and the regime actually had excess volunteers to send back, Khomeini expressed his gratitude to the new volunteers.[107] The economy of the Islamic Republic was also in trouble as the war took its economic and human toll on the country.[108] According to official figures, by 1988 inflation had reached 26 percent, and the unemployment rate was even higher. "These figures," notes one observer, "may not be high by Latin America standards, but are amongst the biggest recorded in Iran during the post-World War II period."[109] The sudden fall in oil prices in 1986 added to the already mounting pressure on the Republic.

Most troubling for the regime, however, was the growing tension and disagreement among powerful figures loyal to Khomeini. Although the clerical leadership had largely succeeded in mobilizing the population in the face of the war and domestic and foreign pressures, and had presented a unified front in times of crisis, as the Musavi years illustrated the leadership was far from monolithic and disagreements existed across a broad range of issues from socioeconomic policies to foreign policy orientation. Thus, by the end of the first decade of the Iranian revolution, the leadership was admitting to past mistakes and carefully suggesting the need for reforms.

On the occasion of the tenth anniversary of the revolution, Teheran Radio put questions regarding the past ten years to the leaders of the revolution. The interviews prompted some interesting and frank answers. When asked what, in retrospect, the leaders would have liked to change, Khamenehi noted that he "would have created a special management school to teach the necessary skills to the revolutionary but inexperienced forces who took over the state administration." Musavi Ardabili mentioned "lack of maturity and clear policies in certain areas such as cultural activities," while Rafsanjani answered "some [of our] ideas were not practical" and that he "would have prevented the war from breaking out." Rafsanjani also hinted that he may have been the person who convinced Khomeini to stop the war with Iraq by saying that "the war lasted longer than anticipated and some of us were opposed to the continuation of the war after 1982."[110] But some, like Ayatollah Hossein-Ali Montazeri, went further in their criticism of the regime and hinted at its secularization:

> We must avoid empty celebrations and deceptive shows. . . . We must learn from our past mistakes because we had slogans in the past that turned out to be mistakes. Today, Islamic ideology has proved that it can govern society from political, economic, and other aspects. But the Islamic jurisconsults and leaders were not involved in government in the past and did not think that one day the government would be in their hands. They studied economics, politics, and sociology less and attached more importance to religious issues. The responsibility for research and analysis of issues required today belongs to scientists and scholars.[111]

So even the Iranian leadership themselves saw the need for change in both attitude and policy. They considered the first ten years of the revolution to be valuable experience for the Iranian clergy, however, it was all too clear that the regime's emphasis on Islam, war, revolutionary discourse, and the persona of Khomeini were insufficient for governing Iran. Thus, regardless of their factional inclination, the leadership had become aware that reforms were imperative.

Perhaps more than anyone it was Khomeini who had woken up to this reality. The Imam seemed well aware that if the regime was to survive, systemic and ideological deadlock had to be dealt and the government conduct its affairs in an orderly and predictable manner. So it became urgent that Khomeini end his illusive gestures to placate the factions; the engine for change was Khomeini himself. Through various decrees from late 1987 until his death, he paved the way for the rationalization of the Islamic Republic. These decrees, in addition to the new constitution and the new leadership, had three important outcomes with regard to the state and the factions. Firstly, Khomeini's proclamations strengthened the populist dimension of the regime (hence its republicanism) at the expense of its religious and revolutionary dimensions. Secondly, by directly intervening in debates and taking sides in the ongoing power struggle among factions, Khomeini clarified his position. Thirdly, the ensuing decrees, plus Khomeini's other decisions such as the acceptance of the cease-fire with Iraq,

set the tone for a less revolutionary, more temperate, and ultimately more pragmatic postwar Iran. One can argue that this period constituted a sixth phase in
Khomeini's theory of the Islamic government, the impetus being once again
the realities of the time.

The first of these decrees came eight months after the dissolution of the
IRP and at the height of factionalism. In December 1987, the minister of labor,
the leftist Abolqasem Sarhadizadeh, asked the Imam whether the government
could provide services such as electricity, telephone, and water for the private
sector and in return ask the private sector to operate within rules and regulations set by the ministry. In a brief response, Khomeini declared that "the government can impose such necessary conditions."[112] With this decree,
Khomeini had once again used his prerogative as the *vali-ye faqih* to issue an important secondary ordinance that built up the position of statists among factions
(the left and the likes of Rafsanjani from the right). The ecstatic Sarhadizadeh
remarked that "thanks to the Imam's ruling, the state hereafter can regulate
prices as well as exercise control over socioeconomic and medical services."[113]

The conservatives were obviously not pleased. On behalf of the Guardian
Council, its secretary Ayatollah Lotfollah Safii wrote a carefully worded letter
to Khomeini asking the Imam to elaborate on his latest edict. Safii asked
whether it was true that the state would now be empowered to replace fundamental (traditional) Islamic laws and (socioeconomic) systems as a result of this
edict.[114] Khomeini responded to Safii by saying "In all instances where people
use public services, the state is unconditionally entitled to receive compensa-
tion. This is true in all areas and not exclusive to what the minister of labor
stated."[115] Khomeini later tried to appease the conservatives by telling Safii
(who later resigned because of this decree), "I have always supported the institution of the Guardian Council and it will never be weakened."[116] Khomeini
had greatly tipped the balance of factionalism in favor of the left. And this edict
was followed by another, more consequential one.

A few weeks later, in an effort to appease the conservatives and in an attempt to tone down the implications of the Khomeini ruling, Khamenehi provided his interpretation in a Friday prayer sermon of the Imam's words. He
maintained that what the Imam meant was that, although the state held a great
deal of power, its actions were limited as it acted within the "parameters of holy
injunctions." Khamenehi elaborated on his interpretation of the Imam's edict:

"For instance, if a factory worker is not being treated fairly by the factory owner, then the state can intervene and take action to ensure that the worker receives fair treatment."[117] Khomeini addressed the president harshly the next day and said, "He clearly did not understand the ruling." In what was arguably the most important decree of Khomeini as far as the state and its dimensions were concerned, the Imam declared:

> The government [state] that is a part of the absolute vice-regency of the Prophet of God is one of the primary injunctions [*ahkam-e avvaliyeh*] of Islam and has priority over all other secondary injunctions, even prayers, fasting, and *haj'*. The ruler is authorized to demolish a mosque or a house that is in the path of a road and to compensate the owner for his house. The ruler can close down a mosque if need be, or can even demolish a mosque that is a source of harm if its harm cannot be remedied without demolition. The government is empowered to unilaterally revoke any shari'a agreement that it has conducted with people when those agreements are contrary to the interests of the country or of Islam.[118]

Indeed, this was the most momentous and highly controversial statement that Khomeini had ever made regarding the three dimensions of the Iranian state. Although Khomeini in theory granted new and unparalleled powers to the *faqih,* he at the same time drastically undermined the religiousness of the regime and bolstered its populist-republican dimension. To the dismay of the conservatives, by providing the central government (the state) with the authority to not only intervene in the economy but the right to use its discretion to suspend even the pillars of Islam, he undermined both the economic welfare and the orthodox religious disposition of this faction. Moreover, by announcing that based on the interests of the regime, such injunctions were not secondary but primary, Khomeini broke from the historical position of the religious establishment in Iran with regard to state ordinances.[119] The decree was by far the most telling indication of how the politicization of the clergy and the realties of the time had compelled Khomeini to make such controversial religious injunctions that would have been inconceivable during the early days of the revolution.

Factions made political capital out of Khomeini's last decree. Rafsanjani said, "Now there should be no debate over what the line of the Imam is." [120] Musavi believed that the latest ruling would "open the hands of the government to deal with difficult issues faced by the country." [121] The response of the conservatives was both composed and judicious. In a series of editorials in *Resalat* on state ordinances *(hokm-e hokumati)*, Ayatollah Ahmad Azari-Qomi discussed the nature and significance of the Imam's ruling. While attesting to its greatness, he endeavored to subdue its impact. By comparing such a ruling to the food and water needed to survive in life, he contradicted Khomeini's decree by categorizing state ordinances not as primary rulings but secondary ones:

> Although important, secondary ordinances are unique in that they are temporary and aim to serve immediate needs [of the country]. Permanent edicts [primary ordinances] are issued by God and the Prophet and are valid until resurrection. State ordinances have always been parallel to holy primary ordinances and not within their framework, and the ruler sometimes issues these ordinances as temporary secondary ordinances such as stopping the *haj'* for a limited period of time. [122]

Another blow to the conservatives and the religious dimension of the Islamic Republic came in February 1988 when Khomeini ordered the establishment of the Expediency Council. Headed by the president, this assembly was to act as a final arbiter between the parliament and the Guardian Council. [123] The members of the new council aside from Khamenehi were Rafsanjani, Mohammad Tavassoli, Mir-Hossein Musavi, Abdolkarim Musavi-Ardabili, and Mohammad Musavi-Khoeiniha. The establishment of this council was sure to undermine the power of the conservative-dominated Guardians Council to reject laws enacted by parliament and thus delighted the left. Khoeiniha asked, "Can we set aside a bill that the Guardian Council has rejected? We must take under consideration the goals of society." That Khomeini aimed at weakening the conservatives with the creation of this assembly was apparent in the content of his decree: "The interests of the regime and the people are among the most important matters, and resisting such interest may undermine the Islam of the barefooted and lead to the victory of the Islam of the wealthy and the arrogant backed by billions from both inside and outside [of Iran]." [124]

In addition to such rulings in religio-political matters, Khomeini issued precedent-setting injunctions in other spheres as well. For instance, in December 1987, after some conservatives in the *howzeh* complained that Iranian TV showed Western films that contained un-Islamic material such as not properly veiled women, he ruled, "Such films are not only religiously acceptable but often educational." He maintained that such programs were permissible "as long as the viewers do not view them with lustful eyes." [125] Eight months later, the Imam ruled that the game of chess and the buying and selling of musical instruments were also permissible so long as they were used for "religiously sanctioned purposes." [126] This ruling created great uproar within the *howzeh* and the conservative ulama in Qom. In October 1988, hojjatol-Islam Mohammad Hossein Qadiri implicitly questioned the views of the Imam by suggesting that, according to the *revayat,* the imams had considered chess as a gambling tool and music as religiously forbidden. In response, Khomeini uttered a particularly harsh criticism of conservatives:"I must express my regret at your interpretation of the holy decrees. Based on your views, modern civilization must be annihilated and we must all go to live forever in caves and deserts. I advise you to consider God and not be influenced by the 'pseudo-religious' and 'uneducated' clergy [*akhunds*]."[127]

Such pestering of Khomeini by the conservatives eventually agitated the ayatollah. In February 1989, Khomeini uttered his most direct and harsh criticism of the conservative camp, by attacking this faction's fortitude:

There are people in the *howzeh* who, while pretending to be highly religious, are eradicating religion, the revolution, and the system. Certain God-less [people] whose aim is to destroy the revolution label immediately anyone who wants to work for the poor and the needy as Communists. Aimed at defeating the revolution, America and [world] arrogance have such people under their thumbs. I have, on numerous occasions, warned of the dangers of these religiously "narrow-minded," "mentally ossified," and "reactionaries." Through their deceit, in universities and *howzehs* these pseudo-religious people destroy the essence of the revolution and Islam from within. With self-righteous faces and in support of religion and *velayat [faqih],* they accuse everyone of irreligiousness.[128]

What was noteworthy in this speech was that for the first time since the revolution, Khomeini explicitly supported *fiqh-e puya*:

> I believe in *sonnati* and essentials [*javaheri*] *fiqh* and agree that it is the correct and proper form of *ijtihad*. However, this does not mean that Islamic *fiqh* is not dynamic [*puya*]. Time and place are two decisive components of *ijtihad*. A thorough [*jame'*] mojtahid must be familiar with the ways and means of confronting the deceits of [Western] worldly hegemonies, culture, and economic systems.[129]

To show how Khomeini altered his views with an eye towards the requirements of the times, and how he maneuvered on issues, this is what he told the *howzeh* nearly two years before: "Religious schooling must be in a way so that *fiqh-e sonnati* won't be forgotten. This is what has kept Islam to this date. *Fiqh* must be kept the same way that it has always been and new *fiqh* is the start of the death of Islam."[130]

Khomeini's attack on the conservatives and his explicit siding with the left was particularly surprising given that four months earlier, in a message that became known as the "Covenant of Brotherhood," he gave his blessing to both camps and proclaimed their interpretations legitimate. Khomeini stressed that "similar disagreements over issues have been quite common among [Shii] jurists," and that, "the doors of *ijtihad* in the Islamic state must always remain open, and so long as the differences remain within such perimeters, the revolution faces no danger."[131] Nevertheless, Khomeini's post-1987 rulings greatly assisted the left and practically ensured victory for this faction in the third Majlis (1988–1992). For the first time since the revolution, Khomeini announced his support for a faction, the left, when four days before the election he called on voters to "vote for candidates who work for the barefooted and not those adhering to capitalist Islam."[132] Conversely, the conservatives warned voters "not to vote for those who are rhetorically advocates of the barefooted but are conceited in spirit." Khamenehi showed his factional inclinations by advising the nation to "refrain from electing those who [only] utter slogans."[133] Mir-Hossein Musavi said for the left, "Those who do not obstruct the executive should be elected."[134] In the end, the third parliamentary election marked a great victory for the left, and its members dominated the leadership of the Majlis: Mehdi Karrubi was first elected deputy speaker and after Rafsanjani's election to the presidency became the speaker; Mohammad Hashemian and Asadollah Bayat, first deputies; Rasul Montajabnia, Mohammad Razavi, Morteza Alviri, Ibrahim Asgharzadeh, Hossein Mozaffari-Nezhad, and Abbas Dozduzani, clerks; and Abdolvahed Musavi-Lari, Nurollah Abedi, Morteza Katirai, commissioners. Prominent conservatives such as Ahmad Azari-Qomi, Habibollah Asgar-Owladi, and Mohammad Yazdi were not reelected.[135]

Constitutional Revisions: The Design of a New Iran

While Khomeini had clarified certain ideological confusion, the institutional clutter in Iran remained. About two months prior to his death and perhaps concerned about the future of the country, Khomeini ordered the establishment of the Assembly for the Reappraisal of the Constitution.[136] He had earlier expressed concern about the adverse institutional imperatives of the state by pointing out "the need to clarify some of the ambiguities in the constitution."[137] Khomeini directed the assembly to look at the executive branch and to find ways for better management and administration of the country. Referring to existing "parallel systems," Khomeini emphasized the need for administrative discipline and systemic order.[138] According to the secretary of the Council of Experts, Ayatollah Ali Meshkini, one of the overall aims of the new constitution was to "create further centralization and order in the regime."[139] The assembly was made up of twenty members appointed by Khomeini and another five to be elected by the Majlis. Once the members were appointed, the assembly divided its task into four committees: issues related to leadership, the executive branch, legislative-executive relations, and the judiciary. When the assembly concluded its task, the new constitution was to dramatically alter the nature and makeup of the Islamic Republic.

Central to the 1979 constitution were articles 107 through 110, which made the *faqih* the most powerful figure in Iran and provided him with veto power over all governmental decisions and laws. More importantly, it specified that the leader had to be a *marja'-e taqlid,* or a source of emulation. The most controversial component of the new constitution was the changing role and ultimately the weakening of the religious leadership of the Islamic Republic. The new constitution put further limitations on the power of the leader by making him consult the Expediency Council before arriving at major decisions (article 110), prohibiting him from making major decisions outside the framework of the constitution. Significantly, according to the new constitution the leader of the Islamic Republic need not be a *marja'-e taqlid,* as article 109 notes the necessary qualifications and attributes of the leader:

1. Academic qualifications necessary for issuing decrees on various issues of *fiqh*

2. Fairness and piety necessary for leading the Islamic nation

3. Proper political and social insight, prudence, courage, authority, and power of management necessary for leadership. In case there are many individuals qualify under the above conditions, the one who has strongest insight in *fiqh* and politics shall be preferred

The new constitution (article 110) provided the *faqih* with new and substantial institutional powers:

1. To determine the general policies of the system of the Islamic Republic of Iran after consulting with the *Majma'-e Tashkis-e Maslahat-e Nezam*

2. To supervise over the good performance of the system's general policies

3. To decree referendums

4. To hold the Supreme Command of the Armed Forces

5. To declare war or peace, and mobilize the armed forces

6. To appoint, dismiss, or accept resignations of:

(a) The *faqihs [foqaha]* of the Guardian Council

(b) The highest authority of the judiciary

(c) The head of *Sazman Seda va Sima-e Jomhouri-e-Islami Iran* (National Radio and TV)

(d) Chief of Joint Staffs

(e) Chief Commander of the Islamic Revolutionary Guard Corps

(f) Chief Commanders of the Armed Forces and Police Forces

7. To resolve disputes and coordinate relations between the three powers

Meshkini revealed that the omission of emulation *(marja'iyat)* from the new constitution was by order of the Imam himself.[140] Rafsanjani reaffirmed this change in the constitution, claiming that it was the desire of no one but Khomeini himself as "the Imam saw the existence of emulation in the constitution to be against the interests of the Islamic Republic and believed that the two worlds of religion and politics require different types of expertise, and at the moment we require a man with expertise in the latter." Aiming to reaffirm Khomeini's vision for the future leadership of Iran and to support Khamenehi as the new leader, Rafsanjani maintained, "Should priority be with a mojtahid who has expertise in social, political, economic, and foreign policy and other fundamental issues of the Republic, or one in a religious seminary with equal religious knowledge but unfamiliar with such worldly matters? Logic and intellect dictate that there is an [obvious] priority here."[141] Members of the assembly were mindful that perhaps no future leader would have the charismatic appeal or religious power of Khomeini and his popular mandate. Therefore, the position of the *faqih* needed to be institutionalized. Khamenehi was a middle-level clergyman, not possessing a great deal of religious power or popularity, and the new constitution had to compensate for his lack of religious credentials. Through the institutionalization of the position of *faqih,* some constitutional power was gained, but the ultimate power exhibited in the charisma and popularity of an almighty authority like Khomeini no longer existed. In short, by politicizing the *faqih,* the new constitution greatly diminished the influence of the religiousness of the state.

With the issue of the leadership settled, the republicanism of the regime received a huge boost through the increase of the power of the presidency and the executive fiat. In the old constitution the president was a ceremonial figure, having little constitutional power and making few governmental appointments, while the prime minister was the de facto manager of the government. The new constitution eliminated the post of the prime minister and greatly increased the legal powers of the president. Article 113 declares, "The president shall be the highest official state authority who is responsible for the implementing of the constitution." In order to pursue these objectives, the president was provided with a host of networks and newly formed posts to shape and direct domestic and foreign policy. Article 126 empowers the president to be directly in charge of the country's financial, economic, and bureaucratic affairs. This is possible because article 124 enables the president to choose cabinet

members independent of the parliament (although the nominations still require their approval). Another crucial article of the new constitution is article
178, which establishes the Islamic Republic's version of the National Security
Council (*Showra-ye Amniyat-e Melli*). Headed by the president, this council is in
charge of setting and coordinating the foreign policy of the Islamic Republic.

The Iranian judiciary was also affected by the regime's drive for more systemic cohesion and integration of its institutions. Publicly, the reason for the
1989 alterations to the judiciary, according to its new head, Ayatollah Mohammad Yazdi, was "the establishment of centralization in the management of the
judicial branches to speed up the investigation of judicial matters."[142] While a
leaner and more effective judiciary may have been the public justification for
the changes in the constitution, the main goal was to provide more autonomy
for the judicial institution and disengage it from the influence of the opposing
high-ranking ulama, who could overrule decisions from the judicial system.
Article 157 of the new constitution abolished the five-member High Court
and replaced it with one chief justice appointed by the *faqih*. According to article 164 of the new constitution, it is the head of the judiciary, rather than the
faqih, who selects the head of the supreme court and the public prosecutor general. In addition, the head of the judiciary is empowered to remove judges from
the bench.

◆   ◆   ◆

By the time of his death on June 4, 1989, Khomeini had left a canon full of ambiguities and contradictions to which his followers could resort to authenticate
their reading of the true Islamic state after he had left the scene. But the reality
was that the unity of word and action (*vahdat-e kalam va vahdat-e amal*) among
his children was nothing but a mirage. His final pronouncements showed that
he reluctantly recognized the need to position the revolution and the country
at the head of a far less religious-revolutionary path. These rulings and the
changes made to the Iranian constitution provided more legal powers for the
republican institutions and further strengthened the populist dimension of the
state, qualities that would ensure the regime's survival after the demise of its
founder and inspiration.

CHAPTER 3

Factions in Post-Khomeini Iran

Renditions and Sources

When the members of the Reappraisal Assembly met to revise the constitution, factions were aware of certain realities. With the death of Khomeini, factional politics in Iran were sure to enter a new phase. His absence was a mixed blessing for the factions. The departure of the final arbiter meant that allocation and distribution of power among the factions and within the conflict-ridden political institutions in the Islamic Republic had to be settled by other means than appealing to Khomeini's final judgment. The left would undoubtedly lose the most as it had relied heavily on his favorable interventions, particularly during Khomeini's last two years.

It was commonly understood that Rafsanjani would become the next president,[1] and that the next leader would be Khamenehi, who was in fact selected by the *Khobregan* a day after Khomeini's death. Due to Khamenehi's support for the conservatives and his anti-Musavi actions, the left was almost assured that the new leader was not going to be kind to them. The conservatives, however, would surely benefit from the developments taking place in Iran at that time. They anticipated having a highly sympathetic leader and a president who, despite his support for certain statist measures, favored a free market economy.

Khamenehi and Rafsanjani were the heirs apparent as much because of their factional affiliations and maneuvering as because of their qualifications. Though well liked by the conservatives, Khamenehi certainly did not have such popularity among the radicals. After his brief scuffle with Khomeini (the January 1988 decree), he presumably had not had much support from the ayatollah. Moreover, as a middle-level clergyman, a *hojjatol-Islam,* Khamenehi

82

lacked the religious qualifications for such a consequential position, given that at the time there were many qualified senior ayatollahs in the *howzeh.* To be sure, inasmuch as the three dimensions of the regime were concerned: religious, revolutionary, and populist, Khamenehi as a leader would hardly be qualified for the first two. Consequently, the only dimension where the power of the new leader could be buttressed was the populist, hence political dimension. Rafsanjani's position was more complex; his ideological stance after a decade of the revolution was a mixed one. From Khomeini's death until the fifth Majlis, he formed an alliance with the conservatives for two main reasons. The first relates to the Iran-gate affair, wherein the left harshly criticized the speaker both for his involvement in the affair and for the fact that he had been pursuing a conciliatory stance (hence the label pragmatic) on foreign policy.[2] However, an open-door foreign policy was critical to Rafsanjani's vision of postwar Iran, making an alliance with the left inconceivable in 1989. The second and more important reason for Rafsanjani allying with the conservatives was that, in his Machiavellian way, Rafsanjani was paving the way for his own leadership in the postwar reconstruction stage. Thus he supported all measures that would help him accomplish his goal; that is, a strong executive branch and an amicable leader with weak religious qualifications who was both incapable and unwilling to issue injunctions that would imperil Rafsanjani's policies.[3]

With all of this in mind, factions aimed to strengthen the institutions that they held or were about to control when writing the new constitution. It is important to remember that the current (post-1989) positions of the factions were constructed during and after this debate: during the debates, the left and particularly the conservatives almost totally reversed their previous views on important issues. In a shrewd political maneuver, the conservatives suddenly became staunch advocates of "individual" rather than collective leadership and—with their candidate about to assume the leader position—of a powerful *faqih.* Moreover, aware of the future presidency of Rafsanjani, this faction began to advocate a strong, highly centralized government, something they had previously opposed. The left, on the other hand, put their weight behind the only institution they dominated at that time, the Majlis and the office of the prime minister. Moreover, while as self-proclaimed *maktabis* the left during Khomeini's leadership were adamant supporters of a strong *faqih,* during the debate in the assembly they repeatedly objected to the increased powers of the *faqih* in the new constitution. In short, factions altered the views they had upheld while Khomeini was alive to fit their immediate interests. The competing interests of the religious and republican dimensions of the regime facilitated these ideological shifts.

The Deliberations

Understandably, the most heated debates took place over the empowering of the executive and the office of leadership. While the two rights emphasized the need to increase the institutional powers of the religious leader, the left argued for a less powerful *faqih*. Ayatollah Ibrahim Amini suggested, "It is true that the Imam enjoyed invincible powers, but what if someone came along [became a leader] and the people did not accept his mandate; then what?" Basically admitting that Khamenehi was not going to have the same overwhelming influence as Khomeini, he continued, "If a leader does not have those kinds of powers, both the executive and Majlis can confront him. . . . The leader must be able to speak the last word." [4] By relying on *motlaqeh* discourse (absolutist reading of *velayat-e faqih*), the conservatives further pushed for a powerful *faqih*. "The leader is like a ruler, not an observer," maintained Amini. "His mandate is equal to that of the Prophet's. Therefore he is not responsible to the people or the Majlis, but to God only." [5] Azari-Qomi even had reservations about the fact that in determining major policies of the regime, the *faqih* had to consult the Expediency Council: "The philosophy behind the *velayat-e faqih* and the leadership in Islamic government is that the *faqih* must not have any restrictions." [6]

Mehdi Karrubi reversed Amini's argument and suggested that to give sweeping powers to one person was extremely dangerous: "The Imam was one of a kind. We do not know who the future leaders will be." [7] Implying that the process of the Khobregan's selection of the *faqih* was undemocratic and possibly factionally determined, the left pointed out that the *faqih* must have a popular base and could not be a "real" *faqih* just because the Assembly of Experts voted for him. Hossein Hashemian (MP) said, "Even the Prophet could not do much before the population at large gave him their mandate." [8] While reaffirming his loyalty to the *velayat-e faqih*, Asadollah Bayat (MP) remarked that "the *velayat-e faqih* is indeed our overall conviction," but he believed that the conservatives' interpretation of this concept (equating the power of the *faqih* to those of the imams and the Prophet) was misleading because "what one can deduce from the words of the Imam is that he did not see the mandate of the *vali-ye faqih* in these extensive lines."[9]

Evaluating the possibility of a presidential system headed by Rafsanjani, aware of Khamenehi's less favorable disposition toward the left-dominated third Majlis, and knowing that they had no influence over the super-bodies, the left aimed to protect the only institution that they would conceivably control in the future, the Majlis. When it was suggested by one of the committees that the number of ministers of parliament should increase by one for each 150,000 increase in population, the left supported the measure: "the Majlis is the cornerstone of the popular will, and an increase in the number of MPs would surely contribute to a more democratic Iran."[10] Conversely, conservatives such as Ayatollah Abbas Ali Amid-Zanjani said, "Such measures do not necessarily lead to more freedom and democracy; in fact, the Majlis could become crowded and difficult to manage."[11] Another area to which the left objected was the suggestion of some conservatives for the *faqih* to have the power to dissolve the Majlis. In defense of the Majlis, Bayat argued:

> The poor Majlis has two authorities, to legislate and to supervise. Its supervision is diluted by article 90. And, if we have a strong presidency without a prime minister, it means the supervision of the Majlis is tantamount to zero. . . . If the Majlis cannot question the president or the prime minister, the only thing that remains for it is imputation. Even here the gentlemen bring up the issue of interest and defense of the regime, so the poor MP is silenced.[12]

After the committee for executive affairs met, the constitution proposal they drew up was clearly partisan. Essentially, the right aimed to abolish the post of the prime minister while the left pushed for maintaining the ceremonial position for the president. Those committee members favoring a strong prime minister proposed the following structure: the president presents a prime minister to the Majlis; the president has the power to propose the removal of the prime minister; the prime minister presents a cabinet for the vote of confidence; the prime minister has the right to remove ministers, and if more than half of the cabinet were changed he would have the right to apply for a new vote of confidence in the Majlis. Others had no need of a prime minister: the president should be the head and sole authority of the executive branch; the president should present the ministers to the Majlis for a vote of confidence, and the ministers would in turn be responsible to the Majlis and the president; and the president would be empowered to remove any of the ministers.[13]

Here too, the left defended the Majlis and expressed its desire to maintain its strength vis-à-vis the executive. Hadi Khamenehi argued that a powerful presidency and a mighty leader would cause a polarization of power. He further added, "In order to distribute powers more evenly we should increase the power of the Majlis in executive affairs."[14] Objecting to an all-powerful president, Musavi remarked, "We should have centralization but we should also have accountability. The rights and freedom of people must be taken into consideration here."[15] In an indirect criticism of the super-bodies and how they curtailed the democratic process of the republican institutions, he said, "Because of institutional imperatives in Iran, unlike democratic countries such as the US, we have yet to achieve a free civil society."[16] Musavi also warned of a possible misuse of power: "It has been proven that, while the original intentions of all revolutions were distribution of power and establishment of people's sovereignty, they [revolutions] all ended up with dictatorships."[17]

The arguments for a strong presidency from the right focused on the "requirement of the times" and the "interest" (*maslahat*) of the regime. Khamenehi believed that in parliamentary systems the president was an ineffectual figure who would not solve the systematic difficulties in Iran. He added, "The interest of the regime calls for a strong director who is surely elected by popular mandate of the people."[18] According to Rafsanjani, "We cannot choose a qualified executive but strip him of the necessary powers. The current condition of the country calls for a strong executive branch." He rebuffed the dictatorship thesis of the left by pointing out, "Our country is not like the US; we have a leader who would prevent such a dictatorship. Do not be afraid of a strong president. The likes of Bani-Sadr no longer exist in the country."[19] In the end, the right-dominated Reappraisal Assembly was able to achieve the objectives of Rafsanjani and the conservatives and restructure the state in a way that heavily favored the positions of the two camps at that time.

The Selection of the New Leader

The mammoth task of finding a successor for Khomeini, imposing as it could have been for the clerical elite, was successfully accomplished by the leadership, and the transition went smoothly, averting potential ideological and political crisis for the regime. The idea of a council of leaders was soon pushed aside. The chairman of the Khobregan, Ayatollah Ali Meshkini, announced that the Imam had informed him that he preferred a single leader to succeed him.[20] It was announced on June 5 that sixty of the eighty-three members of the Khobregan voted for Khamenehi as the next leader. Despite some reservations, Khamenehi was favored by all three factions: For the two rights, Khamenehi was no doubt the best choice. The left expected an ultraconservative senior ayatollah from the *howzeh* to be unsympathetic to the radicals, so they settled for the leadership of Khamenehi. Although the approved choice of all three factions, the new leader suffered from a handicap in addition to his slight religious-revolutionary credentials. Unlike his predecessor, Khamenehi's neutrality was indeed doubtful. In confrontations with Prime Minister Musavi, Khamenehi had shown his pro-conservative tendencies throughout his presidential years by criticizing the radical policies of the left, accusing them of lack of clear planning and too much statism.[21] He also envisaged a more active role for the private sector in the economy while rebuffing accusations of improper links to the powerful merchants of the bazaar:

> The private sector must be involved, alongside the government, in the economy. Those who think that the private sector should not have a role in the economy do not have the proper understanding of the policy of the Islamic Republic, and those who believe that the private sector acts against the goals of the Iranian economy by amassing wealth are [also] mistaken. . . . Those who claim that we support the well-to-do are mistaken and should know that I and all the public officials in the country come from the lower middle classes and understand the problems of the deprived.[22]

It was not surprising, therefore, that the conservatives were most delighted about Khamenehi's selection as the new leader. Newspapers were flooded with congratulatory messages from the conservative camp, all trying to buttress his mandate as the new *faqih* and institutionalize his rulership. The Guardian Council announced its obedience to Khamenehi, declaring his mandate to be both religiously and legally binding.[23] The former minister of labor and *Mo'talefeh* sympathizer, Ahmad Tavakkoli, believed that all must obey the wishes of the new leader.[24] Members of the Bazaar Islamic Guild Society met with the new leader and pledged their support.[25] Knowing that Khamenehi's biggest challenge was potentially the leftist Majlis, Rafsanjani announced that the Majlis must obey the new leader.[26] The leadership of the Qom Seminary and the Islamic Propagatory Organization (*Sazman-e Tablighat-e Islami*) declared that Khamenehi's leadership was an extremely positive development for the future of Iran.[27] Later in 1993, the JMHEQ published a book on Grand Ayatollah Khamenehi in which they hailed the "new Caesar" and declared him as a rightful *marja'*.[28] While congratulating the new leader, the left added that it expected Khamenehi to "follow the Imam's path."[29] As for Khamenehi himself, his message immediately following Khomeini's death was a call for the unity of the nation and the continuity of the path of the Imam.[30]

Since his selection as the leader, however, Khamenehi has been anything but a powerful and commanding *faqih*. He has yet to issue a consequential injunction in either religious or state matters; rather, his injunctions have been modest in significance at best. In 1992, for example, he announced that it was religiously permissible to transplant the organs of a brain-dead person.[31] In 1994, he declared that the use of satellites was permissible as long as they did not cause harm.[32] As to his *marja'iyat*, after the death of Ayatollah Araki (the most senior *marja'* in Qom) in 1994, Khamenehi announced that he prefers to be the source of emulation only for the Shii community outside of Iran. It is no wonder that his religious thesis (*resaleh*) is published in Arabic.[33]

Khamenehi was more willing to intervene in the affairs of the country after 1994: he began to take the conservatives' side in the conflict between Rafsanjani and the conservatives in order to strengthen the position of the traditional right faction. He used his power as a *faqih*, for instance, to reappoint the controversial pro-conservative Mohsen Rafiqdust as the head of the *Bonyad* three times. Khamenehi kept the arch-conservative Mohsen Rezai as head of the IRGC until October 1997, and he replaced Rafsanjani's brother with a known

Mo'talefeh member, Ali Larijani, as the director of the national radio and TV in 1992.

On the whole, however, the real leader in terms of effectiveness and political sway, who set the tone, the policies, and the direction for post-Khomeini Iran was President Rafsanjani. This claim will be illustrated further in the next two chapters, but some of the most pertinent reasons will be explored here. As with most major decisions in the Islamic Republic, the choice of Rafsanjani for president came through the consensus of the clerical elite. This decision that was due to many overlapping reasons. To begin with, the new constitution clearly made the president the key figure in post-Khomeini Iran. Knowing very well that Khamenehi could not fill Khomeini's shoes or nor was he capable of directing the course of postwar reconstruction in Iran, Rafsanjani was the best possible choice.[34] Following the revolution, Rafsanjani presented himself to be more sober, skillful, and pragmatic than other clerics.[35] His judicious positions on issues, his timely and prudent comments, and his numerous efforts to minimize the destructive impact of extremism led to him being held in highest regard by almost everyone in the Islamic Republic.[36] As the following comments of Bazargan indicate, friend and foe alike regarded him with a certain degree of esteem:

> Among Ayatollah Khomeini's supporters, [Rafsanjani] was effective. He did not display much fanaticism and was capable of communicating with intellectuals. He did not have the fanaticism the *akhunds* [derogatory term for the clergy] usually have. Any time we had a conversation with the Khomeini camp, Mr. Rafsanjani was present in those meetings. It was easy to reach an understanding with him. He is pragmatic. . . . He is moderate, very knowledgeable, and a clever man. He is well informed and has good instincts for politics.[37]

Even before his presidency, Rafsanjani's discourse indicated that he recognized the requirements of the time, especially with the reconstruction phase that required reforms in all spheres in Iran. For example, a prevalent (and cynical) view held by many opponents of the regime inside and outside Iran since the early days of the revolution was that Islam was a medieval system and thus incompatible with the realities of modern life. Rafsanjani believed such views were misconceptions about Islam, its ability to govern, and its congruence with contemporary life:

> Today the main conflict between us and our enemies, and the main point of conflict, is that they wish to make present and future generations believe that Islam belongs to 1400 years ago and that today it cannot administer the world under industrial conditions and the advancement of science. If they succeed in preventing us from providing for the material needs and requirements of our people, if our society continues facing difficulties, they will mislead many young people as well as future generations and they will accuse Islam with this unjust accusation. If we succeed and if we prove in practice that the spiritual well-being of mankind is the best possible way and that it can provide for the living needs of the people and keep up with the requirements of the age, we have ensured the greatest victory in the history of Islam. . . . We should and we can create a modern society.[38]

The second major reason behind Rafsanjani's rise to power may well have been Khomeini's trust in him. One can assume that the personal qualifications of Rafsanjani did not go unrecognized by Khomeini. The various important positions delegated to Rafsanjani since the first years of the revolution are testimony to this fact: founding member of the Islamic Republican Party, Khomeini's representative in the High Council of Defense, commander of the armed forces in 1988, and speaker of the Majlis from 1979 until his presidency in July 1989. If one believes the remarks of insiders such as Bazargan, Rafsanjani was perhaps even "the eyes and ears" of the leader. One might surmise that the strong presidency instituted with the new constitution, an element not provided in the first constitution, was especially tailored for the future leadership of Rafsanjani. It certainly had the blessing of Khomeini himself.

Factions in Post-Khomeini Iran

Literature that describes the factions and ideological currents during the Khomeini era tends to be muddled. Usually, the elite within the Iranian polity are categorized according to their economic views and foreign policy attitudes.

Those who believe in a free market economy, are socially conservative, and oppose revolutionary foreign policy are labeled as "conservative," "moderate," or
"pragmatic." The "left" or "hard-liners" support radical economic policies such
as land reform, a state-controlled economy, and other redistributive and egalitarian economic policies in addition to a belief for the need to export the revolution. However, as noted, some individuals in the first category (generally
pro-Rafsanjani people in the Majlis or the IRP) also supported some of the
policies advocated by the left, such as land reform, nationalization, and government taxation. People who followed the line of Rafsanjani are often called "reformists" in analysis of Iranian factional politics. As a rule, however, the
conservatives and the reformers were categorized as one camp: right/moder-
ate/conservative/pragmatic.[39]

Although essentially accurate, these categorizations disregarded certain
overlapping differences among the factions. For instance, although the leftist
were "hard-liners" on economic issues, they were moderate or "liberal" (at least
relatively) regarding sociocultural policies. Or, while some members of the
right (the conservatives) remained moderate when foreign policy issues were
considered, as proponent of traditional *fiqh,* they maintained a hard-line position in sociocultural policies. To add to the confusion, other members of the
right such as Rafsanjani, who adhered to dynamic *fiqh* and liberal sociocultural
policies, actually had far more in common with the left than with other members of the right.

After 1989, the ideological disposition and the makeup of factions under-
went a major transformation. For instance, as was discussed earlier, the conservatives changed their views for almost purely political reasons on certain
religious matters such as the *faqih* and his role in Iran. In addition, 1989 witnessed two major changes in the political landscape—a new constitution and a
new leader—which greatly affected the balance of power and factional politics
as a whole. Some observers took notice of these changes. Siavoshi, for example,
points out the gradual emergence of a new faction made mostly of the new ap-
paratchik-state technocrats assembled around the new president and supportive
of his pragmatic, reformist vision of post-Khomeini Iran. This group included
Rafsanjani's pupils and some members of the left who, after a decade of espousing radicalization of the revolution, had tempered their views.[40] Siavoshi also
signals the gradual rift between the conservatives and the reformists. Like

Siavoshi, Baktiari also indicates a clear split emerging within the two camps in the last chapter of his book on factionalism in the Majlis from 1992 to 1994. However, his categorization of the factions for the period after 1989 remains within the old paradigm of left/hard-liner (pro-Musavi), moderate/pragmatic (pro-Rafsanjani), and conservative (pro-Azari-Qomi), ignoring both the changes and the complexity of the factions in post-Khomeini Iran.[41] Other analysts such as Milani and Ehteshami focus on the "dual leadership" of Rafsanjani and Khamenehi, emphasizing both the continuity of the republic and the unity at the top.[42] As we shall see, however, this is a highly presumptuous viewpoint.

Between December 1994 and May 1995, the left-leaning biweekly *Asr-e Ma* published a series of articles in which factions in the Islamic Republic were reconceptualized. The writer of these articles, Behzad Nabavi (the minister of heavy industry from 1981 to 1988, currently an adviser to Khatami), provided a new interpretation of the left/right moderate/radical classifications of factions. Nabavi's recategorization, the first of its kind after the revolution, differed from the earlier literature on factionalism in that his was a more clinical description of factions and their inclinations. He was also able to incorporate changes that had taken place in the nature, attitude, and composition of the factions. This classification today is considered to be the most accurate and comprehensive picture of the ideological differences within the Iranian polity. Nabavi argues that after the fourth parliamentary election of 1992, one sees a rift with regard to issues and policies among the members of the right (conservatives and pro-Rafsanjanites). These differences, which existed since the early days of the revolution, surfaced after 1989, gradually intensified, and climaxed after the 1992 parliamentary election. The split within the two rights emerged over the type of *fiqh* and the nature of the economy. Some (led by Rafsanjani) espoused dynamic *fiqh,* believed in a more liberal attitude in sociocultural policies, and strove to establish a modern industrial economy that entailed higher taxation, foreign borrowing, and World Bank-inspired structural adjustment policies. On the other end of the spectrum, conservatives such as Nateq-Nuri, Mahdavi-Kani, and Azari-Qomi maintained their support for traditional *fiqh,* the bazaari free market economic system, and a more stringent implementation of the shari'a in cultural life. They opposed state policies of interference in the economy, modern forms of taxation (arguing for the sufficiency of religious taxes), modern banking, and nationalization of various industries. The only area where the two rights remained in agreement was a pragmatic foreign policy.

Nabavi's categorization of factions is largely based on their economic views and the type of *fiqh* that factions adhere to, that is, the traditional-dynamic axis. By 1992, Nabavi argues that due largely to economic views that embraced the economic modernization of Iran, segments of the right (pro-Rafsanjani) began to exhibit what he labels as a "modernist" tendency and shared far more in common with the left than their old conservative allies. Therefore, Nabavi believed that it was more accurate to distinguish the two rights as "modern right" and "traditional right" factions.[43] Because the word "traditional" is too broad to describe all their positions, the traditional right hereafter will be referred to as either the traditional right or the conservative right.

In addition to the division within the rightist camp, Nabavi also points out that by 1992 another faction had emerged on the left side of the political spectrum, the new left.[44] Members of this faction were mostly young ideologues who claimed to be the guardians of the religio-revolutionary principles of the *velayat-e faqih*—without, however, having a clear definition of these principles. The views of the new left, Nabavi maintains, were an odd mix of the left and the right. Like the (old) left, they were strongly anti-American and believed in an egalitarian Islamic Republic. On the other hand, their views in the socio-cultural sphere were in line with the conservatives (traditional right), as they believed in the strict implementation of shari'a and abhorred the infiltration of Western culture into the Islamic Republic.[45] Although Nabavi accurately describes the beliefs of this faction, his terminology is misleading. The term "new left" is today often used to identify the views (or the plight) of socialists and Marxists since the fall of the Soviet Union. This is certainly not the group with whom the Iranian new left would align themselves. Members of this faction uphold views that are a dubious mix of the writings and speeches of Navab Safavi, Ayatollah Morteza Motahari, and Ali Shariati. The primary activity of this faction has been to attack, both physically and verbally, all those opposed to their ideas. As such, because they have far more in common with the fundamentalists/Hizbollahis of the heyday of the revolution, this faction will be identified here as the neo-fundamentalists.

It is common practice for factions to claim to be Hizbollahi or to justify their views and actions by stating that they are in line with the attitude of Hizbollah, therefore, the use of this name must be explored. There is no faction or specific group in Iran that can be referred to as Hizbollahi; it is a term that various individuals and groups have used to declare that they are highly religious and still true supporters of the original discourse of the revolution. Use of this term was most prominent between 1979 and 1981, when it was used by pro-Khomeini supporters both to distinguish themselves from other groups and to suppress opponents of the *velayat-e faqih*. The original leader of the Hizbollah was the leftist Hadi Ghaf'fari, who gathered the highly religious, often poorer segments of the Iranian population and organized them into mobs that brutally attacked participants at anti–*velayat-e faqih* gatherings.[46] They were the bearded men with batons whom Bazargan often criticized for interfering in government activities.

Since that time, a faction may label itself or its actions as Hizbollahi to gain political capital or to discredit other factions; the name implies that one is a true religious-revolutionary individual seeking to preserve the original essence of the revolution. Whether the emphasis is on the religious or the revolutionary depends on the faction wielding the term: due to their radical interpretation of the revolution, for the left a Hizbollahi means being a revolutionary in its classical sense, while for the conservative right a true Hizbollahi is one who is highly religious and jealously guards the religious principles of the revolution. In the fifth Majlis, some of the members call themselves *Majma'-e Hizbollah* (left–modern right) and others *Jame'eh-e ye Hizbollah* (traditional right). Because those espousing this term claim to be protectors of the original values of the revolution, their position is considered unassailable. In fact, to be a Hizbollahi is another source of legitimacy for a faction's views and actions, alongside the *fiqh,* the constitution, and the Imam's agenda. Currently, the neo-fundamentalists call themselves Hizbollahis in their assault upon all things Western and liberal, ranging from improper veiling of women to Western clothing and corrupting movies.

Relying on Behzad Nabavi's categorization, then, the four main factions in post-Khomeini Iran are discussed below and their views explained on two main axes: their convictions on the political, economic, sociocultural, and foreign policies of the Islamic Republic; and the bases on which they justify their views. Before exploring these distinguishing features, however, the following points must be recognized. Firstly, unlike political parties or interest groups, although there are people in each faction who exercise more power and often set the agenda for the respective faction, they are unofficial groups (with the possible exception of the Rafsanjani-led modern right faction); they are not under the authority of a single person. Rather, factions are made up of individuals who hold various positions within the Iranian polity, groups and organizations promoting similar views. In other words, Iranian factions are loose coalitions and alliances of these entities. Secondly, throughout the post-Khomeini era and for purely political, often short-term reasons, factions have modified their views on issues. These fluctuations are usually temporary and are designed to push through a particular agenda in a particular period of time. The focus below will be the prevalent views of each faction; however, the reasons behind some of these exceptions will be explained as they arise. And of course, not all members of a faction share the exact same views on issues at all times. In fact, differences of opinion have caused rifts within factions and the building of alliances with other factions (for example, the split of the two rights and the alliance of the modern right with the left in 1994).

Thirdly, as might be expected given the loose organizational "structure," factions do not have an official manifesto and their views are expressed in proclamations, newspaper editorials, journal articles, parliamentary debate, confidential memos, Friday prayers, and so on. Moreover, as an implicit "rule of civility" of Iranian factionalism, factions generally speak (of each other) in meandering and indirect ways. Therefore, instead of specific names, one hears words such as "some people," "those," "a certain assembly," "a wing." Such implicit exchanges among factions make discourse confusing for observers, and may result in inaccurate interpretations. Therefore, the evidence used to draw conclusions will be presented as well as the deductions themselves.

Fourthly and finally, how can observers tell what person, association, or organization supports what faction? The most obvious indicator is self-proclamation: a group or individual says they belong to a given faction. Another important indicator of factional affiliation is during presidential and parliamentary elections where support is declared for a candidate. Factional affiliation is exhibited in the Majlis through the support for one policy or another and in inter-Majlis elections and appointments, such as the speakership or appointments to various Majlis committees.

Factional Renditions and Views

The different views factions hold on various issues come about in part because of the different sources they use for guidance in determining the role of government and formulating policy. There are four sources that factions use to construe and legitimize their vision of the true Islamic state: religious texts, the ideological legacies of several Islamic scholars active before 1979, the constitution of the Islamic Republic, and Ayatollah Khomeini's teachings. The religious sources, more specifically the *fiqh,* provide factions with ample material to draw on and to authenticate their views. These include the two pillars of Shii jurisprudence: the Qoran and the *Sonna* (the Prophet's pronouncements, or the *Hadith*) in addition to the pronouncements and anecdotes of the imams *(revayat).* One can imagine the wealth of derivations available for the factions seeking to set policy: the holy book sets general guidelines that are elaborated on by the abundance of commentary in the *Hadith* and *revayat* (both texts whose authority is subject to dispute). The initial guidance provided by the texts is then coupled with the discretionary enterprise of Shii *ijtihad,* which can proceed according to traditional *(sonnati)* or dynamic *(puya)* interpretation of the *fiqh.*

The second source for developing a model of the genuine Islamic state are the ideas of previous Islamic ideologues who either actively sought to establish the true system or proposed theories in this regard. The views of these thinkers, which emerged as a response to the Pahlavis' modernization of Iran, were far from monolithic. Although they believed in some sort of Islamic political order where Islamic tenets were observed, they held differing ideas on the authentic model, in a similar way to contemporary factions. In Rahnema and Nomani's terminology, the beliefs of each Islamic thinker and his movement embody what can be called an Islamic "subsystem." [47]

The first and perhaps the most uncompromising of these subsystems was Navab Safavi's *Fedaiyun-e Islam* (devotees of Islam). The major emphasis of Safavi's (d. 1956) subsystem was sociocultural purification of the Iranian culture through eradication of creeping Western cultural intrusions and their replacement with a moral society based on Islamic tenets. Safavi preached strict, to-the-letter implementation of doctrinaire Islam, which meant an extremely rigid social life for Muslims that included prohibition of the use of alcohol, segregation of sexes, and a strict dress code for women. What marked Safavi's subsystem was his belief in the achievements of these goals and willingness to defend them through martyrdom.[48] Today, extremists from the right such as the Hizbollahis and the *Mo'talefeh* base their creed, particularly on sociocultural matters, on Savafi's highly restrictive paradigm.

Another subsystem was that of Mehdi Bazargan (d. 1997). The key words in his subsystem were moderation and tolerance, which combined to make a unique synthesis of Western and Iranian political culture. While Bazargan's main objective for an Islamic regime was also the implementation of shari'a, unlike the forceful implementation in Safavi's case, Bazargan's discourse was largely based on the Qoranic notion of *la ekra-he fil-din* (no coercion in religion), maintaining that Muslims should follow Islamic tenets out of free and conscious will and not through force. Influenced by European liberalism, Bazargan was a firm believer in individual rights and power sharing in the Islamic state, and indeed he exhibited such pluralistic tendencies during his short premiership. More importantly, he keenly believed that the aims of the Islamic regime could be achieved through a Western European-style parliamentary political system.[49] Since the election of Khatami, Bazargan's discourse has become very popular among many from the left such as university students.

More than any other pre-1979 Islamic discourse, the ideas of two thinkers, layman Ali Shariati (d. 1977) and clergyman Ayatollah Morteza Motahari (d. 1979), have inspired Iranian revolutionary forces both before and after the revolution. The impact of the ideas of these men on factions is so significant that to a great extent one can classify the left and the right in the religio-political spectrum of postrevolutionary Iran according to these two subsystems. Shariati was greatly influenced by the Third World radicalism of the sixties and thus was very receptive to Marxist views. However, he believed that Muslims could emancipate themselves from Western imperialism without reading Marx; Shii Islam contained all the progressiveness found in Marxist ideology. (Imam Ali, in particular, spoke in his own way about the struggle of haves and have-nots.) What made Shariati's subsystem more appealing to the somewhat progressive postrevolutionary Islamist intellectuals was the fact that, except for the person of Ayatollah Khomeini, Shariati was distrustful of the conservative, apolitical clerical establishment in Iran.[50] The left in Iran, particularly after the death of Ayatollah Khomeini, has often relied on Shariati's paradigm to justify their revolutionary egalitarian-distributive model of the Islamic state.[51]

Motahari's paradigm has been a useful source for the conservatives (apologists for *fiqh-e sonnati*).[52] According to Motahari, Islam is not a revolutionary religion in the classical sense of Third World revolutions, and is therefore alien to modern ideas of class struggle. In the tradition of conservatives, society is conceptualized by Motahari as an organic unit where divisions within society are justified by the will of God, and change should be gradual and initiated by the elite, specifically the clergy and not the masses. In an Islamic society, argued Motahari, there is no need to impel social justice as such egalitarian ideas are embedded in the shari'a and Islam provides equal opportunity for everyone. In line with Khomeini's phase two theory of an Islamic state, Motahari maintained that the state must be governed by the clergy, as they are the only true representatives of God on earth.[53]

Another source upon which all factions rely when forming their positions on issues and ultimately on the nature of the Islamic regime is the Iranian constitution. The constitution, however, is full of generalities regarding the economic, social, cultural, and foreign policies of the Islamic Republic. In addition, the document itself is replete with contradictions and ambiguities, the most conspicuous being the attempt to give authority to both the religious and republican dimensions of the regime.[54] (Pertinent articles of the constitution are in the appendix.) As a result, because the constitution addresses all three dimensions of the regime, any faction is able to locate enough articles to authenticate their particular views. In particular, the claim can be made that either the populist or the religious dimension has ultimate sovereignty, depending on which constitutional articles are selected. A detailed discussion of the constitution is beyond the parameters of this work. Suffice it to say that, as the following comments by Asghar Schirazi indicate, the constitution enshrines an uneasy coexistence between the religious and populist elements of the Iranian state, a conflict that remains unresolved both in the constitution and among the factions:

Among the many contradictions to emerge from this process [the forming of the constitution], two are fundamental and have had a decisive impact on the development of the Iranian state. The first is the contradiction between the constitution's Islamic legalist and non-Islamic secular elements that flows largely from the claim that a state set up on the basis of Shii law and ruled by Islamic jurists is capable of offering solutions to all problems, not only in Iran but throughout the world, even though the constitution itself incorporates many Islamic and nonlegalist elements. The second is the contradiction between the democratic and antidemocratic elements, arising chiefly from the conflict between the two notions of sovereignty embodied in the document: the sovereignty of the people on the one hand and of the Islamic jurists on the other, a sovereignty the jurists exercise as God's deputies.[55]

Finally, governing principles of the Islamic Republic have been determined from Khomeini's theory of an Islamic state and his pronouncements before the revolution and throughout the first decade of the revolution. Because Khomeini's ideas *(khatt-e Imam)* changed over time, factions have been able to select passages that serve to advocate their own ideas as well as differ over the interpretations of particular passages. The Imam also presented an example of using the religious sources for governing, variously including elements of the constitution, the two *fiqh,* an uncompromising revolutionary stance, and a pragmatic approach in his speeches and decrees. Khomeini modified and remodified the tenets of *velayat-e faqih* through often contradictory (yet timely) rulings, and throughout the first decade of the revolution his oscillation allowed for increasingly discretionary interpretations of his true vision of the fundamental objectives and governing principles of the Islamic state.

The Traditional/Conservative Right Faction: The Conservative Revolutionaries

Religio-political views

For the traditional right faction, the religiosity of the Islamic Republic is its most essential component and the republicanism or the populist dimension of the regime plays a secondary role. The religio-political views of this faction resemble Khomeini's phase two theory of the Islamic state, presented in a January 1988 decree that introduced the concept of *velayat-e motlaqeh-ye faqih*. The JRM upholds the view that "the Islamic Republic is a holy phenomenon where sovereignty and leadership belong ultimately to God, who relegates such powers to the *faqih*."[56] Asadollah Badamchian from the *Mo'talefeh* also stresses that "the Islamic revolution is a Godly one and God must be present to witness and supervise all principles, directions, judgments, slogans, . . .in short everything."[57] "The main purpose of the regime," maintains Ali Akbar Nateq-Nuri, "is the implementation of the words of God."[58] Given the highly religious nature of the Islamic Republic, the traditional right maintains that the *vali-ye faqih*, the biggest symbol of the religiosity of the regime, is the central pillar of the Islamic Republic and all powers must emanate from this center. Members of the JRM seeking election to the fourth Majlis in 1992 stated that "the *vali-ye faqih* as the representative of the almighty on earth must be obeyed by all and it is he who must draw up the ways and means of the *ommat* [Muslims].[59] Some members of the traditional right are in accord with Nateq-Nuri, who—taking the authority of the ruling *faqih* to new heights—said, "During the occultation, the *vali-ye faqih* enjoys the same rights and powers [over the society] as those of imams and the prophet, and his wishes are the commands and duty for all."[60] There is no room to question the decision of the *faqih*, therefore, because, as Morteza Nabavi argues, "The will of the *vali-ye faqih* must be obeyed even if his rulings are wrong."[61]

So in the uneasy balance between Islamicity and republicanism in the Islamic Republic, the conservative right has stressed the subordination of the latter to the former. They disparage the republican dimension of the regime most effectively by downplaying its symbols and emphasizing the secondary role provided to republican institutions by the constitution. For example, Ayatollah Ahmad Azari-Qomi suggested that the Islamic Republic is the de facto personal domain of the *faqih*:

> The powers delegated to the leader in the constitution are the [extension of the] monopoly of the leader in his duties and responsibilities and do not impose restrictions on his powers. . . . [The leader] is like the head of the family

who, although in the division of labor takes the responsibility of outside shopping, he leaves for himself the right to interfere in the house where he has delegated the housework to his son.[62]

It is not surprising that the JRM's constitution sees an extensive role for the clergy in the affairs of the country. Mahdavi-Kani said, "The clergy must not only guide the nation but be directly involved in ruling because, in the Islamic Republic, the clergy is entrusted with the task of insuring that the regime is at all times Islamic."[63] As the representatives of God, their "fatherly supervision" over people should encompass everything, including the sociopolitical affairs of the country.[64] As Asadollah Badamchian stated in an interview, "We all need the guardianship of the clergy as people are concerned about their afterlife and thus need clerical confirmation with regard to their [daily] activities in this life."[65] Besides, as the vanguard of the revolutionary forces, such an all-encompassing role for the clergy is justified, according to Nateq-Nuri: "It was the clergy who masterminded the revolution, who deposed the shah, who gave martyrs and saved the revolution from the likes of the Bani-Sadr."[66]

Ironically, however, although the traditional right espouses such an active clerical role in politics, until the 1997 presidential election (see chapter 5), the majority of its members have staunchly opposed the formation of a clerical political party. The JRM, according to its chair Mahdavi-Kani, will not organize itself as a political party in the modern sense because the society exists "as a spiritual organization whose duty is to intervene in politics, but it does not like to use parties as a means of furthering its own duties."[67] Mahdavi-Kani believes that the clergy enjoys a special status and privilege in Iranian society unlike any other group. Accordingly, the clergy has an independent source of authority because it draws its legitimacy from its holy status approved by the Qoran and the *vali-ye faqih*.[68] Thus, a clerical assemblage such as the JRM has considered itself entitled to act as a political organization, both before and after the revolution, without seeing the need to form a political party.[69] Such anti-political party views are shared by the *Mo'talefeh*. Badamchian, the deputy secretary, believes that modern (Western-style) political parties are political tools used to struggle for more power and influence, which is prohibited in Islam and is tantamount to polytheism *(sherk)*.[70] Another *Mo'talefeh* member, General Secretary Habibollah Asgar-Owladi, believes that, because all members of the society perceive the government of God and the *velayat-e faqih* as the only legitimate political force, all belong to one party, the party of God, and there is no need for another party.[71]

Opposition to a clerical political party on the part of the traditional right is an expedient as well as logical position to hold as it runs counter to the interests of the clergy for two main reasons. Firstly, a political party entails subordination to mundane, state-formulated rules and regulations, which would circumscribe clerical autonomy and action. Moreover, a modern political party may result in not only disagreements but struggle for more power and influence in society within the clerical circle or between the clergy and the society at large. Nevertheless, it is ironic that such negative views of political parties are held by the backbone of the IRP in the early days of the revolution, the JRM and *Mo'talefeh*. At that time the idea of an Islamic Republican Party required some justification as well, provided here by its founder, Ayatollah Beheshti:

> If we define a party as an organization for convoking all the active forces [in society] and perceive it as a [means of] ensuring a social movement, then we can say that Islam and Islamic governments have had parties. The Prophet by indoctrinating Muslims created a party with a party organization and an underground movement. After the Prophet's leadership the [nature of the] party did not remain the same as it took the form of a state/government. By tracing the clandestine movement of *amir-ol mo'menin* [commander of the faithful] in history and providing references to the views of the imams, I have, during the period of 1970–1977, proven that during the period of Shiism and Imamat there was a "party of Imamat."[72]

This expedient interpretation of what constitutes a (religiously) sanctioned political party is enshrined in the constitution of the Islamic Republic. Article 28 of the constitution states that "parties, societies, and political associations are free to assemble so long as they do not contradict or threaten the Islamic tenets of the regime." This article has been interpreted to mean that the regime is entitled to evaluate whether a party's belief is in contradiction with the principles of *velayat-e faqih,* which once again may be a decision motivated by expediency rather than ideology. Indeed, applications from the likes of Bazargan's Freedom

Movement (*Nehzat-e Azadi*) party have been rejected by members of the faction who occupy decision-making bodies, on the grounds that the group does not hold appropriate views on the *velayat-e faqih*.[73]

As was noted earlier, the *Motlaqeh* version of the *velayat-e faqih* theorizes a minimal role for society at large: most people would be categorized as imitators (*moqalled*) rather than sources of imitation (*marja'-e taqlid*). Such a view has its justification. Accordingly, it is implied in this interpretation of the *velayat-e faqih* the society relegates all of its rights to the *faqih*, the embodiment of the eternal legitimacy/sovereignty of the state. Thus, the traditional right considers state, society, and politics in the Islamic Republic to be interwoven. In the government of God, Badamchian maintains, there is pluralism of thought (*tazarob-e afkar*) but not dissension (*tanazo'*) of thoughts. Describing this as "holy social unity" (*towhid-e ijtemai*), he further notes, "Sisters and brothers do not fight, and in case of disagreements they will submit to the will of the *faqih*, hence God."[74] Elsewhere, Badamchian elaborates further on his vision of the holy Islamic society:

> The Islamic society is one where all activities are for God. It begins with God, works for God, and ends with God. . . . There are different views in this society but not a struggle [for power] because everyone works for God. . . . The definition of politics in this society differs from other monotheistic ones. In the West [politics] is for acquisition of status, power, and money. In Islamic society politics is based on the words of the Imam. . . . In this society no one is engaged in politicking [*siyasat bazi*], but all are performing their religious duties.[75]

Another *Mo'talefeh* member, Morteza Nabavi, used a *JIM* editorial to construct his own version of a Lockian "social contract": "The people in this system [*velayat-e faqih*] are assured that the leader has their good in mind and that he uses its political power for the welfare of the public only. . . . As the principle political source in the Islamic Republic, the *vali-ye faqih* through his kindness and knowledge galvanizes them and makes the people obedient."[76]

Given such obedience on the part of society, the utility, role, and function of symbols of the will of the people such as the constitution and the Majlis appear superfluous. In other words, here again the uneasy interplay between religious and republican institutions surfaces. A standard response of the faction to this balancing act has been to point out that the republican institutions are secondary in importance to the religious super-bodies. For example, Ayatollah Mohammad Yazdi (a member of the traditional right) states that the Majlis by itself, without the sanctioning of the *vali-ye faqih* and his supervisory bodies such as the Guardian Council, has no legitimacy or power.[77] Or, drawing again on the *Motlaqeh* discourse, Reza Zavarei (also traditional right) believes that the role and function of republican institutions in Iran differ from conventional establishments. *Hojjatiyeh* sympathizer Ali Akbar Parvaresh argues that the constitution and the Majlis in the Islamic Republic differ from those in other democracies: "In other revolutions people seek to ensure the sovereignty of the nation, but in an Islamic state they seek the implementation of sovereignty of divine laws [hence God], because the people believe that the nation's sovereignty can only be achieved under the beacon of sovereignty of Islam . . . because laws contrived by mankind will ultimately lose their credence."[78] In summary, with such fundamentalist religious views on the part of the traditional right and their emphasis on the Qoran and tradition *(sonnat)*, Behzad Nabavi argues that if there is one faction in Iran that can be categorized as "orthodox" *(osul-gara, bonyan-gara)*, it is this faction.[79]

Economic Views of the Traditional Right: Islamic Bazaar Economy

From the brief history provided in chapter 2 about the bazaar-mosque alliance, the economic views and interests of the traditional right after the revolution are predictable. As would be the case with any faction, the conservatives' views of the alliance between bazaaris and clergy needed religious justification in light of the goals of the postrevolutionary regime. Consequently, from early on the clerical contingent of this faction, particularly through the rulings of the jurists of the Guardians Council (all members of the JMHEQ), pushed through their interpretation of the true Islamic economy.

Outside of the Council, one politically active champion of the economic views of this faction, especially during the first decade of the revolution, was another member of the JMHEQ, Ahmad Azari-Qomi. Well aware of the alternative economic systems that could be implemented in the wake of the revolution, Azari-Qomi began discrediting the left and their desired changes for the economic system of the Islamic Republic. Through extensive editorials in *Resalat,* he supported less government and a free market economy, and further explained what the conservatives meant by nonstatism. Azari-Qomi often referred to various Qoranic verses to substantiate the claim that not only did Islam advocate the sanctity of private property, but in fact the holy book held those engaged in commerce in high regard.[80] Thus, according to Azari-Qomi, a proper Islamic economic system is one in which individuals are provided with the freedom to produce and enjoy the fruits of their labor.[81] "Allowing greater freedom for people to engage in commerce," Azari-Qomi argued, "would cause a flourishing of talents and take a heavy burden off the shoulders of the government."[82] For example, Azari-Qomi thought cooperatives should be in the hands of the private sector and not the state. Redistributive-egalitarian policies such as land distribution, according to him, would lead to nothing but a godless socialist system. Instead, Azari-Qomi suggested, "Based on *fiqh-e sonnati,* the government should lift the limit on land appropriation."[83]

This traditional interpretation of the Islamic economic system was indeed stated by Khomeini in *Hokumat-e Islami,* and he reiterated it immediately after the victory of the revolution.[84] Thus, in 1984 when a bill was presented to the Majlis that aimed to increase government revenue by levying higher taxes on business and commerce, Azari-Qomi opposed the measure, citing Khomeini's opinions in *Tahrir-ol Vasileh* in which he argued for the sufficiency of *khoms* and *zakat,* or tithes.[85] Ayatollah Hojjat, a member of the JMHEQ, has said openly that clerical opposition to modern forms of taxation was due to the pragmatic expectation that the imposition of such taxes would limit the financial autonomy of the ulama, as people would have less money to contribute to religious coffers.[86]

The traditional right continued to hold the same economic views after the death of Khomeini. Since 1989, this faction has further advocated a minimalist role for the state that entails less taxation, fewer regulations, and a free market economy. The bazaaris favor an economic system where they, as middlemen, are free to "import and sell" with the least governmental interference and regulation. To justify such views, Mohammad Reza Bahonar, a powerful member of this faction and currently one of the leaders of this faction in the Majlis, asserts that Iran can never be a successful industrial country: "In the commerce sector, our country has great potential for becoming an international merchant.

I do not have high hopes that at any time [in the future] our industry or agriculture can meet the country's expenditures. However, I do believe that we have considerable capabilities of becoming a connecting bridge of many countries."[87]

In a series of *Resalat* editorial articles entitled, "The Roots of Economic Ill" that appeared in November 1990, Morteza Nabavi criticized the statist policies of the left during the first decade of the revolution and argued for what should be the basic principles of the Islamic Republic in the post-Khomeini era.[88] The timing of the editorials was particularly important because they appeared soon after Khomeini's death, when factions were trying to push through their views on issues and policies. On November 13, Nabavi stated that the real cause behind the economic ills of the country had been that, "rather than relying on indigenous economic forces and capabilities, we have been relying on the statist policies of the central government." The next day Nabavi called for supply-side economics and scorned state interference in the economy, which he believed took away private domestic incentive and caused inflation by limiting supply. Nabavi opposed high government taxes and quoted Azari-Qomi, who said, "The government should not have a free hand on taxation but should tax according to its needs." On November 17, he further disapproved of various aspects of state interference in the economy. An activist, hands-on government that required numerous permits for business activities would not only discourage commerce but would ultimately produce a sluggish economy, maintained Nabavi. The November 19 editorial stated that unemployment was another side effect of a centralized economy. "When there are numerous obstacles to domestic commerce, investment will decrease, and with it, employment." Nabavi also noted that bureaucratization of Iran was another systemic ill as it was a hindrance to the productive economic forces in Iran. He therefore suggested that it was the constitutional duty of the government to decrease the size of the bureaucracy.

Like all factions in Iran, the traditional right must address the issue of socioeconomic justice. Like economic conservatives in the United States and elsewhere, conservatives in Iran believe in letting natural market forces redress economic inequalities. The basic argument of this faction is that their proposed economic system would indeed reduce poverty in Iran through "invisible hands" and the inherent "trickle down" process of Islamic culture and its (traditional) economic mechanisms. Therefore, Azari-Qomi harshly criticized those who supported laws that place limitations on individuals who make a profit through "religiously sanctioned" (shar'i) means, because when individuals (hence, merchants) in an Islamic society become well-off, they will in turn aid the poor and the less fortunate. Based on the traditional *fiqh* and the words of the Imam himself, Azari-Qomi maintains, "It is only through religiously sanctioned ways that we can help the *mostazafin*." Thus, if one limits the religiously sanctioned commercial activities of people, there will be less money for benevolent and charitable endeavors.[89]

It is not just how one addresses economic inequality, but how one defines it, of course. According to the confidential newsletter of the JRM, socioeconomic justice entails "lessening the gap between the rich and the poor" and not the systematic eradication of poverty because absolute equity is nothing but a utopia:

> Attainment of a classless society has never been achieved in history and it will never be achieved. Yet Islam does not allow a sharp gap between classes so that one class rules and another is ruled. . . . In societies where exploitative relations do not exist, there are, ultimately, those who are more diligent, hardworking, and industrious. Such extra efforts should not go unrewarded. The holy Qoran states, "We distributed their sustenance and gave some more than others."[90]

Islam and true Muslims, the newsletter maintained, will attend to the poor without government interference:

> Because sharp class differences are frowned upon in Islam, through measures [stated in the Qoran] such as Islamic taxes [*khoms* and *zakat*], wealth is adjusted [*ta'dil*] in an Islamic society. Islam is mindful of the fact that wealth should be circulated, so that parity of wealth and social equilibrium will be created. . . . Islam does not allow wealth to remain in the hands of the rich and for the poor and the dispossessed to be deprived . . . [because] Muslims are brothers and a brother cannot be oblivious to the hunger of his brother. . . . Based on their capabilities, Muslims are duty bound to provide for the essential needs of the needy. . . . If [the paying of] *khoms* and *zakat* are regularly performed, there will be no poor Muslims.[91]

Sociocultural Views of the Traditional Right: Restrictive Puritanism

The conservatism of the traditional right is further accentuated in their socio-cultural views. More than any other faction, the traditional right emphasizes the preservation of Islamic culture. This means a highly pious lifestyle where Islamic tenets are strictly observed. Consequently, this faction has been wary of reforms and the opening of Iran to the outside world. In post-Khomeini Iran, the traditional right routes its social views through enmity against what it calls the "cultural onslaught" (*tahajom-e farhangi*) of the West.[92] Infiltration of Western culture into Iran, according to the JRM, will spread moral corruption among the youth, accompanied by the danger of a return to prerevolutionary culture.[93] This faction argues that to confront this onslaught, Iranians must take shelter in the Islamicity of the regime. Nateq-Nuri often warns the young against Western cultural influences and suggests that "the best possible way to confront it is through more acquaintance with the Qoran."[94] Reza Taqavi suggests that *fiqh-e sonnati* will preserve and guard the spiritual dimension of the Islamic Republic.[95]

The stringent sociocultural views of this faction are exemplified by their stance on women. A virtuous woman for this faction is one who is first and foremost a good mother, and her role models are famous female Islamic figures such as the Prophet's wife.[96] To spread such ideas in postrevolutionary Iran, the JRM and JMHEQ arrange seminars on women and veiling (*hejab*) in which its forced imposition is suggested and improper veiling (*bad-hejabi*) is condemned.[97] One sympathizer of this faction, hojjatol-Islam Mohammad Faker, had these patronizing words for women MPs when they lobbied for a bill that would give women the same inheritance rights as men: "They have written this bill as if all men are oppressors and all women are innocent. I ask you, the lady Majlis deputy, is this really true? Are you really innocent? One of you is enough to make life a living hell for the other 270 [male MPs]. How could you say all women are innocent and all men oppressors?"[98] The *Mo'talefeh* maintains the same traditional, conservative view on women as the JRM and claims that Iran must protect its pure Islamic culture against possible permeation of Western morality in Iran. According to Mohammad Javad Larijani and Morteza Nabavi, "Western liberal culture is incompatible with Islamic culture, as their yardstick for freedom is unfetteredness [*bi band-o bari'*]."[99] Another *Mo'talefeh* sympathizer, Ali Besharati, emphasized that cultural principles of the Islamic Republic should be based on its Islamicity, and "its preservation must take place through PVPV [propagation of virtue and prohibition of vice]." [100]

The conservative views of *Mo 'talefeh* were the official sociocultural policies of the Islamic Republic from 1992 to 1997 when *Mo 'talefeh* member Ali Larijani was minister of culture and then headed National Iranian Radio and TV, *Mo 'talefeh* member Mostafa Mir-Salim headed the ministry of culture, and Ali Mohammad Besharati was minister of the interior. However, when it comes to sociocultural issues, Ayatollah Ahmad Jannati, an influential member of JMHEQ and the secretary of the Guardian Council, has been the most uncompromising. Jannati says that in an Islamic society, "We must and are duty bound to preserve [proper] veiling of women." [101] On another occasion he warned, "The enemy is trying to destroy our Islamic culture." [102] Speaking at a Friday prayer sermon, Jannati suggested, "If we want to preserve our Islamic culture, it is upon us all, including the ulama and the government, to support true Islamic culture by reinforcing the religious bedrock of people and fighting all those who are anti-Islamic and Western-stricken." [103] As the head of the Headquarters for Vivification of PVPV, whose members are made up of young *Basijis* (highly religious war veterans), Jannati has indeed been able to enforce strict Islamic code in the streets of Teheran (see chapters 4 through 6).

The puritanical attitudes of this faction extend to other public domains as well. Education in the Islamic Republic, for example, must be based purely on moral and Islamic grounds. Reminding university students of their "role in society," a *Resalat* editorial notes, "our students know well that scientific knowledge is not sufficient to manage the country. The executives of the country need piety and virtue." [104] To ensure the Islamicity of the universities, JMHEQ's hojjatol-Islam Mohammad Kharazi believes the *"vali-ye faqih* must have direct supervision over the university . . . to prevent the spread of stray thoughts." [105] And indeed the *faqih* does. As with most public institutions, all Iranian universities have a special office for the representative of *velayat-e faqih* who is actively engaged in making sure that the university curriculum conforms to Islamic tenets. Aside from the devout religious sentiments of its members, one major reason for the traditional right's support of these representatives is that most of them are either members of or are sympathetic to the traditional right (see chapters 4 and 5).

Foreign Policy: Traditional Quietism

The conservative nonrevolutionary views of the traditional right extend to their attitude in foreign policy. The chaos that would result from exporting the revolution would inhibit the interests of the bazaaris, who are better served by open borders and an atmosphere conducive to free trade. When tranquility is preserved, the ulama also benefit because their authority and status within the society depend on the maintenance of the status quo. The revolutionary rhetoric of the conservatives includes criticism of the "great Satan" and anti-American slogans. But although the traditional right criticizes American ideals, they never specifically endorse direct confrontation or the export of the revolution.[106] However, this quietist attitude must be justified within the revolutionary milieu in Iran. In foreign policy issues, too, Islam must be molded to justify another modern conclusion.

An archetypal conservative interpretation of the Islamic revolution by the traditional right is provided by Badamchian in his book, *Recognizing the Islamic Revolution and Its Roots.* Badamchian classifies the Iranian revolution as a "holy revolution," which is undertaken not at the will of or for the people, but for God and to serve his purposes based on the discretion of the *fiqh.*[107] In discrediting the leftist interpretation of the Iranian revolution, Badamchian writes, "Unlike other revolutions, the roots of the Islamic revolution are religious and not economic."[108] Citing the writing of Motahari, Badamchian believes that Islam opposes violent and forceful export of Islamic revolution, and corrects those who favor revolutionary actions in the name of the masses, noting that one should distinguish between "revolutionary Islam" and "Islamic revolution." The former concept indicates that Islam by nature is a revolutionary ideology. This, maintains Badamchian, is simply not the case because contention and struggle should only be undertaken to enforce Islamic tenets and to create the rule of the *faqih,* not to radically and forcefully transform the socioeconomic fabric of the society. Consequently, the words of Islam should be spread in a sedate and rational manner.[109]

In post-Khomeini Iran, the traditional right has pushed through a conciliatory tone in foreign policy in an indirect way and through support for Rafsanjani, who was been the key architect of Iran's pragmatic foreign policy since 1989.[110] Such conservative views become more justifiable after the peace with

Iraq, which signaled a new pragmatic era in the foreign policy of the Islamic Republic. Part of their success was due to their ability to imply that in foreign policy the Imam was indeed pragmatic. Hasan Rouhani, the deputy of Iranian National Security Council (NSC), applauds Imam's pragmatism in signing the Resolution 598 (UN peace resolution) and says, "The basis of Islam is contact and interaction [with the outside world]."[111] Mohammad Imami-Kashani from the JMHEQ downplays one of the radical discourses of the revolution: "Imam Khomeini said that exporting the revolution means simply to spread the word of Islam and does not mean to interfere in the affairs of other countries. This means that the Islamic Republic of Iran wants to apply Islam in a practical way."[112]

There are many instances in post-Khomeini Iran where the conservatives exhibited their conciliatory posture in foreign policy. The traditional right capitalized on every instance where there was a suggestion for normalization with the "great Satan." In a controversial interview with the daily *Teheran Times* in September 1989, for instance, the deputy for foreign affairs, Mohammad Javad Larijani, asked the United States to show its good intentions by condemning its old policies toward Iran and releasing Iranian assets.[113] In another interview with *Sobh,* Larijani said that executing the wishes of the Imam and killing Salman Rushdie "is against international law and not in the interests of the country."[114] Perhaps what best revealed the quietist views of the traditional right was the Gulf War. Immediately after the start of the war, the JRM preached patience and asked the population to refrain from hasty radical actions against the United States.[115] The most recent example of this faction's attitude was Javad Larijani's green light to the West during his trip to Britain in 1997.[116]

The Left Faction: The Populist Islamic Revolutionaries

According to Behzad Nabavi, the views of what is known as the left in factional politics in Iran are in direct opposition to those of the conservative right. This faction supports *fiqh-e puya,* maintains a revolutionary rather than conservative interpretation of the Iranian revolution, espouses a strong centralized and redistributive state, favors a command economy (until the election of Khatami), supports the export of the revolution, and holds a tolerant attitude towards sociocultural and political spheres.[117] Although members of the left, too, believe in the religiosity of the Islamic Republic, they perceive the populist and revolutionary dimensions of the state to be equally important if not more vital than its religiosity. The MRM, the MII, and the Office of Strengthening of Unity (*Daftar-e Tahkim-e Vahdat,* hereafter *Tahkim*) constitute the main groups of this faction.

The MRM has no written manifesto, but the organization has expressed its views through statements and proclamations, particularly through its official daily *Salam,* in addition to the short-lived (1990–1991) bimonthly *Bayan.* Its secretary general is Mehdi Karrubi and prominent members of its central committee are Mohammad Tavassoli, Mehdi Karrubi, Mohammad Musavi Khoeiniha, Ali Akbar Mohtashami, Khatami, Mohammad Hassan Rahimian, Mahmud Doai, Rasul Montajabnia, Asadollah Bayat, Majid Ansari, Mohammad Ali Abtahi, and Abdolvahed Musavi-Lari.[118] The MRM temporarily ceased its activities in December 1995 and resumed activities in February 1997.[119] With the election of Khatami to the presidency in 1997, the MRM and indeed the left in general have been in the ascendancy in the Iranian polity.

The MII began the publication of *Asr-e Ma* in 1994. Through the writings of members such as Behzad Nabavi, Mohsen Armin, and Mohammad Salamati, the MII has been the main ideological think tank for the left in post-Khomeini Iran. A major reason behind the formation of MII, according to its current deputy Salamati, was "to create a political organization that would provide the means for the society at large to partake in the governing of the country."[120] In a nutshell, the views of the MII can be labeled as populist-revolutionary. This is how the manifesto of the MII describes the creeds of the organization:

MII is a politico-ideological organization that, with the belief in the life-giving [*hayat-baksh*] school of Islam and the necessity of enlivened [*zendeh*] and time-conscious [*zaman shenas*] ijtihad in adapting this school to the needs of the times, and by reliance on Islamic lore whose representatives are the *fo-qaha,* the learned [*hokama*], and Islamic pundits, and based on the stated principles of doctrine and within the framework of the constitution and with the acceptance of the principle of *velayat-e faqih,* will strive for the achievement of the following goals: (a) guarding of the principles, values, goals, and achievements of the Islamic revolution that include the Islamic system [*nezam-e Is-lami*] and the constitution, (b) perpetuation, expansion, and deepening of the Islamic revolution in Iran and the world, (c) increase in the ideological-political awareness, moral attitude of the masses and their mobilization for their active participation in revolutionary matters, the society, and their destiny, (d)acceptance of the constitution as the principles and pillars of the system of Islamic Republic that is manifested in the three branches of government.[121]

Although the MRM and the MII make up the backbone of the left, one must mention *Tahkim* as another organization that has been ideologically in line with the MRM and the MII. In May 1980, which marked the beginning of Khomeini's cultural revolution, the Islamic Associations of Students (*Anjo-man-e Islami-ye Daneshjuyan*) were established in Iranian universities to combat the spread of Marxist views.[122] From the outset, some of these student associations held more revolutionary views while other organizations, such as *Jihad-e Daneshgahi* (University Jihad), held far more conservative-religious views. The former associations were unified under the name of *Tahkim-e Vahdat* and gradually diverged from the more religious *jihadis*.[123] The conflict between the two wings in the universities eventually became a proxy conflict between the left and the conservative right (see chapter 5). Since 1991 through their weekly newspaper *Mobin, Tahkim* has been propagating the populist-revolutionary views of this camp in universities in Iran.[124] Three individuals are influential in organizing the activities of the *Tahkim:* Ibrahim Asgharzadeh, Ali Mohammad Gharibani (editor of *Mobin*), and Hashem Aqajari. As we shall see, *Tahkim* and their adherents among university students have been staunch supporters of intellectuals such as Abdolkarim Soroush. Consequently, they have also been battling the conservative right, particularly the representatives of the *vali-ye faqih* and their supporters in universities.[125]

Before stating the major convictions of the left, several points are worth mentioning. During the early years of the revolution, this faction held far more radical positions on issues than they advocated in the period after Khomeini. With the gradual decline of revolutionary fervor in Iran, the left was forced to soften their views after 1989. The collapse of the Soviet bloc was particularly influential in the loss of popularity for statist redistribution policies in Iran.[126] Immediately after the death of Khomeini, the left maintained its earlier radical rhetoric to some degree, mainly to challenge the rise in power and alliance of the two rights (see chapter 4). The second transition took place on the eve of the fifth election when this faction further toned down its views, particularly on foreign policy and economic issues, and made a de facto alliance with the modern right (see chapter 5). The third transition has been taking place since the election of Khatami in 1997, with the left becoming even more pragmatic and nonrevolutionary.[127] What are described below as the views of this faction are their convictions from 1989 until the election of Khatami.

Religio-Political Views: The Islamic Republicans

In theory, all factions in Iran accept and claim loyalty to the concept of *velayat-e faqih*. It is the different renditions of this concept that distinguish one faction from another. The left accepts Khomeini's phase three formulation, *velayat-e intesabi* or Divine Populace (*Ilahi-mardomi*).[128] According to this interpretation, the legitimacy and sovereignty of the regime are drawn not only from its holy dimension but from its populist dimension. The *faqih,* therefore, shares his rule with the populace at large. To win acceptance for this reading, the other interpretation of *velayat-e faqih,* the *Motlaqeh,* must be discredited. According to the left, the conventional understanding of the *Motlaqeh,* and hence the conservatives, has been misinterpreted to mean some sort of despotism of the *faqih,* providing him with absolute power. An interpretation of the words of Khomeini were proffered in *Asr-e Ma*:

> The term *velayat-e faqih* in the Imam's religious writings is used in its broadest/loosest context, and it means the jurisdictions [*ekhtiarat*] of the head of the state in all matters. Thus, the word *Motlaqeh* in *velayat-e motlaqeh faqih* should by no means be understood as political absolutism that, in conventional political usage, is conveyed as despotism. . . . We believe that the theory of a religious state in the Islamic Republic and the constitution, which embodies, in the best possible manner, the two ideas of theocracy and democracy, are shaped based on holy-populist sovereignty rulership.[129]

To support their *intesabi* reading of the *velayat-e faqih,* the left bases its argument on two primary differences that distinguish this faction from the conservatives: their adherence to *fiqh-e puya* and their support for the populist and revolutionary dimensions of the Islamic Republic. Religion, according to the MII, "must adapt to the necessities of the time and the *foqaha*'s rulings must adhere to this."[130] Perhaps the main justification for the left's adherence to *fiqh-e puya* lies in their revolutionary interpretation of the religious movement in Iran. In a two-part article entitled "Islamic Revolution: Its Roots and Consequences," by Behzad Nabavi, *Asr-e Ma* discussed the left's understanding of the essence of the 1979 revolution. The article begins by pronouncing that "revolutions are necessary, inevitable, and a desirable phenomenon for all societies" and goes on to admire the struggle of the Cuban and Vietnamese revolutions against US imperialism. The article then summarizes what the left thinks about the Islamic revolution, its nature, and purpose:

> The dominant ideology of the Iranian revolution was Islam. However, the Islam of the Iranian revolution has fundamental differences with previous traditional [*sonnati*] interpretations. The *sonnati* version perceived the mission of all religions, including Islam, to coordinate the relationship between mankind and God, and secure the afterlife. The Imam, however, introduced revolutionary Islam and religion as a revolutionary school and ideology. . . . The Imam of the revolution laid out [the concept of] *velayat-e faqih* in which he unified religion and politics, and brought to the fore and emphasized the revolutionary mission of religion. The result of all these efforts was the emergence of a revolutionary Islam whose features are an Islam that was combative of injustice, freedom seeking, pro-*mostazaf,* justice and equality seeking, and used progressive *ijtihad*.[131]

In other words, in contrast to the devout religious views of the conservatives, where the goal of the revolution was considered to be the creation and implementation of the government of God, the left saw a far more political (hence populist) role for the revolution. On the left, the goal of the Islamic revolution was understood to be the promotion of grassroots transformation of Iranian society, not merely the top-down imposition of Islamic tenets as stated in the Qoran and the words of the Prophet.

After examining the political and religious positions of this faction, however, one can be forgiven for surmising that in post-Khomeini Iran, the populist-revolutionary left only pays lip service to the concept of *velayat-e faqih*. In fact, this faction considers the power of the *faqih* or the religious dimension to be of secondary importance to its populist dimension, arguing that the *faqih* draws his authority, legitimacy, and thus power from the populace and not from God. Based on such readings, the vision of shared rulership of the Islamic Republic by the left is in stark contrast to the traditional right. The left envisions less power and thus a more restricted role for the *faqih* in the Islamic Republic. Because of the importance placed on the republican component of this shared rulership, the left believes that an all-encompassing *faqih* with unencumbered power is unconstitutional and could in fact lead to totalitarianism. "Principally, the *faqih* is not supposed to think for everyone and present solutions for all issues," argues Mohammad Salamati. "Otherwise it could mean that all institutions, public as well as private, should never be active as their activities may constitute constraints for the *vali-ye faqih*."[132] The MRM is also keen to emphasize such ideas:

> If one is to prevent political and economic chaos in the country, one person must be the final arbiter [*faslol-khetab*] and speak the last word. But this is not tantamount to despotism, because the country has laws and [even] in those instances where the leader says the last word we still have the constitution, [therefore] it is not as if the leader can say whatever he wants. . . . *Velayat-e faqih* ascends from the Islamic state where its limitation and privileges are stated in the constitution that we all must obey.[133]

Naturally, to justify their political and religious views, the left holds dear the constitution and republicanism.[134] For instance, the left points to article 56 of the constitution to highlight the legal limitations placed on the power of the *vali-ye faqih*. This article states: "Absolute rulership over the world and mankind belongs to God, and he [in turn] has put mankind in charge of their social destiny. No one can revoke this holy right from people."[135] Consequently, according to the left, the Iranian constitution (and not the *faqih*) is the "umbilical cord" (hablol-matin) of all political and social activities in Iran and the most important document of national unity.[136]

By accenting Khomeini's populist rhetoric, the left is a staunch supporter of the will of the people and republicanism, as the words of the MRM indicate:

> In the constitution, the pillar for the legitimacy and acceptance of the regime is the popular will. A review of the constitution reveals how the populace and their opinions have been taken under consideration. In fact, all pillars of the regime, even velayat-e faqih, draw [legitimacy] from republicanism. . . . In the constitution, the primary role of managing the country is relegated to the people, and it is the people who bestow these responsibilities on the officials.[137]

The MII similarly maintains that "the Islamicity of the regime emanates from its republicanism."[138] "Our Islamic [political] system is republican and republicanism is its principle pillar. . . . Omission of republicanism is tantamount to omission of religion, Islamicity, and holiness of the system," declared Ibrahim Asqarzadeh from Tahkim.[139] Mehdi Karrubi goes further, and, in direct contrast to the views of the traditional right, maintains that "during the ghaybat, without the vote of the people, the regime does not have legitimacy."[140] Behzad Nabavi rejects the idea that the faqih has unencumbered power because, based on the constitution, all the officials of the country, even the vali-ye faqih are elected by the people, directly or indirectly. Furthermore, he argues that the supervisory power of the faqih over the three branches of the government (article 57) is just that, supervision and not domination.[141]

Support for the constitution and republicanism by the left means advocating the populist dimension of the regime. For example, the left often prides itself on the fact that, in contrast to the elitist views of the conservatives, they are dedicated to creating a more democratic Iran where grassroots participation and power sharing by the people constitute a right and not a religious duty.[142] According to Mohammad Khoeiniha, the publication of the daily Salam by the MRM was aimed to provide a venue for the voice of the people to be heard:

> This newspaper is a tribune for those who do not have the right to speak. . . .
> The more the people are involved in the making and preservation of the

regime, the stronger and more sovereign the regime becomes. We can have a religiously sanctioned regime only when people can criticize the regime. We must never decide for people and tell them what things are good for them to know and what things are not. . . . If one believes that in a religiously sanctioned system such as the Islamic Republic righteousness [*haq'*] belongs to the people, one would not claim to be the guardian [*vali-ye ne'mat*] of the people. Rather, he would perceive the people to be his guardian. He must adapt his activities based on this principle and not decide for the people.[143]

The left is strongly opposed to the conservatives' idea that Iranian society after the revolution must be "taken back in time" to the dawn of Islam. Rather, the left argues that the revolution must provide the society the means of living in a modern age:

The motive behind the [creation of the] Islamic state is the removal of previous restrictions and obstacles in society and the creation of relations that are based on preservation of [society's] interests and well-being, and guarantees an environment that provides the foundations for development and human perfection. . . . [This] can be achieved through the use of man's new findings and tools in order to realize Islamic values and tenets. . . . The device of this realization is *puya* and lively *ijtihad*. . . . It is [only] based on these ideas where the Islamic society with its three features—freedom, social justice, and morality—is formed.[144]

Unlike the conservative right, who believe that society is religiously bound to comply with the wishes of the clergy, the left prescribes independence of thought and action for the population at large: "In the monolithic thought [*tafakkor-e towhidi*], humans are born free and no one has superiority over the other and no one's mandate is binding over the other; *even piety is not a rationale for appropriation and guardianship over the affairs of others.*"[145] Consequently, the left advocates what can be called a kind of "Islamic pluralism." *Salam*'s very first editorial asked all "clergy, Islamic intellectuals, writers, thinkers, university pupils, artists, poets, and critics to help the newspaper to carry out its populist-Islamic wishes."[146] A cornerstone of this pluralistic discourse is the left's support for political parties. In the first issue of *Asr-e Ma,* Mohammad Salamati of the MII announced that the publication of the biweekly is due to the belief that "people's participation is the cornerstone of the Islamic Republic. Towards this aim, free association and establishing parties are essential parts of any democratic society that creates a pluralism of ideas [tazarob-e afkar] and a revolutionary cadre." [147] The idea is that the people, through political parties, civil society associations, and uncensored media, must have the power to "supervise" themselves. [148] According to the MRM's secretary general Karrubi, "Political parties guarantee the [survival of the] Islamic system." [149]

Based on such principles, a democratic Iran is the wish of the left and their religio-political views strongly resemble Bazargan's subsystem. The following citation from Asr-e Ma manifesto illustrates the vision of an Islamic democratic system of the left. While this selection criticizes the Western liberal democracies and their "individualistic" and "nonreligious" predilections, it proposes an idiosyncratic theory of a democratic Islamic system, one that is based on Islam but has a watered-down role for the velayat-e faqih:

> The rule of the people [mardom-salari] that we have in mind differs from liberal democracy. Our version of democracy is a kind of socialization of politics that takes into account the participatory and decision-making role of the people while preserving the rights of the minority. We believe that institutionalization of the participation of the people and a competitive political system are the only means of implanting this democracy. . . . The two pillars of the Islamic Republic in the modern era are freedom of choice in connection with the political system and the belief in Islamic values and goals. A [democratic] legitimate Islamic state can only be achieved through the choosing of the people, thus, absolute and unlimited ordaining/selection has no place in an Islamic society. [150]

Economic Views: Islamic Egalitarianism

On economic issues, the revolutionary discourse of the left is particularly profound. By expressing its concern for the plight of the disinherited, this faction believes that eradication of socioeconomic injustices must be first on the agenda of the Islamic Republic. [151] In fact, this faction believes that after independence, the most important goal of the Islamic state should be the achievement of social justice by eradicating class divisions and preventing the polarization of wealth in society.[152] Like the conservatives, the left believes that it holds the genuine model of the Islamic economic system; the left espouses, as Mehdi Karrubi puts it, "pure Mohammaden Islam [doctrinaire Islam] of the barefooted and not the American brand of Islam of the wealthy."[153] This pure Islam, according to Mohtashami, "means fighting inequality, poverty, and class difference and pursuing socioeconomic justice."[154]

In the early days of the revolution, the oratory and writing of some members within this faction espoused a far more radical position on economic issues. Some of the most celebrated—and controversial—early writings of the MII, which dealt with the rights of the workers and the underclass, were purely based on Marxist analysis.[155] Throughout the first decade of the revolution this faction muscled in its version of pure Mohammaden Islam through Prime Minister Musavi, who espoused a strong redistributive state and supported policies such as high taxation of the rich, government control of the major national industries, rationing of food, and price controls; in short, a sort of Islamic command economy.[156] Musavi said, "The way of Islam is to attend to social justice."[157] "The *mostazafin* are the struggling arms against [world] arrogance,"[158] he said elsewhere, and "the security of the revolution lies in the eradication of poverty and serving the destitute. . . . Capital must not rule and the priority of the regime should be the poor and not the well-off."[159] Although after 1989 this faction toned down its earlier radical views on the economy, the left admits that its members are still receptive to "dependency" and "radical" schools of thought.[160]

The left draws legitimacy for its statist reading of the economic system from article 44 of the constitution, which states that although the economic system of the Islamic Republic must be based on public, cooperative, and private sector interests, there is still call for state ownership of major industries, as well as the nationalization of foreign trade and commerce, banking, insurance, radio and television, railroads, air and sea transportation. By referring to this article, the MRM envisions a critical interventionist role for the government in protecting the *mostazafin* and systematically redistributing wealth in the Islamic society.[161] The need to fulfil the stated principles of article 44 is often emphasized: to obstruct the amassing of unencumbered wealth in the hands of the bazaaris and to prevent the Iranian economy from becoming a capitalist one.[162] The toned-down post-Khomeini position of the MII is that private ownership can be tolerated so long as it does not result in the "rule of the capital." The left believes that in the case of conflict between the two, the public sector must always have primacy over the private.

Sociocultural Views: Islamic Liberalism

In comparison with the traditional right, the left has a far less puritanical interpretation of the sociocultural policies of the Islamic Republic, as they preach tolerance, moderation, and diversity of cultural life in Iran. The discourse of the left on sociocultural issues relies heavily on the novel ideas of the likes of Shariati, who challenged the narrow-mindedness of the conservatives in this area.[163] Leftists are keen to point out that revolutionary Iran must rely on *fiqh-e puya* to protect Islamic culture from ossification, cultural stagnation, and ignorance.[164] One of the Islamic Republic's strongest advocates for reliance on *fiqh-e puya* and the need for the regime to adapt to the modern world has been President Khatami: "Our choice of and dependence on Islam does not mean [that we] return to the precapitalist era and impose a system that resembles those of the Middle Ages under the name of religion. Islam has the potential and the capacity to accommodate all the positive aspects of modern political and economic ideologies, as well as the technological achievements of past and present civilizations."[165] In accordance with its pluralistic views in the religio-political sphere, the left believes that the government must be courteous to intellectuals and supportive of artists and writers, creating a secure environment for them and avoiding censorship in the arts and media.[166] Such convictions, argues the MRM, are ingrained in Islam and represent the goals of the revolution:

> Freedom of thought and respect for the sanctity of the rationality of people has been an important goal of the Islamic revolution. . . . [In an Islamic society,] disagreement is not frowned upon, and if disagreements are presented in a rational and honest manner, not only will Islam not be damaged, but the society will grow much faster. . . . Fortifying Islamic and the revolutionary intellect can preserve the revolution and prove that its logic is stronger now that Islam provides the foundation for a sociopolitical system, and demonstrates its ability to solve various ideological and material societal problems, so that

thinkers and supporters of the revolution and Islam realize that they do not live in a vacuum.[167]

The left has succeeded in implementing some of its progressive views in this sphere through Khatami. In 1980 he was selected by Khomeini to head the daily *Keyhan,* and in 1982 he was appointed by Prime Minister Musavi to be the minister of culture and Islamic guidance. Until his resignation from that post in 1992, Khatami consistently presented an extremely open-minded and tolerant position on sociocultural issues. He repeatedly maintained that the goals of his ministry, and indeed of the Islamic Republic, must be to preserve and legally protect a free, independent, and uncensored media; embrace rather than confront alternative ideas and views; encourage and support all of the arts; and confront (traditional) reactionary patriarchal thoughts.[168] "The future," Khatami once argued, "belongs to logic, rationality, legitimate freedom, and enlightenment. No force can stop thinking and logic."[169]

Differences between the left and conservative right are further highlighted by their contrasting approaches to the Western cultural onslaught. While the left also believes in the possible dangers of this global phenomenon, it offers an alternative method of countering it. Khatami, for instance, believes that closing the cultural perimeter of Iran will result in the closing of the minds of Iranians. He suggests Islamic Iran must confront this onslaught by producing its own enlightenment and intellectuals.

> Only the religious intellectual can fulfil the revolutionary mission and provide a proper model in all areas [of life]. . . . In order to confront the West, we must present a more superior logic. Islam embodies this dimension and we must discover it. . . . Currently we have no option but to discern the ideological nature of the West, choose its positive aspects, and throw away its negative ones.[170]

The left is critical of the regime's treatment of women. Male chauvinism, according to Khatami, "has roots in the beastly attributes of humans. It is regrettable that this has taken on a religious tone, [otherwise] in Islam there is no difference between men and women."[171] A *Salam* editorial refers to the historical struggle of women for their rights and objects to the fact that the Islamic Republic provides only limited rights and freedom to women.[172] The MII emphasizes that in revolutionary Iran breaking the traditional/conservative attitudes regarding women is imperative because Islam and the Prophet intended to liberate and not to "cover" women:

> Unlike the views of the traditionalists [sonnat garayan], we believe that one cannot build a wall between the home and the society. In the contemporary era, the homebound model for women is not only impossible but un-Islamic and inhumane. . . . A woman imprisoned at home and prevented from engaging in social activities under the excuse or the fear of sin or depravity will not only become an inadequate human being, but she will not succeed in performing her role as a mother in today's world. The active presence of women in society is not only a right but a social necessity.[173]

The left is a vehement defender of the young postrevolutionary generation in Iran.[174] This faction advocates freedom of action and thought for university students, specifically challenging the representatives of the *faqih* in universities, most of whom are members of the conservative right or sympathetic to it.[175] Criticizing the intrusive role of these representatives, who under the pretext of guidance and "Islamization of the universities" pry into student activities, *Tahkim* maintains that university students do not need clerical "supervision" and must be encouraged to become highly politicized, not apostles.[176] Instead of force-feeding the young generation with "pseudo-religiosity" and "pseudo-Puritanism," argues the MII, they must be nourished with new ideas.[177] As a result of such support for the autonomy of students, the left has gained some of its most ardent followers from this segment of Iranian society,[178] and indeed *Tahkim* is quite an effective tool in organizing and directing this support.

Although most members of the left hold the abovementioned relatively open views on sociocultural issues, it should be noted that some, like Ali Akbar Mohtashami, maintain an extremely reactionary stance on cultural issues. In his short-lived monthly *Bayan,* for instance, Mohtashami voiced the austere views of the conservative right by warning against the possible dangers of creeping

Western liberal culture and how its banal nature might cause the Islamic culture in Iran to decay.[179]

Foreign Policy: "Death to America"

In a nutshell, the views of the left in foreign policy (until Khatami's election) revolved around the highly celebrated slogan of the Iranian revolution: "death to America." The MII, for instance, insisted that "protecting and guarding the independence and the national sovereignty of the Islamic Republic against US imperialism should be the main foreign policy objective of the Islamic Republic." According to the MII, the US-UK sponsored New World Order must be seen as the biggest danger facing Third World countries.[180] In a pamphlet entitled "The New World Order" published by the MII a year after the Gulf War, Behzad Nabavi offered a detailed analysis of how this discourse is no more than an American scheme to dominate the post-Communist world.[181] Conciliatory gestures toward the United States are naïve; the Gulf War once again showed that the United States will always maintain its hegemonic intentions around the world.[182] The MRM was just as anti-American as the MII. A *Salam* editorial warned all Islamic and Third World countries to create a unified bloc against the imperialism of the United States. In addition, the editorial strongly objected to US-sponsored Middle East peace efforts such as the Camp David accords and supported the anti-Zionist war of liberation of the Palestinian people.[183] The left supported a revolutionary role for the *faqih* in foreign policy: Hashem Aqajari from *Tahkim* said, "Our revolution is like all other revolutions and must be exported. The fact that there is a *faqih* does not change anything."[184] In post-Khomeini Iran, and indeed until the presidential election of 1997, the left saw itself excluded from Iranian foreign policy machinery but remained firmly anti–United States. It will be interesting, therefore, to see how members of the left react to Khatami's latest offer to open a dialogue with the American people, especially since even after the election of Khatami some leftists such as Mohtashami insist that the guiding rhetoric of the Islamic Republic in foreign policy should be "death to America."[185]

It is debatable whether the virtuous views espoused by the conservative right are sincere. For, although this faction presents itself as holy and holding in mind the moral well-being of society, critics of the traditional right maintain that their character and motivations are otherwise. One of the biggest critics of the traditional right is Behzad Nabavi himself. For instance, he asserts that "the traditional right is heedless to republicanism and thus power-sharing in the Islamic Republic, as this faction believes that the preservation of the Islamicity of the regime is its only goal." [186] Nabavi argues that this faction's support at all costs for a highly religious state and society makes them de facto supporters of religious despotism—albeit based on Islamic *fiqh*—found in countries like Saudi Arabia. [187] Finally, Nabavi accuses the JRM of being extremely politically motivated, stating that they should be considered a political party whose aim is to attain more power and not an organization with a messianic mission. [188] Another *Salam* editorial notes that the JRM is more power hungry than others but takes cover in the religiosity of the regime to retain immunity to public criticism. [189] The left often associates the rampant corruption and nepotism in Iran with this faction. [190] The following quote is how the newspaper *Salam* described the JRM:

The JRM has a preparatory cadre-making school called the Al-Sadeq University, a daily newspaper called *Resalat,* an armed militia group called *Jamiyat-e Mo'talefeh-ye Islami,* a propagatory body called *Jame'eh-ye Vo'az-e Teheran* [Teheran's Preachers' Society] and a provisional body called the *Jame'eh-e-ye Anjomanha-ye Islami-e Asnaf va Bazaar* [the Society Islamic Guilds of Teheran's Bazaar]. [191]

Whether or not one trusts the authenticity of the creed of this faction, there is no doubt that the traditional right will enjoy prominence so long as the religiousness and the religious dimension of the regime remains important for the population at large. This faction can exercise its ideological power through its influence in religious establishments (mosques and their preachers, and the *howzehs*) and receives immense financial support from the bazaaris. In a revolutionary society, however, their conservative nonrevolutionary interpretation of the Islamic revolution is bound to put them at a disadvantage compared to the left. Perhaps the major shortcoming of the tenets of the traditional right faction is the incompatibility of its belief in opposing deep-seated socioeconomic and political change with the sentiments of the population at large.

A prominent contemporary theorist of revolutions, Theda Skocpol, defines social revolutions in the following manner:

> Social revolutions are rapid, basic transformations of a society's state and class structures, and they are accompanied and in part carried through by class-based revolts from below. Social revolutions are set apart from other sorts of conflicts and transformative processes above all by the combination of two co-incidences: societal structural change with class upheaval; and the coincidence of political with social transformation. . . . What is unique to social revolution is that the basic changes in social structure and in political structure occur together in a mutually reinforcing fashion, and these changes occur through intense sociopolitical conflicts in which class struggles play a key role.[192]

Skocpol goes on to compare the French, Russian, and Chinese revolutions and illustrates that in all three cases the postrevolutionary regimes shared three common experiences: "a strong centralized state, upper classes losing to lower class groups, and greater popular incorporation into the affairs of the nation."[193] Ultimately, Skocpol argues that these developments are imperatives of (successful) modern revolutions.

The divinely inspired rule by religious elite favored by the traditional right runs counter, of course, to the "imperatives" of populist postrevolutionary regimes. The conservatives appear to have envisioned a revolution where ideological/moral transformation takes place throughout the Iranian society without the socioeconomic and political transformations. This is a problematic mixture of Safavi's and Motahari's subsystem for a revolutionary society. The conservatives envision a social revolution where political change takes place from the top without the social (class-based) transformation. This elitist view of the revolution creates a conflict for this faction because one of the most popular slogans of the revolution was indeed (political) freedom. This ideological paradox now seems to be causing the demise of the traditional right in Iran. After the presidential election of 1997 in Iran, where candidates who supported the populist dimension of the Iranian state gained power, both the ideological and institutional powers of the traditional right are being greatly challenged.

The views of the left have shifted as the traditional right has gained power after 1989, a shift that puts them in opposition to the traditionalists. As stated, the left, particularly the MII, were far more revolutionary; the MII's first few publications analyzed the revolution through an almost purely Marxist conceptualization. Consequently, the economic views of the left were more radical and envisioned practically no role for the private sector in the Iranian economy. In addition, the left were far less supportive of intellectuals and intellectualism and favored a more extensive role for the clergy: although "enlightened clergy enjoy Islamic knowledge, honesty, piety, and mass support, they are devoid of organizational power and the necessary political prudence. . . . The enlightened [*roushanfekr*] may have this political prudence and organizational complexity, but as a rule they lack ideological stability and sound religio–ideological convictions."[194] The most drastic change of the left's view, as noted, took place in their position regarding the *velayat-e faqih*. Until Khomeini's death, the left were the most devoted supporters of the *velayat-e faqih,* and in fact it was they who often scorned the conservatives, the *Hojjatiyeh,* for their lack of dedication to the *faqih.* While the left now admits that their zealous support for the *faqih* was politically motivated and was aimed to pacify opponents of the *velayat-e faqih,*[195] a change in position was also made possible by Khomeini's post-1987 decrees that buttressed the authority of the left. The left suffers from one big disadvantage and enjoys one major advantage. Its disadvantage is that it does not have a high-ranking clergyman (ayatollah) among its ranks: clergy known to be affiliated with this faction are all middle-level hojjatol-Islams. Perhaps the only prominent clergyman that was sympathetic to the views of this faction was Ayatollah Montazeri (heir apparent to Khomeini, dethroned in 1988), who today is marginalized. This handicap means that, unlike the conservative right, the clerical members of the left are less likely to be represented in religious super-bodies such as the Guardian Council, or to be strong candidates for positions of leadership, and are unable to issue fatwas with regard to important issues because these posts require the status of ayatollah. In their favor is a shift in the desires of the population. The left's staunch support for the populist-republican dimension of the regime and its symbols such as the constitution, their liberal attitudes in the sociocultural sphere, and their belief in more freedom of expression and individual rights in Iran are finding more voters among the general population.

The Modern Right Faction: Islamic Modernizers

On January 20, 1996, fifteen members of President Rafsanjani's cabinet announced that they were running for the coming parliamentary election on the platform of "Islamic honor, continuance of constructiveness, and Iran's development [abadi]." The goal of the group was "to continue the postwar accomplishments of Rafsanjani's reconstruction efforts aimed at the political and economic development of Iran."[196] Calling themselves *Kargozaran* (functionaries, servants), Qolam-Hossien Karbaschi, ex-mayor of Tehran and a member of this group, claimed that "their stated course is that of the Imam and the leader" and maintained that their religious-revolutionary credentials stemmed from their postwar efforts, when as part of the government they dedicated themselves to reconstructing war-torn Iran.[197] The self-proclaimed duty of the *Kargozaran* was to work for the welfare of Iran through "creating social justice, [economic] development without the rule of capital, expansion of international relations based on the principles of the revolution, use of experts and reliance on expertise, and creation of a [domestic] environment where ideas can flourish."[198] The most important part of the *Kargozaran's* announcement, however, was the specific statement that they planned to achieve these goals under the direct guidance and direction of Ayatollah Hashemi Rafsanjani. The foundation of the *Kargozaran* officially signaled the public split between Rafsanjani and the conservative right.

The differences between the two rights climaxed over the nature and direction of the Iranian economy. By espousing World Bank–inspired structural adjustment policies, Rafsanjani desired a modern industrial-based economy integrated into the global economy, but the conservatives remained supportive of the traditional bazaar economy.[199] As we shall see in more detail in chapter 5, this and other economic initiatives of Rafsanjani resembled economic policies of the shah, and thus once again the bazaaris found their economic livelihood in danger.

Behzad Nabavi labels this faction, which is comprised mostly of state technocrats and headed by Rafsanjani, as the "modern right." Nabavi places this faction in the right of the political spectrum because of their support for a free market economy. However, they are labeled as modern rather than traditional/conservative because of their economic views and reliance on modern industrial-based infrastructure and dependent capitalist development relying on high taxation, modern banking, and integration into the world capitalist system. In addition, unlike the conservatives, this faction maintains a liberal attitude toward sociocultural life, including relying on *fiqh-e puya*. The modern right emphasizes pragmatism, expediency, and rationalism rather than tradition and conservatism. For the modern right, Nabavi argues, the East Asian Tigers serve as a model for economic and political growth and development.[200]

Since the emergence of the *Kargozaran,* the views of the modern right faction are expressed mainly in the two dailies closely affiliated with Rafsanjani: *Hamshahri* and *Iran.* Additionally, modern right sympathies have been expressed in the short-lived (January 1995–April 1996) weekly *Bahman,* published by Ataollah Mohajerani, and in the daily *Ettela'at,* whose editor, Mahmud Doai, has been very close to Rafsanjani since the early days of the revolution. The views of the modern right are essentially those of Rafsanjani, but this section will focus on the tenets of the *Kargozaran* rather than Rafsanjani's individual beliefs because the next three chapters will discuss his policies in detail.

Before offering this brief account of the creed of the *Kargozaran,* however, Rafsanjani's memoirs, entitled *Combative Era,* must be mentioned. A brief review of this two-volume work is useful at this point, as it reveals insights about Rafsanjani and his views that put the positions of the modern right in context. Reading Rafsanjani's memoirs, one is certainly surprised by some of his comments. For instance, although he states his devotion to the Imam and his ideas,[201] he also indicates that he was "intrigued" by the nationalist movement *Mossadiq,* or Freedom Movement, and in fact he was quite fond of Bazargan.[202] Bazargan's Freedom Movement, believes Rafsanjani, "was a praiseworthy political movement and a proper way of combating [the monarchy]."[203] This, while he specifically mentions that the Imam was staunchly antinationalist and emphasized the Islamicity of the regime.[204] Rafsanjani also seems fond of Western democracies. In recounting his trip to the United States, Rafsanjani regrets that such political freedom in the West is coupled with loose morality and social relations.[205] Another unexpected remark is Rafsanjani's more than tacit support for the ideas behind the shah's White Revolution. Although Rafsanjani believes that the White Revolution was aimed at weakening the influence of the ulama and the Islamic beliefs of the masses, he nevertheless approves of the principle behind reforms such as nationalization of forests, land reforms, and the selling of factory shares to workers.[206] Such views explain his staunch support for similar measures taken by the government after the revolution.

Rafsanjani repeatedly shows his disapproval of the conservatives and their views, particularly the *Mo'talefeh*. He makes a conspicuous effort to discredit the *Mo'talefeh,* their ideas, and discourse of armed struggle. He writes, "During the late 1960s many people believed that armed struggle would play a deciding role in the Islamic movement. However, experience has invalidated such beliefs. . . . We [I] do not give armed struggle a lot of credibility."[207] Rafsanjani also denigrates the *Mo'talefeh* and their violent approach by implicitly saying that this group has overemphasized their role in Khomeini's Islamic movement.[208] In fact, he states that Khomeini was always against violence, particularly armed struggle, and that the Imam in fact explicitly disagreed with the *Mo'talefeh*'s violent approach in cases such as the murder of Prime Minister Mansur. According to Rafsanjani, Khomeini was opposed to killing the shah, even if that meant martyrdom.[209] In short, Rafsanjani's memoirs indicate that he is a pragmatic Islamic nationalist, certainly more of a reformer than a revolutionary. The *Kargozaran,* as we shall see below, has indeed opted for such a moderate, reformist course.

Views of the *Kargozaran*: An Outline

At the heart of the modern right's ideas has been the belief in *towse-'eh* or political-economic development of the regime. The survival of the Islamic Republic, according to Karbaschi, depends on the twin pillars of a healthy industrialized economy with modern infrastructure and well-developed political institutions.[210] In the developmental model proposed by the modern right, the government takes on an active rather than hands-off role in the economy, stimulating growth by intervening to guide the economy, and promoting full employment, export competitiveness, and energy self-sufficiency (which in the case of Iran means diminishing the reliance on oil revenue). In this scheme, the banks play a vital role in attracting and directing capital into small-scale industrial projects.[211] Critical for the success of this plan is an increase in government taxation through major reforms of existing tax laws and of the financial system as a whole. Then the government will undertake fair distribution of income and wealth in society.[212] These principles were enshrined in Rafsanjani's First and Second Five-Year Plans (see chapters 4 and 5).

Members of the *Kargozaran* maintain that their proposed model of economic development will eradicate poverty through systematic and formal means. In an indirect criticism of the conservatives, who believe in tackling poverty through traditional religio-cultural methods, an *Iran* editorial envisions a kind of Islamic welfare state where benefits are systematically furnished by the government: "Although religious alms [*sadaqeh*] and alimony [*nafaqeh*] will help the poor, they will not eradicate poverty. Eradication of poverty and helping the poor are two different propositions. We must create an economic system that will deal with this problem systematically and through increased economic production and employment."[213]

Due to their emphasis on *Towse-'eh,* political and economic development for the modern right are very much intertwined. According to Behzad Nabavi, the modern right embraces "bourgeois liberal democracy" that entails pluralism and power sharing. Like all factions in Iran, the *Kargozaran* states their allegiance to the *velayat-e faqih*. In their first announcement, the *Kargozaran* stated their loyalty to the *faqih* and hoped to achieve their goals "under his mantle and with his blessing."[214] Unlike the conservative right and the left, however, the *Kargozaran,* and indeed Rafsanjani himself, has not addressed the issue of *velayat-e faqih* directly. Rather, the modern right makes systematic and subtle efforts to minimize the significance of the religiosity of the regime, and thus the power of the *faqih,* in two ways. Firstly, the pro–modern right press often stresses the progressiveness of Islam and Shii *ijtihad* in articles on Shii *fiqh*. This can be seen in interviews with high-level ulama who hold progressive views on religion and stress the necessity of *fiqh* to accommodate changes in the contemporary world. For instance, a two-part article in *Hamshahri* entitled "Religion and Issues of Modern Times" suggests that if the Islamic Republic is to achieve its goals, it is imperative that *foqaha* tackle hitherto unaddressed issues such as the population explosion, global warming and pollution, human rights, and women's rights.[215] In a two-part interview with a high-ranking clergyman from the *howzeh, Iran* promotes the idea that the clergy must not be cautious (*ihtiyat*) in issuing new decrees because such hesitation is against the principles of *ijtihad*.[216] "In religious matters" argues another two-part article, "we must support free thinking, questioning [of tradition], and novelty."[217] Surely, the ideas of this faction and their successful implementation require a *faqih* who is dynamic and willing to accommodate changes.

The second way that this faction plays down the religious dimension of the Iranian state is through their support for the republican principles of constitutionalism, free elections, and pluralism. A *Bahman* editorial, for example, argues, "The government should provide for the genuine and credible presence of the people in the system as expressed by the Imam. There is no doubt that the increased participation of the people in the revolutionary scene creates a more legitimate, colorful, and powerful regime."[218] Members of the *Kargozaran* believe in a political environment that welcomes pluralism (*kesrat-gharai*), a competitive party system, an increase in the public's role in the decision-making process, and sociocultural freedoms that include freedoms of expression, the press, and association, within the limits set by the law.[219] A three-part editorial in *Hamshahri* reminds the leaders and the public of those freedoms, which was an indispensable slogan of the revolution, noting that most Islamic teaching was aimed at destroying obstacles to political and social freedom.[220] Like the left, the modern right often quotes article 56 of the constitution and its guarantee of the "God-given right of self-government for the people."[221] An editorial in *Iran* suggests that the revolution has reached maturity and "national interests dictate that we refrain from exclusivist policies and allow people to freely choose their representatives."[222] The modern right accents concepts such as "civil society" and "human rights" and the need for the regime to adhere to these contemporary universal principles[223] in order to maintain its legitimacy and popularity and endure:

> In the contemporary world, we cannot find a political system that does not need the participation of the people even if it [this participation] is exhibitional. Today, it is an accepted international norm for the states to be based on [the will of] the population, and the efficacy of all states depends on the sympathetic presence of people in the political institutions.[224]

To indicate the importance of such principles, the modern right points out the dangers of their absence in Iran. A *Bahaman* article on "fractionalization of [Iranian] society" warned that, aside from the existence of the left-right dichotomy in the Iranian polity, there is a far more important division in Islamic Iran:

> The most active and fundamental rift in Iranian society today is between those who support the religious state and those who do not. In fact, one can speak about the political atmosphere in Iran as being made up of these two blocs: one made of various people and groups who support an active political role for religion [and] the other believing in a regime that is devoid of any particular ideology and is run based on customary [orfi] principles.[225]

The left and modern right share similar views in the sociocultural sphere, with the modern right also emphasizing *Towse-'eh* and its potential positive impact on Iranian/Islamic culture. An editorial in Iran entitled *"Towse-'eh:* Revival of Islamic Culture" argues that development based on science and technology will help advance Iran's Islamic culture.[226] In order to tackle the issue of the Western cultural onslaught, for instance, the modern right believes that the younger generation must not be coerced into becoming religiously indoctrinated into the regime. Rather, says Mir-Baqeri, the president's consultant on youth affairs, the regime must understand the young and provide sound, systematic solutions to their problems.[227] On issues related to women, this faction has found specific tenets of the Qoran and the words of the Imam to suggest that Islam believes in equality and partnership of the sexes, and not their segregation and inequality.[228] Consequently, the participation of women in socioeconomic and political spheres, according to the modern right, "is not a sociopolitical necessity but a fundamental principle [of the Islamic Republic]." Additionally, the modern right is a defender of freedom of the press, stressing that "press censorship is un-Islamic."[229]

The emergence of the modern right is another example of how the diverse ideological components of the regime allow for faction formation and new interpretations of the Islamic state, even though the core ideas (in this case *Towse-'eh*) may be totally alien to previous Shii discourse. The rise to power of the modern right as a distinct faction was due primarily to three reasons. The first, mentioned above, was the disagreement between Rafsanjani and the conservative right faction. The second impelling force was the shared experiences of governance on the part of some members within the leadership (both from the left and the right), and how the imperatives of everyday management of a complex revolutionary country forced them to adapt their earlier positions to fit the realities of modern politics. The third force behind the ascendancy of the modern right was no doubt Rafsanjani himself, who espoused more or less the same views from the beginning of the revolution to the time of the modern right's split and later. While in prison in 1967, Rafsanjani wrote a laudatory book on Mirzataqi Khan (the famous nineteenth-century prime minister whose modernizing policies, interestingly enough, greatly agitated many contemporary high-ranking ulama), which indicates that he held these convictions long before the revolution. In short, Rafsanjani's attitudes and the political and economic views of the *Kargozaran* add up to a vision for the Islamic Republic of a politically and economically modern Iran sanctioned by religious principles.

The Neo-Fundamentalist Faction: The Soldiers of Morality

We believe that Islam is against a capitalist-style economy, amassing of wealth and polarization of society. To confront such corruption we believe that force must be used. We believe that if the *faqih* commanded it, it must be obeyed even if it is against our views and desires. Even the *mojtahedin* must be obedient to the decrees of the *faqih*. As a newspaper this is our line. We believe that [Western] liberal culture can threaten our [Islamic] culture and must be seriously confronted. We have standards in everything and we aim to confront cultural unfetteredness and deviation from the values of the revolution.[230]

These words, by the most well-known member of the neo-fundamentalists, Mehdi Nasiri, at the time on the editorial board of the daily *Keyhan* and the current editor of *Sobh,* sum up the creed of this faction. The rise of neo-fundamentalist groups was largely a response to what some members of the regime (that is, the conservative right) call the "Western cultural onslaught." This faction's self-proclaimed duty is the purification of Islamic culture from this Western cultural conspiracy. Essentially, the clamor of the neo-fundamentalists is that the original values of revolution, such as religious orthodoxy, martyrdom (for Islam), piety, and an ascetic lifestyle have all but disappeared and have been replaced by material greed, indulgence, luxury, and an "unfettered" (be-band-va-barî) and immoral life-style.[231] Moreover, argues this faction, in the face of the infiltration of this corrupting culture, government officials are mere observers. Their task as true guardians of the moral paradigm of the early revolution, therefore, is to defend and propagate the original virtues of the Islamic government espoused by the Imam. If one faction merits being referred to as the club-wielding Hizbollahi in post-Khomeini Iran, it would be the neo-fundamentalists.

In comparison to other factions, the neo-fundamentalists are weaker in that they do not control any of the institutions and their known members have yet to dominate major centers of power in Iran. The structure of this faction is even looser than other factions and is made up of individuals surrounded by cronies who act like a pressure group within the system. While those associated with this faction use similar rhetoric and support each other's actions, by and large they act independently. Moreover, unlike other factions, the neo-fundamentalists do not have a well-defined platform on issues. There are prominent individuals within the polity, including some members of the conservative right, who share similar views on sociocultural issues with the neo-fundamentalists. By supporting the discourse of this faction, the conservatives have been strengthening the position of the neo-fundamentalists and promoting their own political interests at the same time. In fact, the ability of neo-fundamentalists to act in an unobstructed way is due to the indirect support they receive from the conservative right, which is aimed at weakening the post-1994 alliance of the modern right and the left.

The first person to form a distinctive discourse for the neo-fundamentalists, one that was distinguishable from other factions, was Mehdi Nasiri. He joined the editorial board of Keyhan in 1988 at the age of twenty-four and remained there until 1994. When he left Keyhan, he began publishing Sobh in March 1995, first on a weekly basis and then monthly. Since that time he has pursued a crusade against immorality in Iran, reputedly relishing the support of Khamenehi. While at Keyhan, his position on issues at first was in line with the left, strongly anti-American and pro-mostazaf. However, like the conservatives, he supported austere sociocultural measures in addition to believing in forceful enforcement of "proper" Islamic culture.[232] Nasiri has expressed his devotion to the Islamicity of the regime and in numerous editorials attacked the left as those "who under the seductive slogans of republicanism [jomhuriyat] and mass participation are undermining the power of the *faqih,* diluting the Islamicity of the regime."[233] Nasiri has maintained his previous position as editor of *Keyhan* in *Sobh*. In one of the prepublication editions, in a editorial called "Why *Sobh?*" Nasiri began, *"Sobh* aims to play its part in guarding the principles of the revolution and to spread [religious] 'orthodoxy' *[osul-garai]* and fight heterodoxy." He then summarized his views in the following manner:

> My principles are the belief in *velayat-e motlaqeh-e faqih* and the Imam's values, fighting the bloodsucking wealthy, noncompromise with the US, belief in the dynamism of *fiqh* with reliance on the principles of traditional *fiqh,* and a culture without unfetteredness. . . . I am against the actions of the former ministry of culture and Islamic guidance [Khatami] and its sponsoring of Western-infected liberal intellectualism as a cultural model, especially in media and cinema.[234]

Another group within this faction call themselves the *Ansar-e Hizbollah* (the comrades or patrons of Hizbollah, hereafter called Hizbollah or *Ansar*). The known leaders of *Ansar* are Masud Dehnamaki, Hossein Allah-Karam, and Mehdi Shoja'i. The first two publish the biweekly *Shalamcheh* (which rather purposefully came out a year before the last presidential election to discredit the left-modern right alliance), and Shoja'i publishes the monthly *Neyestan*. According to Allah-Karam, the *Ansar* are "groups of young war veterans who, based on their revolutionary-Islamic duty, claim to be carrying out the Imam's will and rectifying existing shortcomings in Iran."[235] The claim of this trio and other Hizbollahi is that they represent the highly religious-revolutionary, mainly poor, segment of the population like the *Basijis,* who since the end of the war have been marginalized and their views ignored in the midst of postwar reconstruction efforts. Young believers who for eight years fought for Islam and its values returned to see that all they had fought for, and indeed what the revolution had represented, had all but disappeared. That is why *Shalamcheh* prints gruesome pictures of mutilated dead *Basijis* at the war front with headlines such as "what have 'you' done for us," and why Allah-Karam warns the *Basijis,* "Brothers, the war has not ended, it has just begun."[236] In its first issue, *Neyestan* announced that the reason for its existence was to "confront the onslaught of the termite-like enemy while the officials are asleep."[237] Speaking on the nature of *Ansar, Neyestan* noted, "the *Ansar* are formed based on the pain felt by those who feel that the revolution and its values and principles are being forgotten and weakened, and that the essence of the revolution is in danger. *Ansar* believe that it is their duty to rely on and enforce such ideas."[238]

Neo-Fundamentalists and Factional Politics

The role played by the neo-fundamentalists in Iran is best understood when placed in the larger picture of factionalism after 1989, particularly the post-1992 developments. (These will be discussed in detail in chapter 5; here is a brief account.) With Rafsanjani's split from the conservatives, his orchestration of the modern right faction, and the establishment of an alliance with the left, the conservatives tried to diminish the power of Rafsanjani by attacking his "liberal" views in the socioeconomic and cultural sphere. By joining this attack against the modern right, the neo-fundamentalists have gained power and effectively acted as a pressure group through their relentless attack on Rafsanjani, particularly on his notion of *Towse-'eh,* which has resulted in economic opening to the West and a less restrictive cultural life in Iran. According to Nasiri, "preserving revolutionary values and principles is vital and should not be sacrificed for the sake of freedom and *Towse-'eh.*"[239] By depicting *Towse-'eh* as a Trojan horse for the displacement of Islamic-revolutionary values,[240] Nasiri and the *Ansar* show disdain for the new technocratic class in the executive branch, scorning their support and import of everything modern, such as Western clothes, cars, and even mobile phones, picturing them as sort of lewd yuppies.[241] The technocrats, maintains Nasiri, "are not compassionate and caring revolutionaries but are simple yes-men."[242]

The economic policies of Rafsanjani are also blamed for the creeping materialistic mentality and social decay in Iran. For example, the making of Kish Island into a free-trade zone flooded with foreign luxury goods, in addition to the relaxed enforcement of moral codes of the Islamic Republic on the island, which included the selling of Western pop music and improper veiling, receives its share of criticism by the neo-fundamentalists.[243] *Neyestan* believes that "*Towse-'eh* is a prescription made for us by the West and propagated by the 'executive' machinery."[244] According to *Ansar*, "political and economic openness in Iran will cause the collapse of the revolution."[245] In one interview, Nasiri went so far as to claim that, due to their liberal ideas, the modern right (Rafsanjani) were anti–*velayat-e faqih* and should not be considered as one of the familiar domestic (*khodi*) forces.[246]

The austere views of this faction about cultural life in Iran are particularly profound when it comes to issues related to women. The fundamentalists maintain that Rafsanjani and his liberal attitudes provide more rights for women than the Qoran and tradition allow. These attacks are especially pointed at Rafsanjani's daughter Faezeh, who since her election to the Majlis in 1995 has called for more freedom and rights for women.[247] For example, Faezeh has suggested that properly veiled girls should be allowed to engage in all sports including sports such as bicycling. *Shalamcheh* responded by painting a caricature of Faezeh and wrote, "If the martyrs knew that 'lady' Faezeh would make such remarks, they should not have gone to war so their families would not have to answer."[248] To combat such un-Islamic practices, the *Ansar* have been taking the law into their hands, beating female bicycle riders and closing down cinemas that show films where women appear in provocative clothing, claiming that their action is PVPV and a response to government inaction in this regard.[249] *Neyestan* has a section on women entitled *nesvan* (a derogatory term traditionally used to refer to women), where writers advocate preserving the traditional Islamic values about women. In one issue, the magazine told reformers, "Please do not defend the rights of our women. Just because foreigners think of us as petrificated, do not force-feed us feminism to please them."[250] The female version of *Ansar*, Sisters of *Ansarollah*, also joins in to criticize the growing feminist sentiment in Iran through street demonstrations in the capital.[251] It is customary for the *Ansar* to organize independent anti-improper veiling gatherings throughout the streets of Teheran where demonstrations dissolve into brutal attacks on incorrectly dressed women.[252]

The *Ansar* and Nasiri are known for their concerted efforts to discredit Abdolkarim Soroush, the Islamic intellectual who since 1991 has been suggesting the need for the separation of religion from politics in the Islamic Republic. *Sobh* has characterized Soroush as the Martin Luther of the Islamic Republic and one of the biggest threats to *velayat-e faqih* in Iran.[253] The physical arm of this faction in the confrontation with Soroush has been the *Ansar,* who, headed by Allah-Karam and Dehnamaki, have organized demonstrations against Soroush during his speeches at universities,[254] claiming that "the ideals and values of revolution are threatened by a group of irreligious intellectuals."[255] The *Ansar* have repeatedly asked the authorities to dismiss "liberal" professors from the universities and replace them with Hizbollahi educators.[256]

Aside from the modern right, the neo-fundamentalists were highly critical of the left. When asked why he had changed the focus of his criticism from the conservatives to the left, Nasiri stated that he supports those who are devotees of the *faqih* and the religiosity of the regime. "When the Imam was alive," maintained Nasiri, "the JRM were not true believers of *velayat-e faqih,* but the MRM were. Later, however, the JRM 'corrected' its view while the MRM's support for the *faqih* diminished."[257] In one of his speeches, Allah-Karam referred to Behzad Nabavi as "the third generation Iranian Communist."[258] One of the biggest confrontations with the left, one that also reveals conservatives' support for the Neo-fundamentalists, came when MP Ali Mohammad Gharibani (editor of *Mobin*) compared the *Ansar* to those hooligan watch dogs who surrounded the shah, referring to them as a "bunch of brainless thugs."[259] In response, the *Ansar* marched through the streets chanting anti-left slogans and issued a manifesto that had three main components: the *velayat-e faqih* is the fundamental principle of the Islamic Republic, the *faqih* must be obeyed, and all must engage in PVPV.[260] Given such principles, in addition to its combat with the modern right and the left, it is no wonder that the conservatives have more than "tolerated" this faction. In line with Nasiri, who believes in the "rightfulness of the actions of *Ansar,*"[261] Torabi from the conservatives attacked Gharibani: "How dare you assault the Hizbollahis who are preserving and protecting the honors [*navamis*] and ideals of the people and the revolution."[262] Morteza Nabavi noted, "Gharibani has been highly discourteous to those who are defending the revolution against the American Cultural Onslaught in this country."[263] Even Mahdavi-Kani joined in to support the *Ansar* by saying that "*Towse-'eh* does not mean that we forget our values and beliefs."[264]

The discourse and actions of the neo-fundamentalists further highlight how the competing ideological dimensions embedded in the Iranian state allow for groups or individuals to claim legitimacy for their views, actions, and ultimately their version of the true model of the Islamic Republic. In addition, the ideological tenets of this faction, a precarious mélange of the views of the left and the right, illustrate that a faction can draft a reading of the Islamic Republic embedded with contradictions, and can have differing interpretations of the key ideological components. For example, as supporters of the barefooted and espousing permanent enmity of the United States, the neo-fundamentalists proclaim to be revolutionary and socioeconomically egalitarian. However, this populist radicalism is in stark contrast to the left who also uphold such convictions. For the neo-fundamentalists, being a revolutionary entails being devoutly religious and obedient to the *faqih* and the clergy as a whole. In other words, they consider themselves as populist *(mardomi),* while they maintain similar cultural views as the conservative rights. The neo-fundamentalists should be identified as the true followers of Navab-Safavi's subsystem in terms of their xenophobia, anti-Western position in the cultural realm, and their belief in clerical rule. Within the overall revolutionary-religious discourse of the Islamic Republic, as these remarks by Dehnamaki and Allah-Karam indicate, the creed of this faction has unassailable attributes: "The *Ansar* are not made up of particular groups or individuals, but fighters combating immorality in the country based on their religious and holy duty of PVPV that all people must engage in, actions that do not need governmental permission."[265] In this regard, perhaps the most telling words of the *Ansar* came in November 1995, when they burned down the Morgh-e Amin book store after it published what they considered to be an un-Islamic book. When their action was condemned by some as total disregard for the law, the *Ansar* proposed their vision of the "true" law of the land and, like all factions in Iran, "rightly" defended their conduct:

> Our actions are PVPV, and therefore we do not need permission because such rights are given to us by the constitution and the constitution considers such actions as a religious national-populist duty. We have not broken any laws. . . . What laws are you referring to? If by the slogan "legal" you want to destroy the Hizbollahi spirit then we ask you: was the essence of the revolution legal? Were people's demonstrations legal? Was the takeover of the US embassy legal? Was the slogan of "exporting the revolution" legal? If by law you mean

the law of Islamic government, we ask you where have we broken the law? Does not the law state that books such as the one published by Morgh-e Amin are prohibited? Is *velayat-e faqih* not the spirit of the constitution and adherence to it a must? Then what are you complaining about?[266]

The Ascension of Rafsanjani, the Alliance of the Two Rights, and the Demise of the Left

1989–92

The rise of Rafsanjani to power was the most significant development in post-Khomeini Iran. Indeed, the years from 1989 to 1996 were arguably the era of Rafsanjani, who skillfully managed to position himself as the architect and manager of a new Iran, gaining for himself the title "Commander of Constructiveness" (*sardar-re sazandeghi*). Factional politics in Iran during this period should be understood in the context of the new agenda setting of Rafsanjani backed by the conservative right and the reactions of others to these changes. With the major religious super-bodies in the hands of the conservatives, and Rafsanjani at the pinnacle of the executive branch, the two rightist factions joined forces to undermine and weaken the spirit, political momentum, and revolutionary discourse of the left. The weakness of Khamenehi enabled Rafsanjani to assume the role previously played by Khomeini, that of setting the direction and principles of the Islamic Republic. The new president strove to implement his notion of *Towse-'eh* through two complementary goals of de-revolutionization and [Weberian] rationalization of the Islamic Republic. The changes instigated by Rafsanjani received a mixed reaction from various factions. The conservative right, particularly the free marketeers of the bazaar who were hard hit by the statist policies of the Musavi years, welcomed the "economic liberalization" policies espoused by the new president. However, Rafsanjani's liberal attitude in the sociocultural realm and his "real politick" approach to foreign policy were initially cautiously tolerated, but later opposed by this camp.

The response of the left, who perceived the de-revolutionization of the Islamic Republic as betraying the goals of the Imam, was the opposite of that of the conservative right. They adamantly opposed Rafsanjani's economic policies and his pragmatic stance in foreign policy but gave their tacit support to his sociocultural views by embracing the ideas of the new minister of culture, MRM member Khatami. The neo-fundamentalists and some members of the conservative right (in particular Ayatollah Ahmad Jannati), on the other hand, totally rejected what they considered to be Rafsanjani's Westernization of the Islamic Republic. It should be noted, however, that although Rafsanjani by and large remained on the side of the conservatives, the ultimate aim of the new president, as the post-1994 years illustrated, was to muster power for his own faction, the modern right. Thus, Rafsanjani sometimes remained nonpartisan in the conflict between the left and the conservative right.

Rafsanjani and the De-Revolutionization of the Islamic Republic

The first decade of the Iranian revolution was essentially a one-man show directed by Khomeini. After the ayatollah's death, the major uncertainty faced by the Iranian leadership was the question of who would define the nature, objectives, and governing principles of the Islamic Republic. Rafsanjani capitalized on this absence of clear direction of the second phase of the revolution to produce what the Islamic Republic sorely needed after the death of its leader: fresh agendas and a new path. While the leadership in the last year of Khomeini's life admitted partial defeat and hinted at the need for fundamental change, it was Rafsanjani who took on the responsibility of producing necessary reforms. Rafsanjani advanced with relative success his reform-minded vision and impelled the Islamic Republic towards pragmatism and compliance with principles previously ignored by the elite. This meant giving precedence to worldly political matters over religious ones, which in turn called for setting in motion a process of "rationalization" of the regime. This required governance through formal rather than informal or personal principles and institutions, a centralized rather than diffused polity, and law and order through the rule-making of the central government rather than through religious-revolutionary institutions. Compliance with these fundamental principles, however, required relinquishing previous rhetoric—and power—in favor of more expedient methods.

The de-revolutionization of the Islamic Republic by Rafsanjani took place on two levels: ideological and institutional. On the ideological level, Rafsanjani attempted to moderate the prevailing extremist discourses of the first decade of the revolution. On the institutional level, while pushing for a more decentralized style of administration, Rafsanjani aimed at increasing the infrastructural powers of the central government, and hence of the republican institutions.

Successful implementation of Rafsanjani's de-revolutionizing of the Islamic Republic meant either doing away with, or providing alternative renditions of, the prevailing discourse and practice of the first ten years of the revolution. For nearly a decade, the Islamic Republic and its leadership thrived on stressing particular religio-revolutionary discourse: emphasizing doctrine over expertise, asceticism over indulgence, export of the revolution rather than realpolitik, redistributive instead of laissez-faire economy, traditional rather than dynamic interpretation of the shari'a in sociocultural life, and a decentralized rather than centralized polity. In short, the old revolutionary modus vivendi and the new direction were incongruous with the new phase of reconstruction in Iran. So Rafsanjani launched a calculated attack on what he perceived to be detrimental religio-revolutionary misunderstanding, not only about the governing principles of the Islamic Republic, but about Islam itself.

For instance, his brand of laissez-faire economy emphasized consumerism rather than austerity: "Asceticism is necessary only under emergency situations, [otherwise] pretension to piety and poverty will become pretentious. Why should you forbid yourself things that God made permissible? . . . God's blessing [ne'mat] is for the people and the believers [to devour]. Asceticism and disuse of holy consumption will create deprivation and a lack of drive to produce, work, and develop [economically]."[1] Rafsanjani criticized other ideas that seemed to be ingrained among Muslims. Citing the Prophet, Rafsanjani said, "Worship and piety without work are not enough. . . . The deterministic and fatalistic idea that God will take care of everything in its [proper] time is a wrong thought that *ommat* is afflicted with."[2] In support of Rafsanjani's political views, his advisor Ataollah Mohajerani explicitly criticized Islamic culture in a series of articles in *Ettela'at* by chastising what he called the "Eastern mentality," labeling "lazy" Third World mentalities as the cause of Iran's backwardness.[3]

Mohajerani suggested that Rafsanjani's discourse would become more effective by suggesting cynicism of the Hizbollahis. The revolutionary Hizbollahis symbolized the milieu of the first decade and all of the changes Rafsanjani perceived as necessary. As the archetype of a revolutionary Islamic person, a Hizbollahi personified a particular phenomenon in postrevolutionary Iran. He was recognized as someone with a distinctive personality who held a unique set of religio-political and sociocultural views. In the political culture of the Islamic Republic, particularly in the first three years of the revolution, these attributes included coming usually from a poor socioeconomic background, zealously supporting the Imam and the Islamic revolution, being unlettered and despising the (Western) educated class, exhibiting a special loathing for anything Western and anyone who held secular Western ideas, espousing an ascetic rather than a lavish and extravagant lifestyle, the belief that one had an independent religio-revolutionary right to act autonomously from the central government in enforcing what he perceived to be the correct Islamic ways, and the right to physically attack opponents of the regime. Lastly, a distinguishing feature of a Hizbollahi was his bearded, scruffy appearance. Regarding the extremist nature of Hizbollahis and their popular cultural image as the accepted model of a revolutionary Muslim, Rafsanjani argued:

God has created in humans an ornamental and beauty-seeking sense and with a disdain of ugliness. . . . This beauty-seeking is a pillar [of Islam]. Now, if we object to beautiful sights it will be fighting nature, something that God did not want. . . . The demeanor of a Muslim, if we want to think in Qoranic terms, must be the most beautifully dressed of all [human] societies. . . . There is a culture that the style of living of priests and Hizbollahis should be unpleasant and ugly. If it becomes a cultural phenomena that being a Hizbollahi means looking unbearable, this is a sin and Islam has fought this. . . . It would defame Islam. . . . Luxury should exist, but not overt luxury. . . . We have religious decrees that you must wear perfume, comb your hair, comb your beard, and wear a clean outfit. The Prophet himself looked at his reflection in water to make sure that he was presentable before his guests.[4]

In addition to the Hizbollahis, there were other revolutionary legacies of the first decade that Rafsanjani considered to be potentially harmful to his new vision for Iran: for example, the highly orthodox *Basijis* fresh from the war would surely object to Rafsanjani's overtures. Similar to the Hizbollahis, the *Basijis* claimed independent religious-revolutionary legitimacy for their actions and were willing to take the law into their own hands. Rafsanjani believed, "While keeping their belligerent spirits, the *Basijis* should be engaged in the phase of economic construction in Iran."[5] Fearing the continuation of the revolutionary milieu of the first decade, the conservative right supported such views and defended Rafsanjani's implicit call for law and order.[6]

Finally, Rafsanjani's new economic direction, *Towse-'eh,* also required a shift in the existing beliefs about the nature of the Islamic economy:

> The goal of Islam is to attend to both the material and spiritual well-being of humans, and Islam has specific plans for this [which involve] an emphasis on work, production, and resource extraction. . . . Islam suggests moderation to accomplish this. . . . There are some people who still believe that Islam and other holy religions do not concern themselves with the material lives of people, that they [religions] have plans for heaven and not for earth. We, as holders of a [religious] school who are in the position of managing a society, must wipe away such misgivings. Especially the younger class listening to [religious] discussions may [wrongly] understand that being a Muslim is tantamount to suffering. This mood must be rectified.[7]

Soon after the death of Khomeini, it became apparent that the new caesar in Iran was Hashemi Rafsanjani and not Khamenehi. While Khamenehi was uttering generalities such as the need to maintain unity and continuity, Rafsanjani was telling the world what specific direction the new Iran would be taking.[8] He put forward his fresh vision for Iran shrewdly but cautiously. The new tone of post-Khomeini Iran was ushered in by the president in his very first news conference following his popular election in July 1989. In a news conference on August 1, 1989, Rafsanjani spoke about his vision for post-Khomeini Iran. Although for obvious political reasons he reiterated that the goals of the Imam and the revolution would stay intact, Rafsanjani skillfully redefined what those goals were.[9] More than anything else, Rafsanjani aimed to convey the message that the revolutionary fervor was over and that the Islamic Republic and the revolution as a whole had entered a new "Thermidor stage," where there was no room for the radicalism of the left or the reactionary tendencies of the conservative elements of the right. By so doing, he set himself and those like him who believed in the need for fundamental reforms clearly apart from the other factions:

> [Revolutionary/religious] slogans are holy, but we should not deceive our people with these slogans or create obstacles to the reconstruction of the country. . . . The Imam's guidance [for postwar Iran] was to relegate the task of reconstruction to the skilled experts without fear of the religiously narrow-minded and the pseudo-revolutionaries, spell out the outline of the primary reconstruction goals, and attend to the families of martyrs with [special] attention to foreign policy and the material well-being of the people within the confines of Islamic teachings.[10]

At the top of Rafsanjani's agenda for a new postwar Iran was economic reconstruction and recovery from eight years of war, made worse by the command economy of the left. For nearly a decade the government controlled domestic prices and imposed a wage ceiling, kept the exchange rate of foreign currencies artificially overvalued, subjected imports to government allocation, required a variety of permits for establishing new industrial enterprises, refused to allow foreign investments in Iran, and provided subsidies for nearly all basic foodstuffs. In addition to these restrictions, the government transferred the management of industries to young inexperienced revolutionaries while nearly a million professionals fled the country.[11] However, according to Rafsanjani, rather than creating a healthy, just, and independent Islamic economy, these doctrinaire statist economic stabilization policies (*iqtesad-e tasbit*) of the Musavi years resulted in economic stagnation, rising unemployment, an increase rather than a decrease in dependency on the West, and chronic, soaring inflation.[12] The key to economic revival, according to Rafsanjani, was a shift to a market economy marked by less state interference and greater reliance on the private sector as the engine for economic growth and development. Rafsanjani pleaded with private investors to enter the market and invest their huge sums of capital for productive purposes. Rafsanjani said, "For economic prosperity and independence, the Iranian economy should direct all of its resources to domestic output," with the major economic goal being increasing exports. The state would have a supervisory role rather than direct control because, Rafsanjani noted, "At the present time we do not see fit for the state to have too much involvement in the economy, and more freedom in commerce will be allowed by the state."[13]

The foreign policy of the Islamic Republic was to undergo its own brand of liberalization. In this realm, Rafsanjani reversed Iran's isolationist foreign policy and scorned the internationalist, export-oriented, and anti-Western stance of the left. Instead of adamantly refusing to deal with the Great Satan, he left open the possibility of future relations: "Our goal was never to export our revolution by force. . . . If people think we can live behind a closed door, they are mistaken. While we must be reasonably independent, we are in need of friends and allies around the world. . . . As long as the United States does not behave itself [adam nashavad, or does not become human], it cannot have relations with us."[14] The open-door foreign policy was opened further when Rafsanjani suggested the need for the return of the expatriates, Iranians previously scorned by the leadership, asking for their participation in the reconstruction of a postwar economy.[15] "We must create a suitable environment for them . . . and should not frighten them regarding the revolutionary milieu of the country," he said.[16]

Rafsanjani's remarks on sociocultural issues indicated an Islamic glasnost: "We will not sacrifice freedom because seeking truth and freedom is the soul of our revolution."[17] On the sensitive issue of freedom of the press, he said, "Criticizing and combating [the regime] are two different things. . . . Criticism is necessary and is to the benefit of the country."[18] On the controversial issue of women, Rafsanjani also made important remarks. Showing disdain for the conservative strains of orthodox Islam and therefore the belief of groups such as the conservative right and the neo-fundamentalists in the implementation of the shari'a on this issue, he said, "Women should not spend their time [just] nourishing. . . . If we restrict them to housework we will not have acted fairly."[19] In a more challenging statement to the conservatives, he said, "Women's education until advanced stages is [should be] emphasized and the actions of the religiously narrow-minded in preventing women from doing so is condemned."[20]

Khamenehi: In Accord with Rafsanjani

As mentioned in the last chapter, Khamenehi became the supreme leader in Iran with the help of Rafsanjani and without possessing the qualifications necessary for such a mammoth position. Given this and his other shortcomings, Khamenehi has not been able or willing to assert his authority in a strong, decisive fashion, unlike his predecessor. Rather than speaking in a specific and commanding manner, his customary practice has been to express his views with a cautious tone in broad, open-ended terms. As the leader and the successor of Khomeini, however, Khamenehi publicly had to maintain certain "politically correct" positions on issues. In line with the accepted rhetoric of the Islamic Republic, the United States remained the main source of the world's great arrogance,[21] Israel had to be removed from the surface of the earth,[22] and the fatwa against Rushdie would remain valid even "if he repents and becomes a devout [Muslim]."[23] As events unfolded, however, it became apparent that the views of the new leader were very much in accord with those of the president.

For the future postwar stability of the Islamic Republic, camaraderie and solidarity between Rafsanjani and Khamenehi was indispensable. Any fundamental difference between the leader and the new constitutionally empowered president would have meant ideological and systemic calamity for the republic. Luckily for the regime, from the outset both Rafsanjani and Khamenehi tried to eliminate any suspicion of friction between them. Immediately after the death of Khomeini, Rafsanjani publicly announced, "There is no dispute between me and Khamenehi." Khamenehi on numerous occasions called upon the entire nation "to support and strengthen the executive."[24] Khamenehi supported the president on all important issues, signaling his approval of the new direction of the Islamic Republic espoused by Rafsanjani and thus taking part in the de-revolutionization of post-Khomeini Iran.

Once again, it is interesting to note that, unlike Khomeini, Khamenehi did not initiate policies. Rather, it was Rafsanjani who announced policies and directions, and Khamenehi suggested his inclinations that—at least until 1994—were in line with and in support of Rafsanjani. He said, "Those who question the constructive efforts of the government help America's arrogance and engage in propaganda [against the regime]."[25] For instance, on foreign policy Khamenehi declared:

The export of the revolution did not mean that we would rise up and throw our weight and power around and begin wars, forcing people to revolt and carry out revolutions. That was not the Imam's intention at all. This is not part of our policies and in fact it is against them. . . . This is what exporting the revolution means: to enable all nations in the world to see that they are capable of standing on their own feet, resisting submission with all of their strength by relying on their own will and determination and by replacing their trust in God.[26]

To legitimize the economic liberalization views of Rafsanjani, Khamenehi said, "We are not following the Western concept of a free market economy. Rather, ours is the proper Islamic approach to fit our needs."[27] Like Rafsanjani, Khamenehi refuted the idea that living under Islam is all about suffering and asceticism:

Islam has plans for both the [earthly] world and the afterlife, and it is binding on government officials to attend equally to the material as well as spiritual matters of people. . . . If we perceive that a utopic society does not attend to the material problems and well-being of the people, it is tantamount to saying that religions, sanctities, and spiritualism do not concern themselves with people's lives, and this is against the explicit calling of Islam and the constitution. The move towards solving people's problems and opening the way for a healthy, prosperous life in which the population enjoys plentifulness and cheapness and facilities, is an Islamic duty on the shoulders of all the country's responsible officials; it is possible and definitely part of the ideals of Islam and our dear Imam.[28]

To become more in accord with Rafsanjani and more compatible with the "requirements of the times," Khamenehi developed less conservative and more tolerant views in the sociocultural sphere as well. Speaking to the heads of Iranian national radio and TV (seda va sima), he said, "You must endeavor to transform in correct and 'practical' ways the lives of the people."[29] In December 1992, Khamenehi assigned a group of prominent clergy and Islamic scholars to find ways of responding to the needs of Muslims based on the shari'a. "Your mission" Khamenehi announced "is to find rational and scholastic answers for the questions raised by the Islamic community today."[30] On issues related to women, while emphasizing the importance of their traditional role in the family, Khamenehi has adopted a tolerant and broad-minded language. Clothed in Islamic terms, he has repeatedly supported the presence of women in decision-making centers.[31] Women, Khamenehi noted, "should be engaged in sociopolitical activities in Iran and the *hejab* should not interfere in such endeavors."[32] In the area of higher education, rather than breeding a doctrinaire cadre, he has said that the job of universities should be "the correct and proper educational training and the creation of professional competence."[33] Finally, like Rafsanjani, Khamenehi uttered his disapproval of certain extremist Islamic behavior. In June 1994 he prohibited head stabbing during mourning, a long-practiced Shii ritual, describing it as an "un-Islamic tradition that portrays Iranians as irrational and superstitious people."[34]

In short, until 1994 when Khamenehi appeared to side more often with the conservative right, Iran experienced the "dual leadership" of Khamenehi and Rafsanjani with the president in the driver's seat. With the leadership and the presidency in line, the right moved to implement what seemed to be their shared vision of a new Iran. However, the difference of opinion between the conservative and modern elements within the right on sociocultural issues and economic policies (such as the higher taxes planned in the First Five-Year Plan) was bound to create friction. These differences were to come to a head over Rafsanjani's goal of rationalization of the regime. This formalization involved an increase of the "infrastructural powers" of the central government, hence the republican institutions, at the expense of the interests of the conservatives. But until late 1993 when the modern right clearly separated itself from the conservative faction, the two rights enjoyed a honeymoon period under the mantle and the blessing of the *rahbar* (leader).

It should be noted here that between the two rights, the conservatives were disliked far more than the modernist faction by the radicals in Iran. Although the left often criticized Rafsanjani's pragmatic policies, these two factions had far more in common than the left and the conservatives. Both the left and modern right maintained tolerant views in the sociocultural sphere and favored strengthening republican institutions, although for different purposes. The main point of contention between the left and the modern right during this period remained the issue of closer ties with the United States. This disagreement was resolved when the left moderated its position on this issue by 1996.

Who Is the Real Successor to Khomeini's Legacy?

One controversy that arose after Khomeini died was which faction's views more accurately matched the Imam's. Factions pondered the Imam's statements on topics such as dynamic *fiqh* and traditional *fiqh,* economic orientations, and relations with the Great Satan, or United States. The debate over *khatt-e Imam* mainly took place, as it did during the first decade of the revolution, between the left and the conservative right. Rafsanjani followed Khomeini's example and presented himself as being above factionalism.

In May–June 1991, a conference on the "Imam's economic thoughts" provided a forum for the two factions to put forward their readings on this issue although, again, in the Islamic Republic a discussion of secular issues did not occur without a religious component. The chairman of JRM, Mohammad-Reza Mahdavi-Kani, maintained that "while the Imam's economic view was class-based, he never favored open class wars." Rather, Mahdavi-Kani continued, "The Imam supported the systematic and gradual eradication of poverty."[35] As for the two *fiqh,* Mahdavi-Kani claimed that the Imam always reiterated, "In religious decrees I follow the *Sonnat* and the book."[36] On the other hand, Asadollah Bayat, the radical deputy speaker of the Majlis, maintained that "until the establishment of a just society, the war between haves and have-nots must continue and indeed this is what distinguishes pure Mohammedi Islam from the American brand of Islam." Moreover, Bayat argued, the Imam shunned the traditional version of *fiqh* in the *howzeh,* and believed that such a *fiqh* is not compatible with the realities of modern times.[37] Bayat's emphasis on the dynamic *fiqh* was shared by other members of the left. For instance, *Tahkim* was strongly opposed to those "pseudo-religious" elements in Iran who rely on traditional *fiqh* and stressed the need for the leadership in post-Khomeini Iran to rely on the dynamic *fiqh.*[38]

The goals of Rafsanjani, reconstruction and development of postwar Iran, also received their share of criticism by the left as they were portrayed as betrayal of the Imam's wishes and the revolutionary doctrine of the Islamic Republic. *Tahkim* condemned those who under the banner of rationalism and realism undermined the revolutionary principles of the regime and how those who adhere to such views labeled opponents as anti–*velayat-e faqih.*[39] A proclamation issued by the MRM on the occasion of the anniversary of the revolution also criticized Rafsanjani's priorities: "The slogan of postwar well-being and comfort is no doubt an enemy plan to destroy the revolution. Material well-being cannot be the goal of an Islamic society. If welfarism replaces justice-seeking, the spirit of the doctrinism [*maktab*] and the worldly revolutionary aspirations of Islam will be destroyed." [40]

In foreign policy and particularly on the issue of US-Iran relations, initially the left maintained an uncompromising stance. Anticipating the possibility of closer ties with the United States, this faction began immediately to scorn the pragmatic attitude of the dual leadership. The MRM referred to the will of Khomeini and declared, "Our animosity towards the United States is irreconcilable and not simply a misunderstanding." [41] The harshest words against the new tone in Iran set by the leader-president axis came from the monthly magazine *Bayan,* published by minister of the interior Ali-Akbar Mohtashami. The first editorial of *Bayan* stressed that the Imam wished for the continued struggle with (world) arrogance and supported the rule of the disinherited. The editorial also emphasized the need to keep a watchful eye on the "narrow-minded" (conservative right) and "the Westernized" (modern right) and that the real Khomeini's Islam is the Islam of anti-US feeling and class wars. [42] In its next issue, *Bayan* went further and implicitly accused the dual leadership's pragmatic overture in foreign policy as pro-United States and antirevolutionary:

> Those people and currents who claim that we should only work within the framework of our country are not knowledgeable about Islam. They are a bunch of liberals and nationalists who have not recognized Islam, the Imam, and his revolutionary ideas. . . . Those who present such talks and theses work in line with the enemy's policy and the United States. If we apply this thesis and forget about the disinherited outside our borders, it would be applying the US thesis. [43]

The argument of the left during this period was that the conservatives were never true followers of Imam and their indirect confrontation with the Imam while he was alive (that is, the ninety-nine MPs and the *Hojjatiyeh* fiasco) was indicative of this fact. Thus, the left tried to taint the credibility of the conservative right and questioned this camp's legitimacy as the conveyor of the Imam's ideas. In April 1991, for instance, radical MPs attacked the integrity of

Ayatollah Ahmad Azari-Qomi, accusing him and his family of corruption and economic wrongdoing.[44] In December 1989, a letter signed by 136 members of parliament accused the conservatives of the *Resalat* Foundation of tampering with the Imam's will by omitting the words "petrifaction" and "pseudo-religiousness" when citing Khomeini's will in their newspaper. These words, argued the radicals, were meant by the Imam to discredit the conservatives and question their sincerity.[45] Throughout this period, the left's claim remained that the two rights were straying from the doctrine of the Imam by "selling out" the revolution. However, without Khomeini's support, the two rights were too powerful for the left, and by the 1992 election the radicals in Iran had (temporarily) departed from the political scene.

As mentioned in the previous chapter, Khomeini's radicalism adversely affected the conservative right, particularly the bazaaris. This faction would clearly welcome a nonradical, weak leader such as Khamenehi. With its members in control of the super-bodies, the conservatives pushed for the strengthening of the institutions of *velayat-e faqih* via support for the new *rahbar*. The policies of the new president were also welcomed by this faction. They were quite content with an open-door foreign policy and a free market economy. Thus, the politically expedient reading of *khatt-e Imam* by the conservatives gave them support for the institutions of *velayat-e faqih*—hence the religious dimension of the Islamic state—under the umbrella of the leadership. In other words, the conservatives' reading of the Imam's teachings became the discourse uttered by the leader and the president. Morteza Nabavi, the editor of *Resalat,* who also believed that the Islamic Republic needed to carry on the Imam's work, summarized that task this way: the need for all "to rely on the tent and pillar of *velayat-e faqih,* avoid discord and ensure the continuity of the system." For Nabavi, "support of the *faqih* is the yardstick for being a revolutionary."[46]

All individuals and groups close to the conservative right voiced their nationwide support for the new president and his programs as well.[47] In addition, against the accusation of the left that Rafsanjani was betraying the true spirit of the Imam's ideas, the conservative camp went out of their way to legitimize Rafsanjani's mandate and rule, stressing that his policies were indeed a continuation of the Imam's. There was even a slogan expressing this sentiment: "obedience to the *rahbar* and support for Hashemi [Rafsanjani]."[48] In praise of Rafsanjani, one conservative MP had this to say:

The Islam that can withstand injustice and produce a pure Mohammedi brand of Islam is that which contains *velayat* and thus we must all bow to the leader and totally obey him. . . . The powerful government of our distinguished and clever brother Mr. Hashemi Rafsanjani, this old companion of the Imam, this confidant of the Imam's secrets [about whom] no one can claim to have been closer to the Imam than Mr. Hashemi, or to be more revolutionary or closer to secrets and political discussions and consultation at the presence of the Imam, this shining face, this strong, clever, and studious element today is at the pinnacle of the executive and we must all try [our best] so he can succeed in his goals.[49]

Factionalism in the Political Sphere

In terms of politics, the discord between the conservative right and the left from 1989 to 1992 resembled that of the Musavi years—the conservative-dominated Guardian Council versus the radical-dominated Parliament—this time, however, without the interventions of the Imam on behalf of the left. The loss of Khomeini's support became more significant for the left when the two most prominent clergy of this camp, Mehdi Karrubi and Mohammad Musavi Khoeiniha, were soon to be marginalized. The institutional power of the radicals in Iran during this period was also to suffer. The de-revolutionization and rationalization of the Islamic Republic by Rafsanjani diminished the power and influence of the *Nehads*—for example, the Martyr Foundation headed by Karrubi, the KII, and the Revolutionary Courts—whose membership the left dominated. Their demise became imminent when the Guardian Council rejected their credentials to run for the fourth Majlis. Thus, the right's aim to monopolize power and bar the "real" *khatt-e Imam* from major decision-making centers became a frequent and justifiable allegation of the left during this period.[50] To fight back against this monopolization of power, the left's strategy was to challenge the conservatives in two areas, the Majlis and the issue of the republicanism versus the religiousness of the regime. In the Majlis, the radicals tried to weaken the conservatives by drafting legislation aimed at curtailing their ideological and institutional powers. In response, the conservatives used their near monopoly in the discretion-prone super-bodies to diminish the sway of the radicals.

The division between members of the right and the left was explicit in the Majlis. One group, which held the majority and whose membership included the radicals, called itself "representatives of Hizbollah and followers of the Imam's doctrine" while the other, supporters of the right, called itself "followers of *velayat-e faqih*." The second group was headed by Nateq-Nuri and deputies Hasan Rouhani and Ali Movahhedi-Saveji; other influential MPs in this group included Reza Akrami, Sa'id Hossieni-Shahrudi, and Hassan Ja'fari. Rightists controlled only one important committee, foreign relations headed by Sa'id Rajai-Khorasani. The left dominated other important ones such as budget and planning headed by Morteza Alviri and defense and military affairs chaired by Mohtashami.[51] Outspoken MPs of the left during this period included Sadeq Khalkhali, Mohtashami, Abbas Dozduzani, Asadollah Bayat, Mohammad Salamati, Ilias Hazrati, Ibrahim Asgharzadeh, Hadi Ghaffari, and, ironically, the brother of the *rahbar* and the editor of the daily *Jahan-e Islam,* Hadi Khamenehi.

The Election of the Khobregan

Modifications made in the laws of candidacy for the Khobregan, or Assembly of Experts, became one of the most consequential events of this period. The debate throughout Iran surrounding the new laws became so heated that it brought the country to the verge of civil war. From mid-July 1990 until March 1991, Iran witnessed a fierce war of words between the factions. In the end, the right succeeded in excluding the left from one of the most important institutions in the Islamic Republic.

On July 15, 1990, the Assembly of Experts announced that it had decided to change two of its fundamental procedural laws. Previously, to be elected to the Khobregan, eligible candidates had to be "fully acquainted with the basis of *ijtihad* and educated at prominent *howzehs* to the degree of being able to discern the competency of candidates for the *marja'iyat* and leadership." The second law that was to be changed stated that "the eligibility of candidates is discerned through the attesting of three well-known teachers in the *howzeh.* However, those candidates about whom the leader has explicitly or implicitly testified regarding their *ijtihad,* and those whose *ijtihad* is recognized and accepted in religious circles, do not need the above attestation by the leader." The proposals were passed to the Majlis to be made into law, where they were modified further. The new version of the first law stated that "to be eligible for candidacy for the Khobregan, candidates must have *ijtihad* to the degree of being able to infer in issues of *fiqh,* and competent enough (religiously) to choose the eligible *vali-ye-faqih* for the position of leadership." The second law was changed to "the source of assertion for the above conditions [eligibility of candidates] is the *foqaha* of the Guardian Council. Those candidates whose *ijtihad* has been explicitly or implicitly approved by the leader do not require the approval of the Guardian Council." Furthermore, candidates had to take a competency test for their knowledge of *fiqh* to be evaluated by the Guardian Council.[52]

This was a clever move on the part of the conservatives. Unless the conservative-dominated Council or the leader (the conservative Khamenehi) attested to the religious qualification of candidates, they would not get a seat on the assembly. Because the left was virtually devoid of high-ranking clergy, the new requirements would insure that a leftist would be unable to set foot in the Khobregan. In addition, by changing the election law just before the beginning of its second term, the conservatives in the assembly insured themselves of another term. To make matters worse for the left, in July 1989 Ayatollah Khamenehi had appointed three conservative members to the Guardian Council: Mohammad Mohammadi-Gilani, Mohammad Imami-Kashani, and Mohammad Mo'men.

The left responded ferociously to the announcement of the Khobregan by calling the actions of the assembly illegal and warned that a movement had begun to destroy the real followers of the Imam.[53] In an MRM memorandum, Mehdi Karrubi angrily argued that these changes "were not part of the guidelines of the Khobregan and were aimed to exclude some people from membership in the Assembly."[54] *Bayan*'s editorial noted that according to Majlis laws the role of Guardian Council is merely supervision and not interference in elections.[55] The left repeatedly asked the *rahbar* to intercede in this matter.[56] When Khamenehi remained silent, the left implicitly accused him of taking sides with the right and not following the true path of the Imam.[57] Another MP had these harsh words against the conservatives: "The corrupt ulama supporting the capitalist leeches and the tyrant feudal lords [*khans*], who on the one hand break the back of God's prophet and on the other hand claim to support God's religion and *velayat-e faqih,* are shamelessly trying to get control of key trenches of the system, especially the Assembly of Experts." [58]

In response, the conservatives justified the actions of the Khobregan by pointing out the divinely inspired, autonomous power of the supervisory bodies and accused the left of creating conflict in the midst of the need for unity. Azari-Qomi believed that the new powers granted to the Guardian Council by the Khobregan would have been the wishes of the Imam himself. The Imam, Azari-Qomi argued, had chosen the esteemed members of the Guardian Council and the Council would eliminate the possibility of any wrongdoing in the Khobregan election. [59] Others referred to article 108 of the constitution and maintained that Khobregan was an autonomous body and had the right to act as it saw fit. [60] As the pressure of the left increased, however, so did the response of the conservatives. The conservative right organized a nationwide effort to delegitimize the left. Demonstrators filled the streets of Qom and Teheran charging the left with being antirevolutionary and anti–*velayat-e faqih.* Chanting "death to anti–*velayat-e faqih,*" the crowd accused the left of endangering the revolution and becoming the mouthpiece of the United States and Israel. [61] The next day Tehran's Guild Society and the bazaaris of Tehran closed the bazaar and scorned those who were, they said, in line with American Islam. Mahdavi-Kani warned the crowd of a faction that was trying to exclude the clergy from the scene. [62]

In the war of words between the two factions, the conservatives once again relied on the discourse of the *motlaqeh* reading of the Islamic state and challenged the left by undermining the populist dimension of the regime. Some of the harshest and most damaging accusations against the left came from MP Ahmad Zamanian, who said leftists were undermining the institution of *velayat-e faqih* by attacking the sanctity of the *rahbar* and the Khobregan. [63] In the same vein, Ayatollah Mohammadi-Gilani announced that disobeying the *rahbar* was tantamount to blasphemy (*kofr*) and that "in the Islamic Republic, the Khobregan, the Guardian Council, and the Majlis act only as advisory bodies to the *vali-ye faqih.* . . . All must give precedent to the will of *faqih* before their own." [64] Finally, Khamenehi stepped into the fray: he came to the support of the conservatives and the new powers of Guardian Council by attacking the left, calling the actions of those who create obstacles for the system "commotion." [65]

In the end, the right succeeded in eliminating from the Khobregan key figures of the left. One hundred and seventy-eight applicants applied for seventy
six seats in the assembly. Of those who applied, sixty-two failed the examina-
tion and seven withdrew their candidacy.[66] Karrubi, Khoeiniha, Khatami, Mohammad Tavassoli, and Abbas Khorasani did not submit applications for the
Khobregan, and the Guardian Council designated Mohtashami, Asadollah
Bayat, Sadeq Khalkhali, and Hadi Khamenehi unfit to run. Khalkhali pointed
out that Karrubi and Mohtashami had been close aids of Khomeini, and he
justifiably asked, "How can the confidants of the Imam be questioned?"[67]
"For us Imam's writing, Imam's narrative is the law," argued Khalkhali.[68] Speaking in the Majlis, Ibrahim Asgharzadeh denounced the conservatives: "Dear
friends, I am sorry to announce that this election has no losers or winners. . . .
What is being sold out here is the honor of the system and the respect of the
revolution."[69]

In the reactions to the proposed changes, the neo-fundamentalists showed
early signs of an alliance with the conservative right when they supported the
conservative right's position in this battle. In a series of editorials against MP
Asgharzadeh in *Keyhan,* Mehdi Nasiri criticized the left: "How can they call
themselves Islamic when all they speak about is one pillar of the regime?"[70]

The election of members of the Khobregan is significant for several reasons. Firstly, it was the most divisive incident to the factions in this period. Secondly, the election of the Khobregan was an archetypal case of how
factionalism operates in the Islamic Republic, that is, through manipulation of
the state institutions. Indeed, as to the popular versus religious, formal versus
informal, and republican versus religious dimensions of the state, this episode
displayed all the dimensions. In addition, the Khobregan election illustrated the
method of factional contention: the use of threatening, negative discourse and
labeling of one another (that is, antirevolutionary, anti–*velayat-e faqih* and pro-
United States)that is politically motivated and without real or contested
grounds. One is struck by the similarities between how the conservatives vili-
fied the left and how, by using similar language, pro-Khomeini supporters during the first few years attacked proponents of Bazargan and Bani-Sadr. Finally,
the Khobregan election exhibited the divide-and-rule approach of Rafsanjani.
By portraying both camps as extremists, he presented the modernists as the
only sensible faction. His view on the Khobregan fiasco was that "the [conser-

vative] right will only be satisfied when the country is returned to its past feudal system, and the left wants the country to be managed as an extremist communist country."[71]

In December 1991, the conservatives were the beneficiaries of another decision of the Guardian Council. They were assured of a victory in the next election when the Council "clarified" article 99 of the constitution. Towards the end of 1991, the radicals in the Majlis had asked the Guardian Council for clarification of the Council's supervisory role in elections, fearing that this approval power would be used against them in the next election. The Council did more than clarify its power when it announced that its supervisory role was "approval supervisory" (*nezarat-e istesvabi*), which meant that all candidates had to be accepted by the Council regardless of approval of the ministry of interior (whom the left controlled). The Guardian Council was supposed to simply "observe" the election; with the new law they gained the power to approve it.[72] As we shall see, this ruling of the Council became the main instrument by which the conservatives eliminated all "unfit" elements in the fourth and fifth Majlis elections.

In the face of the conservatives' ascendancy, the left pursued several largely unsuccessful attempts to hinder the increase of power of the right. In October 1990, members of the Majlis presented a bill mandating the number of candidates running in elections. According to this bill, an election would not be legal unless the number of candidates was double the number of seats available for a given district.[73] This bill would insure that the radicals would not have the same fate as the election of Khobregan; all opposition candidates could not be disqualified. Supporters of the bill claimed that, because the sixth principle of the constitution states that matters of the country should be decided by the people, this would increase and encourage mass participation in the political process.[74] However, after weeks of deliberation, the left could not prove that the bill would indeed lead to more participation and the proposal never received a majority in the parliament.

Another proposal by the radicals, one that created nearly as much controversy as the Khobregan election, was Karrubi's suggestion that the vague term "practical commitment to Islam" be dropped as a condition for candidacy of the Majlis. Knowing very well that the Guardian Council would most likely exploit the vagueness of this term to exclude leftist candidates in the next election, Karrubi argued that such a precondition must be dropped as anyone could swear his allegiance to Islam.[75] In response, Nateq-Nuri argued that the term was crucial for precisely that reason, otherwise "its omission could lead to a parliament run by the lackeys of US and Israel."[76] During further debate between the two camps in the Majlis, familiar accusations were exchanged. Radicals suggested that Azari-Qomi and the conservatives' opposition to this bill was further testimony to how the corrupt clergy, backed by the bazaaris, aimed to monopolize power in Iran. Powerful organizations associated with the conservative right, such as the Qom Seminary Teachers and the Association of Bazaar Guilds, accused Karrubi and the left of questioning the sanctity of Islam and *velayat-e faqih*.[77] The proposal was so controversial and politically damaging for the left that it had to be withdrawn.

In April 1990, the radicals in the Majlis proposed a bill designed to hit the conservatives where it hurt them most, their pockets. They proposed "punishment of saboteurs of the economic system," which aimed to punish those who, through brokerage (manipulating the prices and the economy), matchmaking (*dallali*: taking money from one, giving it to another, and making a commission), and land speculation, amassed great wealth during the war.[78] The law would severely punish or even execute those who, within a short period of time, amassed exorbitant wealth through hoarding and price manipulation. This proposal was obviously meant to hamper the bazaaris, who thrived on this sort of commerce and tradesmanship, because the radicals believed that they were the cause of the current economic crisis in Iran.[79] As when religious questions were involved, the argument started with an interpretation problem: the major objection of the right circled around the question of how much "exorbitant" was and who would determine when it occurred.[80] The conservatives also argued (in a series of editorials in *Resalat*) that the real saboteurs in the Iranian economy would be found in the public sector because it was there where the real roots of economic corruption lay.[81] Nevertheless, after some modifications the bill was passed by the Majlis, and the Guardian Council, after minor alterations of its wording, approved it.[82] Due to the politically sensitive nature of the subject matter, it would have been unwise for the Council to oppose this bill. Besides, with the other wing of the right in charge of the executive branch of government, the bazaaris felt assured that the law would not be implemented to the letter.

Republicanism versus Religiosity

The conflict between the populist and religious dimensions of the state in the Islamic Republic surfaced after the death of Khomeini over the debate over the republicanism versus religiousness of the Islamic state. Throughout the first decade of the revolution, this tension remained diffused through the patriarch's intervention. After 1989, however, the power struggle between the left and right exacerbated the tension. The institutional manifestation of this duality was exhibited through the collision of republican institutions, namely the parliament, on one hand, and the religious super and supervisory bodies on the other.

The climax of the debate over this duality took place in 1991 and 1992, initiated by the left's fear of total elimination from the political scene after the rule change regarding election to the Khobregan. Support for republicanism on the part of the radicals was partially due to their populist values, but also represented a tactical move to prevent the right from seizing control of key superbodies. The view held by most members of the left was that the masses were quite capable of deciding for themselves. According to the radicals, the other factions perceived the population as adolescent, requiring the guardianship of the clergy.[83] According to Ibrahim Asgharzadeh, although the Islamic Republic was a divine system, the regime was ultimately based on popular rule because the direction of power is from bottom to top rather than the other way around.[84] *Salam* argued that according to the constitution, the legitimacy of the regime was based on the will of people and all institutions in Iran, even *velayat-e faqih,* had their nucleus in republicanism.[85] As Mohtashami maintained, even the *rahbar* was not infallible and could make mistakes.[86]

One of the most interesting debates on this topic took place at Teheran University in May and June 1992 between the editor of *Salam,* Abbas Abdi, and Shariar Sarfaraz, a member of the editorial board of *Resalat.* In one sentence, Sarfaraz summed up the conventional *Motlaqeh* views of the conservative right on this issue: *"velayat-e faqih* is above the law, and popular will alone does not secure the legitimacy of the Islamic state."[87] In reply, Abdi maintained that it was the constitution that safeguarded the Islamic state and the legitimacy of the regime therefore was based on the popular vote. Even the fatwas, argued Abdi, were binding only if they were instituted in the form of laws.[88] After a few days of arguments, Sarfaraz finally said, "the American brand of Islam is Islam minus *velayat-e faqih.*" In other words, the conservatives resorted to questioning the loyalty of the radicals to the divine principles of the regime in Iran. In a *Resalat* editorial during the debates, Azari-Qomi criticized the left's halfhearted support of *velayat-e faqih*: "Some claim that they accept the *velayat-e faqih* but say that we have our own minds and if we realize that his decrees are not logical, we will not obey them. This is wrong because in essence it means that the fallible wisdom of a person may be equal to that of the *faqih*. What then happens to the obedience to the *vali-ye faqih*? We must obey the *faqih* even though we are aware that his ruling is wrong."[89]

In support of the conservative right, the neo-fundamentalists scorned the left for advancing the old thesis of the dictatorship of *velayat-e faqih.*[90] Showing clear disdain for the "populist" interpretation of the *velayat-e faqih,* the MP Mohammad-ali Haqqi remarked that the ultimate lawmaker was the almighty himself, and bodies such as the Majlis are merely interpreters of divine laws.[91] Surely, no faction in Iran could yet dare to contemplate questioning this interpretation, therefore the religiousness of the regime, directly. Nevertheless, the debate continued throughout this period and became heated during the campaign for the fifth Majlis. People like Asgharzadeh from the radical camp believed that republicanism was an indispensable component of the Islamic state:

> Our Islamic system is republican, and next to Islamicity, republicanism is principle pillar of our system. According to article 177 of the constitution, the goals of the Islamic Republic and the republicanism of the regime and the management of the country are based on the popular and reli-gious views, which are unchangeable. Hence, the omission of the regime's republicanism is impossible. The omission of republicanism is tantamount to the omission of religion, Islamicity, and holiness of the regime. No excuse for the omission of people's vote or republicanism of the system is acceptable.[92]

Economic Policies: The Isolation of the Left

The First Five-Year Plan (FFYP) of 1989/90–1993/94, which passed both the parliament and the Guardian Council on January 31, 1990, reflected Rafsanjani's vision of the post-Khomeini direction of the Iranian economy.[93] The primary goals of the FFYP were strengthening the defense program, restoration of the old war–damaged industrial infrastructure through structural adjustment policies (*iqtesad-e ta'dil*), improvement of the quality of the public's cultural standards with special emphasis on the younger generation, economic growth aimed at an increase in per-capita income, achievement of social justice, provision of the basic needs of the population, reform of judicial and executive management procedures, the safeguarding of individual and social rights, and a better organized geographic distribution of developmental plans throughout the country.[94] The less ideological and presumably more realistic economic plans were privatization of state-owned industries, downsizing of the state with emphasis on its supervisory rather than interventionist role, an increase in investment in infrastructure and industrial output, gradual reduction on the dependence on oil revenues, and a projected increase in state revenues through taxation.[95] According to Mohsen Nurbaksh, the architect of Rafsanjani's economic policies, the government considered an increase in its revenues to be the most efficient way of handling the problem of an uncontrolled money supply. In addition to the goals listed in the five-year plan, Nurbaksh announced that the government would advocate price decontrol, trade liberalization, deregulation, and the attraction of foreign investments. At the same time, the state would to become more efficient by cutting "unnecessary paper pushing."[96] Due to incentives given to the private sector, the expectation was that the particularly the bazaaris would invest in the industrial infrastructure and cause a substantial increase in domestic economic output.[97]

For the conservative right, particularly the bazaaris, Rafsanjani's postwar economic policies were a breath of fresh air. With little or no state intervention in the economy, they foresaw increasing profits. Even before the announcement of the FFYP, all the leaders of the conservative right, while reiterating Khomeini's plea for unity and reconstruction of the Islamic Republic, announced their unanimous support for Rafsanjani and his economic program.[98] *Resalat* was filled with words of praise for Rafsanjani and his ability to successfully navigate the reconstruction phase in Iran. Habibollah Asghar-Owladi hailed the open-door policies of the president and believed that the skills of Rafsanjani in getting the wheels of the economy rolling were unprecedented.[99] The conservatives, however, were not pleased with government plans to increase taxes, maintaining that previous attempts at tax collection by the government had never succeeded, and that ultimately taxing the rich would harm the economy.[100] The debate over taxation later became a major cause of the split between the two.

The left disapproved of the content of the FFYP. This faction was alarmed by the economic liberalization policies of Rafsanjani and anticipated less republicanism and an Iranian state that cared more about economic output than socioeconomic justice. Moreover, the postwar reconstruction would greatly empower the bazaaris and open the door for foreign (capitalist) investment in Iran. According to *Salam,* the conservatives were behind the new economic policies in Iran, without having an understanding of modern economics. The article argued that the conservatives were trying to compensate for their lost profits, justifying their economic views by drawing on traditional interpretation of *fiqh,* and, by giving priority to primary rulings over secondary ones, creating a pro-market conservative economic system.[101] Khalkhali predicted that in the new economy, the government and the bazaaris planned to divide the country's resources and wealth between themselves.[102] Mohtashami noted in *Bayan* that, although the FFYP claimed that its priority was containing the money supply and creating a stronger economy through increased industrial production, real economic growth would be hindered by the lack of a modern economic infrastructure in Iran and, more importantly, by the quick-cash mentality of the bazaaris. The bazaaris' interests would foster an unhealthy dependence on the West and an economy where the bazaaris got rich through land speculation, hoarding, and manipulation of the exchange rate.[103] The left, as during the first decade of the revolution, favored high government taxation. Thus, while Hadi Ghaffari disagreed with the economic open-door policy of the FFYP, he viewed taxation as the only means of combatting the economic domination of the rich (the bazaaris).[104] Government spokesmen supported such claims by the left, arguing that taxation was an important lever for the state.[105]

Factional disputes over economic issues during this period became fierce at times, but they did not linger as the disputes in the political or sociocultural realms did because of several interrelating factors. To begin with, on economic issues the two rights maintained a unified front. The only faction opposed to the new economic course in Iran, the left, had no one with whom to build a coalition. And after a decade of what most people considered mismanagement of the Iranian economy, the left could hardly justify criticism of new economic plans. In addition, the worldwide decline of socialism damaged the left's credibility in Iran as well.[106] Moreover, it can be assumed that as with cases where the survival and stability of the regime are at stake, factions in Iran tended to forego their own individual or factional interest for the sake of the regime as a whole. The approval of the FFYP by the radical third Majlis clearly proved this point. In addition, compared with the two rights, the radicals in Iran suffered from another disadvantage: lack of a powerful economic base in the country. At the time of the death of Khomeini, the left had ideological influence through university students and Islamic intellectuals, and institutional power in the form of the Majlis and revolutionary bodies such as the Martyr Foundation, the KII, and the Revolutionary Courts. With the exception of the Majlis, however, after Khomeini's death the left was gradually forced to relinquish its influence in these bodies when Rafsanjani initiated his centralization and rationalization policies. The two rightist factions enjoyed the backing of other economic forces in Iran. The conservatives, for instance, were directly or indirectly favored by segments of Iranian society who, as a result of the chaotic economic situation and lack of clear economic direction in Iran during the first decade of the revolution, were pushed into the quick-cash tradesmanship of the bazaaris. Thus, the "import and sell" economy has become a widespread phenomenon leading to the "rule of commerce over production."[107] In addition to the bazaaris, the modernist wing of the right could count on the support of former Iranian industrialists and those Iranians who were at odds with the regime. The first group had suffered under the statist policies of the left and welcomed the promise of Rafsanjani and his aides to return industrial units to the private sector.[108] The second group was weary of the closed economic system espoused by the left and welcomed the possibility of obtaining foreign goods again.

Sociocultural Policies: The Modern Right and the Left versus the Conservative Right and the New Left

The cultural aspect of the Iranian revolution has been a pivotal ideological component of its transformative nature.[109] However, while Khomeini was alive, there were no specific guidelines or laws regarding the sociocultural policies of the regime, as once again he set the sociocultural standards in the country through piecemeal declarations as issues arose. Consequently, factional disputes over the direction and nature of sociocultural policies of the Islamic Republic became just as fierce as the struggle over government institutions. It was over sociocultural issues that a major difference between the two rights surfaced. Moreover, it was over sociocultural issues that the radicals and the modernists shared views. By supporting the conservatives' traditional interpretation of cultural life, the neo-fundamentalists during this period used the opportunity to express their animosity towards Rafsanjani and his Westernization of Iran.

However, it was Rafsanjani who, as the president, was legally able to determine sociocultural policy in the Islamic Republic. Although the FFYP focused on the economic policies of the Islamic Republic, the document did include some generalities about sociocultural issues. Most of the regime's principles and guidelines in this regard were conceived by the High Council for Cultural Revolution (HCCR) headed by the president.[110] The first time after the death of Khomeini that the government officially addressed the sociocultural direction of the country was in May 1991, when Hasan Habibi, a government spokesman and deputy to the president, stressed "the need to encounter cultural issues in a sedate and rational fashion because we live in an open society where various ideas and preferences exist."[111] Before exploring these principles, a few words about the HCCR and its function prior to 1989 are in order.

In June 1980, Khomeini ordered the creation of the HCCR, entrusting it with the task of "setting the overall guidelines for universities based on Islamic culture and principles."[112] However, aside from a handful of laws in the late 1980s, from the time that the HCCR officially began functioning in 1984 until 1989, the council was simply engaged in establishing the "correct" mission for higher education.[113] The Imam himself made pronouncements about policy in other cultural areas. However, Khomeini set up the HCCR as an independent body, so its decisions were as effective as laws without the need for approval by another body such as the Guardian Council or the Majlis. Rafsanjani capitalized on his legal and institutional rights as the head of this important body to introduce the "Cultural Principles of the Islamic Republic" (CPIR) on August 24, 1992, based on the readings of the modern right in this sphere.[114] The liberal theme of this document is immediately evident. Although the CPIR made rhetorical gestures towards traditional Islamic guidelines, the document hinted that a more pragmatic approach to sociocultural issues would be the actual course of the regime. For instance, the introduction said that "cultural height" would be achieved by the unified engagement of "fundamentalist and realistic" leadership.[115] The document suggested that cultural principles of the Islamic Republic should "be mindful of the capacity of the country and the realities [of the time]."[116] In addition, the guidelines explicitly advocated the views of the modern right, which were now distinguishable from the conservative right. Thus, some of the cultural polices the CPIR would confront were confronting superstitions, combatting intellectual stagnation and pseudo-religiousness, spreading the spirit of criticism, and PVPV through wisdom and amiable exhortation (rather than through force).[117]

The most striking point about the CPIR is its declaration that the task of handling sociocultural issues and determining solutions to social problems should be left to the "experts" and not the clergy. In fact, in the seventeen-page manuscript, the word "clergy" was not used even once. The only clergy mentioned was Khomeini, and his words are used in a clever, purposeful, and factionally pointed manner. For instance, the introductory part of the law stresses that the Imam's views were the shining guidelines for the cultural policies. However, the document carefully selected quotes from Khomeini's speeches that were in line with the views of Rafsanjani and the left. It contained sentiments that both Rafsanjani and Khomeini had used to criticize the sociocultural inclinations of the conservative right: "the danger of the petrified and the pseudo-religious," "in the Islamic Republic, except in instances where Islam and honor of the regime is determined by 'knowledgeable experts' to be in danger, no one can impose his ideas on other," "the pen and words have served humanity more than guns."

In addition to its explicit castigation of the conservatives, the CPIR showed disdain for the discourse and actions of the Hizbollahis and the neo-fundamentalists as well. This was highlighted in a section called "Prohibitions" (*monabbahat*). Among the twenty prohibited endeavors are: inappropriate inferences of piety and asceticism in ways that are harmful to (social) growth and progress, disregard for public order, cynicism toward the state, depicting the shari'a as incompatible with modernity, suggesting the incompatibility of piety with expertise, resorting to hasty solutions to social problems that require research to solve, recourse to shari'a to evade law and visa versa, spreading superstitions under the pretext of preserving the national customs or religious ideas, demagoguery that relies on incorrect societal beliefs and customs in the name of support for the deprived or in the defense of religion, and not interrogating those who independently interpret and execute the laws.[118]

Clearly, the CPIR is vague and open to discretionary interpretations. As far as displaying the complex interplay among factions across organizations and institutions, the CPIR is a significant episode. The faction in control of the executive branch (modern right) used its legal and institutional authority to undermine and challenge the sociocultural agenda of other factions while pushing through its own policies and values. For instance, the CPIR's numerous explicit suggestions that experts should decide the fate of cultural life in the Islamic Republic are in direct contrast to the ideas of groups such as the conservative right and the Hizbollahis who favor men of religion as the legitimate arbiters in this realm. Furthermore, the *monabbahat* were primarily warnings against future extremist and autonomous actions of the Hizbollahis/neo-fundamentalists, actions that ultimately undermine the authority and rules of the central (republican) government. Finally, the new sociocultural direction in Iran espoused by the modernists was to become a fundamental cause of the split into two rights and of physical confrontation between the officials of the central government and the Hizbollahis.

The essence of the guidelines espoused by the CPIR was the to advance a more socioculturally tolerant Iran, primarily through the efforts of three people: the president, his brother, Mohammed Hashemi, as the head of Iranian radio and TV, and Khatami, the minister of culture and Islamic guidance. Rafsanjani made certain that he conveyed his moderate attitude to the conservatives. Speaking at a gathering of Friday prayer imams, he asked them to be more tolerant of the youth and refrain from resorting to harsh consequences because "through suppression, pressure, and threat we can only partially preserve the outer facade of our society."[119] In an address to the Association of Preachers of Teheran, the president reminded them that "Islam is the religion of forgiveness and leniency and not harshness and intolerance."[120] Rafsanjani appeared keen to allow more freedom of expression for the arts and artists in general, promoting a more eclectic view of the arts. In November 1991, he had this to say to the cultural seminary of the Organization for Islamic Propagation, a Qom-based conservative center for the promotion of "Islamic culture": "The religiously narrow-minded and the extremists do not value subtlety in art, believing that art must be presented in a dull and dry manner. . . . Our artists' goal should not only be to please the ulama and the doctrinaires; we must think of the need of the younger generation and have goals that are far more worthy and all-encompassing." [121]

In the cultural realm, Rafsanjani was particularly weary of the confrontational methods used by the likes of the *Basijis* in implementing what they believed to be the correct Islamic cultural norms in Iran. The *Basijis* are under the command of socioculturally extremist conservatives such as Ayatollah Ahmad Jannati, the head of the Headquarters for the Vivification of PVPV (*Setade Ihyaye Amre be Ma'ruf va Nah-ye az Monkar*). With this factional affiliation, the *Basij* could challenge Rafsanjani in both his ideological and institutional de-revolutionization efforts. Like the Hizbollahis of the neo-fundamentalists, the *Basijis* claim to be the guardians of Islamic morality. By claiming independent legitimacy based on the religio-revolutionary principles of the state, the *Basij* often acted autonomously from the central government. Rafsanjani frequently admonished the *Basij* on the need to safeguard the cultural principles in Iran in a more "delicate" way. [122]

Rafsanjani's message of more tolerance in the cultural sphere was transmitted by his brother Mohammed Hashemi through what some conservatives and extremist elements such as the Hizbollahis and the neo-fundamentalist in Iran considered to be nonrevolutionary and liberal programs on Iranian radio and TV. The main complaint against Hashemi was that by showing Western movies and programs directed at a wealthy audience rather than at poor people, Iranian TV ignored the views of the Hizbollahis and *Basij*. By promoting Western culture, such programs undermined the Islamic-revolutionary culture in Iran. [123] Hashemi responded by rebuking the accusers as unfair and claimed that he was a victim of factional disputes. [124] In turn, he was accused of acting for his own faction's advantage. The left, too, criticized Hashemi for his partisan direction of this important governmental body. [125]

As a prominent member of the MRM since his appointment as the minister of culture and Islamic guidance in 1982, until his resignation in 1992, Khatami was influential in moderating the extremist aspect of cultural life in Iran. In comparison to the austere views of the conservatives and the neo-fundamentalists in sociocultural spheres, Khatami's attitude can be considered as relatively progressive and liberal. Throughout his term, Khatami made remarks on the need to establish an Islamic state based on pluralist ideas that he believed are ingrained in Islam. Emphasizing that restrictive and exclusionary attitudes toward those with different ideas to that of the regime would ultimately lead to a dictatorship, Khatami maintained that "freedom of thought and respect for intellectual honor are among the primary goals of the revolution."[126] Khatami also held a different position on the proper "revolutionary-Islamic culture" and Iran's struggle with Western secular ideas and the "cultural onslaught." Rather than hostile confrontation with the West, Khatami believed that Islamic Iran must create its own intellectual force because "it is the religious intellectual that can provide powerful logical [cultural] alternatives to that of the West."[127] Consequently, he said, "We should not perceive intellectualism [roushanfekri] as immoral and futile. . . . Enlightenment is based on consciousness and change, both of which Islam heeds."[128]

One conclusion Khatami drew because of these views was that the media should be independent as it symbolized the rights, freedom, and sovereignty of the people.[129] In 1990, for the first time Khatami established a "press jury" to investigate issues involving the media fairly and legally and remain outside of factional and personal grievances and interpretation.[130] Khatami also acknowledged that the regime has its share of opponents but believed in tolerating them and being proud of doing so.[131] As a result, civil society in Iran during the Khatami years relished some freedom. Iranian media experienced a substantial increase in number of publications, operated under less censorship, and were allowed to be more critical of the regime. The number of newspapers and journals rose from 102 in 1988 to 369 in 1992.[132] In 1991, Khatami announced that during his ministership, close to 8,000 books had been published, three times the number published before the revolution.[133] Iranian arts such as music and cinema also flourished under Khatami. Films by directors such as Mohsen Makhmalbaf and Abbas Kiyarostami won international awards. Moreover, although many of these films dealt with highly controversial subject material, the ministry of culture and Islamic guidance permitted them to be released.

The conservatives and the neo-fundamentalists challenged the new cultural tone in Iran. Mehdi Nasiri from *Keyhan* dedicated his newspaper to fighting the increasing laxity of sociocultural life in the face of the Western cultural onslaught. In a series of editorials in April 1992, *Keyhan* complained that the actions of the ministry of culture and Iranian TV were aimed at spreading Western liberal ideas in Iran. In addition, these editorials suggested that, through propagating such poisonous ideas, some people in Iran were implicitly arguing that the Iranian regime was a dictatorship.[134] In another *Keyhan* editorial marathon in March and April 1992, Shahriar Zarshenas wrote that the attitude of certain intellectuals Western-inspired willing to write freely and supporting a particular concept of culture and development (*Towse-'eh*) would ultimately destroy the genuine revolutionary movement in Iran. In yet another *Keyhan* editorial, entitled "What Music," the writer suggested that hidden hands were at work to bring back satanic (*taquti*) music.[135] The neo-fundamentalists and other extremists did not confine their criticism to verbal opposition. Believing that the government was not doing enough to stop the Westernization of Iran, they attacked newspapers and magazines they considered responsible for inflicting Western immorality in Iran.[136] The kind of secular art and culture that was creeping into the Islamic Republic and spreading Western moral corruption, a *Payam-e Inqelab* article argued, was contrary to the Imam's words.[137] Perhaps the main justification used by groups such as the neo-fundamentalists to criticize Western cultural imports to Iran was Khomeini's various comments on the "proper" revolutionary-Islamic art:

> The only accepted kind of art is that of pure Mohammadi Islam, the Islam of the poor and the disinherited, the Islam of those who suffered. . . . An art is beautiful that hammers modern capitalism and blood-sucking Communism and destroys the Islam of comfort, luxury, and the painless wealthy . . . in one word, American brand of Islam. . . . The only kind of [permissible] art is the one that teaches confrontation with the blood-sucking world-eaters headed by America and the Soviet Union.[138]

Due to their alliance with Rafsanjani, the conservatives at first tolerated the president's liberalism in sociocultural issues and remained rather docile. By mid-1992, as the conservatives moved to completely uproot the left, however, opposition from the ultraconservatives in the traditional right camp against Khatami peaked. One of the most outspoken opponents of the prevailing cultural tone in Iran was Jannati, who initiated a crusade against the ideological de-revolutionization of Rafsanjani and "liberal"-minded officials such as Khatami. As the secretary of the powerful Guardian Council, the head of the Organization for the PVPV, and the director of the powerful Organization for Islamic Propagation, Jannati was indeed a powerful figure in the Islamic Republic. Jannati strongly opposed government initiatives by the executive branch that were replacing the Hizbollahis in government with technocrats.[139] He also capitalized on his influence in religio-revolutionary bodies to weaken the rule-making powers of the executive. For instance, a few days after Rafsanjani commented on the need for the regime to be more relaxed on the veiling of women, a rally masterminded by Jannati brought thousands to the streets of Teheran to protest improper veiling (bad-hejabi).[140] To further challenge Rafsanjani's mandate in the cultural realm, Jannati called on the Basijis to take the law into their own hands and insure proper Islamic behavior in the country even if this led to their imprisonment.[141] The secretary of the Guardian Council considered the policies of Khatami and other liberal officials to be spreading a corrupt morality throughout the country, and he warned the nation that a "creeping movement" under the title of art was undermining Iran's religious values.[142] Clearly furious about the relative freedom of the press, he proclaimed that "under the banner of freedom, liberal writers and artists cannot live in this country."[143]

The conservatives tried their best to move sociocultural life in Iran back in a more conservative direction by condemning the improperly veiled and the Westernized segments of Iranian society. In January 1990, marchers called the "Vanguard of Chastity" (afaf) organized numerous demonstrations against the secular culture of the West.[144] Gradually other conservatives began expressing their disapproval of the increasing cultural liberalism in Iran. A Resalat editorial in March 1991 indirectly referred to the likes of Mohsen Makhmalbaf and questioned the wisdom behind allowing a few filmmakers to ridicule the lifestyle and beliefs of devout Muslims.[145] Ayatollah Mohammad Fazel Lankarani, a powerful Qom Seminary teacher, asked the president to admonish the ministry of culture, whose actions were "uprooting the revolution."[146] Morteza Nabavi of Resalat accused Khatami of neither being in line with the views of the rahbars on the need to confront the Western cultural onslaught nor a genuine Hizbollahi.[147]

Khatami responded to the conservatives and neo-fundamentalists with adjectives such as "petrificated" and "reactionary," challenging and sneering at their views on sociocultural issues. He particularly opposed the backward stance of those "who believe that the place of women is at home, when the Imam believed that women should be present and active in society and help spin the wheels of the country." In further reference to the restrictive attitude of the conservative right, Khatami noted, "Imagine a society where sports, music, films, books are highly restricted or banned; how can you organize such a society?"[148] In Islamic Iran, issues related to women have been among the most controversial, often generating heated debate in the country.[149] When it came to the status of women in society, Rafsanjani was clear: "Women can become philosophers, actors, scholars, Friday prayer imams, researchers, and writers. Not only do these things not contradict chastity [of women], they are a means of propagating chastity."[150]

To help fulfill such ambitious goals, Rafsanjani established various organizations to deal with socioeconomic and cultural problems of women in the Islamic Republic. For instance, the Women's Social-Cultural Council was established in 1989 to undertake "nationwide programs that would eliminate structural and cultural injustices faced by women."[151] In 1991, Rafsanjani created a special bureau in the executive branch to deal with matters related to women and appointed Shahla Habibi as its head.[152] Another prominent figure in Iran involved in women's issues was the head of Iranian judiciary, Ayatollah Mohammad Yazdi. Yazdi frequently maintained that "women's rights under Islam have been misinterpreted as Islam believes in the equality of the sexes."[153]

One issue where the conservatives and modernists stand in direct opposition is over women's *hejab*. While conservatives are stringent on the *chador*, the long head-to-toe cover, as the only acceptable attire for women, modernists take a more tolerant position on this matter. During a congress on *hejab* in December 1991, both Rafsanjani and Khamenehi expressed leniency in this area and considered any attire that would provide sufficient covering for women (that is, a scarf and a long dress) as sufficient *hejab*.[154] Two days later, Grand Ayatollah Mohammad Golpayegani, a prominent member of the JMHEQ, seized upon this opportunity to not only endorse the *chador* as the only permissible kind of covering for women but condemned the prevailing liberal atmosphere in the country:

Westerners are attacking the *chador* by presenting it as an impediment to women's progress in political and social life. . . . I warn you Muslim people that in order to destroy our youth's Islamic identity, world arrogance is campaigning through the spread of moral corruption and under the disguise of art, music, trashy press, and improper *hejab*. . . . With these evil thoughts, the enemy has penetrated all public life and is attacking Islamic values, describing the teaching of Islamic culture as petrifaction.[155]

As with other members of the left, Khatami could not withstand the opposition that mounted against him, and he was forced to resign in July 1992. Khatami's replacement was first Mohammad Ali Besharati and later Mostafa Mir-Salim, both known *Mo'talefeh* members. Hashemi was succeeded by Ali Larijani, another *Mo'talefeh* sympathizer. For the next four years, the conservatives pursued more restrictive policies in the sociocultural realm, illustrating further how the direction of policy on basic issues fluctuates due to factional maneuvering.

Foreign Policy: Pragmatism on the Rise and Radicalism on the Decline

As noted earlier, Iran's less revolutionary and more pragmatic overtures in foreign policy have generated the most interest among the scholars of post-Khomeini Iran. Indeed, the statements of the dual leadership following the death of Khomeini were a clear indication that the leadership had realized that the Islamic Republic could neither export its revolution nor remain in international isolation. Bearing such realities in mind, the Islamic Republic strove to wipe clean the previously held image of the "outlaw state."[156] Consequently, since the death of Khomeini, Iran has tried to stop making enemies and pursue a rapprochement policy aimed at establishing friendlier ties with the outside world, particularly with European countries.[157] This nonconflictual attitude was frequently reiterated by Rafsanjani: "In our foreign policy and in the formulation of our relations with the countries of the world, we support the policy of respect for international regulations and are committed to the policy of nondomination and nonacceptance of domination."[158] The revisions made to the constitution dramatically altered the endeavor of making foreign policy in the Islamic Republic and provided the necessary footing for the implementation of the views of the leadership. Here was another area where Khomeini's method of making individual pronouncements on particular issues had to be routinized and institutionalized. With this in mind, and because a more centralized and administratively ordered Iran was a primary goal of the new constitution, it was hoped that with the establishment of institutions such as the National Security Council (NSC), Iranian foreign policy would be conducted in a more systematic and formal manner than it had been previously.[159] In other words, spontaneous and impassioned conduct such as the taking of hostages and unofficial street demonstrations had to be curtailed because, as Sa'id Rajai-Khorasani, a close foreign policy adviser of Rafsanjani believed, such "populist-revolutionary" actions are both an extension of factionalism and damaging to the interests of the regime:

> Where in Islam do they pursue the act of conducting foreign policy through the propitiating rhetoric of irresponsible channels or through the demonstrations of a bunch of inexperienced excited young men on the street? . . . No country conducts its foreign policy in the context of open domestic ideological discord. On the contrary, they conduct it in a delicate way so that foreigners will not know their intentions and internal ideological differences.[160]

As in other areas of policy making, factionalism has played a crucial role in both the making and direction of Iran's foreign policy. Here, too, the methods of factionalism were practiced: factions in control of relevant bodies used institutional and legal powers to advance their interests and justified them through the use of discretionary interpretations of religious texts. The Iranian foreign policy machinery after the 1989 constitution was comprised of the foreign ministry, the president, the leader, and the NSC. Since 1989, these offices have been under the heavy influence of the right. In addition to Khamenehi and Rafsanjani, the *rahbar* and president, the foreign minister, Ali Akbar Velayati, was a staunch supporter of the conservatives.

The pragmatic stance of the dual leadership in Iran has been indispensable in making a judicious and prudent foreign policy. The decisions of the NSC, for example, must have the approval of both the *rahbar* and the president. In the new foreign policy machinery of the Islamic Republic, therefore, the left had little sway. The only institutional device in the hands of the left that could possibly impact foreign policy was the Majlis. However, the efficacy of the Majlis in this realm is confined to legislative oversight and approval or disapproval of international agreements (constitutional provisions 113–132). Consequently, as in the economic and political realm, during this period the right was able to dominate the left. The left's lack of institutional representation, however, has not meant that radicals have not been able to pester the right.

US-Iranian relations are one issue where factional disputation has been heated; there has not been a unified stance over time. As with other issues, prior to 1989 the official policy of the Islamic Republic was the de facto prerogative of Khomeini. Moreover, the war with Iraq from 1980–88 became the focus of all factions' foreign policy rhetoric. Following the death of Khomeini, it became evident that Rafsanjani desired closer ties with the United States. Such desire on the part of the president was publicized obliquely in an article entitled "Direct Negotiations," where Atollah Mohajerani hinted at the need to establish better relations with the United States via the release of hostages in Lebanon. "Times have changed," argued Mohajerani. "We must give priority to helping release the hostages." [161]

As expected, such a bold overture received a broad spectrum of responses. A *Jomhuri-ye Islami* editorial called such remarks "naïve and disrespectful to the revolutionary honor.[162] The neo-fundamentalists believed direct negotiations with the oldest enemy of Iran were tantamount to the abandonment of *velayat-e faqih* and dancing on the graves of the martyrs." [163] *Keyhan-Havai* argued that while, as a rule, it was acceptable for Iran to better its relations with the outside world, Israel and the United States should be exceptions.[164] Not surprisingly, the conservatives supported the possibility of future ties. A *Resalat* editorial suggested that the Islamic Republic would benefit from such "movements" *(taharrok)* in foreign policy for three main reasons: changes that have taken place in the world order, the emergence and rise of (powerful) Islamic zones throughout the globe, and the fact that as a key player in the region, Iran should consider itself powerful enough to speak even with its worst enemy.[165]

The idea of closer ties with the United States certainly appealed to the pragmatists within the Iranian polity as well as with some segments of Iranian society.[166] The more secularly inclined (Westernized) segments of Iranian society such as the intelligensia capitalized on the new tone uttered by Rafsanjani and openly called for a more realistic stance toward the United States. Some of the most controversial words were those of Sa'idi Sirjani, who, in a *Ettela'at* editorial after Mohajerani's comments, praised the more logical and open-minded views of the new president. In support of Rafsanjani, he said, "It is a sour reality that with slogans such as 'death to America,' the United States will neither disappear nor change its injustices. . . . Fighting such an enemy requires [economic] self-reliance and rational actions." [167] For a few weeks Sirjani's article, which set Rafsanjani and the modern right apart from other factions, created another war of words in Iran. The JRM scorned those who were creating divisions within the Iranian leadership [168] while the neo-fundamentalists warned about a conspiracy that was pushing the president toward the West. [169] However, a cordial relationship so soon with a country that symbolized all of what the Iranian revolution stood against seemed preposterous. Thus, after days of heated debates in the press and the Majlis, Khamenehi called such suggestions premature and unwise. [170]

The next time factional infighting over the direction and nature of Iran's foreign policy reached a head was during the Kuwait crisis. Soon after the start of "Operation Desert Storm," the MRM condemned US actions in the Persian Gulf, suggesting that Iran should stand solidly behind Iraq, and in the case of an Israeli attack on Iraq, the Islamic Republic should call *jihad* against the Zionist regime and the United States. [171] Rafsanjani also denounced US adventurism but proclaimed, "Iran will not interfere unless its interests are endangered." In addition, the president called upon the people to "keep calm and refrain from emotional advances." The next day, the NSC officially announced Iran's neutrality in the war. [172] In line with the position of the dual leadership, the conservatives of the JRM refrained from proposing extreme actions against the United States. The JRM used the crisis to once again propagate their official line. On the occasion of its thirteenth anniversary, the JRM called for unity under the pillar of *vali-ye faqih* and support for the president while scorning those who created a rift in this unity. [173]

The left used this opportunity to accuse the right again of conservatism and betrayal of earlier revolutionary rhetoric. Khalkhali's attitude was that "we have always said 'death to America' and 'death to Israel.' Now we have to live up to these slogans." [174] Mocking those simple-minded groups who underestimated the United States's larger imperialist goal in the region, the MRM suggested that Iran would be the next Iraq.[175] In the end, however, the radicals failed to alter Iran's policy of active neutrality in the Gulf War. Thus, the Kuwait crisis was, as one observer noted, "A Victory for the Pragmatists."[176] Iran's neutrality during the Gulf War set the precedent for a less adventurous and nonrevolutionary foreign policy. Excluded from the corridors of power, the radicals lost their biggest opportunity to (re)radicalize Iranian foreign policy. The left continued to remain marginalized until 1995 when they formed their historical alliance with the modern right during the fifth parliamentary election.

Finally, the fatwa issued by Khomeini against Salman Rushdie should be mentioned.[177] For the left, the fatwa could have been used as a political tool against the pragmatic foreign policies of Rafsanjani. Fearing the possibility that the right might amend or rescind the decree, on the first anniversary of the Imam's fatwa, Mehdi Karubi said, "Salman Rushdie will be executed. The Imam's decree is holy and eternal."[178] The next day other members of the left such as Mohtashami and *Tahkim* maintained that "defending the Imam's decree is tantamount to defending Islam."[179] Rafsanjani, however, had this to say on the issue: "An enlightened Muslim should not be afraid of a book. . . . It is nothing. A book may be written that puts forwards a correct or incorrect wisdom, but the encounter must be logical. . . . Everyone who has read it says it is a worthless book. . . . The Imam's view was one of a [religious] expert."[180]

CHAPTER 5

The Split of the Two Rights and the Alliance of the Left with the Modern Right

The coalition of the two rightist factions was short lived. The strife over the nature of the postwar economy was the key issue for the split within the right. To be sure, the conservatives had been opposed to the imperatives of Rafsanjani's *Towse-'eh,* the creation of a modern industrial economy similar to those of the newly industrialized countries in Asia, even before the revolution. It soon became apparent that the alliance had been no more than a marriage of convenience, and both factions had tolerated each other's differences for the sake of immediate political interests. Except for their shared belief in a free market economy and less adventurism in foreign policy, the two factions had fundamental differences. With the discord over the direction of the economy, therefore, the two rights were left with little if any in common. The conservatives, however, seemed to have the upper hand. By challenging Rafsanjani's economic policies, the conservative right set out to eliminate the president and dominate the political scene in the Islamic Republic. With election of Nateq-Nuri to the presidency in 1997, this strategy would have proved successful.

The position of Rafsanjani thus became dangerously precarious. He had made the grave mistake of isolating the left, with whom he shared many sentiments, and he was now being purged by his old allies. Consequently, the president was left with no option but to turn back to the radicals. Luckily for him, the left had toned down its rhetoric and was far less radical by the time of the fifth parliamentary election. Also, because many members of the modern right were former radicals, and because the left had always disdained the bazaaris, an alliance between the left and the modern right *(Kargozaran)* became not only feasible but vital for the survival of both factions. The election of Khatami impaired the dominance of the conservatives and illustrated the success of the new alliance. What the post–1996 events once again illustrated was that the pivotal figure behind major power shifts in Iran had been Rafsanjani.

The Parliamentary Election of 1992

Members of the left were cognizant of the fact that they were going to miss Khomeini's support; they did not know to what extent until the parliamentary election of 1992, when they were booted out from their last corridor of power. With the Imam's departure from the scene, the two rights (dominating the executive, the leadership, and the super-bodies) moved to disqualify the left almost altogether from the political stage in Iran. In the process of ascertaining the suitability of candidates, the Guardian Council and its nationwide supervisory committees designated as unfit nearly half of the influential candidates from the left. Once again, the discretionary decision making by the institutions of the religious dimension enabled one faction (in this case the alliance of two), to enfeeble the rival faction.

Two factors in particular were influential in the left's defeat. First was the Guardian Council's 1991 interpretation of article 99 of the constitution, where the council construed its legal authority over elections as supreme and all-inclusive, involving supervision as well as the power to disqualify candidates determined to be unfit. Second was Khamenehi's full-fledged backing of the conservative right, particularly the new powers of the Guardian Council. Speaking to the supervisory committee of the council nearly two months before the 1992 election, Khamenehi essentially gave its members carte blanche to dismiss the eligibility of candidates from the left, handing them the excuse of removing those opposed to *velayat-e faqih*:

> Observing the [rule of] law is of course important. However, one must find the language of law and its parameters. This discretion can only be accomplished by those like you who know the laws very well. If some one speaks and writes in opposition to the views of the *faqih*, he is anti–*velayat-e faqih*. People [candidates] must be pure and pious. Although some people are good-natured, it is obvious that they act partisan [*khatti*], and this is not good. As a rule, therefore, it is better if you do not select these people. If there is no proof

or evidence against them [being opposed to the *velayat-e faqih*], you can act based on your own knowledge.[1]

The left was quick to recognize the coming danger. Mohammad Musavi-Khoeiniha stressed the need to allow people to freely choose their candidates because, as the Imam repeatedly maintained, "The regime belongs to the people and they are their own guardians."[2] Declaring that the nation would not stand injustices to the true children of the revolution, Mehdi Karrubi warned the Guardian Council that it "must be careful not to act one-sidedly or support any one group or current. If the Guardian Council acts factionally biased, we will complain to the leader and inform the people."[3] A *Salam* editorial entitled "Judgment or Supervision" called upon the Guardian Council to act within the scope of the law and not according to the personal preferences of its members, underlining articles 156 and 157 in which the "popular will" is emphasized as the justification of its opinion.[4] A MRM proclamation entitled "The Majlis Faces Two Dangers" alerted voters of the possible pitfalls of the coming parliament: "One current is sinister, anti-religious, and aims to portray Islam as incapable of administrating the country; the other is mentally petrified and reactionary and does not tolerate any views aside from its own narrow-minded one. . . . The Majlis, as the most important support [of the system], must defy both erroneous currents."[5] The proclamation went on to declare that the task of the next Majlis must be the preservation of the true Islamic nature of the regime, the implementation of the constitution, the protection of the disinherited, prevention of the rule of capitalist leeches (conservative/traditional right supporters), and confronting world arrogance headed by the United States. The next day, however, the Guardian Council announced that from the 3,150 registered candidates, 1,060 of them, including 30 incumbents, had been declared unfit to run for parliament.[6] Five days earlier Khamenehi had referred to the left as "those seditious [*fetnehgar*] people who have always caused trouble for the government and told lies in their newspapers," adding, "People should not vote for these candidates."[7] Among the people disqualified by the Guardian Council were key figures from the left: Asadollah Bayat, Hadi Ghaffari, Ibrahim Asgharzadeh, Atefeh Rajai (the wife of the former prime minister), Ayatollah Sadeq Khalkhali, Abolhasan Haerizadeh, and Behzad Nabavi.[8] Behzad Nabavi among others asked the Guardian Council the reasons for his dismissal.[9] Ayatollah Ahmad Jannati responded with the usual platitudes. "We could not jeopardize the interests of the people by allowing unvirtuous people to enter the Majlis. Thus, the supervisory committees used caution and disqualified those with dubious qualifications." Jannati went on to say that the main reasons for candidates' rejection were financial wrongdoings and moral corruption, but he did not provide specific details.[10]

In response to what was clearly an onslaught by the two rights, the left (MRM, MII, and *Tahkim*) joined forces and created the Great Coalition (*I'telaf-e Bozorg*), nominating thirty candidates from Teheran for the upcoming election; chief among them were Karrubi, Khoeiniha, Mohammad Tavassoli, Ali Akbar Mohtashami, Abdolvahed Musavi-Lari, Morteza Alviri, Sa'id Hajjarian, Abbas Dozduzani, Morteza Katirai, Abolqasem Sarhadizadeh, Mohammad Salamati, and Mahmud Doai. The slogans of the coalition became the Islamicity of the regime, full implementation of the constitution, support for the disinherited, and confrontation with reactionaries.[11] Interior minister Abdollah Nuri announced that "an open [unrestrained] election indicates the sovereignty of people, while a restricted one indicates the division between the state and the people. . . . We should never think that the choice of the people is flawed."[12] In a strongly worded declaration, the Great Coalition tried to undermine the integrity of its rival factions:

> The Coalition staunchly opposes the improper use of "parallel institutions" that weaken the Majlis and obliterate people's rights. We also announce our opposition to those currents who under the pretext of privatization help the creation of a "bazaar economy," as it will devastate the disinherited. . . . The Coalition is against foreign borrowing from the World Bank and IMF and provisions of any kind of funds from the imperialists, as they are contingent upon political concessions.[13]

The conservatives and Rafsanjani not only defended their positions and the decisions of the Guardian Council but questioned the loyalty of the anti-*faqih* leftists who, since the death of the Imam, they claimed, had consistently harassed (in Farsi, "put a spoke in the wheels of") Rafsanjani and the government. In one of the most memorable speeches ever made by an official in Iran, Ayatollah Abolqasem Khazali told a crowd in Qom, "We will open the file of the minister of state [Mohtashami] and see if he has been the mouthpiece of the United States and the *Monafeqin* [Mojahedin-e Khalq] and if so, we will not let him enter the Majlis. Yes, we will not let you. You who want to weaken the leadership and the regime. . . . So long as we have the power, we will not allow such morons [*avazi*] to enter the Majlis and we will spray them with DDT!!!"[14] Mahalati, deputy for the Headquarters of Friday Prayer Leaders remarked, "We should not vote for those who disrespect the leader and the esteemed members of the Guardian Council."[15] Criticizing the seditious words and writings of "certain people," Mohammad Raisi, Teheran's prosecutor general said, "Candidates must realize that their legitimacy and indeed the legitimacy of all institutions in the country stems from *velayat-e faqih,* and if they are not believers in the *velayat-e motlaqeh-ye faqih,* they are not the true representatives of the people."[16] Ayatollah Ahmad Azari-Qomi stated, "The true interpreter of the thoughts of the Imam is the esteemed leader and we must pay attention to what he says. Any other interpretation is wrong and astray."[17] According to Nateq-Nuri, "Although it is important for an MP to have sociopolitical acumen, he must first and foremost give credence to *vali-ye faqih* and support the regime wholeheartedly."[18]

All the "satellites" of the JRM also expressed their opposition to the leftists and offered their own views on the "proper candidates." A *Mo'talefeh* memorandum expressed the belief that "the most meaningful trait of the MPs should be embracing *velayat.* The Imam said that seditious people [Khomeini was referring to the conservatives] who imperil the work of the government should not enter the Majlis."[19] In support of the JRM and the pro–*velayat-e faqih* candidates, the Society of Islamic Guilds of Teheran also issued a proclamation. The Society was keen to emphasize the revolutionary character of the bazaar. The proclamation mentioned the bazaaris' two hundred years of financial support for the clerical establishment, in addition to quoting Khomeini's words: "Without the support of the bazaar, the revolution would not have succeeded."[20] The JMHEQ issued a proclamation in which members such as Ayatollahs Ali Meshkini, Mohammad Fazel Lankarani, and Jannati warned the nation against those who were trying to break up the unity of the regime.[21] Lankarani believed that in disqualifying certain candidates, the Guardian Council and all the supervisory committees had acted within the parameters of the law.[22]

Khamenehi and Rafsanjani had their share of criticism of the left. "Some are aggrieved by Islam and the Islamic government. We will not count on them," declared Khamenehi.[23] Rafsanjani said, "The enemy exaggerates the shortcomings and the problems of the country. People should not fall prey to such empty slogans as it is the enemy's plot."[24] In a Friday prayer sermon, he further scorned the left and defended the mandate and leadership of Khamenehi:

> At present, world arrogance is doing two things. It is distancing the people from the government while itself deviating from the line of Imam. For the sake of popularity, these people are crying out that the Hizbollah has been marginalized or that the supporters of the true doctrine of the Imam are being estranged. This is used by the foreigners against us. They blow up the economic problems and have become a mouthpiece of foreigners. . . . Did not the Imam himself before departing draw and plan things and mend the constitution so that our current leader would come to power? Well, is this not the real doctrine of the Imam?[25]

The JRM ran under the slogans of following the Imam's doctrine, obedience to the leader, and support for Hashemi, and had thirty candidates from the *Mo'talefeh,* Society of Islamic Engineers, and clergy from the JRM. The supporters of this ticket were the Society of Teheran Preachers, *Mo'talefeh,* the Society of Islamic Engineers, the Zeynab Society, and the Society of Islamic Guilds of Teheran.[26] A proclamation on the declared "Positions of JRM" included the following campaign slogans: the most priceless asset of the Islamic revolution is *velayat-e faqih* and obedience to Khamenehi, opposition to those who publicly support the cause of the *mostazafin* and the barefooted but in reality act against their interests, and a deter-mined confrontation with the Western cultural onslaught and the pseudo-intellectuals.[27]

After the first round of elections (April 10), 120 MPs were elected. Of the incumbents, 54 (20 percent) were reelected and 141 lost their seats.[28] The left accused the "conservative establishment" of resorting to nationwide election improprieties.[29] In some districts the Friday prayer leaders, who are selected by the mosque affairs committees, had praised the conservative candidates and denounced others as enemies of *velayat-e faqih.*[30] The minister of state, Abdollah

Nuri, announced that in some cities, the number of votes counted was higher than the total population of the district.[31] MP Rasul Montajabnia told the Majlis, "The United States and world arrogance are certainly pleased with the election results."[32] Nevertheless, the various maneuvers by the conservatives and their negative campaigning paid off. By the end of the second round of elections (May 8), even those candidates from the left who were allowed to run for the Majlis, such as Mohtashami, Karrubi, and Hadi Khamenehi, were not reelected. The only high-profile figures from the left who reentered the Majlis were Mohammad Reza Tavassoli, Majid Ansari, Ali Mohammad Gharibani, and Ilias Hazrati.[33] The balance of power had shifted in favor of the conservative right, which allowed the right to select the leadership of the Majlis. The speakership of the new Majlis went to Nateq-Nuri while Hasan Rouhani and a known *Mo'talefeh* member, Ali Akbar Parvaresh, were elected as the first and second deputies.[34] The chairmanship of committees also changed. For example, budget and planning, legal and judicial affairs, and foreign affairs committees went to Hossein Hoseini-Shahrudi, Ali Asghar Baqani, and Hasan Rouhani, respectively.[35] Trying to appear both nonpartisan and pro-*mostazaf*, Khamenehi reminded the new Majlis of their main duty: "Your most fundamental task should be eradication of poverty and support for the *mostazafin* and the barefooted. You should also put the country's interests before your individual and factional interests."[36]

The Coming of the Split within the Two Rights

With the dominance of the two rights (pragmatists or moderates as they were called at that time) over major centers of power, the parliamentary election of 1992 would in theory mark the end of factionalism, and the Islamic Republic would be on a more predictable and stable path. This understanding was implicit in Rafsanjani's speech before the first session of the fourth Majlis when he stated, "People had voted for unity at the top and a Majlis that cooperates with the executive."[37] Surprisingly, however, the conservative-dominated Majlis immediately began to criticize the president. The Majlis pointed to weak economic indicators and blamed the poor economy on the president's policies and on the incompetence, widespread improprieties, and misuses of power by his entourage, the technocrats. In turn, the majority of the MPs believed the solutions to the economic ills and administrative venality in the country rested on closer supervision by the Majlis over the activities of the executive branch, slowing down the pace of the ambitious plans of *Towse-'eh,* and replacing the Western-educated technocrats with a more doctrinaire cadre. Moreover, now it was the conservatives who were concerned about the plight of the disinherited and who were complaining about how various government policies were "breaking the backs" of economically vulnerable segments of the Iranian society. But before describing how the new Majlis challenged Rafsanjani, it is important to know why it did so. Although it appeared that the conservatives were seeking socioeconomic justice for the poor, their own livelihoods were being undermined by the new economic policies instigated by Rafsanjani and the increased role of the central government in the economy.

The first FYP had some success in achieving its objectives.[38] In 1989/90, Iran's GDP in real terms grew by 4.2 percent; the following year it increased to 11.5 percent and to 8.6 percent in 1991/92,[39] exhibiting an average growth of 7.5 percent for the first three years of the FFYP.[40] By the end of 1993, the government succeeded in reducing unemployment to 11.4 percent of the workforce.[41] Annual government revenues rose by 10.5 percent in 1989 and by 31 percent in 1992; the 1992 deficit of 857 billion rials was a substantial decrease from the 1986 figure of 1375 billion rials.[42] Industrial activities were revived, and industrial output showed an average growth of 12.8 percent.[43] The sale of non-oil exports increased from 1,241,463 million rials in 1989 to 3,438,129 million rials in 1992. This figure was further increased to 5,137,216 million rials and 7,454,099 million rials in 1993 and 1994, respectively.[44] The most impressive achievement of the FYP, however (by Third World standards), was the increase in taxes collected by the government; tax revenues became the fastest growing component of government revenues in the FYP.[45] In May 1992, it was announced that tax revenues during the first FYP had surpassed the expected amount and accounted for more than 40 percent of the government's revenues.[46] According to Mohsen Nurbaksh, the minister of economics and finance, figures for 1989 through the first half of 1992 were: 20 percent, 69 percent, 63 percent, and 40 percent for the respective years.[47]

By the end of the first FYP, however, negative economic indicators began to have a deleterious effect on the goals of the FYP. Most damaging of all was inflation, which by 1992 was running at about 50 percent.[48] The main reason for the steep inflation rate, the government argued, was that liquidity during the first three years of the FYP had increased nearly 83 percent while the aim of the FYP was to reduce it to 35 percent.[49] According to Morteza Alviri, the head of Majlis budget committee, "From the victory of the revolution until 1992, cash liquidity has increased eighteen times."[50] Many observers of the Iranian economy asserted that the most devastating effect of increased liquidity was that more than half of the population became engaged in quick-cash entre-preneurial trades; only 6 percent of the work force was employed in the pro-ductive sector.[51]

Other economic difficulties, such as the budget deficit, were primarily due to two important factors: lack of investment by the private sector (in particular bazaaris) in industrial projects, and the liquidity at their disposal. Mohammad Hossein Adeli, the governor of the central bank, noted, "The 9 billion dollar deficit of 1991, for example, was because in that year we had 28 billion dollars worth of imports as opposed to 17 billion in exports."[52] The minister of eco-nomics and finance maintained, "Nearly all the increase in domestic output was due to government projects and activities, and the private sector had no share in it."[53] Anticipating a positive response to its privatization efforts, the govern-ment had placed the shares of three hundred companies and production units in the Tehran's stock exchange. However, the shares of only fourteen companies were bought by the private sector.[54] In other words, the majority of domestic companies remained in the hand of the state, which according to one MP, numbered around 2,500 by 1993.[55]

Although the private sector bore the lion's share of the economic adversi-ties during the first FYP, the government accepted partial responsibility for the unfavorable economic indicators such as inflation, as it was fueled by state ex-penditures on major projects of *Towse-'eh* and a 10 percent rise in consumption encouraged by the state.[56] Nevertheless, it was apparent that rather than invest-ing in domestic industrial projects, the private sector or the bazaaris had ex-ploited the unfettered import policies of the government to make huge profits. As a *Payam-e Imruz* editorial concluded, it was the bazaar and its well-entrenched system that was behind the chronic high inflation and economic predicament in Iran. The editorial scorned this medieval economic system, which employed nearly half the work force (the service sector), produced literally nothing, yet had a near monopoly in price setting and the distribution of goods:

> A large segment of importers, forward purchasers [salaf-khar], wholesalers and wholesale dealers, middlemen, cargo dealers [bardaran], warehouse owners . . . act on their own regulations and according to their own interests. Their network is unofficial but extremely powerful and closely intertwined, and within it, the numerous [layers of] handing-over [of goods] is constantly reinforced. The directors [of this system] deal with big numbers and colossal earnings. Their interest rates are exorbitant, their dealings complex, and their profits grand. They have never favored a strong independent national economy and continue their traditional way of conducting commerce without yielding to supervision and inspection by the government. They perceive it as their right to freely set prices and have autonomy of action. Although not visible from the outside, they are so well-rooted inside [the country] that they can easily sabotage government regulations.[57]

According to officials, this kind of arcane exchange amounts to nearly half of all commercial activity in the country.[58] The bazaar system adversely affected public-sector employees and fixed-income groups in particular. In words of one MP, "Today, the daily income of a small trader [kasabeh] is more than the monthly salary of a government employee, and a one-day commission of a middleman or a retailer is more than one year's income of one family."[59] By mid-1991, therefore, the government had no option but to change its economic policies, and Rafsanjani himself was the first to disclose this shift. Speaking during "Government Week," he was highly critical of the avaricious bazaaris and their petty bourgeois clients: "By interfering in the supply of goods, the government will control the prices. We were hoping that such activities would not have been necessary and that supply and demand would automatically stabilize prices. Later, we realized that we must interfere in the economy . . . traders and entrepreneurs did not behave in an honorable way."[60] From mid-1991 onward, the government instigated new initiatives designed primarily to tighten the country's economic belt and exercise more control over the direction of the economy. This shift—which among other policies included more government regulations, increasing revenues from public services, import restrictions, and increased tariffs and quotas—gradually began to undermine the bazaar economic system.

One of the most important directives was to involve the banks and banking system more intensively in the economy in order to exercise some control over the activities of the private sector. In this regard, the government significantly deregulated the banks, allowing them to open foreign currency accounts inside as well as outside the country, and to increase investment in various projects.[61] In September 1992, central bank governor Adeli announced that by the end of the first FYP, the currency exchange-rate system would be fixed.[62] Efforts were made to attract foreign capital for domestic projects, and in the summer of 1992, various officials announced that Iran was safe for foreign investment and the government would support, protect, and guarantee safe investments without imposing any limitations.[63]

Other regulation changes directly increased revenues. The utility charges for telephone, post, water, and electricity were increased dramatically. In 1992 the minister of Post Telegraph and Telephone (PTT), Mohammad Gharazi, announced that postal costs would increase by 100 percent.[64] The ministry of economics announced that with few exceptions, all importers of goods must pay a 5 percent custom tax before their goods were released from customs. Given that the value of goods at customs was based on the floating currency exchange rates, importers would pay far more than 5 percent.[65] At the same time the government also decided to look after its employees. In February 1992, with the help of the leftist Majlis, a new law on direct taxation was passed that raised the exemption ceiling significantly for public sector employees.[66]

These new government initiatives and the aim of the second FYP were summed up by Minister Nurbaksh in his first speech before the new Majlis. Acknowledging that the policy of "unrestricted imports" was no longer a viable alternative for the country, he told the MPs that the government had realized the need to reconsider its original open-door policy and intended to exercise more control over imports and market mechanisms. Instead, he announced, "The driving engine behind the economy will be investment in and emphasis on industrial production and growth and not distribution and consumption." He also noted that the government aimed to fund various economic projects by raising customs duties, tariffs, tolls, and taxes.[67] Naturally, the government's new directives placed the interests of the two rights at odds with each other as they would surely undermine the economic viability of the bazaar economic system. Aside from the powerful bazaari merchants, this system had become the lifeblood of the postrevolutionary service sector and included "petty traders, street peddlers, foreign currency dealers, and people involved in a whole list of illicit or extralegal activities from selling foreign cigarettes to buying and selling government-issued ration coupons."[68]

◆ ◆ ◆

As noted in the previous chapter, Rafsanjani's vision for the next phase of post-war Iran included both institutional and ideological de-revolutionization. This entailed a shift from a diffused polity towards a more centralized political structure, a notion that became enshrined in the constitution. The return of the increased role for state in the economic realm is better understood in connection with this centralization because the institutional changes that took place after 1989 were part of the "rationalization" of the Iranian polity. Centralization took place largely under the pretext of eliminating duplications by merging parallel institutions and providing better governmental management. The real reason for it, however, was to bring various revolutionary bodies under greater state (central government) control and, in many ways, to subdue their revolutionary characters and functions.

For obvious security reasons, the armed forces were primary targets for centralization. In 1989 the Ministry of Defense and Armed Forces Logistics (MDAFL) was established through the amalgamation of the IRGC and the regular armed forces.[69] To justify the merger, Rafsanjani remarked, "The merger of the armed forces was the wish of the Imam and the esteemed leader."[70] With the creation of the MDAFL, the regime minimized the possible threat from the revolutionary IRGC and, by ranking its cadre, moved a step closer to professionalizing the IRGC and ultimately toward further unification of the armed forces. While resentment between the IRGC and the regular army still exists, the two bodies have been brought closer through more cooperation and joint military actions.[71] The unification of the armed forces continued when, in June 1991, the Islamic Republic's Law Enforcement Forces (*Niruhaye Intezami*) was created through the merger of the KII with the gendarmerie and the police, bringing them under the supervision of the ministry of justice.[72] Various government ministries have also been combined, including the mergers of the ministries of industry and heavy industry, mines and metals, and construction jihad and agriculture, to name a few.[73]

Some of the *Nehads* were highly resentful of their merger with government bodies. As with most *Nehads,* the KII, for example, maintained the importance of its revolutionary-religious credentials and functions in the regime and pointed out its legitimate right to be considered as an independently functioning organ outside the jurisdiction of the central government.[74] With the merger imminent, the KII pleaded with the Majlis to reconsider its initiative, arguing that its administrative style was based on religious duty rather than bureaucratic rationality, and therefore the merger would strip the KII of its true essence.[75] In contrast to Rafsanjani's claim regarding the merger of *Nehads* with the parallel government institutions, the KII believed that the Imam had always been opposed to the bureaucratization of the *Nehads.*[76] Once the merger was under way, the KII criticized Rafsanjani's de-revolutionization of the country and warned, "A creeping revolution against the Islamic revolution is under way that is an enemy's plot against our Islamic culture." The editorial specifically referred to Rafsanjani's brother who was spreading Western culture through national radio and TV programs. The editorial also chastised those members of the government who were formulating the cultural policies the editor viewed as sinister, calling them lewd technocrats.[77]

These mergers had their share of outbursts of factionalism. The left, whose members had a strong presence in the IRCG and the KII, objected to their mergers. Ilias Hazrati (MP), for instance, said, "The merger of the KII will greatly diminish the revolutionary dynamism of the country."[78] Arguing in the same vein, Abolhasan Haerizadeh told the Majlis, "In order to preserve the revolutionary spirit of the country, the KII is a far more reliable body than other forces, and its merger will result in destroying true Hizbollahi forces in the country."[79] Mohtashami said that "if we lose the KII, we will lose our revolutionary identity."[80] What obliged the left-dominated Majlis to vote for the mergers were the claims made by the conservatives and Rafsanjani that it was the wish of Khomeini prior to his death, and of Khamenehi.[81]

Immediately after Khomeini's death, the two rights shared common interests in de-revolutionizing Iran both ideologically and institutionally; but by 1991, however, a conflict of interest was surfacing in the sociocultural realm:

the direction of the economy and the role of the state in it. While the conservatives continued to desire a hands-off state, for Rafsanjani the success of the five-year plan depended upon the increased role of the state. The need for an interventionist state in the economic realm, combined with the imperatives of *Towse-'eh*, required a well-institutionalized, central government with powerful infrastructure. This goal resurrected an old fear among the conservatives: the emergence of an industrial state. Bit by bit, Rafsanjani began to advance the need for the increased predominance of the republican institutions, striving (given the weight and efficacy of the religious dimension) to create a modern autonomous central government. In October 1991, for example, he said, "Paying taxes is a religious as well as a national duty and is tantamount to paying your dues to society. It must be explained to the people that taxes are the right of the state, otherwise the wheels of the country will be halted." [82] Under the pretext of the need for order and stability, he remarked on another occasion, "Chaos is not compatible with Islam. The Prophet always maintained that Islam is the religion of order and order is a fundamental pillar of our religion." [83] Rafsanjani's most important speech regarding the importance of the role of the state in Iran was made in April 1992 when he clearly separated his views from those of the conservatives with regard to the significance of the role and function of state in society:

> States have been an indispensable endeavor in Islamic societies and human societies in general. Some people and currents argued against the need for a state, but subsequent experiences and events have proved them wrong. The holy book has said that even if the leaders are lewd, their existence is far more advantageous for the society than the chaos that their absence could lead to. ... The existence of government and administration, and the enterprise of managing societies is an imperative and holy principle. [84]

A modern state requires its own trained cadre and as noted earlier, Rafsanjani was keen to emphasize that the successful implementation of his economic policies required reliance on secular experts and expertise rather than revolutionary-religious credentials. He wished to capitalize on all human resources, even those opposed to the regime outside Iran. In his New Year's message of 1994, Rafsanjani addressed educated Iranian former patriots and called upon these "scientific assets" to return home, maintaining that "the current reconstruction stage requires the participation of all Iranians abroad, even those who had previously committed wrongdoings."[85] This emphasis on expertise and administrative capabilities was conspicuous in his cabinet selections for both 1989 and 1993. Most of the twenty-three cabinet members of 1989, which he called the "cabinet of reconstruction," were "highly educated with degrees from American and European universities," Rafsanjani proudly told the Majlis.[86] The composition of Rafsanjani's first cabinet was a mixture of the left and the president's old associates. Rafsanjani made important ministerial changes by replacing hard-core leftist members of the Musavi cabinet with his own close associates in key posts such as economics and finance (Mohsen Nurbaksh), heavy industry (Mohammad Reza Ne'matzadeh), agriculture (Isa Kalantari), health (Reza Fazel), and energy (Bijan Zanganeh); and he balanced the cabinet by selecting less extreme members from the left as ministers of Islamic guidance (Khatami), petroleum (Mohammad Aqazadeh), labor (Hossein Kamali), and interior (Abdollah Nuri).[87] In 1993, only two clergy (Ismail Shushtari, justice, and Ali Fallahian, intelligence) were chosen by Rafsanjani for the cabinet, as compared with four in 1989. Of the twenty-three cabinet members in 1993, eight were MDs or Ph.D.s and nine were engineers.[88]

Thus, with regards to economic policies, the attitude of Rafsanjani's technocratic cadre was hardly pro-bazaari (hence the vote of confidence from the left-dominated third Majlis for his 1989 cabinet). Although they were supporters of the Islamic regime, many of the nominees had been educated in the United States, so the vision of technocrats such as Nurbaksh and Adeli in the economic realm was a modern one. Those in the modern right who had served under Musavi, former leftists, were long-time opponents of a bazaar economy. The post-1989 views of Morteza Alviri were typical of many members of the left who, after years of radicalism, had moderated their views and joined Rafsanjani's technocratic cadre. Alviri explicitly criticized the profit-hungry bazaaris and was an adamant proponent of diminishing their powers, blaming them for Iran's economic impasse. In an interview with *Keyhan,* he said, "The government is after those who make 700,000 tomans overnight." He further remarked, "We are faced with people who say that government must be administered through revenues from *khoms* and *zakat* and perceive any kind of taxation as anti-shari'a. . . . Thus, they favor a feeble state [central government]."[89] On another occasion he said, "It is unacceptable that 10 percent of the population owns 63 percent of the country's wealth."[90] The new statist government initiatives and the growing animosity between Rafsanjani and his old allies no doubt pleased the likes of Alviri, brought the left closer to the president, and further paved the way for the future alliance between the modern right and the left.[91]

In short, the real reasons behind the assault of the fourth Majlis against the government were the policies instigated by Rafsanjani including high taxation, an export rather than import oriented economy through integration in the global market, and the modernist views of the architects and executors of these policies (such as Nurbaksh, Adeli, and Alviri) in the economic realm. In other words, the posturing of the conservatives about Rafsanjani's policies in the new Majlis described below was no more than another instance of factional theatrics. To be sure, as the following passage from an insightful *Iran-e Farda* editorial suggests, by 1993 the opposition on the part of the conservative right faction to the imperatives of *Towse-'eh* was because they resembled the economic policies of the prerevolutionary regime:

> This current will support the existing economic policies so long as they do not lead to the reemergence and dominance of foreign capital and a dependent industrial development in Iran. They are not inclined to lose their preferred position attained after the war as this current has not forgotten how the US-sponsored Shah reforms [the White Revolution] of the 1960s led to the rise of dependent industrial capitalism in the country, and how the commercial capitalist bazaaris lost their economic predominance and autonomy. The kind of industrialization favored by this faction is one where the financial control and ownership of industrial development remains in the hands of traditional commercial capitalists. This faction leans on traditional *fiqh* and religious leadership [Khamenehi] and in this way objects to any decision or efforts that would shift power and the management from the religious leadership to the management of the skilled and the experts.[92]

In the first session of the fourth Majlis, Rafsanjani played into the hands of the conservatives by admitting the existence of economic hardship in the country. "Economic development is not achieved painlessly," he announced. "It is a lengthy process and will have its own victims."[93] Capitalizing on such remarks, the MPs began their protestations. While calling some of Rafsanjani's efforts honorable, MP Lotfollah Ghanavati said, "Development and its associated measures such as high taxation have resulted in high inflation and are breaking the backs of the disinherited and the vulnerable segments of society."[94] MP Forushani noted, "The chronic inflation and the heavy burden of taxes and other charges such as water, gas, and phone, in addition to paper pushing and bribery in the bureaucracy, have made the life of the disinherited burdensome. Corruption is rampant in government offices and is threatening the country. . . . This is the blood message of the martyrs."[95] By referring to the "debt trap" common in Third World countries, foreign borrowing and investments in the country were also rejected as solutions. An editorial in *JIM* maintained, "The experience of other Third World counties such as Latin America and Africa clearly shows that foreign investment has had devastating affects on the national economy. They [foreigners] only think about themselves."[96]

To truly discredit the "Rafsanjanites," a concerted effort was made by the conservatives to taint the moral inclination of the technocrats and, tacitly perhaps, that of Rafsanjani himself. According to Ahmad Pishbin, "By replacing the war veterans, the poor, and the Hizbollahis with indolent and callous technocrats, the enemy has placed his pupils in key positions in the country and is defeating the revolution. . . . Officialdom is the right of highly devout people."[97] The speaker, Nateq-Nuri, stressed the virtues of religiousness over expertise and emphasized the importance of PVPV. To sanction his view, he remarked, "One of the worries of the esteemed leader is the isolation of Hizbollahi forces in some government agencies."[98] Nateq-Nuri's words were also significant in that it indicated the beginnings of the split in the dual leadership: although he criticized Rafsanjani, he also indicated that his faction, the conservative right, was upholding the views of Khamenehi. MP Kamal Daneshiar attacked the moral credentials of three primary ministers behind Rafsanjani's economic policies: "The planners of our 'macroeconomy,' in particular the heads of the Central Bank, the ministry of economics and finance, and the MBO, were all educated in the West. Thus, they are devoid of the same spirit of the disinherited. In fact, thy are rarely seen to associate with the *mostazafin*."[99] In an interview with *JIM*, Mohammad Javad Larijani and

Morteza Nabavi indicated the differing sociocultural visions of the two rights when it came to development:

> Some people believe that development means attaining high scientific and technological achievements and is the solution to all of our problems. To achieve this goal, we must have social permissiveness and the system must become "liberal." They also claim that the religious culture of the Islamic regime is not conducive to development and that we have to import the culture of *Towse-'eh*. . . . They support freedom, so do we. But we have a different view of freedom. Our standard includes morality and theirs is unfetteredness.[100]

It is worth noting here that gradually the term "liberal" experienced another shift in its connotation. The modern right was classified with this damaging label, a designation that not only distinguished their factional inclinations (pro-Rafsanjani) but also their cultural and moral dispositions. Even one of the most celebrated ideological imprints of the regime, the Hizbollahi, fell under this marker. While the Hizbollahis that the left in the third Majlis accused the two rights of marginalizing were the left-leaning *maktabis* and their followers, now the conservative right was calling their own constituents—the religiously orthodox members of society and all those who made up the bazaar economic system—as Hizbollahis. Once again, the discourses within the regime shifted to fit a faction's political purposes.

To constrain the independence and autonomy of the government, the conservatives, who previously thought of the Majlis as no more than a place for the consultation of Islamic elite, became defenders and protectors of the Majlis and its constitutional powers. Now that the conservatives were in the majority in the parliament, they had a different view of what the role of the Majlis could be. According to the majority of the MPs, one of the most effective ways to oversee public mismanagement and corruption was for the Majlis to use its constitutional rights of supervision over the activities of the executive. MP Busheqi reiterated this legal right of the parliament and warned officials, "They must better serve the faithful and we [MPs] are determined to fully carry out our legal rights."[101] Mohammad Qasem-Kia disapproved of the excesses of government agencies such as the ministries and government-financed industrial enterprises and pointed out how the unchecked increases in rates for government services were hurting the people. To prevent further "autonomous" and uncontrolled actions by the government, he also maintained that the Majlis must carry out its legal and constitutional duty of tight supervision over state activities.[102] Another MP, Hasan Shakhesi, remarked: "One can observe that in emptying the pockets of the people, some government agencies act with total autonomy. It is the custom today for government organizations to reach self-sufficiency without taking into consideration the livelihood of the people."[103] As will be discussed below, the Majlis used such statements to alter—and greatly impair—Rafsanjani's economic plans.

The Conflict over the 1993/1994 Budget Proposal

The goals of Rafsanjani's proposed budget for 1993/1994 were to further the government initiatives that were in progress and challenge the autonomy of the bazaar economic system by shifting its hold on the country's capital to the government and the banks. The proposed budget was designed to increase revenue by 50 percent through taxes, boost exports, and augment the role of banks in the economy by allowing them to issue government bonds and offer competitive interest rates for savings. To silence his critics, Rafsanjani announced that government subsidies of essential goods for the following year would be doubled.[104]

One of the most distinctive components of the new budget was its reliance on a fixed-rate currency policy. In a move that Adeli and Nurbaksh called an "economic revolution," the government announced that, beginning in the next calendar year, the price of the rial would be fixed against the dollar at 1450 rather than at the artificially held low rate of 70. It was claimed by both men that this would stabilize the rial and discourage further imports, encourage investment in domestic industrial projects, and provide more order and predictability for both investment and the economy as a whole.[105] Needless to say, the immediate results of this policy were the devaluation of Iranian currency and higher inflation.[106] In the Majlis, Rafsanjani stressed that despite opposition to the new direction of the economy and recent policies of the government, he would "firmly stay the course." He condemned those who wished to keep prices low through imports and asked, "For how long can we do this? Gradually, there will be no foreign currency and no money. . . . It is easy to spend oil money, buy goods, and create a broker [*dallal*] economy. This will destroy our economic infrastructure and cause the country's backwardness."[107] This theme of "hardship now but welfare in the future" hereafter became the cornerstone of the modern right's economic discourse.

As anticipated, the budget proposal for the 1993/1994 fiscal year was challenged by the Majlis, particularly the proposed 86 percent increase in the government's budget and the fixed currency rate. Hossein Hosseini-Shahrudi, the new head of the Majlis budget committee, believed that the budget was overly ambitious given that many projects of the first FYP remained incomplete. He objected to the colossal funding appropriated to government agencies and projects under the pretext of research and education when the new monetary policy was sure to lead to inflation and a black market for the dollar. "Do not furnish billions and billions of rials to the government without knowing how and what they are going to spend it on," he concluded.[108] Mohammad Reza Bahonar (MP) approved of the fixed-rate currency initiative but asked, perhaps rightly, "in the light of declining oil prices and increasing foreign debts of the country [estimated at $30 billion], how the government could ensure that it would have enough dollars to inject into the market to prevent a further inflationary trend in the economy."[109]

The new budget and the first FYP had its defenders as well. For example, by itemizing the achievements of the first FYP, Ali Mobini-Dehkordi maintained that "most crucial objectives of the FYP have been accomplished, so let's stay the course."[110] By pointing out that the Keynesian model is the prevalent economic system in the world today, Rajab Rahmani stressed the need for the government to intervene in the economy. He also defended the budget increase for state-run companies because "they ultimately produce goods for the domestic market and the people."[111] The government also defended its taxation and fixed-rate currency policies. Roghani-Zanjani (the head of MBO), asked the MPs, "How can the government and various ministries accomplish their expected tasks without having sufficient funds?"[112] Mohsen Nurbaksh wanted to create a more manageable economic environment and said, "We hope that by fixing the exchange rate, the demand for currency will diminish and we can balance our budget and deal with the economic problems more effectively." As an example of a successful government measure, and probably to rub salt into the wounds of the bazaaris, he reminded them, "Bank savings since 1989 have doubled. This capital at the disposal of the banks can provide an opportunity for investments and loans." [113]

After deliberations over the generalities of the budget, the Majlis debated specific articles for a week. On January 30, 1993, they approved a watered-down version of the budget that decreased the government portion, especially the allocation for government agencies and ministries, by more than 10 percent.[114]

After seeing the difficult time the Majlis and the conservatives gave the president on the budget, one might ask the question again: Why would a group formerly supportive of Rafsanjani so quickly turn their backs on him and become critical of the president? To this question, Morteza Nabavi had a sly response:

> They ask us why you [conservatives] who entered the Majlis under the slogan of support for Hashemi are now pestering the government. What is the difference between you and others who did the same thing? [Because] we want his programs to succeed and therefore we say that the administrators must be pious, morally proper, and acceptable to the people. . . . We say for the success [of these programs] the government, ministers, and officials must use the utmost care when dealing with the country's resources and coffers, refrain from extravagance, fortify the Hizbollahi and the *Basiji* forces and not those who are oblivious to the revolution. . . . These words are all part of the covenant that the esteemed leader has framed.[115]

The Split in the Dual Leadership

In the midst of increasing tension between the two rightist factions, another crucial rift was taking place between the president and the leader. In expressing dissatisfaction with the new socioeconomic direction of the country and the cultural imperatives of *Towse-'eh,* Khamenehi gradually began siding with the conservatives. It is difficult to ascertain with any degree of certainty the reasons behind Khamenehi's move. Nevertheless, a few possibilities come to mind. Khamenehi was well aware that he enjoyed neither the politico-economic footing of Rafsanjani nor the well-established religious and socioeconomic base of other powerful conservatives. He had neither religious credentials and followers nor strong connections to the bazaaris. In this precarious position, solidifying Khamenehi's power meant choosing sides in the conflict between the two rights. Given his unrelenting disagreement with the left, plus the fact that after 1992 the conservatives seemed destined to dominate the political scene in Iran (and because perhaps Khamenehi did not wish to remain in the shadow of Rafsanjani), strengthening his ties with the conservative right seemed a prudent choice.

One of Khamenehi's first direct criticisms of Rafsanjani and the technocrats came in October 1992, when, along with the conservatives, he complained about depravity in government offices and said, "Some [in the system] mock the Hizbollahis and their religious virtues, but if we spend billions on development projects and ignore moral issues in the country, all the achievements amount to nothing." [116] Two days later, his words were even harsher:

> If I find out that officials have abandoned PVPV I shall personally defend it. The responsible officials and the administrators must provide the environment for the implementation of PVPV. . . . The enemy is claiming that during the period of reconstruction, revolutionary spirit and morality must be put aside. The enemy is advertising that the postwar period and the reconstruction phase is the time of the demise of revolutionary fervor and that it is time to go back and live the oblivious life of some countries. Is this the meaning of reconstruction? It surely is not. [117]

During the debates over the 1994/1995 budget and the second FYP, Khamenehi provided the conservatives in the Majlis with the justification needed to modify Rafsanjani's plans when he said, "It is true that [in reconstructing the country] we should rely on experts and expertise, but the system must be ruled by Islamic thinking and holy thoughts." [118] On another occasion he remarked, "If there is no social justice, nothing is accomplished." [119] In his New Year message of 1994, Khamenehi warned the "pragmatics and technocrats" against the detrimental affects of complacency. [120] In one of his most partisan comments, Khamenehi illustrated the new conservative support for the authority of the Majlis when he said, "Based on their legal authority, the MPs must engage in guiding the government and prevent mistakes. . . . We should not defend any mistakes committed by the government and the administrators."[121] Finally in May 1994, he ordered the ministry of intelligence and the state's Audit Office to investigate financial improprieties in government offices.[122]

In solidifying the mandate of Khamenehi and his newly developed rift with Rafsanjani at this critical juncture, the leader received much support from members of the JMHEQ and the JRM. Nateq-Nuri threatened the modern right, "Those who do not accept the words of the leader should know that there is another revolution on the way."[123] Azari–Qomi declared, "All institutions of the regime such as universities, religious seminaries, legislative assemblies, mosques, Friday prayer leaders, economic and political centers . . . are the dominion of the leader."[124] *Towse-'eh* also came under attack from the JMHEQ. According to Rasti-Kashani, "Under the excuse of completing big development projects, the poor and the disinherited should not be sacrificed."[125]

Rafsanjani's Second Term

For Rafsanjani's second run for president in 1993, the conservatives reused their slogan from his 1989 election, "Support for Hashemi." A few days before the election, Nateq-Nuri called Rafsanjani "highly intelligent, sociopolitically knowledgeable, and an astute leader."[126] The JMHEQ echoed these compliments.[127] The conservatives supported Rafsanjani during this election for three main reasons. First, there was no other credible, viable candidate. For the conservatives at that point in time, Rafsanjani was still a valuable asset against any possible challenges from the left. Second, even the conservatives knew that at that juncture the survival of the system, and therefore of the factions themselves, depended on a competent leadership. Khamenehi did not have their confidence in this regard. As Nateq-Nuri himself admitted later in the Majlis, "Since the death of Imam, the ship of the country has been navigated by the only person who could have done it, Mr. Hashemi Rafsanjani. No one knows and can tackle the problems of postwar Iran better than him."[128] Finally, the majority (if not all) of the conservatives at that time did not yet desire to appear to want direct control of the executive. Even later, when some influential conservatives such as Nateq-Nuri and Asgar-Owladi sought to further politicize this faction by supporting Nateq-Nuri's candidacy for the presidency, other members such as Mahdavi-Kani and Azari-Qomi objected and resigned from their posts in the JRM and *Resalat*.

When the election results were announced, Rafsanjani's second mandate was hardly impressive compared to his first term; the 10 million or 63 percent of the votes that he received attested to this fact. The remaining votes went to the other two conservative candidates, Ahmad Tavakkoli (4 million) and Abdollah Jasbi (1 million).[129] The election results were not only a sign of Rafsanjani's decreasing popularity but indicated the decline of the legitimacy of the regime as a whole. Only 55 percent of the nearly 30 million eligible voters had cast votes, as opposed to 70 percent in the previous election.[130] The conservatives used the turnout and the final margin to try to rein in their candidate. Abbas Ali Amid-Zanjani hinted that while the low turnout was in no way an indication that the population was unhappy with the president, "Maybe the people were trying to tell something to Mr. Rafsanjani. Maybe they were saying that you needed to listen more carefully to what they wanted, which was that the current path needed reconsideration and that there was a need to have managers with more Islamic credentials."[131] In his acceptance speech in the Majlis, however, Rafsanjani firmly stood behind his political, economic, and sociocultural tenets. For example, his second priority after "guarding Islam, spirituality, and morality," he announced, was his pledge to "the issues of freedom, democracy, and the individual and social rights of the people." He also reiterated his goal of establishing social justice not through traditional methods such as subsidies and handouts but by creating a modern economic system that tackled the issue systematically.[132]

The first confrontation between Rafsanjani and the Majlis during his second term came when the Majlis refused to give its vote of confidence to the minister whom the MPs held responsible for the existing economic crisis, Nurbaksh. Even before the election, conservatives both inside and outside of the Majlis had signaled to the president their desire for substantial reshuffling in his cabinet.[133] MP Ahmad Nasri reflected the mood of the Majlis when he said, "The expectation of the Majlis from the president is to take under consideration the current composition of the Majlis and discard those ministers who are not in line with himself and the Majlis. It is enough to take a vote in the coming days and find out which ministers the Majlis is opposed to."[134] MP Farajollah Afrazideh remarked, "We like Hashemi, but how long will his ministers make up for their incompetence by overspending? The [real] support for Hashemi on the part of the MPs is to bring to his attention that some of his ministers are incompetent and introduce to him more competent ones who are in line with *velayat*."[135] Two ministers in particular were under attack: Abdollah Nuri, a member of MRM and the minister of state, and as already noted above, Nurbaksh. Nuri was criticized for his ineptitude and partisan actions and comments. The disturbances in some cities during the summer of 1992 were used as an excuse by MP Baratali Mohammadifar to denounce Nuri: "a good minister is one who can carry out his rugged duties successfully."[136] In addition, Mohammadifar insisted, "The minister of state is conspicuously exhibiting his tendency to oppose revolutionary spirit and is unfriendly and rude to Hizbollahis."[137]

In August 1993, Rafsanjani introduced his new twenty-three-member cabinet to the Majlis. The new composition of the cabinet was an indication that, except for economics and finance, the conservatives had succeeded in compelling Rafsanjani to change the head of the ministries that they were particularly sensitive about: state (Ali Besharati), commerce (Al-Ishaq), education (Mohammad Ali Najafi), higher education (Mohammadi Golpayegani, Khamenehi's adviser on cultural affairs), and Islamic guidance and culture (Ali Larijani, Khatami's replacement).[138] A week later, when Rafsanjani spoke in support of his new cabinet, while he made no mention of Nurbaksh, he admitted that the reason for the cabinet reshuffling was his awareness that the old ministers would not receive the necessary votes for confirmation.[139]

The next two days the MPs spoke in favor and against the new cabinet. The most highly praised ministers were Golpayegani, Besharati, and Larijani, and the most objections were against the incumbent Nurbaksh. MP Mohsen Kohkan remarked, "All the current economic predicaments in the country are caused by the government's weakness in managing fiscal policies, and the behavior of the banking sector."[140] "Mr. Nurbaksh, you have fixed the rate of currency, but what are your plans for its side effects such as inflation? What have you done for the vulnerable segments except raising their taxes?" asked MP Abbasali Zali.[141] In the end, the Majlis gave its vote of confidence to all the ministers except Nurbaksh.[142] Later, Rafsanjani introduced Morteza Mohammad-Khan for the post and he did receive the necessary votes.[143] Asgar-

Owladi set the tone for the next cabinet by reminding the new ministers of the need to act in line with Islam and with the wishes of the *faqih*. In addition, he emphasized that government offices must be filled with Hizbollahis. "This is both a serious recommendation and a warning," he added.[144]

Factionalism over the Second Five-Year Plan and the 1994/1995 Budget

On December 21, 1993, Rafsanjani submitted the budget proposal for fiscal year 1994/1995 and the second FYP simultaneously to the parliament. While the Majlis approved the budget in less than two months, the debate over the FYP began in August 1994 and was not approved until December; thus, the country was technically without a socioeconomic plan for a year. By the time of the submission of the two plans to the Majlis by Rafsanjani, the dispute between the two rights was becoming more pointed. Despite the objections of conservatives inside and outside of the Majlis to the new economic direction set by the president, it appeared that not only would the modern right maintain its course, but that the government in fact aimed to further supervise, control, and in essence discipline the private sector. Nurbaksh believed that due to the tradition of quick-cash commerce in the country, the private sector would not invest in infrastructure projects unless they were compelled to do so.[145] Or, in the views of Morteza Mohammad-Khan, "The best policy for [economic] adjustment is taxing the rich."[146] The new direction was set by Rafsanjani himself when he spoke about his vision for the new FYP:

> In the second FYP, the government will put further emphasis on social justice and the general welfare of society. The creation of this welfare lies in more production and a healthier distribution of goods. In the first FYP, we tried to create this welfare through imports and filling the market with goods. But now we want to protect the consumer, destroy the diversity of prices, eliminate unofficial channels of distribution, and eradicate hoarding.[147]

Influential figures from the conservative right, who for political reasons had so far remained supportive of Rafsanjani, began to directly challenge the president and the modern right. After 1993, Nateq-Nuri, Asgar-Owladi, and to some extent Morteza Nabavi became the helmsmen of this faction and more senior members of the conservative right such as Azari-Qomi and Mahdavi-Kani took a back seat. Instead of Azari-Qomi, now it was Asgar-Owladi who wrote pro-bazaari and antistatist editorials in *Resalat;* and in place of Mahdavi-Kani, Nateq-Nuri became the de facto speaker of the JRM. Both men moved to impel the conservative right faction, significantly its clerical wing, towards direct rule with the ultimate aim of monopolizing power by eliminating Rafsanjani and the modern right from the political stage in Iran. Because to all intents and purposes the left was already politically incapacitated, Nateq-Nuri's victory in the next presidential election would have shut out the rest of the competition. Their political cushion in this endeavor became the discourse of *velayat-e motlaqeh-ye faqih* and support from Khamenehi himself.

In addition to the old rhetoric, the conservatives called for less statism and more involvement of the people in the economy, advocating some sort of self-defined "economic populism," to free the bazaar from the incursionary policies of the state. According to Asgar-Owladi, "The Imam said if a task can be done by the people the government should not do it. A leech-like public sector is the most dangerous thing for the system."[148] In a three-part editorial in *Resalat* written in opposition to taxation, Asgar-Owladi categorized excessive taxes as a form of state despotism.[149] Increasing foreign influences in the forms of companies and expatriates experts were also condemned by him. Asghar-Owladi believed that government initiatives aimed at attracting Iranians abroad to come back were against the will of the people and the spirit of the revolution. "It is wrong to assume that Iranians living in the risqué culture abroad will ever become Hizbollahis. We cannot brainwash them," he maintained.[150] By pointing out their admired status in the traditional Iranian society, Nateq-Nuri defended the bazaaris against accusations of corruption:

> The bazaar in Islamic culture has always been regarded as a focal point of cultural, social, and economic activities. . . . Due to the gathering of all traditional segments of the Iranian society in a place called the bazaar, even the ulama set up religious schools next to the bazaars. . . . As a result of the influence of this Islamic culture, contentment, trustworthiness, and honesty are prevalent in the bazaar, and the emergence of true Islamic movements from the bazaar is a testimony to this fact.[151]

The arena where the conservatives systematically challenged Rafsanjani, however, was in the Majlis when they fractured the president's economic plans. As in the 1992/1993 budget, the goals of the 1994/1995 budget and the second FYP were to raise fuel and energy prices substantially in order to finance various government projects, to control liquidity through selective credits offered by the banks and tighter fiscal controls, to further restrict imports by increasing tariffs and customs, and to decrease subsidies gradually with the ultimate aim of their elimination.[152]

In challenging the FYP and the budget, familiar words were uttered by the conservatives in the Majlis. MP Ali Movahhedi-Saveji observed, "We must learn our lessons from the past. I think that after the war and during the first FYP we have not successfully decreased the role of the state."[153] Objecting to the proposed new taxes, Mohammadbaqer Bahrami (MP) asked, "Why don't you raise taxes in the government sector? Where are the account sheets of state-run enterprises, and why don't we check if they pay taxes or not?[154] Another MP, Abdollah Nouruzi, expressed skepticism over the projected revenues from oil given the constant decline in oil prices.[155] Ahmad Nikfar placed the blame for inflation and liquidity in the currency on the banks and "their commercial activities and thirst for more money." He also argued that "to confront inflation, the import of goods must be in the hands of the private sector and not the state."[156] Ali Naqi Khamushi remarked, "With all the economic problems that we have, there is no option but to tighten our belts and cut costs. . . . We say that next year government ministries and agencies must cut their excesses and refrain from unnecessary purchases. Government expenditure must be frozen at last year's level." He went on to suggest that the budget should be cut by 10 trillion rials, which the Majlis did in the end.[157] Finally, in support of the plight of the poor, MP Ghanavati said:

Given the difficult conditions that vulnerable segments [of society] are under, and the expected inflation that this budget will cause, I must feel worried and oppose it. Perhaps if there was a mechanism to control increases in taxes, tariffs, customs, prices of electricity, water, petrol, and so on, I would not have been. Experience has shown that in the name of taxes and various charges, the rich and suppliers of government services raise their prices, and those on fixed incomes who the budget has neglected have to pay them.[158]

In deciding the fate of the new budget, the conservatives finished where they left off with the previous budget plan, further constraining government activities and giving the private sector as much control and influence over the economy as possible. The MPs succeeded in bringing the actions of the central government under more Majlis control, as well as in slowing down Rafsanjani's *Towse-'eh*. The total budget was cut by nearly 10 percent.[159] Taxes on state-run enterprises were raised, and MPs decided that any budgetary change on their part or for the banks must first be approved by the Majlis.[160] Except for electricity, the Majlis opposed increases on fuel costs.[161] Finally, the Majlis decreased travel expenses allocated to government employees.[162]

In setting the mode for the debate over the second FYP, Asgar-Owladi, the chairman of the budget committee, stated, "The committee's guide for reviewing the FYP will be the leader's axiom of social justice."[163] Combating social injustices and obeying the leader's wishes became the grounds on which the Majlis revised the government's plans. Thus, what the budget committee found objectionable in the FYP was that the plan did not effectively deal with the issue of social justice nor did it represent the country's Islamic values, two fundamental components that the leader had emphasized. The budget committee believed that rising fuel costs and decreasing subsidies would severely affect the lives of the poor and fixed-income populations. The committee also stressed that rather than emphasize industrial growth, the axis of the plan should be agriculture.[164] As far as privatization was concerned, MP Hasan Ghasghavi reflected the general attitude of the Majlis when he said, "State monopolies have never been successful. Experience has shown us that without the existence of competition, increase in production is not possible."[165]

The Majlis decided to revoke all exemptions of customs, tariffs, and taxes of ministries, government companies, and state-run enterprises. One supporter of this law, MP Mohsen Yahyavi, remarked, "The underlying spirit of the new law is to create healthy competition between the public and the private sector in supplying goods and services."[166] In the same session, the Majlis obliged the same government bodies to obtain all their needed products from domestic suppliers. Purchases from foreign markets were allowed only if goods were not available in the country. The government was also required to lift its import monopoly on essential goods "except those that are critical for the survival and stability of the regime."[167] The Majlis also did its utmost to slow down industrial development in the country. It substantially (50 trillion rials) reduced the budget for various development projects, and the money was injected into agricultural development projects. The argument was that instead of huge industrial projects, underprivileged areas must be looked after first. Thus the allocated budget for agriculture nearly doubled, and rather than a gradual elimination of subsidies, the Majlis decided to increase the government's suggested amount by one third.[168] In short, the final verdict of the Majlis was an extensive modification of Rafsanjani's vision of *Towse-'eh*. This was implicitly admitted by Asghar-Owladi: "The structural adjustment policies must be continued, but we thought they should be at a slower pace."[169]

With the rejection of the FYP by the Majlis, the conservatives' efforts to monopolize power and subdue or even eliminate Rafsanjani became conspicuous. As MP Qasem Sho'leh-Sa'di told *Salam,* "An insidious current intends to weaken and compete with the president. However, Mr. Rafsanjani is a man of battles, turmoil, and crisis. Therefore his purge is not an easy task."[170] In addition to perceiving the attack against the president, the left believed that the budget committee and the MPs disassembled the government's FYP, restored the supremacy of the bazaar in the economy, created further obstacles for economic development, and paved the way for the future political dominance of the conservative right: "The second FYP was passed by the Majlis based on the policy of 'bazaar economy' and less emphasis on *Towse-'eh*. Thus [structural] adjustment policies lost their only justification, increased economic development. . . . Unlike the president who put all his capital on the success of the economic policies, the majority faction in the Majlis had an eye on the [next] parliamentary and presidential elections."[171]

In response to the conservative's method of policy implementation in the Majlis, Rafsanjani instigated a war of attrition on the bazaar and the bazaaris. His first endeavor was the creation of the Committee for Adjustment of Bazaar (*Komiteh-ye Tanzim-e Bazaar*) in May 1994. Headed by the president, the two main objectives of the committee were to control price fluctuations in the market and to combat brokers and middlemen involved in the distribution and selling of goods. The committee's first move to control prices was to order all guilds, importers, and producers to place price tags on their products. The committee also decided that the government would determine the prices of eighteen essential goods.[172] Two days later, in an editorial in *Resalat,* Asgar-

Owladi harshly criticized government policies in general and the latest initiatives in particular, and once again blamed the government for inflation, maintaining, "Such measures can only succeed with the cooperation of the guilds in the bazaar." [173] On the same day in *Resalat,* Sa'id Amani (the director of the Society of Islamic Guilds of Teheran's bazaar) also said that price control needed long-term planning and certainly the cooperation of the guilds. [174] On May 23, 1994, the government sponsored a bill in the Majlis that would severely punish overcharges. In objecting to the bill, Nateq-Nuri remarked, "The Majlis has always supported the fight with overchargers, but at this point it seems unnecessary and will not solve anything." [175] In an editorial in *Resalat,* Asghar-Owladi expressed similar beliefs: "We will solve nothing by controlling prices—the government, which controls 85 percent of the economy, must make the people in charge of buying and selling of goods." [176]

Rafsanjani did not retreat, however. In September 1994, the government placed the ministry of commerce in charge of further supervision and control of goods in the market and made it responsible for arresting and punishing hoarders. [177] The following month, Rafsanjani announced in a Friday prayer sermon:

> We are ready to fight profiteers and hoarders with the same resolution that we fought the war [with Iraq]. Historical injustices and violations take place within the environment of commerce, distribution, and exchange of goods. True social justice can be achieved here by combating these injustices, and the success of the second FYP is contingent upon supervision of the bazaar. I warn those who in one way or another are involved here [in the bazaar] to stop this path; we do not intend to agitate producers, wholesalers, and petty traders, but goods must be offered based on their true cost. . . . The administrators of distribution and those engaged in commerce should know that this is serious, and as the president I am personally behind it. [178]

Similar words were uttered a month later: "The battle against profiteering and price fixing will continue until the existence of an 'Islamic bazaar.' We will not retreat and believe that the amelioration of our economic system is not possible without adjustment of the bazaar." [179]

In the fall of 1994, the government announced that it had created a special committee made of up ministers from economics and finance, oil, industry, agriculture, and construction jihad. The tasks of the committee included supervision of the provision and distribution of essential goods for public factories, organizing and regulating distribution channels, providing sufficient funds for creating government-run chain stores for direct supply of goods to customers, controlling overpricing, and determining the fair prices of goods.[180] The goals of the new *Refah* (welfare) chain stores were "to provide and distribute goods that the public needs and do away with unnecessary middlemen and protect domestic producers and consumers."[181] The principle founders of *Refah* were the three banks, National, Commerce, and Export, plus the municipal government of Tehcran and the state-run insurance companies, *Alborz* and *Asia*. Speaking to the country's bank managers, Rafsanjani said, "There is still ample room for the banks to attract more money and provide more facilities for the people."[182]

The *Refah* initiative was a clever move on the part of the government and Rafsanjani. They realized that policies such as price control and price fixing would not be enough to do away with the well-entrenched system of the bazaar, so through the creation of the *Refah* chain stores, the government began competing with more traditional retail shops.[183] At the same time, the government decided to redirect the flow of capital from the bazaar system into public-sector bodies such as the banks, thus containing the financial livelihood and autonomy of the bazaar. In May 1994, the government announced all purchasing of all goods from abroad had to be registered and go through the banking system, as the banks would be exclusively in charge of all ordering, receiving, and custom clearance of the goods.[184] In October 1995, the Central Bank announced that buying and selling of foreign currency outside the banking system or authorized foreign exchange brokers were considered illegal.[185]

The conservatives responded in predictable fashion. According to the Society of Islamic Guilds of Teheran, the new *Refah* stores would severely hurt the traditional system of distribution of goods and cause economic hardship for many merchants and small shopkeepers.[186] Asgar-Owladi's editorial in *Resalat* labeled such sweeping roles for the banks in the economy as un-Islamic. "The banks in our holy system have become just as money hungry as those infidel banks in the previous regime," he said.[187] In another editorial, he said, "The unencumbered and self-centered ways in which the officials act is one of the main reasons why we have not completed various projects of the FYP."[188] Nateq-Nuri believed that the state should not be directly responsible for rendering social justice. Rather, he argued, "The best way to achieve social justice is to increase financial assistance to revolutionary *Nehads* such as the *Imdad* Committee [headed by Asghar-Owladi]."[189] On another occasion, Nateq-Nuri maintained that "efforts at price setting of goods will not do miracles because the country is overflowing with goods."[190] In an editorial entitled "A Self-Centered Administrator," Asghar-Owladi maintained, "In pure Mohammadi Islam, the administrator should not allow himself or the people around him to overlook religious rulings and act as if they had the mandate of a *faqih*." By reminding Rafsanjani that the leader was Khamenehi and not him, Asghar-Owladi implicitly suggested that such significant directives on the part of the state must have the backing of the leader.[191]

After examining the government's financial records, the state's Audit Office announced that a bloated public sector was the main cause of the increase in cash liquidity. State-run enterprises were purchasing goods at the government-discounted rate of foreign currency and selling them at market prices.[192] Such accusations led to the arrests of many government officials such as bank managers and those supervising state enterprises.[193] The Teheran municipal government also became a target for these arrests, and many officials close to the mayor were imprisoned for bribery and mismanagement of funds.[194]

Denouncing the cultural underpinning of *Towse-'eh,* the neo-fundamentalists joined the conservative right's attack on the modern right. By pointing out that Iranian culture is devoutly religious and traditional, and that the country's well-being depends on a traditional economy, an article in *Keyhan-Havai* maintained, "For the sake of economic dynamism, growth, and output, we should not undermine our traditional nationalist culture and economic system."[195] Mehdi Nasiri accused the government of lacking a clear plan for the Iranian economy.[196] The president was accused by *Sobh* of being the cause of the current economic predicament as it was he who has been championing the culture of consumerism and overindulgence.[197]

By 1995 the economic conditions had further deteriorated, but the government told people that it was their "national duty" to endure the current hard times for further prosperity.[198] However, as the next parliamentary election approached, the Majlis's attacks against the government intensified. The months of January through March witnessed some of the fiercest attacks by the Majlis against the government and its agencies. Ahmad (MP), the brother of Nateq-Nuri (speaker of the Majlis), voiced his strong opposition to businesses under government control that raised their prices frequently and said, "It is not acceptable that the president places all of his political capital on fighting price hikes and the economic mangers raise the prices of goods of state-run production output."[199] Another MP, Mohammad Ali Karimi, spoke about mushrooming bureaucratic corruption and said, "Clothed under the name of government, the enemies of Islam have contrived a complex economic policy to destroy the system."[200] Although they complained about price fixing, inflation, and economic terrorists, the Majlis refused to pass a bill put forward by the government that would have increased the punishment for those found guilty of economic wrongdoings.[201] According to Mohammad Reza Bahonar, "Such policies require lengthy studies and expert analysis.[202]

By this point, the relationship between the two rights was irreparable. The conservatives were not going to change their position and neither could Rafsanjani. The president had no option but to seek other alliances; by himself, he could not implement any of these policies, so he moved to the left. The left, recognizing the coming opportunity, watched the fight with pleasure.

Factionalism in the Sociocultural Sphere

Factionalism in this sphere must be viewed within the larger framework of factional politics. By the time of the appointment of a new minister of culture and Islamic guidance, the conservative Ali Larijani, the traditional right had decisively won the fourth parliamentary election. In their drive towards dominating the political scene, this faction rallied around the leader, gradually moving to isolate and weaken Rafsanjani and impair *Towse-'eh*. Khamenehi supported the conservatives and did his share to boost the position of this faction within the Iranian polity; the unseating of Rafsanjani's brother as the head of Iranian national radio and TV was a case in point. Until 1996, when he split from the conservatives and allied with the left, Rafsanjani had no alternative but to yield to the pressures of his old allies. As a result, during this period the Islamic Republic witnessed the systematic undoing of Khatami's agenda in the cultural sphere.

In July 1992 Rafsanjani introduced *Mo'talefeh* member Ali Larijani to replace Khatami as the head of the ministry of culture and guidance.[203] As expected, the new minister was enthusiastically received by the conservatives. Reza Taqavi praised Larijani's doctrinaire credentials, especially his "total obedience to the principle of *velayat-e faqih*."[204] Ali Movahhedi-Saveji thought that the new minister was well suited to rectify the un-Islamic policies of the previous minister of culture by, for example, preventing the publication of books that "promote secular and morally corrupting ideas in society." He had one more dig at Rafsanjani: "In setting the framework for cultural life in Iran, the ministry must take its general directives from the *foqaha,* particularly the esteemed leader."[205]

Larijani also received support from conservatives outside the Majlis. *Resalat* welcomed the replacement of the previous minister whose "liberal" policies provided "an umbrella for the march of the soldiers of the cultural onslaught in Iran."[206] A group of scholars from JMHEQ also acclaimed the new appointment and further emphasized that "assertion of the cultural guidelines of the country must be the task of the ulama and the religious seminaries."[207]

Immediately after his appointment by Khamenehi, Larijani presented himself as an open-minded person, maintaining that his ministry would respect pluralism of ideas and cultural diversity because "an open [cultural] environment will result in the flourishing of the society."[208] Larijani's tolerant tone, however, was replaced by conventional conservative discourse when he outlined the goals of his ministry before the Majlis nearly a month later. The main mission of his ministry, noted Larijani, would be to confront the Western cultural onslaught, whose decadent music, art, and clothes had permeated Iranian society.[209] To repel this onslaught, he added, "The foundation of our cultural policies must become holy Islamic learning."[210] Instead of making films with "colorful" and "superficial" contents, for example, Larijani believed that Iranian cinema must produce films that reflect true Islamic culture. In the area of filmmaking, Larijani noted, "We must leave the door open for the doctrinaires and the Hizbollahi filmmakers."[211] The main focus of Larijani's speech was to make certain that the views and policies of Khatami and his intellectual cronies were discredited:

> Recently, free thinking [azad-andishi] has been tantamount to inattention to religious values, to a degree where for the stray-minded pseudo-intellectuals, doubting the righteousness of the Islamicity of the government is progressiveness, and the belief in executing religious decrees and following Islamic ulama is a kind of petrifaction. I believe that such mechanisms will cause the beheading of freedom. The freedom that entails the sweet smell of charitable deeds and enlightenment should replace the foul swamp where the corrupt are nourished. True and praiseworthy freedom, which is the holy tradition, must be vivified. To surrender to the enemy's onslaught is not freedom; it is unpatriotic and irreligious.[212]

Larijani's speech in the Majlis also contained factionally pointed comments aimed mainly at questioning and undermining the president's efforts in this area while at the same time calling for more involvement for the conservative "establishment" and the leader. For example, Larijani remarked, "I believe that we have yet to create an Islamic cultural foundation for social relations in the country. The ulama, the Khobregan, and the Majlis must produce such a foundation and it must be part of the plans of the *Towse-'eh*." In a further indirect criticism of the more liberal-minded Rafsanjani, Larijani said, "I must admit that more than anyone, our great leader has realized the dangers of the cultural onslaught and has striven to elucidate and combat its adverse affects."[213]

Having set the stage for a new cultural life in Iran, and backed by Khamenehi, Larijani and the conservatives proceeded to implement their vision of proper Islamic culture. On November 22, 1992, Khamenehi's newly appointed conservative deputy of the HCCR, Mohammadi Golpayegani, presented a plan for combating the cultural onslaught. The HCCR was keen to emphasize that this plan must tackle various dimensions of the onslaught such as clothes, theater, films, and broadcasting. The council also directed the ministry to employ more doctrinaire staff, and they called upon the ministry to increase its "guiding" and "supervisory" roles in society. Finally, the council provided a more active role for the representatives of the *faqih* in the universities in order to buttress the revolutionary-religious spirit of university students.[214] Among the new objectives of the "Reappraised Goals and Duties of the HCCR" were the spread of Islamic culture in society, purification of cultural spheres in the country from Western culture, and the transformation of universities and cultural centers into venues for creating doctrinaire personnel.[215]

Larijani complied with these demands. Decree by decree, he directly involved institutional strongholds and members of the conservative camp in shaping sociocultural policies in Iran. In the name of defending and preserving the Islamicity of the regime, cultural activities in Iran were to be closely scrutinized and, if necessary, restricted. In December 1992, the ministry of culture made public some of its plans and declared that the government would inject more funds into the mosques and use these religious centers as primary cultural headquarters.[216] In February 1993, Larijani noted that more use should be made of mosques to enhance the religious knowledge and awareness of the population at large.[217] In April of the same year, the ministry of culture declared that mosques' trusteeships would be issuing permits for such things as printing and publishing houses and video clubs.[218] In September, the ministry announced that forty cultural centers would be erected in Teheran mosques to fight against the Western cultural blitz.[219] The ministry also promised to support doctrinaire filmmakers or those who made films that supported the revival of Islamic values in the country.[220] Disapproving of banal popular music that was produced in Iran, Larijani ordered the cancellation of those music classes that promoted such music.[221]

Larijani defended and justified the ideological underpinning of his ministry's actions, criticizing at the same time the Western culture and its so-called liberal tenets. According to Larijani, more restrictive policies were justified because "if we in the Islamic Republic restrain freedom it is because our Islamic line of thinking has in mind the well-being of the society."[222] "Freedom," in the words of Larijani, "must be a tool for achieving spiritual growth in society and not the cause for its downfall."[223] Thus, according to Larijani, if by printing improper material a magazine or a newspaper misused this freedom and surrendered to the cultural onslaught, "it should not expect support or leniency from the ministry."[224] On another occasion he noted, "The mere existence of democracy and freedom does not mean that a culture is praiseworthy."[225] Speaking at the fourth conference of information ministers of nonallied nations in June 1993, he remarked, "Under the pretext of cultural, political, and economic liberalism, and based on their limited and politically motivated views, the planners of the New World Order aim to eradicate religious values, tradition, culture, and the civilization of the South, and destroy cultural diversity around the world."[226]

The words and actions of the ministry of culture were supported by prominent conservatives. Nateq-Nuri also believed, "The doctrinaire forces must be called to confront the cultural onslaught of the enemy, whose primary aim is to separate the younger generation from the religion of the Imam and revolutionary values."[227] In a letter to Khamenehi, the JMHEQ announced its readiness to cooperate with the new minister. Ayatollah Fazel Lankarani, secretary of the JMHEQ, applauded the activities of the ministry of culture and the manner in which Larijani aimed to cleanse the culture in the Islamic Republic.[228]

One important consequence of the conservatives' hold on the policymaking machinery of sociocultural life in Iran was that, in emphasizing the need to preserve the Islamicity of the regime and the religious dimension of the Iranian state, this faction began championing the concept of PVPV and its associated discourse as a means for achieving this faction's political objectives. To be sure, reliance on the unassailable notion of PVPV was the most effective way that the conservative right could challenge what it perceived to be the liberal views of both the left and Rafsanjani. In their endeavor to promote PVPV, the *Basij* became the physical arm of the conservative right. First, however, in order for the *Basijis* to be legally engaged in forcefully imposing proper Islamic culture, they needed to be formally recognized. Thus, in November 1992, the Majlis passed the "Law of Legal Protection for the *Basijis*" aimed at "empowering the *Basij* to assist the Law Enforcement Forces in fighting crimes in the country." According to this law, "Like the agents of the Law Enforcement Forces, if witnessing a crime the *Basij* would be entitled to undertake appropriate measures such as arresting the criminals and delivering them to proper authorities."[229] Thus, the increasing role of the *Basij*-mosque axis, blessed by Khamenehi, became an important sociopolitical lever for the conservatives.

The conservatives strongly advocated the need to involve the *Basij* in enforcing proper morality in the country. By pointing out that the passage of this bill was the wish of Khamenehi himself, conservatives such as Mohammad Ali Movahhedi-Kermani, the representative of the *vali-ye faqih* in the Center for

Mosque Affairs, maintained, "The presence and propagatory role of the doctrinaires and those who are the rightful and loyal forces of the regime is necessary to combat individuals who are disrespecting Islamic decrees."[230] Mahdavi-Kani emphasized, "The *Basijis* must be the guardians of the revolution's policies and its true values and the vehicle for implementing the policies sketched by the leader."[231] As expected, the *Basijis* went beyond turning in moral offenders. Newspapers reported that young *Basijis* had cruelly arrested and taken to their headquarters mostly young cultural and moral offenders for reasons ranging from improper veiling to "cultural unfetteredness."[232] In their defense, the commander of the *Basij* maintained that they should be considered official government agents and claimed, "As the pivot of combating cultural onslaught, the *Basijis,* through executing PVPV, must carry out Islamic rules."[233]

Here too, what further bolstered the actions of Larijani and the puritan discourse of the conservatives was the support of the leader himself. To be sure, Khamenehi had gradually shifted his earlier moderate tone in the sociocultural sphere, and he began speaking in line with the conservatives, championing the cause of cultural purification in Islamic Iran. Thus, he often emphasized the need to preserve and protect the Islamicity of the regime, even if this meant imposing restrictions. "In an Islamic society," pronounced Khamenehi, "arts must be in line with Islamic principles and deviation of any kind is not acceptable." Supporting the more restrictive policies of the ministry of culture, he added, "there must be freedom but this does not mean that we allow the operation of the kind of press that executes the plans of the enemy within the country."[234] On issues of women, Khamenehi noted, "Islam approves of women working, but this should not interfere with their primary role as mothers and caretakers of the family."[235] Khamenehi also assisted the conservatives' moral crusade by appointing prominent conservatives to key positions. In September 1993, for example, he selected a prominent *Mo'talefeh* member, Mostafa Mir-Salim, as the secretary of the HCCR.[236] Perhaps the most consequential decision of Khamenehi in this regard, however, was to buttress the power and authority of the ultra-conservative Ayatollah Ahmad Jannati in the sociocultural realm.

In March 1992, Khamenehi appointed Jannati as Teheran's Friday prayer imam.[237] In return, Jannati used this important public position as a powerful mouthpiece for the conservatives' cause. A standard sermon of Jannati reaffirmed the need for the Hizbollahis to be active in the sociocultural scene in

Iran, as "it is they who are the true guardians of Islam."[238] In June 1993, Khamenehi further boosted the power of Jannati by selecting him to form the Headquarters for the Vivification of PVPV (*Setad-e Ihya-ye Amr-e be Ma'ruf va Nah-ye az Monkar,* hereafter *Setad*).[239] As the title of the body indicates, the conservatives believed the PVPV had been neglected and needed rejuvenating. By August, Jannati announced that the *Setad,* whose recruits were nearly all young *Basijis,* would instigate a nationwide effort to enforce proper Islamic culture at the behest of the leader. Essentially, this meant "unleashing" the *Basijis* as the moral soldiers of the Islamic Republic, more specifically the conservative right faction. Knowing very well that the actions of the *Setad* and the *Basijis* would challenge the jurisdiction of the Law Enforcement Forces, Jannati noted, "We do not want to weaken the government, but people must refrain from un-Islamic behavior. To ensure this, the *Basij* and the Law Enforcement Forces must be actively involved."[240] In support of the *Setad* and its moral mission, Khamenehi proclaimed, "The impact of PVPV in an Islamic society is more powerful even than jihad."[241] Unlike Rafsanjani, who believed that after accomplishing their task in the war the *Basijis* should engage in construction efforts to rebuild the country,[242] Khamenehi perceived the role of the *Basijis* to be "present in all public spheres particularly to protect revolutionary-Islamic values."[243]

The conservative right were concerned that the universities, where the left via *Tahkim* enjoyed much support among the students, could potentially challenge their purification efforts. Consequently, Khamenehi initiated a crusade aimed at purging the universities of un-Islamic influences. The stage for the Islamization of higher education, however, needed to be justified. First and foremost, this meant increasing the role of the representatives of the *faqih*. A proclamation issued in April 1992 by the office of representatives of the *faqih* in universities warned against increased moral and religious laxity in the universities and called for the mobilization of all university and seminary students to fight this rising danger. By implicitly referring to the left and their supporters in universities, the proclamation said, "By promoting concepts such as 'enlightenment' and 'logic,' those defeated in the political scene are poisoning the environment of the universities."[244] Therefore, Jannati said that the representatives of the *faqih* must be more involved in the affairs of the universities. Again, having in mind more control over the leftist *Tahkim,* he said, "Student associations must be under the supervision of the clergy, otherwise their Islamicity cannot be verified."[245] The leader also uttered his disapproval of the weakening of the Islamic spirit in universities and emphasized the need to replace the "ambivalent" mentality of the intellectuals with that of "revolutionary-*Basij*" spirit.[246] In November 1992, Khamenehi ordered the implementation of "The Plan of Submission to Thy Khomeini" throughout the universities in Iran. The plan was aimed to "organize and direct Hizbollahi cells in universities in order to carry out PVPV."[247]

Such schemes and the use of *Basijis* to enforce proper Islamic culture were backed by prominent conservatives like Nateq-Nuri and Ayatollah Abolqasem Khazali, who both believed that such endeavors were necessary to protect higher education from the increasing dangers of cultural and moral decay.[248] In addition, Larijani and other officials from the ministry of culture reiterated the need to use the *Basijis* to enforce Islamic morality in the country, and they began to promote the idea that the proper culture in Iran was that of the *Basij*.[249] In October 1993, "in order to spread revolutionary values," the ministry of culture announced it was going to expand and coordinate its activities with the *Basij*.[250] In short, by the end of 1993, the conservatives, backed by Khamenehi, had orchestrated a well-coordinated effort to turn back the clock of cultural life in Iran. In this endeavor the conservative right could anticipate much support from the ministry of culture and other conservative-dominated centers of power such as the ministry of state (Ali Besharati) and IRGC (Mohsen Rezai). Besharati and Rezai repeatedly praised the activities of Larijani, announcing their readiness to collaborate with the ministry of culture.[251] The conservatives' cultural crusade was further advanced by two additional key appointments by Khamenehi.

As noted, aside from opposing the liberal policies of Khatami, the conservative right also opposed the programs aired by national radio and TV in Iran. Their criticism of Rafsanjani's brother continued in this period and ultimately resulted in his "resignation." In September 1993, a group of MPs led by Ali Akbar Parvaresh began criticizing national radio and TV programs and issued a report on their un-Islamic content, citing Western movies and music. In response, the Majlis passed a bill to investigate the national radio and TV and inspect the following: whether revolutionary and Hizbollahi forces were employed by these public bodies; if their programs were in line with the shari'a;

and to ascertain if radio and TV were spreading Western culture among the population and corrupting the minds of the youth.[252] The result of the investigation was read in the Majlis a month later and contained the following observations. The investigative committee believed that the programs were neither revolutionary nor Islamically inclined but the contents were often neutral. In addition, the committee believed that the majority of films shown on Iranian TV were foreign films that were not only offensive to but indirectly mocked the Islamic values and culture. In addition, the employees of both organizations were not true Hizbollahis. In fact, one of the committee's complaints was that both radio and TV employed too many women. Finally, the committee found the financial records of both bodies full of improper usage of funds.[253]

In incriminating Hashemi, the biggest difficulty faced by the Majlis was that the Imam, prior to his death, had personally approved and in fact praised the conduct of Hashemi and the programs in radio and TV. This problem, however, was rectified when the conservatives found another declaration made by Khomeini. Mohammad Reza Bahonar stated, "The Imam in his will has said that officials should not misuse his support for them. . . . Thus, if the actions of some people were at one time approved by the Imam, this does not give them life-time insurance." [254] Bahonar continued, "Many of our people and organizations such as the JRM, the Society of Islamic Engineers, the Society for Islamic Culture, the Zeynab society, the Society of Islamic Guilds of Teheran, the representatives of *vali-ye faqih* in the universities and the *Basij,* have all condemned the actions and words of Mr. Hashemi." Nateq-Nuri claimed that the leader was displeased with the actions of Hashemi and gave the Majlis the prerogative to undertake the necessary actions.[255]

In response, Mohammad Hashemi scorned the MPs for playing factional politics, and in fact accused one of the MPs of being connected to the outlawed *Mojahedin-e Khalq.*[256] Hashemi's retaliation greatly antagonized the conservatives. Nateq-Nuri announced that he had met with the leader and had received his support and was told by him that the Majlis was entitled to take necessary measures against improper actions of any government ministry.[257] Later, when Hashemi resigned, Khamenehi replaced Hashemi with Larijani.[258]

In sociocultural issues, Larijani's replacement, Mostafa Mir-Salim, was even more puritan than his predecessor. In the ministry of culture, Mir-Salim was perceived as a truly socially rigid individual, although highly respected for his honesty.[259] Mir-Salim spent many years in France and received a masters degree in mechanical engineering from the Oil University in Paris; since the victory of the revolution he has held key positions in the Islamic Republic.[260] The new minister was quick to pronounce his own devout religious and parochial views, signaling at the same time that he would continue the work of Larijani. He also believed that "the only way to confront the cultural onslaught is to enliven the true holy trenches, the mosques."[261] "The ministry of culture," maintained Mir-Salim, "will support only those films that deal with topics such as the holy war [with Iraq] and the cultural onslaught."[262] In February 1995, Mir-Salim announced that his ministry would support Qoranic scholars.[263]

Mir-Salim was incited by the conservatives to "cleanse" the press in Iran. Immediately after his appointment, the conservatives expected the new minister to support doctrinaire men of pen and restrict the activities of those without such qualifications. In a lengthy editorial, *Resalat* proposed that the ministry of culture reevaluate the existing press law. The editorial argued, "Under the slogan of freedom of thought and expression, and without any restrictions, some secular-minded intellectuals are parading in Iran." The editorial argued, "The existing press law contains clauses that deal with those who insult individuals and addresses their legal rights, but what if someone insults the religious convictions of people?"[264] Mir-Salim bowed to such demands, and indeed the hallmark of his tenure as minister was the ministry of culture's efforts to curtail freedom of the press in the Islamic Republic by supporting those whom the ministry considered to hold devout religious sentiments and restricting the publication of those with stray thoughts. Thus, Mir-Salim made it clear that he would protect and support publications that "exhibit and spread the *Basiji* culture."[265] In September 1994, the ministry of culture disclosed that publishing permission would be furnished only to those with religious-nationalist qualifications.[266] "Journalists," argued Mir-Salim, "must possess morality and religious beliefs."[267] Mir-Salim's deputy, Ash'ari, believed that only those who exhibited proper moral credentials should enter the world of the press. He further added that if the ministry restricted press freedom, it was because "we want to prevent people from falling into a well."[268] According to Mir-Salim, restrictions and limitations prevent ideological corruption/decay. Moreover, he believed, "Journalism is not a profession. Rather, it must be perceived as an ideological mission aimed at confronting the cultural onslaught."[269]

A trademark of Mir-Salim's tenure as minister therefore became the closure of "improper" papers and journals. The weekly *Havades* was accused of publishing demagogic and superficial stories and its publishing permit revoked.[270] In February 1995, the press supervisory committee ordered *Jahan-e Islam* to be closed. The daily was accused of printing materials that were both "disquieting to the public mind" as well as being disrespectful to the leadership.[271] The paper had published an interview with Ali Akbar Mohtashami, powerful member of the MRM, in which he was critical of both Rafsanjani and Khamenehi.[272] When Abbas Abdi, the editor of *Salam,* began publishing his memoirs, he was arrested, tried secretly, and imprisoned for one year. The memoirs were too "revealing" about politics and personalities in Iran.[273] The doors of other papers such as *Gardun, Bahman, Payam-e Daneshju,* and *Aineh-ye Andisheh* were closed under similar pretexts.[274]

Both ministers of culture defended the actions of the ministry. After the Hizbollahis physically attacked the bi-monthly *Kiyan* for printing articles by Soroush (a "liberal" thinker, highly critical of the regime), Larijani defended their acts: "The press should not write materials that aggrieve the Hizbollahis."[275] Morteza Nabavi also implicitly supported the behavior of Hizbollahis by suggesting that "the liberal press mocked the Islamic culture in Iran."[276] Finally, in one of his most controversial comments, Mir-Salim said, "Under the press law, there is freedom of the press. But some do not have the necessary discernment [*sho'ur*] to know what to do with this freedom or how far to go with it."[277]

The policies of the ministry of culture were greatly resented by the opponents of the conservative right faction. The MRM stressed, "Confronting the cultural onslaught cannot be achieved by force through authoritarian measures."[278] According to a *Salam* editorial, the words and actions of the ministry were part of larger political plot of a "certain faction" to monopolize power in Iran and impose its views, "particularly now that the three bodies responsible for cultural policies in Iran [the ministries of culture and radio and TV, and the Organization for Islamic Propagation headed by Jannati] are under its control." "Thus," the editorial continued, "the rhetoric of 'cultural onslaught' is no more than a ploy to discredit the actions of Khatami and turn back the clock of cultural life in Iran."[279] The president joined the group willing to criticize the current sociocultural policies in Iran. Speaking to officials from the ministry of culture, Rafsanjani said, "We must not show contempt towards our writers and scholars as they must feel secure and write their views freely. . . . If they cannot [write freely], they had better not write at all." [280] On another occasion Rafsanjani said, "Preventing the press to publish the truth will not solve the country's cultural problems." [281]

Mir-Salim, however, did not yield to pressure. For instance, in June 1995, 214 members of the film industry wrote a letter to Mir-Salim strongly objecting to the skewed policies of the ministry of culture. The signatories requested the lifting of the "restrictive and surveillance like" attitude of the ministry. [282] In response, the ministry of culture defended its methods by once again claiming that supervision and restriction in an Islamic society were necessary and virtuous. Rebuffing the accusations of the "liberal" artists, Mir-Salim maintained that "cultural policies in Iran are based on Qoranic principles and the wishes of the people." [283] Khamenehi also showed contempt for the films praised in some quarters when he said, "It does not impress me if we win foreign awards because these films often have dubious agendas." [284] In a two-part interview with the daily *Keyhan,* Khakbbazan, Mir-Salim's deputy, further vindicated such views. His comments on the proper nature of Iranian cinema captured the restrictive-puritan essence of the sociocultural inclination of the conservative right:

> Supervision is based on the values and goals of the system and in fact is a watchful eye of our ideological regime. The purpose behind supervision is the implementation of revolutionary aspirations of the people. . . . We expect Iranian cinema to be the most chaste cinema in the world, and chastity must be observed everywhere, in dialogue, glances [between actors and actresses], and interaction in front of as well as behind the scenes. . . . We shall deal harshly with those who liken religiousness with patriarchy and tradition. [285]

Factionalism over Foreign Policy

Aside from the few incidents mentioned below, factionalism in foreign policy during this period was by and large unexpressed, given that neither of the two rightist factions in control of the foreign policy machinery sought adventurism on the international stage. After its failure to reradicalize the Islamic Republic during the Gulf War, and because of its absence from major centers of power, less radicalism was displayed by the left as well. This was also due to the fact that by 1994 the left had moderated its views. Thus, Foreign Minister Ali Akbar Velayati was correct when he observed, "With regards to foreign policy, there is not a great deal of difference of opinion among the domestic forces." [286] To be sure, when it came to foreign policy, factions had reached an impasse as they were aware that the Islamic Republic must come out of isolation. In this respect, relations with the United States remained the biggest symbolic obstacle: the few bursts of factionalism in this sphere revolved around United States–Iran relations, as this debate remained the most controversial issue of Iranian foreign policy. The growing discord between the two rights affected this issue as well. Instead of the left, it was now the conservatives who pestered Rafsanjani every time he made accommodating remarks to the Americans. As far as the conservatives were concerned, better relations with the United States signified the return of former citizens and possibly prerevolutionary industrialists, Western cultural infiltration, more industrialization, and the demise of the commercial bourgeoisie.

During this period, Rafsanjani continued to make conciliatory gestures to the Americans. For example, in a June 1994 interview with reporters, he said:

> I have always been opposed to completely breaking our ties with the United States. They provide us with much needed spare parts and we sell them petrol. Therefore, our economic ties have never been completely halted and some kind of dialogue must always exist. Although we pursue pragmatism in foreign policy, we will not be the first to initiate further dialogue with the Americans. They must first show good will by unfreezing our assets in America. [287]

Close associates of Rafsanjani went even further, however, and made proposals that perhaps Rafsanjani could not make publicly. For economic reasons, Hossein Mar'ashi, a close aid to Rafsanjani, believed in direct negotiations and even full diplomatic relations with the United States. [288] It was another accomplice of Rafsanjani who instigated the most heated incident of factionalism during this period. In October 1993, Majlis MPs were appalled that Sa'id Rajai-Khorasani, Iran's former representative to the UN, had privately submitted a letter to Khamenehi in which he suggested the need to reestablish ties with the

United States. MP Mohammad Qomi used the opportunity not only to denounce the idea of rapprochement with the United States but to attack the modern right in general and the fact that they were not following the wishes of the Imam or Khamenehi: "Although the liberals such as the followers of Freedom Movement are marginalized, there are people who, under the pretext of the need to aid the reconstruction phase, foreign borrowing, pragmatism, and rationality, are considering the repugnant idea of relations with the Great Satan. . . . They must be mindful that obedience to the leader must be in action and not simply lip service."[289] In support of Qomi, Nateq-Nuri further remarked, "We obey the leader who is adamantly opposed to better relations with the United States."[290] A few days later, Khamenehi declared, "Relations with the United States at this stage are neither possible nor beneficial [for the country]. They [Americans] have yet to show a genuine change in their position towards Iran."[291] Some members of the conservative camp, however, were far more vociferous on this issue. Abolqasem Rezai said, "Our confrontation with the United States is unavoidable, and everything will be decided in this battle. . . . The United States has not stopped its treacheries, and we have not given them our last word."[292]

Although the conservatives publicly maintained an uncompromising position on this issue, as evident in the actions of its members and the discourse of the Iranian foreign ministry, their opposition was another case of factional theatrics aimed at weakening Rafsanjani. For example, with regard to the Rushdie question, Foreign Minister Velayati said, "The fatwa is one thing and sending a group to kill Rushdie is another. . . . Our government will not send anyone to England or anywhere else [to kill him]."[293] Another example of the conservatives' quietism in this sphere came in 1993 on the anniversary of the hostage taking at the American embassy. In the Majlis, Ilias Hazrati complained to the minister of state about not allowing students from *Tahkim* to organize an anti-American rally at Teheran University.[294] In response, Besharati supported the ministry of state's decision, objecting to the fact that *Tahkim* refused to join the ceremony organized by the ministry for this occasion.[295] The truth was that the ministry was not inclined to see the students from *Tahkim* organizing a fervent ceremony. This became evident when Besharati said that the ceremony sponsored by the ministry was a "well-behaved gathering of no more than one thousand Hizbollahis."[296]

The Fifth Parliamentary Election of 1996

By 1995, factions and factionalism had entered a new stage. Although in theory the two rights were still in alliance, given the rising tension between Rafsanjani and the conservatives, there were no real alliances among factions at that time. The conservative right had successfully isolated the left, entangled the modern right, and, given the institutional predominance of the conservatives bolstered by Khamenehi's backing, they seemed destined to monopolize power. By forming an alliance with the left in the fifth Majlis, however, Rafsanjani once again dictated the power configuration in the Islamic Republic.

Although technically on the opposite sides of the factional spectrum, the modern right and the left always shared a common ideological base such as the belief in more political freedom and moderation in the sociocultural sphere. In addition, ever since the victory of the revolution, when it came to the economic realm, both factions espoused a modern industrial economy. The left stressed state-initiated industrialization and the modern right was keen on the participation of the private sector, but there was enough concordance that Rafsanjani could support left-sponsored measures during the first decade of the revolution and the third Majlis vote for Rafsanjani's FFYP. In other words, the possibility of alliance was, as Behzad Nabavi himself noted when classifying factions a year before the fifth election, always conceivable: "There are major similarities between the modern right and left; they both believe in rule of law and sociopolitical freedom. . . . Although there are differences of opinion [on other issues], such common factors are extremely important." Nabavi also disclosed the possibility of a future alliance between the two factions when he revealed that many members of the modern right who had once belonged to the left were contemplating the possibility of a common platform with the left for the coming election.[297]

Aside from ideological similarities, by 1994 three other factors had brought the two factions closer: less radicalism on the part of the left, more statism from the modern right, and the newly developed shared interest in confronting the onslaught of the conservative right—or what *Asr-e Ma* labeled the "traditional right's monopolistic onslaught." The MII believed all factions must join forces and prevent what the organization thought would be a calamity not only for the factions but for the entire system.[298] Less ideological radicalism and more pragmatism were exhibited by both the MRM and MII, which implicitly meant the vindication of Rafsanjani's policies. The MRM, for example, began suggesting that it was time for the leadership to refrain from extremism and zealous revolutionary demeanor.[299] The MII's first proclamation about the fifth election gave its approval of the direction of the economy. Significantly also, in line with the economic course espoused by Rafsanjani, the MII maintained that it accepted the economic participation of the private sector though not, however, its domination.[300] In another proclamation, the MII maintained, "For the sake of the self-sufficiency and independence of the country, we believe in the need for a 'productive' private sector."[301] The left also became less critical of Rafsanjani. On the eve of the fifth election, for instance, Mohammad Salamati noted, "Although we are against the economic policies of adjustment, we hold Mr. Rafsanjani to be a constructive individual for the system and the revolution."[302]

What perhaps still divided the left and the modern right was relations with the United States, although many members of the left had softened their views on this issue as well. A telling example was a June 1994 *Jahan-e Islam* editorial that called upon the leaders to reconsider their policy towards the United States:"Iran cannot live in an [international] vacuum and be oblivious to the realities of the world." The editorial also asked for "all anti-US slogans to be dropped."[303] Even the MII showed signs of moderation in its attitudes in foreign policy by accepting the necessity of conditional links to international organizations such as World Bank:"We believe that if the interests of the country are preserved, presence in world organizations could be a beneficial and positive development."[304] In short, due to the anti-bazaari, statist measures of Rafsanjani after 1992, combined with less radicalism exhibited on the part of the left, by 1995 the left had become moderate more and the modern right less conservative, making some kind of coalition not only feasible but indeed necessary for the survival of both factions.

For the modern right, the best political campaign for the coming election was boasting about the achievements of the first FYP and its commander in chief, Rafsanjani. The president paid numerous visits to different parts of the country and flaunted the realization of various projects of *Towse-'eh*. On one occasion, he said, "The conditions of people's lives has really changed, and everywhere I go, I see more contentment and satisfaction, all due to the FYP that dramatically changed the face of the country."[305] The front pages of the two pro-Rafsanjani dailies, *Hamshahri* and *Iran* often displayed the majestic looking Rafsanjani at the beginning of various developmental projects. At the same time, the two papers condemned those who disparaged the postwar economic development in Iran. One editorial in *Iran* suggested that the people were appreciative of the advances made in the country and that they held realistic expectations from their leaders. By comparing Rafsanjani to Mirzataqi Khan, the editorial noted, "All great men in Iranian history have faced opposition from those who put their own interests before those of the country."[306]

Aside from espousing concepts such as individual freedom and civil society (noted in chapter 3), to push through its modernist views against its old allies, including Khamenehi, the modern right initiated a calculated scheme aimed at subjugating the religious dimension of the regime to its republicanism. This entailed constructing a more dynamic interpretation of Islam and questioning the absolutist reading of *velayat-e faqih*. For example, in June 1996, *Iran* published a two-part article entitled "The Meaning of Society According to Imam" in which the writer compared Khomeini with Durkhiem and Marx and argued, "While the Imam was a highly religious person, he upheld a modern democratic vision of the Islamic Republic." Quoting from various writings and proclamations of Khomeini, the article concluded that the Imam believed that "in a true Islamic society modern ideas coexist with traditional values."[307] With regards to the religiousness–republicanism rumpus, the most controversial piece published in the Iranian press was an interview with Mehdi Haeri-Yazdi in *Hamshahri* on Islamic government, where he explicitly rejected the underlying tenets of Khomeini's *velayat-e faqih,* or at least its *Motlaqeh* version: "Governance [*hokumat*] is no more than deputyship [*vekalat*] and any time you feel that your deputy has committed treachery, you replace him. . . . The kind of true democratic Islamic government that I construe is deputyship. . . . After the *Hijra* of the Prophet from Mecca to Madina, the people of Madia 'elected' him as the head of the state."[308]

The interview sparked heated debates among factions. *Resalat* vociferously expressed its astonishment at how the mayor of Teheran was allowed to campaign for the anti-Imam political forces.[309] The next day, an editorial in *Resalat* maintained, "The idea that an Islamic government is tantamount to true democracy and that true democracy means deputyship [of the *faqih*], is nothing more than political liberalism."[310] Even before the publication of Haeri's interview, *Asr-e Ma* had implicitly questioned the underlying justification of the *Motlaqeh* reading by the conservatives, criticizing their lack of commitment to people's democratic rights.[311] The op-ed section of *Salam* supported Harei's views and stressed that the writer of the *Resalat* editorial "has [mistakenly] construed the *velayat-e faqih* to be an undisputed part of our religion. . . . Among the Shii clergy, this [the topic of *velayat-e faqih*] has been the subject of debates."[312] The clergy of the JMHEQ naturally could not remain silent in the ongoing debate. Mohammad Imami-Kashani said, "The clergy are the 'specialists' of Islam, and Islam minus its specialists and its brain will result in perversion."[313] According to Hossein Rasti-Kashani, "Those who are trying to omit religion from the political scene are determined to bring back Western culture and influence."[314] *Salam,* responded that it was widespread corruption among the clergy that had resulted in the spread of such controversial ideas and that "the decision for the presence or absence of the *clergy* in the scene is the people's."[315]

The emergence into the public eye of this controversial debate was significant for two reasons. First, it broke perhaps the biggest taboo in the Islamic Republic and set the stage for future deliberations on the topic of the *velayat-e faqih*. Second, the left and the modern right had arrived at another understanding, this time on the most fundamental principle of the regime. And the declared position of the left on this issue was another case of a faction manipulating the dimensions of the regime based on the political realities of the time. As Mohammad Javad Larijani observed:

> When the Imam was alive, the left accepted *velayat-e faqih* as the principle of the regime. In fact, they confronted anything and anyone who questioned this principle. After the passing of the Imam, however, this belief began to slowly change, and they began advancing discussions of "sovereignty from below" and "sovereignty from the top." As if the principle of *velayat-e faqih* was gone with the Imam; but *velayat-e faqih* is a permanent political edifice of our regime. . . . Among our friends from the left, there is a group that completely

set aside this principle, and they may even believe that a liberal or secular state is preferable.[316]

Thus, as far as the conservative right was concerned, there was only one distinguishing ideological line of demarcation among the factions running for the election: for and against *velayat-e faqih*. According to an article in JRM's confidential bulletin, "A Look at the Active Political Current in the Election," there were two currents running for the election, "one comprising those in line with *velayat* and those outside this line. The second current was said to be made up of members of the old left and the liberals [Rafsanjanites], neither of which believe in the religiousness of the regime or the presence of the clergy." The article also suggested that already an implicit alliance between the anti-*velayat* forces had been established, and the creed of this alliance included disbelief in religious rule, an inclination towards Western political theories, doubting the *velayat-e motlaqeh-ye faqih*, and opposition to an active clerical role in the system.[317] Labeling them as anti-*velayat* became the cornerstone of the conservative right's negative campaign strategy against the two rival factions.

An example of the conservatives' assault against the left was a four-part editorial in *Resalat* in the summer of 1995. The first editorial once again questioned the religious convictions of the left and implicitly suggested that due to its devout religious tenets, the conservative right was the rightful heir of the Islamic revolution: "Our revolution is a holy phenomenon. If there is a reward [in this revolution], it belongs to the most religious and those who obey Gods laws."[318] Asserting that the result of the fourth election clearly showed that the views of the traditional right are those of the people, the second editorial said that by opposing the conservative right, the left was opposing the will of the people.[319] In a similar vein, the next day's editorial suggested that any opposition to the Guardian Council and its extensive supervisory powers was a disregard for the position of the *faqih,* who strongly believed in the uprightness of the council.[320] In the July 2 editorial, *Resalat* not only called *Asr-e Ma* an "antirevolutionary publication," but it disputed the left's claim that it was in favor of democracy. In reference to the Musavi years and figures such as Azari-Qomi, this editorial reminded the left, "During your reign [of the Majlis], you did not allow prominent ulama, whose duty is to express their opinion on issues, to utter a word in opposition to you."[321] In the editorial entitled "The Sovereignty of the People," the conservatives defended their new discourse of economic populism and castigated the statist views of the left as tantamount to ignoring the rights of the people to make their own decisions.[322]

In February 1995, the JRM issued a proclamation entitled "An Analysis of the Current Situation of the Islamic Revolution." It indicated the end of the alliance of the two rights:

> From the point of view of the people, those who are not in accord with the guidance of the leader are not qualified for important posts. Those who do not have a clear position with regard to the United States and because of their dereliction when it comes to a sworn enemy of Islam must know that their views are not in line with the leader or the Imam; thus they cannot have a rightful influence on the political stage in the country. . . . *Towse-'eh* is only possible by preserving religious values and those who seek *Towse-'eh* without the moral scope are writing a liberal prescription for the country. . . . The pragmatism seen in government organizations is neither religiously based nor legal. No interest is greater than the preservation of holy values.[323]

In the autumn, the conservatives began their political campaign for the coming election. Nateq-Nuri, who after the resignation of Mahdavi-Kani became the most prominent public figure of the JRM, asked people not to vote for "those who speak about the separation of religion and politics because their proposed model of government is a Western-style political system. You should know that Islam without the clergy means an American brand of Islam."[324] In November 1995, *Mo'talefeh* published its own memorandum on the election in which Asgar-Owladi, Badamchian, and Bahonar declared the organization's allegiance to JRM in the coming election. The memorandum was also marked by antiliberal sentiments: "The murmur of many kinds against religion, *velayat-e faqih,* and the clergy are heard from the enemy and world arrogance. This is a new commotion instigated by the liberals. The people must be vigilant and keep in mind the guides of the just *faqih.*"[325] In February 1996, the Society of Islamic Engineers (JIM) also deplored the liberals and announced its support for the candidates of the JRM.[326] Other JRM satellites such as the Zeynab Society, the Teheran's Preachers Society, and the Society for Islamic Guilds of

Teheran had harsh words against those who wanted to separate religion from politics and announced their support for the JRM in the coming election.[327] The *Ansar-e Hizbollah* issued their own election memorandum on the eve of the first round of voting. The *Ansar* asked the Guardian Council to prevent the election of lackeys of world arrogance, technocrats, and liberals. They believed that the most qualified candidates are those who categorically support the *velayat-e faqih,* are at the service of the disinherited, and do not think about reaching the "the gates of great civilization" before achieving in social justice.[328] Finally, the conservative right began warning the public about the possible alliance of liberals as Morteza Nabavi did in interview with Nasiri of *Sobh:*

> The previously radical left now has liberal tendencies. . . . Together with the modern right they do not place emphasis on *velayat-e faqih,* rather, their ideal [regime] is a Western one. From the definition of freedom to the basis of regime legitimacy to cultural matters, they think like the liberals and explicitly believe that you cannot govern and progress through Islam. . . . In opposition to religious orthodoxy, the two have common positions. Where we differ from them is that what for us constitutes the foundation for the legitimacy of the regime is doubtful for them. . . . At the end, the left and modern right will intersect and the new left and traditional right will remain orthodox.[329]

This interview was also significant as it unveiled a new development taking place within the conservative camp, a development that had ramifications far beyond the upcoming election. When talking about the views of the conservatives at this juncture, Nabavi remarked, "I admit that at that time [the early days of the revolution] we felt that we could manage the society based on primary ordinances. This was wrong. With the door-opening rulings of the Imam with regards to *velayat-e faqih,* we corrected our views and now we believe that in running the country, the government should be authorized to have 100 percent authority and power."[330] These words were indicative of the emergence of a group within the conservative right who believed in politicization of the clerical wing of this faction, espousing their direct political rule.

The new discourse was aimed at providing a justification for victory in the coming election and the future presidency of Nateq-Nuri, thus ensuring monopolization of political power in Iran by the conservative right. The latest overture was opposed by many in the faction, as exhibited by the resignation of Mahdavi-Kani and Azari-Qomi. In the summer of 1995, the former announced his resignation from the speakership of the JRM.[331] He attributed his resignation to his opposition to the politicization of the clergy in the JMR, noting, "The clergy have always been like a father to all people and thus should not establish an organization that accepts the membership of some while it rejects those of others." In a statement that suggests why the Shii establishment had previously opposed direct political rule by the clergy, he said, "Do not create a situation where the clergy would require permission from the ministry of the state for their activities."[332] A few months later, Azari-Qomi abandoned his post in *Resalat,* claiming that he was being barred from writing in the newspaper by the likes of Asgar-Owladi who supported the latest change in the ideological direction of this faction. Azari-Qomi said he had been told, "You are well-versed in religious matters and are entitled to issue opinions on that realm, but we are more acquainted with political and economic questions, so it is us who must write in the paper."[333]

To make their ascendancy a fait accompli, the most insolent effort made by the conservatives was once again to exploit the discretionary powers of the Guardian Council. In the summer of 1995, the Majlis passed a bill that further extended the supervisory powers of the council over elections. The new bill expanded the powers of the council to be "unequivocal throughout the duration of the election and with regards to all matters."[334] While the conservatives once again backed such measures by referring to the Guardian Council as the rightful ultimate source of legal authority in the country,[335] Mohtashami and others believed that the power-hungry conservative right faction was displaying its true, unsightly tyrannical face.[336] Ironically, however, rather than trying to appear impartial, some members of the Guardian Council even began to state publicly their factional inclination. Reza Zavarei, the newly selected civilian jurist of the council and a known *Hojjatiyeh* sympathizer remarked, "As a rule, in the coming election the people will vote for the candidates proposed by the JRM, whose revolutionary demeanor has been proven."[337]

As expected, the emergence of *Kargozaran,* the alliance between the left and the modern right, received a mixed reaction from factions, with the left embracing the new group and the conservative right and the new left strongly objecting to it. The status and position of the new group was difficult to categorize as members neither claimed to be a political party nor did they announce that its members wished to run for the Majlis in the next election. The *Kargozaran* simply declared its readiness to continue to work for the system and asked people to participate in the election. Nevertheless, the conservatives raised numerous objections. Asgar-Owladi claimed that due to their positions in the government, any political activity on the part of the members of *Kargozaran* would undermine the constitutional principle of separation of powers between the executive and the legislative branch.[338] MP Mohsen Kohkan implied the possibility of future improprieties by this assemblage, asking, "How do we know that they will not misuse their position and political clout in the election?"[339] Bahonar said the proclamation was against the law, without, however, specifying which law.[340] According to Morteza Nabavi, the group had questioned the authority of the leader when they suggested that the next Majlis should be under the leadership of Rafsanjani.[341] Speaking for the *Mo'talefeh,* Asghar-Owladi stated that the organization believed the actions of the *Kargozaran* would be detrimental to the regime. Calling the *Kargozaran* "the group who clandestinely operated during Musavi," he predicted that this would endanger the unity of action and word in the executive as well as the legislative branch and cause divisions in the country. Badamchian, on the other hand, noted, "In my opinion, this will take away the affairs of the country from those in line with *velayat* and place it into the hands of the religious liberals."[342] About 150 MPs in the Majlis wrote a letter to Nateq-Nuri and expressed their opposition to the *Kargozaran*. Asking the group to apologize to the nation, the signatories believed that the group was suggesting that the country would stop growing and blossoming after Rafsanjani.[343]

During the *Kargozaran* episode, the division within the conservatives became more pointed. Mahdavi-Kani supported the emergence of *Kargozaran* and the technocrats in general by saying, "The political destiny of the people must be placed in the hands of those who have sociocultural and economic acumen. . . . If a person is highly religious but does not have political acumen, he will not be useful for the Majlis."[344] In turn, addressing the IRCG, Nateq-Nuri said, "Liberalism is a real threat for the country and it must be eradicated. . . . The building of a few roads and bridges and the completion of some developmental projects is not tantamount to upholding revolutionary values."[345] On

another occasion he said, "The enemies of the Islamic revolution aim to infil-
trate the notion that the country needs experts and not clergymen. . . . The
main goal of the enemy is to shelve revolutionary values by omitting *velayat* and
the rule of religion. . . . Those who enter the Majlis must be pious, brave, religiously orthodox, and doctrinaire. The notion that economic development requires political development is highly dangerous."[346] Rafsanjani placed the
blame for the emergence of the *Kargozaran* on the JRM and Nateq-Nuri himself. The president revealed that he had asked the JRM to put the names of a
few of his ministers and close assistants in its ticket, but once Nateq-Nuri and
members of the JRM refused, Rafsanjani gave permission to the *Kargozaran* to
announce their existence.[347] The modern right also accused the conservatives
of seeking exclusive power in Iran and of fearing opposition in the Majlis. A
Hamshahri editorial asked the conservatives, "With what wisdom or fair-
mindedness and based on what law can you deprive people from engaging in
vital affairs of the country? . . . Your real fear is of your opponents entering the
Majlis."[348] The *Kargozaran's* third proclamation emphasized that "their aim was
not to omit a current or create division in the system, but rather, strengthen the
Majlis and create a more pluralistic environment in the country."[349] Various
comments made by the *Kargozaran* also showed that by then, the divisions
within the two rights were irreparable and that the views of the modern right
and the left had further intersected. A *Hamshahri* editorial wrote about the
conservatives:

> Their [economic] theory calls for massive acquisition of wealth through unre-
> strained capitalism and involves huge income discrepancies where capital and
> wealth are "trickled down" from the wealthy to the poor. . . . Do those who
> place social justice at the top of their covenant and scorn supporters of *Towse-*
> *'eh* know that any kind of social justice is not possible without taxing the well-
> off, closing the source of colossal effortless profits made by certain segments of
> society, and adjusting the system of income in the country? And [do they
> know] how giving handouts through oil money is an ephemeral policy and
> detrimental for the regime. . . . Should it not be said to the people that the ef-
> fortless profits of a few brokers are made through the exertion of political
> pressure of a certain camp and that these people do not pay even a minuscule
> amount of taxes for the huge sums that they make?[350]

Except for Mohtashami, who suggested that the latest development was another ploy by the president to maintain power,[351] the left warmly received the
Kargozaran. Mehdi Karrubi, a powerful member of MRM and former speaker
of the Majlis, welcomed this dedicated group of individuals and believed their
presence would cause the election to have greater public interest.[352] Although
the *Tahkim* held the *Kargozaran* responsible for many of the economic ills in
Iran, it nevertheless welcomed any group that would confront the conservatives
in the Majlis.[353] Ilias Hazrati declared, "The epoch of avariciousness was
over."[354] Musavi-Lari criticized the conservatives' questioning the motives of
Kargozaran and said, "These people have always been at the service of people."[355] Joyfully declaring the "the defeat of the monopoly," *Salam* predicted
that with the entrance of the *Kargozaran,* the majority faction would lose its
dominance in the next Majlis.[356] According to Abdollah Nuri, the message of
the *Kargozaran* was an invitation to all people to participate in the election.
Thus their views were in line with the revolutionary slogan of "freedom."[357]
Asr-e Ma suggested that those with skills deserved to rule, and that they could
confront the reactionaries.[358] Behzad Nabavi also hinted at the possibility of an
alliance between the left and the *Kargozaran:*"There is some understanding between the line of Imam and the *Kargozaran*."[359]

In the fifth election, the participation of two new groups is worth noting.
Just before the fifth election, the conservatives received a kind of ideological
support when a new group pronounced its existence: the Society of Defense of
Revolutionary Values (*Jam'iyat-e Defa' az Arzesh-ha-ye Inqelab,* or *Arzeshha* for
short), headed by Mohammad Reyshahri, the former minister of intelligence.
Reyshahri announced the goal of *Arzeshha* to be "setting in operation a strong
organization made up of all forces who believe in *velayat-e faqih* and want to defend revolutionary values."[360] In its election memorandum, *Arzeshha* declared
total obedience to the *faqih* and announced its readiness to fortify the holy values of the Islamic Republic.[361] The new group issued a thirty-member list of
candidates, the majority of whom were from the JRM and the rest MRM and
independent candidates. Prominent among them was Ahmad Purnejati, the as-
sistant to the head of radio and TV.[362]

The second new group was ten members of Bazargan's Freedom Movement who registered for the election. Five candidates passed the filters of the
Guardian Council,[363] but they withdrew their candidacy in protest of the rejec-

tion of the rest of the members of the group.[364] Finally, it should be mentioned that a few months earlier, the MRM had announced that because of the manner in which its members were treated by the conservatives and the Guardian Council during the fourth election, the organization was not going to issue an independent list of candidates for the coming election.[365]

Unlike the previous election, Khamenehi tried very hard to appear nonpartisan. He blessed the new group and said, "The bravery of entering the arena of constructiveness is greater than fighting the enemy at the war front."[366] In fact, trying to play his role as a unifying leader, Khamenehi said, "The classification of the domestic groups into left, right, modern, traditional. . . ,was a foreign plot to destroy the unity within Iran."[367] Moreover, just before the first round of election, Khamenehi's office announced that the leader did not order the Guardian Council to reject or accept any candidates.[368] As far as the election was concerned, he told the Guardian Council, "In screening the candidates, you must follow the law and not your personal preferences."[369] Rafsanjani emphasized, "The next election must take place without any discrimination, as no interest is greater than the credibility of the regime."[370] The speaker of the Guardian Council, Imami-Kashani, hinted at the possibility of favoritism on the part of the council, however, when he announced, "The basis for the approval or rejection of candidates would be their total and true allegiance to Islam, the system, and *velayat-e faqih.*"[371] He also said, "The blade of 'unequivocal supervision' of the Guardian Council is the blade of due process of law."[372]

In their efforts to eliminate opponents, the conservatives wished to make the most out of their sway in the council and their presumed unassailable religious discourse. Morteza Nabavi stressed, "The Guardian Council should not allow those who under the pretext of democracy strive to degenerate the revolution and Islam."[373] According to the JMHEQ, "The representatives of the people must be chosen from those who will make guarding the *velayat-e motlaqeh faqih* their first and most important duty."[374] Along the same lines and perhaps unaware of the contradiction implied in his statement, when reiterating the views of the JRM, Nateq-Nuri remarked, "A legitimate and acceptable Majlis is one which is independent and obedient to the leader."[375]

Of the 5,359 registered candidates, only 3,228 passed through the council's filters.[376] Thirty members of the left including Hadi Ghaffari, Abbas Dozduzani, Mohammad Ali Gharibani, and Mohsen Armin (editor of *Asr-e Ma*) were rejected by the council.[377] In response, the MII, the Council for Islamic University Teachers, the Council of Islamic Teachers, and some members of the MRM created the Coalition of the Line of Imam, forming a list of candidates made up of the likes of Majid Ansari, Abdollah Nuri, Rasul Montajabnia, Behzad Nabavi, Mohammad Salamati, and Sa'id Hajjarian.[378] In order not to appear fully apart, the modern right and the conservative right issued two lists of candidates. The one from the *Kargozaran* included ten candidates from the list of the JRM including Nateq-Nuri, Movahhedi-Kermani, Movahhedi-Saveji, and Doai, in addition to MRM members Nuri and Ansari, the House of the Worker candidates Abolqasem Sarhadizadeh and Alireza Mahjub, and independent candidates Morteza Alviri and Faezeh Rafsanjani. The JRM issued another list that, aside from the ten in the list of the *Kargozaran,* was made up of members from its satellite organizations such as *Mo'talefeh,* the Zeynab Society, and JAM.[379]

After the first round of elections (March 8), from Teheran only Faezeh Hashemi Rafsanjani and Nateq-Nuri received the necessary votes for a seat in the Majlis and the rest of the seats awaited the second round. Nevertheless, factions began to claim victory. Declaring "the defeat of the monopoly," the MII announced that only 41 of 140 candidates from the conservative camp received the necessary votes to run for the second round.[380] JRM declared that 70 percent of its candidates from districts outside Teheran entered the second round. *Salam* maintained that the three main tickets (JRM, *Kargozaran,* and the left) had received equal numbers of votes. Prominent figures from all three groups who entered the second round and ultimately the fifth Majlis included, from *Mo'talefeh*-JRM-JAM axis, Hasan Ghafuri-Fard, Reza Taqavi, Hasan Rouhani, Morteza Nabavi, Bahonar, Movahhedi-Saveji, and Abbas Sheybabni; and from the left-*Kargozaran* axis, Abolqasem Sarhadizadeh, Behzad Nabavi, Ali Reza Mahjub, Majid Ansari, Abdollah Nuri, Mohammad Salamati, and Morteza Alviri.[381] Given that fifty new faces had gone to the second round, victory for any one faction was difficult to substantiate. However, the balance was changed when the Guardian Council annulled the election results of sixteen districts.[382] This precedent-setting action meant that the conservatives were not about to receive the necessary seats for a majority in the next Majlis. Jannati, secretary of the Guardian Council, announced that the rejected candidates had used their financial power and personal clout to garner votes and that they had promised their constituents absurd promises if elected.[383] Imami-Kashani, a member of the Guardian Council, noted, "The nullification of the election of some districts was aimed safeguarding the real votes of the people."[384] In the end, though, the actions of the council once again favored the conservatives; they ended up winning enough seats to hold the leadership in the Majlis. The speakership went to Nateq-Nuri, the deputyship to Rouhani, the commission heads went to Movahhedi-Kermani, Reza Taqavi, Mohammad Reza Bahonar, Hasan Ghafuri-Fard, and Ali Movahhedi-Saveji.[385] In the new Majlis, the conservatives established a faction called the Society of Hizbollah (*Jame'eh-ye Hizbollah*),[386] and the *Kargozaran*-left axis formed the Assembly of Hizbollah (*Majma'e-e Hizbollah*). *Asr-e Ma* reported that the latter camp controlled seven Majlis committees.[387] Factions now turned their attentions to the coming presidential election.

The Presidential Election of 1997

The first factional move for the presidential election of 1997 came from the modern right, when some of its members such as Atollah Mohajerani and Hossein Mar'ashi proposed that the constitution be amended and Rafsanjani run for a third term in office. (In addition to the constitutional amendment, the action required the approval of the leader and the Expediency Council.) This, they argued, would ensure a continuation of a successful course of reconstruction. Both believed that this was what the population desired.[388] Given their newly formed alliance with the left, the *Kargozaran* perhaps thought that they would receive the backing of leftist forces, particularly when members of the left continued to voice their support for Rafsanjani and *Towse-'eh* after the election of the fifth Majlis.[389] The initiative by the Rafsanjanites, however, was unsuccessful. Perhaps knowing that they had a chance of their own in the next election, the left politely maintained, "Given the caliber of Mr. Rafsanjani, he can be appointed to another equally important position in the country."[390]

The conservatives, on the other hand, adamantly opposed any changes. Bahonar believed "any tampering with or suggestions for change in the constitution must be initiated by the leader." He accused the *Kargozaran* of trying to divide the country into those for and against Rafsanjani.[391] According to

Movahhedi-Kermani, "Such actions are against the spirit of the constitution." Having in mind a candidate of his own, Nateq-Nuri, he further noted, "Besides, we have more qualified people in the country than Mr. Rafsanjani to fill the post."[392] According to Badamchian, "This would be a slap in the mouth to the leadership of the regime and the people if we say that no one but Rafsanjani can continue the path of constructiveness."[393] Nateq-Nuri praised Rafsanjani but also said, "It is not in the interests of the regime, nor does the leader want it."[394] Given the negative response, Rafsanjani finally put an end to the debate by saying, "At this point, I do not see it to be in the interests of the regime to change the constitution."[395]

For their part, the conservatives initiated their own effort to push through the candidacy of Nateq-Nuri. They sounded so righteous and so sure about the election of Nateq-Nuri that many members of this camp began explicitly suggesting that there was no need for a multi-candidate presidential race: foregoing the formality of an election would maintain continuity at the top, and the consensus of the country was in favor of Nateq-Nuri. This was particularly the discourse of the Mo'talefeh and JIM. In an interview with Iran, for example, Badamchian stated, "If everyone observes their religious duty, we [the people] can reach a consensus on the more advisable [aslah] candidate and thus avoid the need for a competitive election as was the case in previous elections with Mr. Rafsanjani."[396] According to Ghafuri-Fard, "If other factions introduce anyone but Nateq-Nuri, it will create ideological dissension in the country."[397]

Despite all the hubbub created by the conservatives about Nateq-Nuri, the first faction to officially announce its support for a candidate was the left. In July 1996, the Assembly of Hizbollah in the Majlis and all the organizations of the Line of Imam political spectrum announced they would support the candidacy of Mir Hossein Musavi (the former Prime Minister) in the coming election.[398] The selection of Musavi was a clever move by the left. Well-aware of the division within the conservative right, by backing a candidate so soon the left forced the rival faction to do the same thing and perhaps intensify the conflict within that camp. The debate over whether or not the JRM should announce a candidate had been evident in the remarks of Nateq-Nuri a year earlier when he implicitly announced his wish to run for the office. When asked about his political aspirations in the coming presidential election, he had said, "I have never been after post or status, but if the leader obliges me I will

not evade the responsibility." [399] He criticized those clergymen who chose political isolation and relinquished their political responsibilities by saying,
"Whether they want it or not, people perceive this group as responsible for the
affairs of the country, good or bad." [400] Singling out Mohammad Reza Mahdavi-Kani (former chair of the JRM), he said, "Some clergy think about themselves as pious and knowledgeable and are proud that they are apolitical. This is
not a right mindset. We must enter the [political] fore and work for the people." [401] Given the apparent conflict within the conservative camp, and perhaps
because they still had not reached a consensus on whether or not to introduce
a candidate, the cunning move on the part of the left worked. The day after
Salam announced the news about Musavi, *Resalat* pronounced that *Mo'talefeh*
and *Hamsu* supported Nateq-Nuri's candidacy. [402] It was unprecedented that the
two satellites of the JRM would support someone without the JRM announcing first. A month earlier, Nateq-Nuri had reiterated that the JRM must take
the lead and draw up a path for the country. [403]

It was evident therefore that impelled by the *Mo'talefeh,* the Nateq-Nuri-
Mo'talefeh-Hamsu axis of the conservative right faction was not only acting independently of the JRM but was taking the initiative for this faction. Such a
move needed justification, however. *Mo'talefeh* maintained that it had decided
to be more involved in the "political stage in the country." [404] Interestingly
enough, the new axis of the conservative right began advocating the need to
establish political parties in the Islamic Republic. According to Nateq-Nuri,
"Parties are necessary for the country. However, they must draw their legitimacy from the *velayat-e faqih.*" [405] Emphasis was also placed on the independence of the organizations and individual members within the faction. For
instance, Nateq-Nuri said, "When I say if I am obliged [to run for the presi-
dency] some people assume that I am waiting for the esteemed leader to oblige
me. . . . I have recently changed my words and have said if I feel it a duty [I shall
enter the presidential race]." [406] Hasan Ghafuri-Fard suggested that "although
the *Mo'talefeh* has always supported the JRM, it has always been independent of
it." [407] Asghar-Owladi reminded everyone, "The *Mo'talefeh* was formed prior to
the JRM and its independence dates back to that time." [408] Ali Abbaspur, the director of *Hamsu,* said the same thing about the organization he headed. [409]
Those members from the JRM such as Movahhedi-Saveji who supported the
new axis stressed, "Not everyone who is a member of the JRM must accept all

the decisions made by the society."[410] To buttress the actions of the axis, Badamchian announced that Imami-Kashani (Mahdavi-Kani's replacement as the chair of the JRM) supported the presidency of the Nateq-Nuri.[411]

The division within the conservative camp became further evident when, rather than the usual practice of JRM issuing a declaration in support of a candidate, it was the speaker of the society, Reza Taqavi, who announced his support for Nateq-Nuri.[412] It was not until May 10, 1997, that the JRM officially declared its backing of Nateq-Nuri.[413] In November 1996 Nateq-Nuri had implied that both the JRM and the JMHEQ supported his candidacy when he said, "A heavy responsibility has been put on my shoulders by the JRM and the JMHEQ."[414] Although Nateq-Nuri implied that he had received the backing of JMHEQ by saying that Ali Meshkini and Ibrahim Amini approved of his candidacy, the JMHEQ had not officially announced their support for him at that time. In fact, Amini, the deputy of the JMHEQ, had resigned over the debate on whether the society should back Nateq-Nuri.[415] The satellites of the JRM such as JAM, *Mo'talefeh,* and *Hamsu* publicly claimed that the JMHEQ supported the candidacy of Nateq-Nuri since the autumn of 1996,[416] but it was not until May 1, 1997, that Mohsen Kharazi proclaimed that the JMHEQ would support Nateq-Nuri in the coming presidential election.[417] Even then, prominent members of the JMHEQ such as Ayatollah Mas'udi revealed that although the JMHEQ discussed supporting the candidacy of individuals for the coming election, many members of the organization did not wish to support Nateq-Nuri or anyone else for that matter. Mas'udi said, "The status of the society demands it [the JMHEQ] to be above mundane politics. The society belongs to all people and the clergy as a whole must not become involved in party politics and be placed in opposition to the society."[418] In an interview with *Salam,* Mas'udi further revealed that the JMHEQ was pressured by the *Mo'talefeh* to support Nateq-Nuri, and he added, "Those who want to direct the JMHEQ in a certain direction are committing treachery."[419] What is more, according to *Kar va Kargar,* in the session where the JMHEQ decided to support Nateq-Nuri, prominent figures such as Lankarani, Meshkini, Khaza'li, Jannati, Mohammadi-Gilani, and Mo'men were not even present, and other influential figures such as Makarem-Shirazi refused to back any candidate.[420]

In the end, however, for the sake of the survival of the conservative camp, the majority of its members presented a unified front for the presidential election. For instance, in a show of solidarity, Imami-Kashani, Mahdavi-Kani, and Nateq-Nuri appeared together on an occasion where the new chairman of the JRM maintained, "To persevere in the achievement of the Islamic revolution, the clergy must be united, present, and closely linked."[421] Just before the election, Mahdavi-Kani declared Nateq-Nuri to be the most appropriate candidate.[422] In fact, to ward off challenges by rival factions, on the eve of the election Mahdavi-Kani became once again the helmsman of the conservative right faction in opposing the "liberal" candidates in the election. As the chair of the JRM, Mahdavi-Kani had a father figure status among the conservatives. After objecting to the politicization of the clergy he resigned. But to save the right from divisions, he came out in support of Nateq-Nuri. Moreover, perhaps to reestablish the fact that the JRM was the nucleus of the conservative right faction, he responded to the push for power on the part of the *Mo'talefeh* by stating, "The *Mo'talefeh* does not have that kind of weight in our society [that they claim to], and they themselves recognize this."[423]

While the conservatives were occupied with campaigning for Nateq-Nuri, in October 1996 the MRM announced it was resuming its political activities. According to Rasul Montajabnia, "Now that the truth about the real intentions of the other faction [conservative right] has been made known, the MRM has decided to reenter the political stage and create a more pluralistic environment for the presidential election."[424] The MRM also announced that their decision was based on the request of many groups such as the Line of Imam and some members of the Assembly of Hizbollah in the Majlis. In addition, the assembly also made it known that their preferred choice for the election was Musavi.[425] The *Kargozaran* welcomed the decision of the MRM. In the words of Mohajerani, a close aid of Rafsanjani and a member of the *Kargozaran*, "The participation of the MRM would surely cause the presidential election to flourish."[426] The *Kargozaran* also declared that they contemplated supporting the candidacy of Musavi, in addition to being interested in people such as Hasan Habibi and Hasan Rouhani if they decided to run.[427] Because the left and the modern right had newly formed a coalition in the Majlis, it was predictable that they would support the same candidate in the upcoming election. Until the end of December 1996, however, the two factions did not commit to this explicitly. In the meantime—and perhaps to keep the conservatives off balance—members from both camps signaled the possibility of advocating only one candidate. In early December 1996, Hossein Mar'ashi revealed, "The possibility of the coalition between *Kargozaran* and MRM exists."[428] According to Majid Ansari from the MRM, "The two camps could reach a point of synthesis."[429] After many rounds of such exchanges, on December 22, 1996, Mohammad Hashemi announced that the *Kargozaran* had accepted the offer of the MRM for a coalition.[430] Aside from having common ideological grounds, the main reason for the coalition between the two factions, as Sa'id Hajjarian put it, was "confronting a faction that was inclined to monopolize power."[431]

In October, however, Musavi announced that he had decided not to run for the presidency. He provided no explanation of his decision.[432] The proposed candidacy of Musavi had been most likely a tactical move on the part of the left, to create disquiet in the conservative camp as well as to test the factional waters. In addition, it was necessary to gauge the strength of public opinion with regard to the popularity of a candidate from the left. Arguably, this faction was suspicious that the regime was not yet ready for a civilian president. Musavi became the groundbreaker for the next candidate that the left had in mind, Mohammad Khatami, the current president. In November 1996, the daily *Jomhuri-ye Islami* revealed that there was some mention in "political circles" about the candidacy of Khatami.[433] The following month, some members of left such as Mohtashami attested to this fact,[434] and in January 1997, Khatami officially announced that he was running in the coming presidential election.[435] The MII, *Tahkim,* and the Assembly of Hizbollah of the Majlis all declared their support for Khatami.[436] In a statement that indicated the possible future support of the *Kargozaran* for Khatami, Mohajerani remarked, "The wisdom and grace of Mr. Khatami will make him a most popular president."[437] On April 13, 1997, the *Kargozaran* officially declared Khatami as their candidate.[438]

As to why the *Kargozaran* chose not to introduce a candidate from within the group, three major reasons come to mind. Firstly, the *Kargozaran* did not have anyone of the caliber of Khatami to present as a candidate. Secondly, after his tenure as minister of culture, Khatami's antiestablishment liberal views and policies were extremely popular with the people of the country. Finally, politicians such as Mohajerani and Rafsanjani himself were close to Khatami and admired him. It is therefore understandable that when declaring their support for

Khatami, the *Kargozaran* maintained that the former minister of culture and Islamic guidance was the only one who shared Rafsanjani's vision and would continue in his footsteps.[439]

The views Khatami expressed during his political campaign were very much in line with the discourse of the president. He once said, "The constructive path of Mr Rafsanjani must continue." In accord with Rafsanjani, he also believed in the need to rely on experts regardless of their political inclination and ideological credentials.[440] Khatami's support for a more politically open Iran was evident in an another speech when he said, "Economic development must be accompanied by political development." In another sign of support for the economic direction instigated by Rafsanjani, he added, "The state must possess the necessary infrastructure in order to take on a prominent role in the economy."[441] Khatami's campaign had two important campaign messages: to woo the young people of Iran, and to emphasize the rule of law and the primacy of the constitution. He advocated the need to create a civil society in Islamic Iran.

Well aware that the young were disaffected by the restrictive sociocultural policies of the conservatives, Khatami's view was that "rather than estranging them, we must involve the young in politics, economics, and the affairs of the country."[442] Perhaps indirectly addressing the conservatives and warning them that the young might become dissident or worse if pushed too far, he said, "A society that resorts to force will face instability."[443] "Youth," he added, "is not an enigma but an advantage."[444] It was no wonder that the bulk of those who not only distributed election pamphlets advocating Khatami's candidacy but also joyfully celebrated his victory in the streets of the capital were all young people.

Needless to say, when it came to sociocultural matters, he maintained the same views during his campaign that he had held during his previous tenure as minister of culture. His other message for the election was extension of the left's views with regard to the importance of the republicanism of the regime. In this respect, his most celebrated political axiom was the law, more specifically the constitution. He had a particular political purpose in mind when he espoused these two concepts of the law and the constitution. Khatami intended to undermine the institutions of power for the conservatives and question their religio-political views, hence the absolutist reading of *velayat-e faqih*. Thus, the left was bringing into focus once again the dichotomy of republicanism versus the religiousness of the regime, and supporting its populist/republican dimension. On numerous occasions, Khatami stated the most important task of the new president was to uphold the constitution and safeguard the individual rights of the citizens.[445] While asserting his faith in *velayat-e faqih,* Khatami skillfully challenged the *Motlaqeh* version. For example, while on one occasion he said "the *velayat-e faqih* is the pillar of the Islamic Republic," he also stated, "One of our [the regime's] missions is the institutionalization of the Islamic system based on the constitution, and the acceptance of the constitution as the foundation of our political system." He criticized those who "think that they hold a monopoly on the correct reading of the *velayat-e faqih.*"[446]

Interestingly enough, the conservatives also exhibited more tolerant views. Morteza Nabavi said, "We believed in political freedom. In fact, it is those who believe in a centralized economy that cannot be supporters of political freedom."[447] Nateq-Nuri emphasized "while preserving the Islamic values of the country, the need to use the experts and rely on expertise."[448] To the lingering accusations that the conservative right were monopolistic, he responded "do not worry, we are not monopolistically inclined; those who accuse us are doing it for political purposes."[449] Nateq-Nuri also changed his stance to a more moderate position on cultural issues. In one interview he said, "We must do something about our erroneous culture when it comes to women."[450] In what looked like a self-incriminating statement, he said, "Some people compare us with the Taliban [the regime in Afghanistan] and say if elected, I will make wearing the *chador* compulsory. This is a lie, as although I believe that the *chador* is the preferred kind of veiling, observing the minimum [covering] is sufficient."[451] At this stage it was important to the conservatives that they had a more pluralistic sounding public voice. They had been alarmed by the result of the fifth parliamentary election. Although they had finally received/secured a majority in the Majlis, their victory was far from convincing. The fact that the two prominent figures of this camp, Habibollah Asgar-Owladi and Asadollah Badamchian, were not elected made them realize that society was no longer inclined to accept their conservative views. In the face of the more progressive views of Khatami, they saw the need to present a more liberal exterior. However, the conservatives did not retreat entirely from their support for *Motlaqeh* views. In fact, the conservative camp took the issue of allegiance to the *faqih* into a new dimension when many members of this camp suggested that candidates must be immersed (*zowb*, literally "melted") in *velayat*.[452]

The debate over the issue of the *velayat-e faqih* remained civil until late January when, in an interview with *Mobin*, Hashem Aqajari, an influential figure from *Tahkim*, made an extremely controversial observation. When discussing "political participation in the thoughts of Imam Ali," Aqajari maintained, "Legitimacy and rightfulness are two [different] matters. Rightfulness is an inner matter. The Imam Ali of course thought of himself as having the divine right [*haq'*] to rule . . . but he never allowed himself to impose his rule on the people without their consent. . . . Political legitimacy is an exterior matter, and it stems only from the people's allegiance."[453] Aqajari had provided a highly controversial analysis of one the basic tenets of Imamat. His words caused the return of Mahdavi-Kani to the political scene and resulted in negative campaigning. This also led, for the first time after the revolution, to prominent figures in Iran directly insulting each other. This was Mahdavi-Kani's reaction to Aqajari's statement:

> Doubting the principle of *velayat-e faqih*, its foundations, and the disbelief in its all-encompassing character, [giving] precedence to republicanism of the regime over its Islamicity, [speaking about] the sovereignty of the regime from the top to bottom, abstruse religious debates, bringing to the public fore the issues of expertise [over doctrinarism] under the pretext of support for the rule of law, suggesting that the constitution is the pivot of the regime and speaking about national covenant and championing popular sovereignty and political participation, as if the people have not being partaking in the affairs of the country; all appeal to the alternative thinkers and the enemy. . . . The discussions about and undermining of the *velayat* of *Amir-ol Mo'menin* [Imam Ali] and enfeebling it for political purposes and for the sake of tantalizing the population in a paper that calls itself supporter of the Line of Imam, is extremely hazardous and for me intolerable. . . . These are the same words that were uttered in the early days of the revolution by liberals such as Bani-Sadr who wanted to completely omit *velayat-e faqih* from the constitution. . . . They [the left] disregard all the assertions of the Imam about *velayat-e faqih* and cling to this sentence mentioned by the Imam, "I select the government with

the support of the people," or "the gauge is the will of the people." . . . I fear that the episode of constitutional revolution might be repeated.[454]

The words of Mahdavi-Kani instigated a heated round of factional outbursts. The response of Khatami was to ridicule the politically unenlightened conservatives: "The idea of putting the leadership and the law [constitution] face to face, which some people are trying to do, is dangerous and has its roots in not understanding the civil society. . . . In a civil society people must be free and no one has the right to accuse anyone of being liberal and anti–*velayat-e faqih*. We must accept the general will."[455] A few days later Khatami maintained, "If the people are [allowed] to be present [on the political stage], the Constitutional Revolution will not be repeated. . . . Anyone who has accepted the Republic has also accepted republicanism, Islamicity, and *velayat-e faqih*."[456] Karrubi accused Mahdavi-Kani and the conservative right of politicking and voiced his opinion that the previous chairman of the JRM suffered from overweening arrogance regarding his power and position:

> Some gentlemen perceive themselves as the guardian [*ghay'em*] of the people and think they should decide for the people. . . . [However,] as the Imam said, it is they who are [our] guardians. The gauge is the people's will. . . . It is constantly repeated, "I will not allow in a Shii country". . . . Are you the head of this country? Are you, the esteemed clergy, a source of emulation or the leader that you issue a fatwa for your followers? What strategy is this that every time I feel the interests of my political group are in danger, I cry Islam is in danger, the clergy are in danger, the country is in danger?[457]

According to Hadi Khamenehi, "To separate the broad spectrum of groups of Line of Imam from the leadership and the *velayat-e faqih* is a grave mistake and treachery."[458] The most discourteous words against Mahdavi-Kani came from Khoeiniha, who said, "What element of the rule of *velayat-e faqih* is shaky today that few fools want to reinforce it?"[459]

A political tactic used by the conservatives was to begin suggesting explicitly that Nateq-Nuri was the favorite of the leadership—and particularly Khamenehi—to bolster their chances in the presidential election. "I think with regard to [the presidency of] Mr. Nateq-Nuri, the leadership has reached a consensus," remarked Badamchian.[460] Although Khamenehi appeared neutral by saying that all candidates were good and virtuous, he also added, "In selecting the next president, the ulama are a trusted and an acceptable reference for the people."[461] Given that the majority of the clergy were sympathetic to Nateq-Nuri, it was not difficult to ascertain that he himself favored the speaker of the Majlis. To try and weaken the claims of the conservatives, members of other camps proclaimed that the leader did not have favorite candidates.[462] *Resalat* responded by quoting Khamenehi as saying, "Of course I have a preference among the candidates." Three days before the election, Mahdavi-Kani was quoted as saying, "We guess that the esteemed leader favors Mr. Nateq-Nuri."[463] As the election date neared, fuelled by the belief that the "conservative establishment" would never allow Khatami, who disdained the conservatives, to win, the general consensus was that Nateq-Nuri would be the next president. There were also rumors that election vote counting would be rigged in favor of Nateq-Nuri. The fear was then that the general public would believe these rumors and not bother to go to the ballot boxes in large numbers. Once again, Rafsanjani steered the course of events in the Islamic Republic, this time with a speech in a Friday prayer. In warning the nation about election improprieties, Rafsanjani said:

> The administrators of the election procedure must act in a way so that the minds of people will be at ease. . . . The results [of the election] are the people's will, even though there may be people who might want to change the votes to get their candidates elected. This action would undermine the faith of the people in the system. . . . Any action endeavoring to alter the votes of the people is the biggest crime and treachery against a system that relies on the people for [solving] its problems. . . . I have not announced my choice and I hope neither will others.[464]

Rafsanjani's comments forced Khamenehi to come out and say that he would not allow any illegalities in the election.[465] This reassured people that their vote would actually count and made any wrongdoing that might have been planned impossible given the atmosphere that had developed after the assertions of the president and the leader. If one considers how different things could have been if Khatami had not been elected, then Rafsanjani's remarks altered the course of postrevolutionary history in Iran.

On May 23, 1997, the electorate went to the polls to select the next president from among the four candidates approved by the Guardians Council (Reyshahri, Khatami, Nateq-Nuri, and Zavarei). Three days later, the newspapers announced that Khatami had won the presidential election by a landslide.

CHAPTER 6

Factional Politics under Khatami

Civil Society versus Guardianship Society

The dividing politico-ideological line within the Iranian polity and among the factions became more distinct in the aftermath of Khatami's election—the May 23 Epic as it became known. Those who embraced the message of the Epic—the left, the modern right, Islamic intellectuals, and progressive clergymen (the May 23 Front),[1] stood against those opposed it—the conservative right/neo-fundamentalist axis, and, as the public perceived it, Khamenehi. Hojjatol-Islam Mohsen Kadivar depicted accurately the dispositions of the two camps when he identified the first—those who believed in power sharing, independent grassroots associations, political parties, the rule of law, and individual rights and freedom—as supporters of "civil society" (jame'eh-ye madani). He labeled the second camp—which embodied sociocultural ossification, pretentious religiousness, reactionary-elitist tendencies, and a disregard for society's rightful claim to power—as defenders of "guardianship society" (jame'eh-ye velai).[2]

Factionalism, however, retained its place on the political stage. By exploiting their institutional sway, the conservatives moved to exclude members of the rival factions from the corridors of power and weaken their newly found power. At the same time, they accused the president and his supporters of secularizing Iran in the name of democracy and freedom. As we shall see, this faction ultimately resorted to violence against Khatami's supporters. Conversely, the May 23 Front bashed the forces of conservatism for their parochial and dogmatic sentiments that were not only incongruent with the realties of the Iranian society but impeded Iran's progress towards an Islamic democracy.

Aware of the tremendous backing that he enjoyed among the population at large, Khatami pushed through reforms that strengthened the republicanism of the regime. The ensuing factional debates bared once again the two maladies that have inflicted the Islamic Republic since its inception: the regime's two ideological dimensions provided the structure for contrasting factional discourse and factionalism, and the true nature of the Islamic Republic, as well as the goals of the revolutionaries in Iran, still remained dichotomous and disputed. Makeshift readings of the principles and objectives of the Islamic Republic have became the hallmark of Iranian politics.

The Precarious March of the May 23 Movement

While the defeated factions endeavored to explain their biggest political setback yet by portraying the election of Khatami as a vote of confidence for the regime of *velayat-e faqih,* reflecting its democratic character,[3] the victors stressed that it was not business as usual and much more should be inferred from the May Epic. The vote for Khatami, argued the left, was testimony to the fact that the Iranian people now believed the legitimacy and sovereignty of the regime emanated from the "general will."[4] For the MII, Khatami's election renounced the conservatives' rendition of Islam and Islamic politics and illustrated that Iranian society espoused a "democratic" reading of Islam:

> The people voted for an Islam that not only does not see a contradiction between religion and freedom, democracy, human rights, and civil society, but believes that these [modern] concepts can find their true meaning in Islam. An Islam that recognizes the rights of the citizens and discerns the legitimacy of the regime to be based on their consent . . . construes the *vali-ye faqih* to be an elected and lawful leader. One who is the symbol of the country's unity and leads the revolution based on the wishes of people and within the confine of the constitution. . . . May 23 was a vote for such a reading of Islam.[5]

To weaken the *Motlaqeh* reading, and the ideological–institutional predominance of the conservatives and the neo-fundamentalists, the vanguard of the May movement constructed an unprecedented liberal-populist interpretation of Islam and the objectives of the revolution. To that aim, they spelled out a legalistic and constitutionally bound role for the *vali-ye faqih* and detailed a religiously sanctioned civil society. Aside from the president himself, influential figures from the left and the modern right such as Behzad Nabavi, Abdollah Nuri, Ataollah Mohajerani, Abdolkarim Sorush, and Mohsen Kadivar orchestrated a concerted effort to infuse their conception of democracy, civil society, and its associated concepts into the religio-political discourse of the Islamic Republic by ideologically sanctioning—hence Islamicizing—these essentially Western-secular concepts. In reinforcing the significance of the populist-republican dimension further, the May 23 Front construed the four sources of factional doctrine to assert that society's right to self-rule and self-determination, pluralism, the constitution, and the rule of law forge the ideological and institutional axioms of the Islamic Republic.[6] The MII, for example, implied that an Islamic state could have a variety of structures and may be contrived through many different forms and practices. For, while the Qoran, the Prophet, and the imams provided general guidelines for an Islamic state to observe—that is, justice and upholding Islamic tenets—they did not produce specific edicts on its nature and policies. Thus, the argument went, Muslims are entitled to select freely their preferred political system and its modus operandi.[7] Sorush and Kadivar broached the idea of the need to design a more pluralistic Islamic society in Iran and postulated that although the ultimate truth of Islam is eternal and known, there could be many ways of arriving at the truth. And, because the discovery of the truth entails discerning right from wrong, the society must enjoy "religious pluralism" for various viewpoints to be debated.[8]

Khatami accented people's constitutional-religious rights to determine their fate and supervise their own affairs while retaining the basic principles of Islam.[9] Criticizing the "mentally ossified current" who "says yes to Islam but no to the people,"[10] he reaffirmed his preelection promises and pledged to uphold the constitution, protect people's constitutional rights, and instill the rule of law.[11] The president maintained that one of the most important achievements of Imam Khomeini to prevent dictatorship and despotism was the institutionalization of the rule of law, asserting further, "The strength of the Islamic Republic stems from the freedom and individual rights that people hold under the constitution."[12]

Of all the ingredients of Khatami's political discourse, his promise to create a civil society in Islamic Iran was potentially the most controversial because he and his followers were burdened with the arduous task of religiously sanctioning this concept. The May 23 Front delved into the texts to find a reading of civil society that was both non-Western and in line with the Islamic-Shii tradition. Ataollah Mohajerani argued that Muslim rulers—the Prophet, the imams, and Khomeini—were historically legitimate leaders only inasmuch as they procured the consent of the people.[13] Mohsen Kadivar and Abbas Abdi pronounced that an Islamic civil society would not resemble its Western counterpart because "Iranians are religious people and thus the associations and institutions they set up will indeed be based on religious and not secular principles."[14] It was on such inferences that the MII conceived of an Islamic civil society different from those found in the Western world, one that is formed based on the fundamental principles of civil society but adheres to Islamic tenets.[15]

The president and his patrons were aware that the materialization of their new populist-democratic vision of Islamic politics was conceivable only if the power of the conservatives—via the religious super-bodies and an unassailable *faqih*—was curbed.[16] In a well-documented book on the thoughts of Shii *foqaha,* including Khomeini himself, as well as on the Qoran, the Prophet, and the imams and their sayings, Mohsen Kadivar arrived at two main conclusions with regard to *velayat-e faqih:* the (absolute) guardianship of the *faqih* over the lives of the people is devoid of historical, religious precedent, and the *faqih* should be an elected (*intekhabi*) and not an appointed (*intesabi*) official.[17] Khatami paid homage to the *vali-ye faqih* but implied a supervisory-guidance role for the leader, who, as a "symbol" of national sovereignty and unity, drew his power and legitimacy from the society and the constitution.[18] Khatami's periodic declaration that all officials of the regime should be held accountable for their actions regardless of their status was an implicit suggestion that no one, not even the *faqih,* was above the law.[19] Others, such as the MII, endorsed such views by stressing the significance of republicanism and the constitution:

> The constitution is based on Islamic thought and the people's will. The legitimacy of the Islamic regime and *vali-ye faqih* is elected based on the articles of the constitution and should not be considered to be above law. . . . *Velayat-e faqih* is not a post relegated from God. He is an elected official within the con-

fines of the constitution and religion. The constitution is the only guarantee of *vali-ye faqih*'s power.[20]

Finally, the civil society camp in November 1997 received an unexpected boost in their ideological battle with the conservatives when Ayatollah Hossein Ali Montazeri assailed the *Motlaqeh* reading of the Islamic Republic, blasting Khamenehi and the conservatives for creating an un-Islamic autocratic system. Montazeri questioned Khamenehi's religious qualifications as a source of emulation and compared the extravagance and the corruption of the present regime with that of the toppled monarchy. He cautioned the *faqih* not to meddle in the affairs of the popularly elected president, and in turn advised Khatami, "If I were you, I would go to the leader and tell him that, with all due respect, 22 million people voted for me while everyone knew that you preferred another candidate [Nateq-Nuri]. It means, therefore, that the people have rejected the existing order."[21] Although the conservatives uttered their usual rhetoric in support of Khamenehi and his mandate as a rightful *faqih*,[22] Montazeri's assertion was a significant blow to the leader's already blemished public standing.

Khatami's twenty-two-member cabinet, introduced to the Majlis in August 1997, reflected the alliance of the left and the modern right formed during the presidential election.[23] The president kept this conspicuous partisan makeup when he selected his deputies.[24] Opposition to his choice of cabinet was fierce, with most of the criticism directed at two of the proposed ministers. The proposed Islamic guidance minister, Ataollah Mohajerani, was condemned for his previous hints about the need to renew ties with the United States and other liberal views,[25] while Abdollah Nuri, Khatami's choice for interior ministry, seemed destined not to receive a vote of confidence from the Majlis as his commitment to the concept of *velayat-e faqih* was questioned by the MPs.[26] Remarkably though, and despite public anticipation to the contrary,[27] the Majlis approved all the cabinet members.[28] This was a tremendous victory for Khatami and shattered conservative hopes of having a rubber-stamp Majlis.[29]

Not surprisingly and in view of Khatami's preelection pledge of greater cultural openness in society, the public waited enthusiastically to see whether Mohajerani would introduce major reforms in his ministry or simply yield to pressures from the conservatives. To his credit, rather than toning down his views,[30] he embarked on some of the most tolerant and progressive cultural policies ever enacted in the Islamic Republic. Following in the footsteps of Khatami, who maintained that "guidance" in the ministry of culture should not translate into persecution and "guardianship" of thinkers,[31] Mohajerani announced that he planned to "transform the ministry of guidance into a ministry of culture." In a direct reference to his predecessor, Mir-Salim, he pledged that "his ministry will not lie in ambush to trap artists or writers."[32] Significantly, Mohajerani announced that no censorship or auditing of any kind would be imposed on printed materials before they were published.[33] With the encouragement of Mohajerani and his deputy Ahmad Borgani, the first Assembly Guild for Writers and Journalists of the Press was established in December 1997. Khatami hoped that this association would answer one of the most important needs of civil society, and Borgani believed that "the establishment of this assembly is a step towards breaking the paternalistic attitude that existed towards the press."[34]

Indeed, what became the hallmark of Mohajerani's ministerial legacy was the mushrooming of pro–May 23 publications, for which the ministry generously issued licenses.[35] The press became the voice of the civil society camp and was used as its primary lever to demand more cultural freedom from the establishment.[36] Subsequently, the sociocultural realm became the principle arena of factionalism, and the "liberal" media the main focus of conservative onslaught. New newspapers such as *Jame'eh-e, Tus, Neshat, Khordad,* and *Sobh-e Imruz* and weeklies such as *Rah-e No* and *Aban,* together with *Salam, Iran-e Farda, Asr-e Ma,* and *Kiyan,* both agitated and provoked the jurisconsult camp by debating controversial religio–political topics that the conservative establishment held as sacrosanct.[37] Feeling increasingly exposed and challenged, the conservatives accused the guidance ministry of supervisory laxity over materials that were "destabilizing" the regime. The civil society scheme, they argued, was nothing more than a virulent plot to secularize Islamic Iran.[38]

The Response of the Conservatives: From Containment to Coercion and Violence

Although immediately after the presidential election the conservative right supported Khatami's presidency,[39] it soon went on the offensive. The response of the conservative camp to the new ideological challenge posed by the May 23 Front was to take its customary refuge in the regime's religiousness and the *Motlaqeh* reading, vindicating their own "divinely inspired" but elitist views. For Ayatollah Abolqasem Khazali, nothing was more loathsome than religious pluralism and the suggestion that the essence of religion could be debated outside the seminary.[40] The idea of a popularly elected *faqih* was unthinkable for Ayatollah Abdollah Javad Amoli:"This implies that the society is entitled to unseat and appoint even the prophets. How, then, do we respond to Qoranic verses?" he maintained.[41] A *Resalat* editorial entitled "The Right of Governance in a Guardianship Society" reminded its readers of the imperfection of human-made laws, thus the requirement of the holy supervision of the *faqih*.[42] Unlike other officials in Iran, the *vali-ye faqih* is appointed and not elected, another editorial of the daily expounded.[43] Other prominent conservatives such as Ayatollah Mohammad Yazdi spoke of the all-encompassing role and the unlimited rights the *faqih* enjoys under the constitution.[44] The conservatives also considered emulating Western-style democracy, which embodied un-Islamic sentiments such as human rights and gender equality, as undermining the moral pillars of the revolution.[45]

The conservatives' arguments against the republicanism of the regime continued. In May 1997, a letter to the leader the *Mo'talefeh* suggested that the Expediency Council should meet and delete "Republic" from the name of the regime and rename it "Islamic Justice Government" (*Hokumat-e Adl-e Islami*). In reference to Khatami and his supporters, the *Mo'talefeh* warned that some groups infatuated with Western ideas were implicitly seeking to do away with the Islamicity of the country.[46] *Ansar-e Hizbollah* called the new president Westernized, conceding that their support for Khatami was simply out of respect for the leader.[47] Finally, sensing his power seriously at risk, the leader himself took an unusually strong public stand against the May 23 Front. Similar to Khomeini's January 1988 decree where the Imam construed *velayat-e faqih* to be a main pillar of (Shii) Islam, Khamenehi categorized his rule as being derived from the Qoran, the sayings of the Prophet, and the imams, thus implying that unquestioned obedience to the *faqih* was a religious duty.[48] He also scorned secularizing forces for plotting against Islam and the regime:"The epoch of adhering to Western prescriptions has passed. The enemies of Islam are seeking to separate religion from politics. Using seductive Western concepts such as political parties, competitive pluralist political system, and bogus democracy, the Westernized are trying to present a utopic picture of Western societies and portray them as the only salvation for our Islamic society."[49]

The president's unprecedented popular mandate and a combative press were no match for the institutional might of the conservatives, and no one expected them to concede the power bases they had fought so hard to establish. Khatami's opponents retained control over the supervisory bodies, the judiciary, and the legislature, as well as the IRGC and other powerful revolutionary bodies, not to mention Khamenehi's backing. Once again, and perhaps more vividly than in any period in postrevolutionary Iran, Khatami's election laid bare the harsh truth that the hierarchical nature of the Iranian state, and the modus vivendi of the Islamic polity, were powerful counters to the popular will and provided the battleground for factionalism. Khatami's lack of "real" power was often reiterated by the civil society camp to dispute the legitimacy of conservatives' power and depress people's expectations about what the president was actually capable of doing.[50] Outspoken people from this camp emphasized the sweeping and unbridled powers of the leader and the supervisory bodies, implicitly suggesting the need to make the Iranian polity more "democratic" if the popular will, represented by Khatami, were to be reflected in policy making.[51] Others, such as the secretary of the MRM, publicized the fact that Khatami faced difficulties in implementing his reforms due to lack of cooperation from various state organizations.[52]

Unable to mar the president's popular image or his democratic message, the conservatives decided to make use of their institutional-legal privileges and weaken Khatami by purging those close to him. Tehran's mayor Gholamhossein Karbaschi was the first victim. Charged with embezzling billions and wasting public money on what the rightist court called "dubious developmental projects," he was arrested in April 1998.[53] Nearly three months later, the court sentenced Karbaschi to five years imprisonment, forced him to pay the government huge fines, and barred him from holding public office for ten years.[54] Upon appeal, and through Rafsanjani's behind-the-scenes lobbying, his sentence was reduced to two years.[55] It was all too evident, however, that the whole affair was a factional fight. Though there was no doubt that—as with nearly all government institutions in Iran—Karbaschi's office was corrupt at some level, as supporters of the mayor pointed out, Tehran's municipality was certainly far less corrupt than conservative-dominated organs such as Rafiq-dust's Disinherited Foundation (Bonyad).[56] To be sure, except among the bazaaris involved in land speculation, whom the mayor taxed very highly, Karbaschi was immensely popular in Tehran for his achievements, effectiveness, and forthright style of administration.[57] Most of the population shared the views of Behzad Nabavi who maintained that Karbaschi paid a heavy price for supporting Khatami during the election. He had placed generously the entire machinery of the Tehran municipal government at the service of Khatami and his men, as well as contributing financially to his campaign. Of equal importance, argued Nabavi, was that "the defeated faction wants to emotionally mutilate and dishearten the executive and the May 23 Movement."[58]

Karbaschi's arrest was significant for other reasons. Firstly, it marked an increased role in the activities of the judiciary and its head, Ayatollah Mohammad Yazdi, in subjugating the May Movement, particularly the liberal press. Yazdi became the guardian of the tenets of *velayat-e faqih* and the religious rectitude of the regime through a discernible ideological shift to the right. It was the judiciary (religious courts) and not the justice ministry (republican government institution) who organized and carried out the whole Karbaschi affair by capitalizing on the equivocal legal-constitutional nature of the Iranian polity.[59] The Karbaschi episode also reassured the conservatives that they could rely on support from Khamenehi in their antireform enterprise,[60] as the leader offered open support for the actions of the judiciary.[61]

The Karbaschi debacle was a dress rehearsal for a more impressive move. As a well-known and steadfast reformer in charge of the government's most important executive body, the Ministry of State, Abdollah Nuri had the potential of becoming a real menace to the conservatives. He immediately incurred their wrath by dismissing and removing many rightist officials in the ministry.[62] His refusal to dismiss Karbaschi[63] not only angered the conservatives but was perceived as opposing the wishes of the leader himself. However, though all these factors played a key part in Nuri's removal, his support for Montazeri was the offense that Khamenehi could not overlook.[64] In June 1998, thirty-one MPs, headed by Mohammad Reza Bahonar, asked for the impeachment of Nuri, accusing him of an inability to maintain social peace during the Montazeri incident, causing unrest and destabilizing the situation in the country through his support for the mayor of Tehran, and making unsuitable appointments in the interior ministry.[65] One hundred and thirty-seven MPs voted for his removal, while a hundred and seventeen voted against the motion, with eleven abstentions.[66] A defiant Nuri, who was selected by Khatami as his first deputy advisor for political affairs the same day he was impeached, said a week later, "The people should consider this impeachment as a serious warning to the democratic movement, as it displayed the opposing camp's real intention towards the May 23 Movement."[67] In late July, his replacement, the moderate MRM member Abdolvahed Musavi-Lari, secured a vote of confidence from the Majlis despite conservative reservations.[68] The conservatives' campaign eventually backfired. It made Karbaschi and Nuri "martyrs" of democracy and Khatami the "oppressed."

Now, instead of trying to simply block the liberal program, the conservatives looked determined to turn it back; the pro-Khatami press began reporting a much larger and more organized scheme to eliminate Khatami and obliterate the entire civil society project by "far-right circles" made up of extremist elements in the conservative camp. Reportedly, these circles were masterminded by the Mo'talefeh and included extremist elements from the IRGC, the information ministry, the judiciary, and the head of Iranian national radio and television, Ali Larijani. The speculation among Khatami's people was that their ultimate goal was to unseat Khatami through some sort of political coup.[69] With this ultimate goal, the plot was to sponsor enough mayhem in the society at large to portray the president as incompetent and a danger to the survival of the regime. This, in turn, would require military (IRGC) intervention under the pretext of maintaining order in the country. Khatami's close associates and liberal activists, whose views were deemed as undermining the religious foundations of the Islamic Republic, were to be intimidated, threatened, and possibly eliminated.[70] In this endeavor, the neo-fundamentalists—eventually labeled "pressure groups"—would serve as the far right's "physical arm." Alongside Resalat, the daily Keyhan and its editor, Hossein Shariatmadari, championed the ideological crusade of the far-right groups in Iran. Finally, a religious reading that would justify resorting to violence against the enemies of Islam was furnished by few ultra-conservative clergy, particularly by Ayatollah Mohammad Yazdi and hojjatol-Islam Mohammad-Taqi Mesbah Yazdi. The former continued his attacks on the "unfettered press" and the way it was "diluting" velayat-e faqih, noting that true Islam calls upon Muslims to stand firm against such people.[71] In exploring the "political philosophy of Islam" and criticizing those who were disseminating secular ideas, Mesbah Yazdi maintained, "Freedom is not absolute, and humans have conditional freedom. We must accept all the teachings of Islam without questioning them."[72]

In November 1997, the deputy of IRGC, Mohammad Baqer Zolqadr uttered the first of a series of the IRGC's threatening remarks aimed at intimidating the May 23 movement. He said "IRGC will react swiftly to anything that would threaten this holy regime," asserting, at the same time, that the IRGC had the right to engage in nonmilitary matters in the country.[73] Intimidation soon hardened into the threat of violence. In April 1998, the new head of the IRGC,[74] Rahim Safavi, told his men in Qom he had the following words for the liberals and their newspapers:

> These days newspapers are published that are endangering national security and are in line with the words of the enemy and the United States. . . . I have told Mr. Mohajerani that your way [allowing press freedom] is endangering national security; do you know where you are going? . . . I am after uprooting antirevolutionaries everywhere. We must behead some and cut out the tongues of others. Our language is the language of the sword and seekers of martyrdom. . . . The interior ministry is behind Montazeri's mayhem.[75]

Such endeavours were not only supported implicitly by prominent leaders of the "circles,"[76] but by Khamenehi himself. The leader told the people that "today the enemy is striking Islam from home,"[77] and encouraged them to confront "the new plot hatched to destroy Islam."[78] It was with such prompting that Safavi said "When I see a conspiratorial, cultural current underway, I give myself the right to defend the revolution against it and my commander, the esteemed leader, has not prevented me [from doing so].[79] Khamenehi became increasingly hostile to the liberal press and in an unusually harsh tone he spoke in a way more and more aligned with the new discourse of the far right: "Freedom is not absolute and is confined by the rules set by Islam. I warn against misuse of freedom by certain sections of the press. Prevention of such devious acts is not difficult but I wait and see what responsible organizations will do. This is another warning on my part and officials must find out and punish newspapers that are crossing the line."[80]

Silencing the voices of the May Movement became the order of the day, and newspapers were closed down one by one. The justification was similar in each case, with accusations that the papers were spreading lies, publishing materials that threatened the security of the regime, and undermining the Islamic virtue of the republic. *Jame'eh* was ordered to stop publishing after the court interpreted the publication of Safavi's speech as revealing state secrets, and the articles on corruption in the *Bonyad* and of Rafiqdust as lies.[81] *Tus,* the newspaper started almost immediately after the closure of *Jame'eh* by the same staff, was closed in September 1998.[82] Judge Mohsen Ijhei, reportedly one of the ringleaders of the far right, announced that the tone of *Tus* was a danger to the regime after the daily published a controversial interview with the former French president Giscard d'Estaing.[83] The weekly *Adineh* was also closed for spreading lies and publishing materials that were considered morally unacceptable.[84] Violence against the civil society camp moved to another level when prominent members of this camp were physically attacked. In January 1999, Hizbollahis attacked the daily *Khordad,* physically intimidating the staff.[85] In early January, Nuri and Mohajerani were beaten up by a group who later admitted to belonging to the Hizbollah,[86] and Hadi Khamenehi was physically beaten a month later.[87]

In order to maintain the moral virtues of Iran, the young, particularly university students, become the objects of a new round of physical attacks by the *Basij* and the Hizbollahis[88] following comments made by Khamenehi and Yazdi who called for an increase in their activities to preserve Islamic values in the universities and on the streets.[89] The conservatives also silenced the students' most popular religious mentor, Mohsen Kadivar, who had crusaded against the principle of *velayat-e faqih*.[90] In a very controversial interview with *Asr-e Ma,* he said, "The leader is not immune to criticism and individuals have the right to disagree with his actions."[91] The Special Court for the Clergy accused Kadivar of spreading lies and unsettling the public mind and sentenced him to one and a half years in prison. The court's decision infuriated the May 23 Front, particularly students, who carried banners saying, "We think like Kadivar, so you can arrest us, too."[92]

Khatami's reaction to the conservative onslaught was initially measured, but he eventually took up a much more critical stance. He bitterly attacked the extremist right-wing groups for their actions, saying that they cannot run a country by creating fear. He constantly reiterated that Islam is a religion of tolerance, not of fear and aggression, and emphasized the need for respect of others and their opinions.[93] However, he refrained from directly confronting the right. Knowing very well the conservative plan to provoke pro-Khatami supporters a violent response, he warned his supporters that "the enemy wants to say that there is no order and security in the society."[94] But the president's tone soon became harsh as the Islamic Republic witnessed its most disastrous situation yet.

In fall of 1998, a series of murders of secular intellectuals shocked the country. In November, Bazargan's minister of labor, the nationalist Darush Foruhar, and his wife were brutally murdered in their home.[95] This was followed by the suspicious deaths of Majid Sharif, Majid Mokhtari, and Mohammad Ja'far Puyandeh, all writers and intellectuals who had planned to re-create a secular-minded writers' academy.[96] The murders offered gruesome evidence for the reformists' theory that the far right would stop at nothing to succeed in its anti-Khatami moves. They pointed out that the recent murders aimed to scare all "alternative thinkers" in the country while simultaneously portraying Iran as a dangerous place due to Khatami's inability to maintain order. This was designed to deepen the chaos.[97] The president responded by ordering the information ministry to investigate the case, promising to do his utmost to find the perpetrators.[98] For the first time since the conservative actions began, he spoke as strongly as his own hardline supporters, blaming the "Fascist pressure groups who want to present an image of danger and disorder in the country."[99] Such a position meant Khamenehi had little choice but to support a full and credible investigation into the matter.[100]

The reaction of the far right was an unapologetic combination of farfetched explanations. While blaming foreign forces for the murders, they implicitly approved of the killings, labelling the murdered intellectuals apostates.[101] Others such as Asgar Owladi suggested that the government was incapable of preserving security and protecting the people.[102] But the most ridiculous theory came from Ruhollah Hosseinian, after the information ministry announced that it had arrested a few of its members for the killing.[103] In an interview with *Keyhan,* the head of Iranian National Islamic Archives alleged that far-left elements from the Khatami camp who had turned against the revolution and the imam were the perpetrators of the killings. He, too, quite explicitly, justified the killing of the apostate writers.[104] A week later the information ministry announced that the people arrested for carrying out the murders were "rogue" elements from the ministry who had acted alone and without the knowledge of the minister, Qorban Ali Dorri-Najafabadi.[105] This statement did little to convince anyone of the truth, and he resigned a month later, to be replaced by Ali Yunesi.[106]

Regardless of whether or not the perpetrators and their bosses are brought to justice, this affair has had a deep impact on the regime and on Iranian politics generally. Khatami demonstrated his political clout by persisting in his ultimately successful campaign to force the information ministry to acknowledge the participation of its own people.[107] The murders also stained the image of innocence and infallibility previously upheld by the regime. Given that such killings could not have taken place without the permission or at least knowledge of senior officials within the regime, the incident has created an Iranian style "Watergate," with Khatami and the left pushing for all the facts to come out, and everyone waiting to see where the trail will lead. Depending on who is implicated, the consequences for the regime could be immense. As Behzad Nabavi said in an interview with *Salam,* it means that the left's accusations of a rightist plot to terrorize reformers and bring down Khatami have been borne out by the facts, and we now have a convincing example of the antireformist strategy:

> The basic goal of the right from the start was to present Khatami as the antithesis of [Islamic] "values" and "stability" of the regime, to show that if political development and civil society were institutionalized, security and order would disappear in society. They also want to create more opposition against the discourse of the May Movement. By opposing the slogans of freedom and civil society against Islamic values and the revolution, they expect naturally to bring out some *maraje',* ulama, and religious masses against Mr. Khatami, recruiting forces at the same time. . . . The aim is to steer society to a point where people would say "despotism is a good thing and we do not want freedom" . . . and to say that "we consent to anyone who establishes stability and order."[108]

Conclusion

As the Islamic Republic enters its third decade, factional politics have evolved into more than a power struggle among competing ideological blocs; it is conceivably the base of politics in Iran and an integral component of the political process. Understanding the complexities of Iranian factionalism lies in recognizing the interplay of the embedded ideological dimensions of the regime—the religious, the populist, and the revolutionary—and the institutional workings of the Iranian state. The ideological dimensions embody the multiple aspirations of the postrevolutionary regime, and each faction's discourse is made up of the amalgamation of the components of one or more dimensions. The hierarchical Iranian polity, however, becomes the arena and instrument of factional politicking. Regardless of their vision of the structure of the true Islamic state, and depending on their position within the state institution, factions have used the multidimensional nature of the state, the Iranian constitution, the views of Islamic activists, and the ambiguous legacy of Ayatollah Khomeini to advance their readings on issues and policies.

Factional disputes over politics in Iran accent the biggest irony of the postrevolutionary Islamic regime. The unifying force and strength of Khomeini and his disciples in the face of domestic and foreign challenges—the Islamicity of the regime—has become the main source of contention leading to the republic's current predicament. Aside from toppling the monarchy and implementing Islamic tenets, Khomeini and his followers had at best a vague notion about the day-to-day workings of the next regime. And the inability of the clergy to provide solid, Islamically sanctioned solutions to the country's problems only became more conspicuous as the revolution stabilized and questions arose concerning everyday matters of governance in a more politically seasoned society.

266

From early on, the debates between the two dominant factions in the political spectrum—the left and the right—represented the main difference among Khomeini's pupils: populist-revolutionary vs. elitist-conservative. The latter faction held the upper hand, however. The powerful alliance of bazaar and mosque, which had longstanding historical precedent, argued for a free market economy that had grounding in the traditional practice of Shiism. Emphasizing the traditional interpretation of *fiqh,* or Islamic jurisprudence, the conservatives upheld their doctrine by citing the Qoran, the decrees issued throughout history by the clerical establishment at large, and the words of Khomeini himself. The right relied on the same sources to advocate austere sociocultural policies as well as a political elitism that recognized the clergy as having the divine right to rule and the *faqih* as the "apolitical" guardian of the system.

What the postrevolutionary period clearly illustrated was that ambiguities of the constitution and fluid interpretations of Islam allowed factions to create new platforms as well as to form alliances between rivals while holding to their claim of being doctrinaire. The governing elite after a decade had yet to introduce to the population a clear image of the regime and its policies in different spheres. Lingering problems made all factions realize the need for major shifts in both ideology and practice. By the time the third Majlis was assembled, the patriarch had become far less ideological. His rulings prior to his death as well as his wish to amend the constitution favored the position of the left and the Rafsanjanites, the modern right.

This paved the way for a more pragmatic, less ideological, and ultimately less religious Iranian state. Bearing in mind the factional balance of power, the fate of Islam, the religiosity of the republic, and above all the survival of the regime, Khomeini skillfully charted a postrevolutionary course. Following Khomeini's footsteps, Rafsanjani's de-revolutionization of the regime was essentially a "revolution from above," at first with the support of Khamenehi and the conservatives. By further opening the "open doors of *ijtihad,*" he gradually introduced a more liberal interpretation of sociocultural policies, extensively privatized the Iranian economy, and championed greater political openness, which all contributed to the ability of the regime to adapt to the realities of time. Indeed, aside from Khomeini, Rafsanjani has been the most pivotal political personality in postrevolutionary Iran. It was the policies of this former president who paved the way for the reformist president Mohammad Khatami, who, if he continues on the path he has begun, could be the next key figure.

A legitimate question at this juncture is whether any faction's views are more consistent with the prevailing interpretation of modern Shiism. Although among Shii opinion setters (the ulama, Islamic activists, and scholars) there have been diverse opinions with regards to sociocultural, economic, and political questions, historically one is able to detect certain themes and precedents. For instance, with regards to sociocultural issues, the puritan stance of the conservative right has been the more widespread creed among Islamists, who espouse views more or less in line with Navab Safavi's system. This interpretation dates from the mid-nineteenth century, when the ulama and the majority of the religiously orthodox masses opposed Western cultural penetration in Iran, opposition that continued during the reign of Pahlavis. Indeed, cultural purification became one of the main objectives of the Islamic revolutionary movement in Iran.

On the left, the contemporary sociocultural discourse in post-Khomeini Iran is hardly a conventional Shii discourse. Prior to 1989, most members of the left were just as puritanical as the conservatives. Many members of the MII were organizers of the club-wielding Hizbollahis of the heyday of the revolution, and the likes of Khatami were exceptions rather than the norm. Even today, people with views such as Khalkhali and Mohtashami remain highly parochial. So not only do the left's current relatively progressive views and their endorsement of notions such as civil society and women's rights lack historical precedent, but these views are a definite break from their earlier stance on sociocultural issues. The anti-conservatism of the left in the sociocultural realm is at variance with historical Shii conviction and with the Imam himself. Here, too, however, the multifaceted dimensions of the regime and the "open doors" of *ijtihad* have provided the left with the opportunity to not only alter its earlier positions but to put forward a divergent thesis.

As noted in chapter 1, the clergy, with the exception of Khomeini, can hardly be considered revolutionary politically, and, like the church men of the West, historically they have sought to influence political power rather than assume it directly. Political activists such as the *Mo'talefeh* and the views of left-leaning thinkers such as Shariati, who opposed the Pahlavi dynasty, should be interpreted as pressuring the government to change its un-Islamic policies, not as clamoring for a full-fledged revolution. That being said, the analysis of the political views of the left and the right during the first decade of the revolution and after Khomeini's death begs explanation. While Khomeini was alive, the religio-political views of the conservative right (views that were in line with the predominant historical position of the clerical establishment) were similar to the views of the *Hojjatiyeh:* a supervisory and watchful guardianship role for the ulama and not their direct rule. At the same time, because of Khomeini's precedent-breaking views that called for the revolutionary political activism of the clergy, the left espoused direct involvement for the ulama in politics. Following the death of Khomeini, when the conservatives welcomed a sympathetic *faqih* and enjoyed a majority in the super-bodies (see chapters 3 through 5), they began advocating religious rule more strongly. The left shifted towards supporting stronger republican institutions after the departure of Khomeini and the changes in the balance of power and political structures in Iran. Once again, the multidimensional nature of the regime facilitated shifts in the views of both factions on religio-political issues.

Economically, a conservative pro-private ownership and free market reading of the Islamic economic system has solid historical foundations among Shii mujtahids and thinkers, including Khomeini himself.[1] Even those like the progressive ayatollah Mahmud Taleqani, who espoused a more radical interpretation of the Islamic economic system, upheld the right of private ownership as long as society's welfare was not imperiled.[2] Although socioeconomic justice is exhorted by Islamic jurists and polarization of wealth frowned upon, the notions of economic justice and equality and their attainment methods are open to a variety of interpretations. And again, these broad values do not dictate a specific role for government: when it comes to the role of the Islamic state in the economy, the inferences of the mujtahids are nebulous and idiosyncrasy. The Islamic government, they argue, should interfere in the economy and maintain equity and justice only when there is an absolute necessity, discerned of course by the *vali-ye faqih* or the *foqaha*.

So except for its current politically motivated position on *vali-ye faqih*, the conservative right faction can claim that its paradigm of an Islamic state is in accord with both the historical stance of Shiism and Khomeini's discourse prior to and immediately after the victory of the revolution. Given their historical political and economic interests, it is clear why the "traditional" interpretation is both desired and defended by the bazaar-clergy axis where socioeconomic policies are concerned. Therefore the new breed of Islamists, made up of young middle-level clergy and lay revolutionaries, the left, faces an arduous task to advance its unconventional readings of Islam on various issues in the face of the right's well-drawn, historically supported views. This faction has endured mainly due to Khomeini's edicts and sporadic aid, as well as with Rafsanjani's support for the socioeconomic policies that were put forward by the radicals in the Majlis.

The Elite and the Unintended Consequences of the Revolution

As is the case with most revolutions, the leadership in Iran encountered some unforeseen situations. These realties have forced the revolutionaries Iran to change, adopt, and transform fundamental ideologies, regardless of their factional inclinations. Two important developments come to mind in this regard. The first is the transformation in the status of the Iranian clergy. One element that enabled the clergy to persist as a powerful social force in Iranian history was their role as protectors of the masses against the actions of the state. Indeed, fighting the secular powers was a crucial element in clerical popularity in Iran. Following the revolution, however, the ulama acquired a new status, that of statesmen. This transformation is of paramount importance, for it transposed the clergy's relationship with the population at large. Now, instead of being a class in opposition to the state, they found themselves to be the representatives of the very same institution. Indeed, greater than factional politics, the involvement of the clergy in government bared a far more profound paradox for the clergy and Shii establishment in Iran: radical political posturing vs. quietist-conservative demeanor. As the government and statesmen, the clergy were compelled to pursue policies that all states must pursue in order to govern effectively. The need to carry out the affairs of state compelled the clergy to define and redefine religion and justify their new "hands on" role in society, in contrast to their historical role. Nowhere is this paradox more conspicuous than the cracks created in the historical alliance of clergy and the bazaar. The more Iran was forced to modernize culturally and economically, the more strain was placed on this relationship.

Another harsh truth to which the revolutionaries had to succumb was the realization that contemporary Iran bears no resemblance to the Islamic society of the time of the prophet. The Islamic Republic is ultimately a modern nation-state with all of the problems and complexities associated with a Third World country. As such, the simplistic and utopian picture of an Islamic government espoused by the clerical elite was incompatible with the realties of contemporary Iran. There are important imperatives and governing laws to which all contemporary states must adhere in order to survive and endure both domestically and internationally, and the Islamic Republic is no exception. What is more, in order for the clergy to manage successfully the affairs of a contemporary Iran, they had to learn the art of modern statesmanship, a novel experience indeed for the clergy. This lack of managerial experience on the part of the clergy was undoubtedly a key factor in their modest performance after the revolution, and certain injudicious—or even outlandish—decisions of the leadership must be attributed to this factor.

The ambiguous ideological and systemic edifice of the regime has allowed factions to change their stance in order to adapt to the political realities of the time. But as the revolutionary years passed, the governing elite came to realize that success—even survival—in the contemporary world necessitated closely complying with certain fundamental imperatives, regardless of their ideological disposition. For the leadership in Iran this meant that religio-revolutionary rhetoric had to be superseded by more expedient methods of governance, that the supremacy of mundane worldly political matters over religious and ideological ones be established, and that the state be ruled through formal rather than informal principles. In Weber's terminology, the regime's survival rested on its "rationalization," which was initiated by Khomeini and later taken up by Rafsanjani and now Khatami. This rationalization ultimately could mean a more democratic Iran. There are good reasons to believe that quasi-democratic Iran may be evolving into a full-fledged democracy; the will of the people and not the elite's will is likely to have the final say in the future, given that the unobstructed authority of the leader and the supervisory bodies are being challenged by the population at large and not just the more liberal members of the elite.

Although the Islamicity of the regime is the source of factional politics, the regime's viability over time also depends considerably on it. For although Shii jurisprudence and *velayat-e faqih* make the Iranian polity a fertile ground for factional politics, they also serve as its safety valve. As we saw, *ijtihad* allows for opposing factional readings of issues and the creation of policies that will lead to ideological disputes. At the same time, it grants the clergy, and above all the *faqih* who enjoys supreme and unbridled power and can employ *maslahat* (interest) of the Islamic society and state, the power to issue edicts that break up deadlocks. The January 1988 edict by Khomeini was a case in point. Paradoxically, the highly individual, discretionary exercise of *ijtihad*, coupled with the unencumbered powers of the *faqih*, actually provides the regime with a great deal of flexibility, maneuverability, and, ultimately, resiliency. However, these two features, *ijtihad* and the discretionary powers of the *faqih*, can be the cause for great shifts in disposition and policies. While Khomeini's edict served the immediate interests of the regime, it eventually became a tool for the faction in power to advance its political ambitions. At that time that meant the conservative right, and the result was to make the government far more repressive.

However, the 1997 presidential election should be an alarm for all factions in power that the society will no longer accept oppressive measures. Khatami's election indicated that Iran is witnessing the emergence of a contesting civil society, producing serious challenges for a regime already under pressure. The regime is not entirely to blame for current conditions in Iran: any young government would struggle to cope with a lengthy war, international pressures, or a decline in revenues due to falling oil prices. But the clerical elite bear the lion's share of responsibility for their predicament. Aside from lacking a consensus on the nature of the revolutionary-Islamic regime, the leadership promised too much, too soon, and for too many people, ignoring their own as well as the country's limitations.

Current pressures from the Iranian people ultimately will lead either to accommodation or resistance on the part of the leadership. The former scenario entails major changes in the nature of the Iranian theocracy, both ideological and institutional, while the latter is bound to create clashes between the state and society. The poor performance of the Iranian regime has transformed it from a proactive state into a reactive one. Early popularity of the elite allowed the leadership to pursue various policies without shaking the public's close-to-unanimous support. Now, in many ways, it is the society that sets agendas and the state that must react accordingly. Arguably, the regime has recognized both its own limitations and the important fact that it must respond to the demands of a politically experienced revolutionary society. At the same time, given the current structure of the Iranian state, the predicament of the regime remains just as much institutional as ideological.

Appendix

Notes

Glossary

Bibliography

Index

Articles from the Constitution
of the Islamic Republic of Iran

On the overall essence of the Islamic Republic:

ARTICLE 2—The Islamic Republic is a system based on faith in:

1. The One and only God *(There is no God but Allah)*, His exclusive Sovereignty and Legislation and the necessity of submission to His command.

2. The Divine Revelation and its basic role in the exposition of laws.

3. The concept of Resurrection and its constructive role in the course of evolution of Man towards God.

4. The justice of God in the Creation and Legislation.

5. Perpetual Imamat and leadership and its fundamental role in the perpetuation of the Islamic Revolution.

6. Eminent dignity and value of Man, his freedom coupled with his responsibility before God.

On the "Method of Government in Islam" the constitution states:

From the viewpoint of Islam, government is not a product of the class system or individual or group domination but it is the crystallization of political ideal of a nation that has same ideology and religion and organises itself to move, in the process of its ideological evolution, towards the final goal [movement towards Allah]. . . . In creating the political foundations on the basis of ideological interpretations which in itself is the basis of organising a society, the pious men shall bear the responsibility of government

(Source: Constitution of the Islamic Republic. Directorate-General of International Agreements Pub., 1995)

and management of the country. Legislation, which is indicative of standards of social management, shall follow on the course of Koran and traditions of the prophet. Therefore, serious and minute-supervisory by just pious and committed Islamic scholars (just faqih) is necessary and indispensable. Whereas the objective of government is to foster the growth of Man in such a way that he progresses towards the establishment of the Divine Rule. . . . The Constitution, in view of this direction, shall lay the ground for such participation by all members of society in all stages of political and fateful decision-making so that in the course of evolution of Man, every individual would be involved in growth, development and leadership. This in fact is the realization of the concept of government on earth by the oppressed.

Important article pertaining to the religious dimension of the regime:

ARTICLE 56—God Almighty has absolute sovereignty over the world and Man, and He has made Man the master of his own social destiny. No one can divest Man of this divine right or apply it in the service of interests of a particular individual or group. The Nation shall exercise this God-given right in the manner set forth in the following articles.

ARTICLE 110—Functions and Authorities of the Leader:

1. To determine the general policies of the system of the Islamic Republic of Iran after consulting with the Majma'a-e Tashkhise—Maslahat-e-Nezam.

2. To supervise over the good performance of the system's general policies.

3. To decree referendums.

4. To hold the Supreme Command of the Armed Forces.

5. To declare war or peace, and mobilize the armed forces.

6. To appoint, dismiss, or accept resignations of:

a) The Faqihs of the Guardian Council.

b) The highest authority of the Judiciary.

c) The head of Sazman Seda va Seema-e Jomhouri-e-Eslami Iran.

d) Chief of Joint Staffs.

e) Chief Commander of the Islamic Revolutionary Guard Corps.

f) Chief Commanders of the Armed Forces and Police Forces.

7. To resolve disputes and coordinate relations between the three powers

On law: its making, process, and implementation:

ARTICLE 4—All laws and regulations including civil, criminal, financial, economic, administrative, cultural, military, political or otherwise, shall be based on Islamic principles. This article shall apply generally on all the Articles of the Constitution and other laws and regulations. It shall be decided by the jurisconsults of the Guardian Council whether or not such laws and regulations conform to this article.

ARTICLE 156—The judiciary shall be an independent power that protects individual and social rights, shall be responsible for the implementing justice and shall carry out the following functions:

1. To examine and pass judgments in respect of litigation, violations, complaints; to settle lawsuits, resolve hostilities and to take necessary decisions and actions in respect of that part of matters of personal status to be laid down by law.

2. To restore public rights and to promote justice and lawful freedoms.

3. To supervise the proper implementation of laws.

4. To uncover crimes, to prosecute and punish the criminals and implement *Hodoud* (penance by the lash) and the Islamic codified penal provisions.

5. To take suitable measures for preventing the commission of crime and to reform the offenders.

ARTICLE 8—Inviting to do good deeds, directing to do what is lawful or good and enjoining not to commit what is unlawful or bad shall be a public and reciprocal duty of all people vis-à-vis each other in the Islamic Republic of Iran, of the Government vis-à-vis people and vice versa. Conditions and limits thereof shall be determined by law.

Politics and political process and political parties

PREAMBLE—The executive branch of the government must strive to create an Islamic society. Thus, surrounding it with any complicated bureaucratic system, that slows down the attainment of this objective shall be rejected from the Islamic point of view. Therefore, the bureaucratic system, which is a product of the Taqhouti (satanic) rule, shall be strongly rejected so that an executive system with more speed and efficiency may be created for carrying out administrative obligations.

ARTICLE 57—The sovereign powers in the Islamic Republic of Iran consist of the Legislature, the Executive and the Judiciary, which shall be exercised under the absolute Velayat-e Amr va Imamat-e Ommat in accordance with the following articles of this law. These powers shall be independent of each other.

ARTICLE 6—In the Islamic Republic of Iran the affairs of the State shall be managed by relying on public opinion, through the elections such as the election of the president, representatives of the Majlis-e Shura-e Eslami members of councils and the like, or through referendum in cases set forth in other articles of this law.

ARTICLE 26—It shall be allowed to form parties, societies, political or professional associations, and Islamic or other religious societies of the recognized minorities, provided that they do not violate the principles of freedom, independence, national unity, Islamic standards and essentials of the Islamic Republic. No one may be stopped from participating in them or forced to participate in one of them.

Sociocultural: media, women, individual rights

PREAMBLE—Women shall enjoy greater rights for the reason that so far they had suffered more oppression at the hands of the *Taghouti* (satanic) regime. Family is the fundamental unit of society and the focal point of growth and elevation of Man. Ideological and idealistic concurrence in the setting up of a family, which is the main factor of growth and evolutionary movement to provide opportunities to attain his objective. Under such approach of the family unit, woman will cease to be "a mere object" or "a work tool" in the service of propagation of consumerism and exploitation and regaining her enormous and worthy role of motherhood for bringing up pioneer and ideological Man, she is a companion of men in the battlefield of life. Consequently, she will assume greater responsibilities and enjoy greater value and esteem from the viewpoint of Islam.

ARTICLE 21—The Government shall be required to guarantee the rights of women in all respects, by observing the principles of Islam, and shall carry out the following:

1. To create suitable environment for the growth of personality of Woman and to restore her material and moral rights.

2. To protect mothers, particularly during the period of pregnancy and custody of children, and to protect children without guardians.

3. To create competent courts for preserving the existence and survival of family.

4. To create special insurance for widows, elderly women, and women without guardians.

5. To grant guardianship of children to worthy mothers for protecting the children's interests, in case there is no legal guardian.

PREAMBLE—The mass media [radio and television] in pursuit of the evolutionary course of the Islamic Revolution, must be in the service of propagating Islamic culture. To this end, it must try to benefit from healthy encounter of various thoughts and views. However, it must seriously refrain from propagating destructive and anti–Islamic attitudes. It is the duty of all to abide by the Articles of this law which regards the freedom and dignity of Man as its main objective and paves the way for evolution and perfection of Man.

ARTICLE 23—Investigation of one's beliefs shall be prohibited. No one may be offended or reprimanded simply because of having a certain belief.

ARTICLE 24—Publications and the press shall have freedom of expression unless they, violate the essentials of Islam or public rights. Its details shall be set forth by law.

ARTICLE 29—It shall be the universal right of all to enjoy social security covering retirement, unemployment, old age, disability, destitution, accidents and calamities, and health, medical treatment and care services through insurance, etc.

ARTICLE 30—The Government shall be required to provide free education and training for the entire nation up to the end of high school education, and to expand the means of free higher education up to the level of self-sufficiency of the country.

ARTICLE 31—It shall be the right of every Iranian individual and family to have a house suitable to his needs. The Government shall be required to carry out this article with due observance of the priority of those who are more needy, particularly the villagers and workers.

PREAMBLE—Freedom of speech and expression of ideas must be guaranteed at the seda and seema [radio and TV] with due observance of the principles and criteria of Islam and the interests of the country.

Economics and economic system:

ARTICLE 44—The economic system of the Islamic Republic of Iran shall be based on public, cooperative and private sectors, with proper and regulated planning . . . Ownership in the aforesaid three sectors, insofar as it conforms to other articles in this chapter, does not surpass the limits of Islamic laws, causes economic growth and development of the country, and does not harm the society, shall enjoy protection of law in the Islamic Republic.

Details of regulations, scope and conditions of the three sectors shall be determined by law.

ARTICLE 47—Private ownership acquired legitimately shall be respected. Regulations thereof shall be determined by law.

Foreign policy:

ARTICLE 152—The foreign policy of the Islamic Republic of Iran shall be based on the negation of excreting or accepting any form of domination whatsoever, safeguarding all-embracing independence and territorial integrity defense of the rights of all Muslims, non-alignment with domineering powers and peaceful and reciprocal relations with non-belligerent states. The Islamic Republic of Iran regards the happiness of Man in the Human Society as its aspiration and recognizes independence, freedom and the rule of right and justice as the right of all the people of the world. Therefore, while completely refraining from any interference in the internal matters of other nations, it supports the rightful struggle of the oppressed people against their oppressors anywhere in the world.

ARTICLE 154—The Islamic Republic of Iran regards the happiness of Man in the Human Society as its aspiration and recognizes independence, freedom, and the rule of right and justice as the right of all people of the world. Therefore, while completely refraining from any interference in the internal matters of other nations, it supports the rightful struggle of the oppressed people against their oppressors anywhere in the world.

Notes

Introduction

1. The conventional notion of a clash between Western and non-Western cultures was proposed by Harvard University scholar Samuel P. Huntington in his 1993 article "The Clash of Civilizations."

2. See, for example, Khatami's speech before the United Nations on September 20, 1998, where he suggested the need for a constructive "dialogue of civilizations" *(Salam,* September 22 and 23, 1998). He expressed the same views on the anniversary of his election to the presidency *(Salam,* May 24, 1998).

3. See his Friday prayer sermon in *Ettela'at,* January 6, 1999.

4. *Ettela'at,* September 26, 1998.

5. Tucker (1975, 301).

6. In the Russian case, the struggle was among the Bolsheviks, Mensheviks, and a host of other groups ranging from constitutional monarchists to moderates and socialists. Ultimately the Bolsheviks were able to consolidate power. The revolutionary forces of the Chinese Revolution also had their share of differences. The revolutionary movements of the nationalist Kuomitang and the Chinese Communist Party emerged at the same time and soon became allies in the anti-warlord struggle, at first agreeing to unite and work together for a "nationalist, democratic revolution." The alliance soon disintegrated and China experienced civil war from 1947 to 1949; Mao and the Red Army were the victors. A detailed account of the struggle among the revolutionary forces in the Russian Revolution is discussed in Rabinowitch (1968). On China, see Sheridan (1975, particularly chap. 2).

7. For a brief but accurate description of the anti-Shah revolutionary forces, see Hooglund (1986).

8. The Chinese polity after the victory of the revolution, for example, was plagued by factions and factionalism (Nathan [1973]).

9. Skocpol (1979). The thesis of Skocpol's classic study on revolutions is that one common outcome of all modern revolutions has been a highly centralized and ideologically coherent state.

10. Ilias Hazrati in *Mashruh-e Mozakerat-e Majlis-e Showra-ye Islami* (Parliamentary Debates of the Islamic Consultative Assembly); hereafter referred to as *Parliamentary Debates.*

11. The best and most accurate account of the views and the make-up of factions in post-Khomeini Iran was published in the Iranian biweekly *Asr-e Ma* (Our Epoch) in the winter and spring of 1995. My own categorization of the factions throughout the book is primarily based on these articles (see further chap. 3).

12. The concept of a redistributive state here is one where the state undertakes an active role in allocation of resources in society in order to implement socioeconomic justice (Nozick 1974, 149–82).

13. It should be noted that the left upheld such radical views throughout most of the postrevolutionary years but has greatly moderated its views since the election of Khatami, who belongs to this faction (see further chap. 6).

14. "Conservative" here is used in its broadest and classical definition: emphasis on tradition and its role in society, acceptance of class cleavages in society, the belief in the "natural right" of certain groups and individuals to rule, gradual rather than abrupt social change instigated from the top by the elite, an organic view of society, and the belief that what is good for the elite is good for society as a whole (Aristotle 1962).

15. According to Mohsen Nurbaksh, arguably the main architect of post-Khomeini economic policies in Iran, "except for omitting interest [*reba*], the Islamic economy has not produced a specific path or solution for the economy" *(Bayan,* 1991, no. 2: 48).

16. On the nature of Iranian polity, see the excellent study by Schirazi (1997).

17. In this book, the term "state" is used strictly in its Weberian institutional sense. According to Charles Tilly, a state in its institutional conceptualization is "an organization which controls the population occupying a definite territory insofar as (1) it is differentiated from other organizations operating in the same territory; (2) it is autonomous; (3) it is centralized; and (4) its divisions are formally co-ordinated with one another" (Tilly [1975, 70]). See further chap. 1.

18. Siavoshi (1992).

19. Entessar (1994).

20. Baktiari (1996).

21. For example, the Guardian Council, a twelve-member body, is constitutionally empowered to supervise all parliamentary and presidential elections and to determine whether candidates are "Islamically fit" to run for office. See further chap. 1.

22. Although well-respected, Khamenehi has neither the religious qualifications nor the charismatic appeal of Khomeini. See chaps. 4–6.

23. By discussing factionalism in the Majlis, Baktiari's book is limited to one, albeit critical, sphere of factional conflict.

Chapter 1. The Islamic State in Iran: From Theory to Reality

1. *Khotut-e Kolli-ye Andisheha-ye Imam Khomeini* (Imam Khomeini's Line of Political Thought), 39–45; hereafter referred to as *Khotut.*

2. Ibid., 44–51.

3. Khomeini (1942, 44–45 and 180–90).

4. *Khotut* (1994, 223–24).

5. On political conservatism of the ulama, see Reza Sheikholeslami (1986). For perhaps the best two accounts of clergy-state relations in Iran, see Algar (1969) and Akhavi (1980).

6. Khomeini (1942, 186).

7. For instance, following the announcement of the six decrees of the shah's White Revolution in 1962, which included controversial policies such as voting rights for women and land reform, Khomeini requested in a letter addressed to "His Royal Majesty" for "His Majesty to kindly do away with such un-Islamic laws in the country." He signed the letter "Al-dai," or well-wisher *(Sahifeh-ye Nur* [The Book of Lights], 1: 37; hereafter referred to as *Sahifeh*. This is a twenty-five-volume collection of Khomeini's speeches, comments, and important writings). Tehran, Government Publication, 1982.

8. For a good summary of the events and activities of Khomeini leading to the revolution of 1979, see *Khotut* (1995, 56–73).

9. Khomeini 1978, 30–31.

10. Ibid., 20–21.

11. Ibid., 92–93.

12. Ibid., 58–62.

13. Kadivar 1997.

14. For instance, Shaykh Morteza Ansari, arguably the most prominent nineteenth century marja', construed the role of the ulama to be that of "issuing fatwas, arbitration of disputes, and appropriation *(tasarrof)* of properties and persons" (Amanat 1988, 98–102).

15. Enayat 1986, 65.

16. In January 1988, Khomeini declared that *velayat-e faqih* constituted one of the primary rulings of Islam and that the *faqih* relishes such an extensive mandate over the lives of Muslims that if he deems it necessary, he is even entitled to (temporarily) halt pillars of Islam such as prayer and the *haj'*. For the context of decree, see *Ettela'at,* January 8, 1988. For the significance of this ruling, see chap. 2.

17. Bazargan *(Velayat-e Motlaqeh-ye Faqih,* 88–154). Bazargan also argues that none of the previous high-ranking Ayatollahs have envisioned such an all-encompassing role for the *foqaha.*

18. Khomeini (1978, 36).

19. Ibid., 52–58.

20. Ibid., 53–54.

21. Ibid., 58. Arguably, then, Khomeini opposed a republican form of government in its Western secular meaning.

22. Zubaida (1989, chap. 1); see also Ayubi (1991, 18–34 and 48–69).

23. Ayubi (1991, 5).

24. Khomeini (1978, 26–27).

25. See Tilly's definition cited in the introduction, note 17.

26. Vincent (1987, 58).

27. Khomeini (1978, 58).

28. Tabari (1983, 63).

29. Khomeini (1978, 34–37).

30. *Sahifeh,* 4: 169.

31. Ibid., 2: 260.

32. Ibid., 3: 27.

33. Ibid., 4: 206. For similar comments, see also 3: 107.

34. Kadivar (1997).

35. This was later admitted by Bazargan (1984, 84–87).

36. For two detailed accounts of clerical monopolization of power, see Menasheri (1990) and Bakhash (1984).

37. The resistance was orchestrated by people such as Hadi Ghaffari, who was the key organizer of what became known as the Hizbollah. See Ghaffari's memoirs (1984, particularly 400–434).

38. *Ettela'at,* July 5, 1979.

39. See Milani (1988).

40. The term "fundamentalism," or "fundamentalist," in the context of politics of the Islamic revolution is muddled in the literature. Generally, however, it refers to those devout religious segments of the population who believe in the implementation of the words of the Qoran to the letter and/or reject the secular milieu in Muslim countries. Ghaffari's Hizbollah would fit this categorization. On fundamentalism, see the ambitious project of University of Chicago's Marty and Appley (1990).

41. Hojjatol-Islam Hasan Lahuti, the first head of the IRGC, announced that the goals of the *Pasdaran* as the guardians of the revolution based on pure Islamic tenets are combatting all anti-revolutionary and anti-Islamic elements in the country *(Ettela'at,* April 5, 1979).

42. The KII extended its government-like activities to such a degree over several months that at one point the daily *Keyhan* announced, "The KII has taken charge of the country's affairs" (February 19, 1979). Needless to say, the paper was highlighting the extent to which the KII was duplicating government actions rather than being in charge of the government. Two weeks later, another headline in *Keyhan* read, "The revolutionary KII is selecting city officials" (March 4, 1979).

43. Before going to Qom for what ended up being a temporary stay, Khomeini instructed Bazargan to make attending to the plight of the poor his top priority by, for example, exempting them from paying for water or electricity, and to do his outmost to wipe societal cleavages *(Ettela'at,* February 28 and March 1, 1979).

44. On this, see Abrahamian's excellent book (1993).

45. According to Ali Naqi Khamushi, the first director of the *Bonyad,* the revolutionary body executed the rulings of the Islamic Revolutionary Council and not the government and aimed to assist the industrial sector to get back on its feet while minding the disinherited with housing, health, and education *(Ettela'at,* October 7, 1979).

46. The ultimate goal of the *Imdad* Committee was the eradication of poverty while providing educational, health, and other forms of assistance to the poor and the needy, particularly in the rural areas of Iran *(Ettela'at,* March 6, 1980).

47. One the most violent attacks was in summer 1979 at Teheran University where the Hizbollahis stormed a gathering of leftist forces and supporters of Bani-Sadr, savagely beating the participants *(Ettela'at,* June 29, 1979).

48. *Ettela'at,* June 23, 1979. Hizbollahis attacking opponents of clerical domination became widespread from the summer of 1979, especially during the time of the drafting of the constitution, which placed the *velayat-e faqih* into the Islamic Republic.

49. *Ettela'at,* September 24, 1979.

50. Menasheri (1990, 265).

51. Mohajerani (1982, 76).

52. On numerous occasions, Bazargan and his ministers stated that expertise rather than religio-revolutionary credentials would be the criteria for choosing members of the state apparatus *(Ettela'at,* March 30, 1979 and *Keyhan,* January 31, 1980).

53. Bazargan notes that this anti-statist (central government) view was so prevalent that even street cleaners and servants deemed anything that the government did as elitist and reformist (Bazargan [1995, 89–90]).

54. Teheran Radio, BBC World Broadcasting Service, June 28, 1979.

55. *Keyhan,* April 3, 1979.

56. See *Ettela'at,* July 30, 1979 for the statement of the governor of the providence of Hamadan declaring his resignation. See also Bazargan's complaint in *Ettela'at,* May 29, 1979.

57. More than once, Khomeini complained about the satanic *(taquti)* ways in which the government was running the country. For the Ayatollah, the central government was not acting according to the Islamic-revolutionary aspirations of the masses *(Ettela'at,* August 18, 1979).

58. Teheran Radio, May 28, 1979.

59. *Ettela'at,* May 26, 1979.

60. *Ettela'at,* June 11, 1979.

61. *Ettela'at,* July 2, 1979.

62. *Ettela'at,* August, 2, 1979.

63. For the names of the members of the assembly, see *Surat-e Mashruh-e Mozakerat-e Majlis-e Barresi-ye Nehai-ye Jomhuri-ye Islami-ye Iran* (Minutes of the Debates of the Council of the Final Review of the Constitution of Islamic of Iran), 1:221–24; hereafter referred to as *Mozakerat*.

64. *Mozakerat,* 1:39.

65. Ibid., 1:312–16.

66. Ibid., 1:43.

67. Ibid., 1:41.

68. Ibid., 2:50.

69. Ibid., 1:310–11.

70. Ibid., 1:317.

71. Ibid., 1: 64–65.

72. For the text of the proposed article, see ibid., 2: 879.

73. Ibid., 2: 889–91.

74. Ibid., 2: 883–88.

75. Ibid., 2: 887.

76. Ibid., 2: 900–902.

77. Ibid., 2: 922.

78. Ibid., 2: 918–21.

79. Ibid., 2: 899–900.

80. Ibid., 2: 913–16.

81. The Constitution of the Islamic Republic of Iran (Directorate-General of International Agreements, 1995), 12.

82. Ibid., 29–30.

83. *Ettela'at,* February 8, 1989.

84. This analysis of the Iranian constitution benefits from the studious works of Schirazi (1997) and Madani (1995).

85. This is the categorization made by Schirazi (1997, 73–75).

86. Interview with Mohammad Baghai, the representative of the *vali-ye faqih* in Shahid Beheshti University, in *Resalat,* December 29, 1990.

87. *Keyhan,* June 30, 1989.

88. Mann (1995, 913).

89. During the debates about the drafting of the constitution, Bani-Sadr introspectively observed, "How can we be certain that the infallible *(ma'sum) faqih* will not err?" Khomeini's arbitrary designation of imam after the revolution was simply aimed to boost his religious and political mandate among the highly orthodox masses. The mandate of Khamenehi as a benevolent leader is far more controversial. He was a lower-ranking cleric (a hojjatol-Islam) risen overnight to the position of Ayatollah mainly to avert possible leadership crisis (see chap. 3).

90. The first declaration of the IRCG, for example, stated that "the country's laws must be based on divine laws and anything to the contrary will not be accepted and tolerated" *(Ettela'at,* April 17, 1979).

91. The leadership of the IRCG specifically announced that they would take orders only from Khomeini and the Revolutionary Council *(Keyhan,* April 17, 1979). During the debates over the drafting of the constitution, the consensus was that as the guardians of the religiosity of the regime, the IRCG and not the Western-trained army were the trusted armed forces in the country (Mohammad Rashidian and Hasan Taheri-Gorgani in *Mozakerat,* 2: 930–31).

92. *Hamshahri,* April 18, 1996.

93. *Hamshahri,* June 4, 1998.

94. *Salam,* February 4, 1996.

95. Poggi (1990, 102).

96. For two insightful works on Shiism and Shii *ijtihad,* see Momen (1985, 172–96) and Heinz (1991, 60–127).

97. Rahnema (1997, 118–19).

98. By saying that the supervisory bodies are prone to factionalism, I am not suggesting here that all the decisions made by these bodies are factionally based. No faction can afford to appear or act partisan at all times. Nevertheless, when it comes to areas where the vital interests of a given faction are at stake, partisan decisions are highly likely. At times during the first decade of the revolution, the conservative members of the Guardian Council even disregarded the publicly announced wishes of Khomeini himself (see chap. 2).

99. See *Salam,* March 11, 1997, and *Shalam-che,* December-January 1997–1998.

100. *Ettela'at,* July 8, 1983.

101. See the three-part articles on the Martyr Foundation in *Ettela'at,* March 16–18, 1991. See also *Keyhan,* October 15, 1989.

102. *Ettela'at,* October 7, 1979.

103. See *Asasnameh-ye Bonyad-e Mostazafin* (The Constitution of the Foundation of the Disinherited), 2–3.

104. *Ettela'at,* November 11, 1982.

105. *Ettela'at,* January 4, 1983.

106. *Ettela'at,* January 22, 1984.

107. *Jl,* January 21, 1984.

108. *Ettela'at,* January 21, 1985.

109. *Ettela'at,* November 10, 1983.

110. *Jl,* August 8, 1983.

111. *Ettela'at,* November 30, 1983.

112. *Keyhan,* August 13, 1984.

113. *Ettela'at,* September 26, 1984.

114. *Ettela'at,* August 2, 1985.

115. *Keyhan,* November 25, 1986.

116. *Ettela'at,* February 26, 1986.

117. *Ettela'at,* February 18, 1989, and September 7, 1989.

118. *Ettela'at,* January 2, 1985.

119. *Ettela'at,* January 13, 1989.

120. *Ettela'at,* July 23, 1984.

121. *Ettela'at,* March 10, 1990.

122. *Resalat,* November 26, 1990.

123. *Resalat,* October 6, 1990.

124. *Resalat,* November 1, 1990.

125. *Ettela'at,* December 23 and 24, 1990.

126. *Ettela'at,* October 6, 1990.

127. *Ettela'at,* January 27–28, 1991.

128. *Keyhan,* October 10 and 12, 1992.

129. *Salam,* July 30, 1993.

130. *Keyhan,* July 1, 1995.

131. *Hamshahri,* September 30, 1995.

132. *Payam-e Daneshju,* February 19 and March 4, 1995.

133. *Resalat,* April 6, 1995.

134. *Hamshahri,* November 23, 1995.

Chapter 2. Factional Politics in Khomeini's Era: 1981–89

1. See Baktiari (1996, 108–15).

2. For Rafsanjani's remark, see *JI,* September 18 and 19, 1984; for Khamenehi's, see *JI,* September 22 and 24.

3. For example, it was members of this faction such as hojjatol-Islam Mohammad Musavi Khoeiniha, the prosecutor general at the time and later the director of the daily *Salam,* and Abbas Abdi, the editor of the daily, who masterminded the storming of the American embassy on November 4, 1979.

4. For a radical interpretation of the Iranian Revolution where dynamic *fiqh* is emphasized, see the manifesto of the Crusaders of the Islamic Revolution *(Mojahedin-e Inqelab-e Islami)* (1992).

5. For a conservative interpretation of the revolution in Iran and the suggestion that the Islamic Republic should not deviate from reliance on traditional *fiqh,* see Badamchian (1995, particularly 67–79 and 101–19).

6. As will be explored further in chap. 6, the debate over the two *fiqhs* has sharpened greatly between the religious conservatives and the Khatami camp since his election to the presidency in 1997 and is currently the main line of demarcation among the factions.

7. Aside from the public support for each other's views on issues, since 1989 the three have supported the same candidates in presidential and parliamentary elections. The last presidential election was a case in point. In July 1996, the *Mo'talefeh* pledged their loyalty to JRM, its politico-religious guide, and announced its support for the society's candidate, Nateq-Nuri *(Resalat,* July 29, 1996). The JMHEQ pledged their support for Nateq-Nuri in May 1997 *(Iran,* May 1, 1997).

8. Following the election of Khatami, who belongs to the left-leaning *Majma'-e Rouhaniyun-e Mobarez,* the power of this faction has greatly decreased. See chaps. 5 and 6.

9. In a nationwide poll on March 5, 1995, the daily *Keyhan* concluded that nearly half of those who participated believed that the JRM was the most powerful political organization in the country. For perhaps the only comprehensive study of the JRM, see Darabi (1995).

10. Ibid., 100–104; see also Ziba Kalam (1993, 267–68).

11. Darabi (1995, 298–304).

12. Ibid., 307.

13. Ibid., 310–16.

14. *Kar va Kargar,* October 22, 1996.

15. On the June 5 uprising, see Rouhani (1982, 115–544).

16. The origins of the *Mo'talefeh,* its members and organization is discussed by one of its original founders, Mehdi Araqi (1995, 192–262). *Mo'talefeh* bankrolled Khomeini's movement through its "charitable" donations, a point emphasized by Araqi (1991, 150). See also the memories of another *Mo'talefeh* sympathizer, Jalalodin Farsi (1994, 120–26).

17. *Resalat,* June 13, 1996.

18. Araqi (1991, 165–77).

19. Ibid., see also Asadollah Badamchian recalling the events in *Ettela'at,* June 16, 1996.

20. *Bahar,* February 21, 1996.

21. Ashraf (1997, 1).

22. Keddie (1966).

23. There is much literature on the Constitutional Revolution. For the best primary sources in Persian, see Kermani (1967), Kasravi (1974), Malakzadeh (1974). English sources include Brown (1910) and Martin (1989).

24. Lambton (1955, 125–48).

25. Algar (1969).

26. Martin (1989, chaps. 3 and 4).

27. Lambton (1987, 102–6 and 278–84).

28. Ashraf (1997, 6–8) and Gilbar (1977).

29. Ashraf (1981, 5–10).

30. Ashraf (1997, 7).

31. Ibid., 17–27.

32. Pahlavi (1980, 156).

33. Ashraf (1991, 23–27).

34. Parsa (1989, 102–22).

35. Ibid., 92–93.

36. In his letter to the shah complaining about the White Revolution, Khomeini wrote, "Creation of these cooperatives will destroy the Iranian bazaar" (Rouhani [1982, 230–31]).

37. Parsa (1988, 124–25).

38. Nateq and Adamiyat (1977, 11–200); see also Gilbar (1977).

39. Hazim-el Islam Kermani's day-to-day record of the discussion among the revolutionary forces of the ulama and the merchants maintained that the major complaint of the bazaaris was the higher taxes imposed on them by the state and the new customs duties they had to pay the government (1967, 1: 243–73 and 280–327).

40. Nateq and Adamiyat (1977, 309), for instance, provide ample evidence that since the mid-nineteenth century, merchants made two demands of the state: first, that they should be free from state regulations on their commercial activities, and second, that they be protected from foreign competition. Powerful *tojjar* in Iran often asked the Qajar kings to allow merchants and

commerce to function in their "natural state," which for the bazaaris meant less state regulation and a hands-off policy by the central government. This is, for example, what the richest merchant in Iran, Aminol Zarb, demanded from the Qajar government.

41. Baqi (1983). This an invaluable book that discusses the views of the *Hojjatiyeh,* and makes a strong case that these officials are members of the society.

42. Ibid., 260–64.

43. For instance, immediately after the victory of the revolution, Ahmad Azari-Qomi was reported to have said, "Until the appearance of the *Mahdi* we cannot establish an Islamic government" (ibid., 75). Some members, like Khazali, gave interviews in which he provided detailed information about the views and proclamations of the *Hojjatiyeh* (ibid., 58, 172, 236–37). What raised more suspicion about the affiliation of Azari-Qomi and Khazali with the society was the fact that they never criticized the *Hojjatiyeh* publicly.

44. *Keyhan,* July 23, 1983.

45. *Majmu-e ye Bayaniye-ha va Ettelai-ye-ha-ye Sazman-e Mojahedin-e Inqelab-e Islami* (Collection of Announcements and Proclamations of the MII), 11–15; hereafter referred to as MII proclamations; see also the MII's proclamation in *Ettela'at,* April 6, 1979.

46. *Ashenai ba Mavaze-e Sazman-e MII,* 10–14.

47. The new members included Asadollah Lajvardi, Hashem Amani, and Mohammad Reza Bahonar. See *Ettela'at,* April 21, 1983.

48. *Mavaze'-e Ma,* Tehran: IRP pub., n.d., 28.

49. Ibid., 297.

50. Ibid., 81–86.

51. Ibid., 57–80.

52. *JI,* February 8, 1984.

53. *Keyhan,* July 18, 1980.

54. *Ettela'at,* March 10, 1981.

55. *Resalat,* June 18, 1987.

56. Baktiari (1996, 66–70 and 80–84).

57. Ibid., 81.

58. Ibid., 80–84.

59. Interestingly enough, one of the people who strongly opposed the appointment of Velayati was Khatami, who questioned his capabilities as well as his credentials. Khatami later disapproved of the conservative stance of Velayati by criticizing the "inactive" foreign minister (*Keyhan,* October 31, 1980).

60. *Keyhan,* October 30, 1981.

61. *Keyhan,* April 8, 1981.

62. *Ettela'at,* October 6 and 26, 1982.

63. *Ettela'at,* October 10 and November 5, 1982.

64. *Ettela'at,* October 27, 1982.

65. *Asheni ba Majlis-e Showra-ye Islami-ye 1360* (Familiarity with the Islamic Consultative Assembly, 1981 records), 11.

66. Even after the revolution, many senior ayatollahs such as Mohammad Reza Golpayegani expressed their disapproval of such statist measures, arguing, "Any interference by the state in property ownership was against Islamic tenets and Shii practices" *(Ettela'at,* April 10, 1980).

67. *Majmu-e ye Nazari-yat-e Showra-ye Negahban; Dowre-ye Avval 1359–1365* (Collection of the Opinions of the Guardian Council; first period 1980/81–1985/86), 68; hereafter referred to as *Nazari-yat*. For the text of the law, see 69–72.

68. Ibid., 1:73–74.

69. Ibid., 1:79–80.

70. Ibid., 1:161–73.

71. Ibid., 1:160–61.

72. Ibid., 1:174–75.

73. Ibid., 1:178–79.

74. *Resalat,* October 23, 1985.

75. *Ettela'at,* December 18, 1983.

76. *Ettela'at,* April 20, 1984.

77. Baktiari (1996, chap. 3 and 99–144).

78. Ibid., 117–18.

79. *Ettela'at,* August 27, 1984.

80. Menasheri (1990, 32), Baktiari (1996, 119).

81. Baktiari (1996, 119).

82. Ibid., 124–27.

83. *Ettela'at,* September 7, 1985.

84. *Ettela'at,* September 29, 1985.

85. *Ettela'at,* October 13, 1985.

86. *Ettela'at,* October 14, 1985.

87. This number was often used by the left in post-Khomeini era to question the conservatives' loyalty to the Imam (see chaps. 4 and 5).

88. *Ettela'at,* October 18, 1985.

89. *Keyhan-e Havai,* November 25, 1986.

90. *Ettela'at,* December 21, 1986.

91. *Keyhan-e Havai,* November 25, 1986.

92. *Iran-e Farda,* October–November 1992, 38–49.

93. *JI,* August 21, 1983.

94. *JI,* August 3, 1984.

95. *JI,* May 2, 1987.

96. *Asr-e Ma,* August 17, 1994.

97. *Keyhan,* October 9 and 11, 1986.

98. *Ettela'at,* February 3, 1987.

99. *Ettela'at,* April 4 and 6, 1988.

100. *Ettela'at,* April 13, 1988.

101. *Ettela'at,* April 14, 1988.

102. *Ettela'at,* May 8, 1988.

103. *Keyhan,* April 6, 1988.

104. *Ettela'at,* May 4, 1988.

105. *Ettela'at,* April 1, 1988.

106. *Ettela'at,* April 5, 1986.

107. *Ettela'at,* May 10, 1986.

108. On the human and economic cost of the war, see Hooshang Amirahmadi (1990). According to Amirahmadi, by 1987 the cost of the war was around $18 billion and the total economic cost around $309 billion.

109. Pesaran (1992, 110).

110. Teheran Radio, February 8, 1989.

111. Teheran Radio, February 14, 1989.

112. *Ettela'at,* December 8, 1987.

113. *Ettela'at,* December 9–10, 1987.

114. *Ettela'at,* December 11, 1987.

115. *Ettela'at,* December 17, 1987.

116. *Ettela'at,* December 31, 1987.

117. *Ettela'at,* January 9, 1988.

118. Ibid., English translation from Teheran Radio, January 8, 1988.

119. Traditionally, the *mojtahids* had issued state ordinances as secondary injunctions when they perceived the interest of Islam and/or society to be in danger; Ayatollah Hasan Shirazi's fatwa against the use and sale of tobacco in 1891 was such a case. On the subject of state ordinances, see *Ahkam-e Hokumati va Maslahat* (State Ordinances and Interests). For various definitions of state ordinances suggested by the foqaha, see 58–65 and 71; for the need of issuing state ordinances in an Islamic government, see 37–50.

120. *Ettela'at,* January 9–10, 1988.

121. *Ettela'at,* January 10, 1988.

122. *Resalat,* January 12, 1988.

123. *Ettela'at,* February 8, 1988.

124. *Ettela'at,* May 30, 1988.

125. *Ettela'at,* December 31, 1987.

126. *Ettela'at,* August 10, 1988.

127. *Ettela'at,* October 5, 1988.

128. *Ettela'at,* June 20, 1988.

129. Ibid.

130. *Ettela'at,* January 26, 1987.

131. *Ettela'at,* October 30, 1988.

132. *Ettela'at,* April 4, 1988.

133. *Resalat,* April 7, 1988.

134. *Ettela'at,* February 21, 1988.

135. *Salam,* May 28, 1991.

136. *Ettela'at,* April 26, 1989.

137. *Ettela'at,* December 4, 1988.

138. *Ettela'at,* April 27, 1989.

139. *Keyhan,* June 12, 1989.

140. *Keyhan,* June 10, 1989.

141. Ibid.

142. *Keyhan,* October 30, 1990.

Chapter 3. Factions in Post-Khomeini Iran: Renditions and Sources

1. This was explicit in comments made by him as well as other members of the assembly. See *Surat-e Mashruh-e Mozakerat-e Showra-ye Bazneghari-ye Qanun-e Asasi-ye Jomhuri-ye Islami-e Iran* (Debates of the Reappraisal Assembly of the Constitution of the Islamic Republic), 1: 251; hereafter referred to as Reappraisal Assembly.

2. Baktiari (1996, 134–38).

3. It is commonly known that, behind the closed-door meeting of the Khobregan, it was Rafsanjani more than anyone who lobbied for Khamenehi's leadership.

4. Reappraisal Assembly, 1: 298.

5. Ibid., 1: 296–99.

6. Ibid., 2: 672–74.

7. Ibid., 2: 678–81.

8. Ibid., 2: 678–81.

9. Ibid., 2: 661.

10. Ibid., 2: 404.

11. Ibid., 2: 406–8.

12. Ibid., 1: 223–28.

13. Ibid., 1: 435–36.

14. Ibid., 1: 280–89.

15. Ibid., 1: 259–72.

16. Ibid., 1: 273–77.

17. Ibid., 1: 450–52.

18. Ibid., 1: 217–23.

19. Ibid., 1: 246–52.

20. *Ettela'at,* June 12, 1989.

21. *Chahar Saal-e Dov'om* (The Second Four Years), 44. This book is a collection of Khamenehi's speeches and pronouncements during his second presidential term.

22. Ibid., 372.

23. *Ettela'at,* May 7, 1989.

24. *Ettela'at,* June 1, 1989.

25. *Ettela'at,* June 8, 1989.

26. *Ettela'at,* June 17, 1989 and June 22, 1989.

27. *Resalat,* June 29, 1989.

28. *Marja'i-yat az Didgha-he Foqaha va Bozorgan* (Source of Emulation from the Views of the Notables and the *Foqaha*).

29. *Ettela'at,* June 10, 1989.

30. *Ettela'at,* June 17, 1989.

31. *Ettela'at,* February 21, 1992.

32. *Ettela'at,* May 28, 1994. Interestingly enough, in 1995 the Majlis prohibited its use and possession.

33. *Ajwabul Estefsarat* (Questions to Quarries).

34. Ayatollah Abbas Ali Amid-Zanjani said, "We looked around to see who has more experience and who could be a good navigator and thought that Mr. Rafsanjani was the best person for the job" (personal interview, August 1996).

35. For a sample of his earlier views, see *Khotbeha va Jom-'e ha* (Sermons and Fridays). This book is a collection of all Rafsanjani's Friday prayer sermons from July–September 1981.

36. During the early days of the revolution, more than once Rafsanjani called upon the revolutionary bodies to refrain from extreme actions. In October 1979, for example, he scorned the hasty executions ordered by the revolutionary courts and called for the power of these courts to be curbed *(Ettela'at,* October 9, 1979).

37. Milani (1995, 226).

38. *Ettela'at,* April 24, 1989. English translation from Teheran Radio, April 24, 1989.

39. This is how Akhavi (1987), Behrooz (1991), Siavoshi (1992), and Ehteshami (1995) have categorized factions in Khomeini's era.

40. Siavoshi (1992, 28–29).

41. Baktiari (1996, 185–233).

42. Ehteshami (1995, 45–76); Milani (1995, 219–23).

43. The modern right and conservative right are discussed in the following issues of *Asr-e Ma:* January 11 and 25, February 8, May 31, 1995.

44. *Asr-e-Ma,* December 28, 1994; February 22, 1995; April 5, 1995.

45. *Sobh* editorial, October–November 1997.

46. *Ettela'at,* June 23, 1979. Hizbollahis attacking opponents of clerical domination became widespread from the summer of 1979, especially during the time of the drafting of the constitution, which placed the *velayat-e faqih* into the Islamic Republic.

47. Rahnema and Nomani (1990).

48. For a firsthand account of Safavi's views and actions, see the memoirs of one of his ardent followers, Araqi (1991, 17–153); see also Rahnema and Nomani (1990, 79–83), and Kazemi (1985, 118–36).

49. On the political life of Bazargan, see Barzeen (1995); on his religio-political views, see his *Intezar az din az Didgah-e Mohandes Bazargan* (Interpretation of Religion from the Perspective of Engineer Bazargan); see also Bazargan (1984).

50. Major works of Shariati include *Islam-shenasi* (Knowing Islam); *Insan, Marksizm va Islam* (Humans, Marxism, and Islam); and *Tashayo '-e Alavi va Tashayo '-e Safavi* (Shiism of Alavi and Shiism of Safavi).

51. See, for example, the editorials in *Salam,* September 17–19, 1994.

52. In justifying his conservative interpretation of the revolution in Iran rather than, for example, relying on Khomeini's views, Badamchian often refers to the ideas of Motahari and his conservative views on Islamic government (1995, 77–79 and 104–11).

53. Motahari notes, "I agree that revolutions take place because of deprivations and they are the war between the rich and the poor, the exploited and exploiter; but this is not a holy war. In the Islamic Revolution, the battle is not class based but between right and wrong [*haq' va batel]*" *(Piramun-e Inqelab-e Islami* [On the Islamic Revolution], 18). Another of Motahari's major works is *Shenakht-e Inqelab-e Islami* (Knowing the Iranian Revolution) (Teheran: n.p., 1982), particularly 50–58 and 192–200.

54. Amir Arjomand (1993).

55. Schirazi (1997, i).

56. See the comments of Mahdavi-Kani on the occasion of the anniversary of the revolution in *Resalat,* February 7, 1996.

57. Badamchian (1995, 103).

58. *Ettela 'at,* January 31, 1994.

59. See the JRM's statements on the eve of the election of the fourth Majlis in *Ettela 'at,* March 18, 1992.

60. *Salam,* March 17, 1991.

61. *Sobh,* June 20, 1995.

62. *Khotut* (1994, 316).

63. *Resalat,* May 1, 1992; Mahdavi-Kani was speaking about the 1992 Majlis election.

64. Mahdavi-Kani in *Resalat,* January 31, 1996.

65. *Abrar,* December 24, 1995.

66. *Khabar-Nameh-e ye Jame'eh-e ye Rouhaniyat-e Mobarez (mahramaneh)* (Confidential Newsletter of the JRM), no. 22 (August/September 1995): 295; hereafter referred to as JRM newsletter.

67. *Resalat,* July 3, 1993.

68. *Salam,* February 22, 1996; see also JRM newsletter, January-February 1996.

69. Nateq-Nuri in *Abrar,* January 16, 1994.

70. *Iran,* January 10, 1996.

71. *Resalat,* December 30, 1995.

72. Darabi (1995, 130).

73. Schirazi (1997, 129–32).

74. Badamchian (1995, 106–7).

75. *Iran,* January 8, 1996.

76. *JIM,* March–April 1992.

77. *Resalat,* December 9, 1987.

78. *Resalat,* August 3, 1995.

79. *Asr-e Ma,* January 25, 1995.

80. *Resalat,* November 10, 1985.

81. *Resalat* editorials in December 12, 13, and 17, 1987.

82. *Resalat,* February 15, 1986.

83. *Ettela'at,* June 23, 1979.

84. On modern taxation, for instance, he maintained his 1971 views that "similar to the time of Imam Ali, religious taxes are sufficient and just ways of taxing an Islamic nation" *(Ettela'at,* June 21, 1979).

85. *Ettela'at,* December 13, 1984.

86. *Ettela'at,* June 22–23, 1979.

87. *Sobh,* February–March, 1996.

88. *Resalat,* November 13–17, 1990.

89. *Resalat,* (prepublication issue) February 9, 1984.

90. JRM's newsletter, January 1996, 95–96.

91. Ibid., 98–102.

92. This term is used to scorn the infiltration of Western values and culture into the Islamic Republic and the fear of replacing traditional Islamic ways of life in Iran. It refers to moral issues such as improper veiling of women and more open gender relations; Western clothes, arts, and cinema; and secular thoughts in university education. See the collection of speeches by Khamenehi on this subject collected in *Farhang va Tahajom-e Farhangi* (Culture and Cultural Onslaught).

93. JRM's newsletters, August/September 1995, 37–39; and January 1995, 36–40.

94. *Salam,* January 19, 1994.

95. *Sobh,* February 20, 1996.

96. *Resalat,* January 9, 1991.

97. *Resalat,* October 24, 1985.

98. *Hamshahri,* January 5, 1998.

99. *JIM,* August 29, 1992.

100. *Ettela'at,* September 15, 1993.

101. *Resalat,* January 12, 1991.

102. *Resalat,* March 9, 1992.

103. *Ettela'at,* November 6, 1991.

104. *Resalat,* December 8, 1990.

105. *Resalat,* December 10, 1990.

106. JRM's newsletter, November–December 1995, 127–38.

107. Badamchian (1995, 61–70).

108. Ibid., 73–77.

109. Ibid., 108–15.

110. On Rafsanjani's foreign policy, see Hunter (1992).

111. *Resalat,* December 27, 1990.

112. Teheran Radio, April 29, 1991.

113. *Teheran Times,* September 3, 1989.

114. *Sobh,* July 11, 1995.

115. *Ettela'at,* February 3, 1991.

116. In his trip to London just before the 1997 presidential election, Larijani confidentially assured the Labour government that if the candidate of the conservative party, Nateq-Nuri, is elected, this faction will pursue a "moderate" and accommodating foreign policy towards the West. He maintained that supporters of the other camp (the left) would maintain a radical position on foreign policy *(Hamshahri,* February 22, 1997; *Resalat,* February 17, 1997).

117. *Asr-e Ma,* April 5, 1995.

118. *Ettela'at,* April 14, 1988.

119. *Salam,* December 10, 1995, and February 27, 1997.

120. *Asr-e Ma,* October 19, 1994.

121. *Asr-e Ma,* October 19, 1994.

122. In their first proclamation, the *Anjoman* announced their support for purging unwanted anti-Islamic elements from the universities *(Keyhan,* April 21 and May 13, 1980).

123. Bazargan (1984, 103–11).

124. See *Tahkim's* support for Khatami's election bid in *Mobin,* May 12 and 26, 1997.

125. In May 1996, for instance, *Tahkim* confronted the representatives of the *faqih* at Amir Kabir University for not allowing Soroush to give a lecture *(Salam,* May 9, 1996).

126. The left has occasionally admitted this point. See, for example, *Asr-e Ma,* December 30, 1995.

127. Khatami's overture toward the United States after his election in 1997 is a case in point.

128. *Asr-e Ma,* January 19, 1996.

129. *Asr-e Ma,* July 24, 1996.

130. *Asr-e Ma,* June 14, 1995.

131. *Asr-e Ma,* February 22, 1996.

132. *Asr-e Ma,* August 18, 1994.

133. *Salam,* March 5, 1992.

134. See the editorials in *Salam,* February 28, 1991, and *Asr-e Ma,* October 2, 1994.

135. MII manifesto, 37.

136. *Salam,* April 6, 1995.

137. *Salam,* March 17, 1992.

138. *Asr-e Ma,* April 5, 1995.

139. *Parliamentary Debates,* November 13, 1990.

140. *Salam,* February 8, 1996.

141. *Keyhan,* December 24, 1996.

142. *Asr-e Ma* editorial, July 26, 1995.

143. *Salam,* May 13, 1991.

144. MII manifesto, 9–10.

145. Ibid., 9.

146. *Salam,* February 9, 1991.

147. *Asr-e Ma,* October 2, 1994.

148. *Asr-e Ma,* December 14, 1994.

149. *Ettela'at,* December 12, 1995; he made similar comments in *Salam,* February 8, 1996.

150. *Asr-e Ma,* August 27, 1997.

151. *Salam* editorial, July 28, 1993.

152. *Asr-e Ma,* April 5, 1995.

153. *Keyhan,* July 18, 1990.

154. *Bayan,* no. 1, June–July 1991.

155. See the MII proclamation on Workers Day (no. 5), 62–64. The MII used concepts such as the masses *(khalq),* anti-imperialism, and bloodthirsty capitalists in its politico-economic analysis; see also their proclamation no. 6, 68–76.

156. See, for example, his speech before a Friday prayer sermon in *Keyhan,* July 30, 1986.

157. *Ettela'at,* September 19, 1991.

158. *Ettela'at,* August 31, 1986.

159. *Ettela'at,* August 29, 1987.

160. *Asr-e Ma,* April 5, 1995.

161. *Salam,* July 28, 1993.

162. Interview with Mohammad Salamati in *Salam,* February 24, 1992.

163. *Asr-e Ma,* June 14, 1995.

164. *Salam,* July 28, 1993.

165. *Keyhan,* November 26, 1990.

166. On the mission of the press, see *Salam,* May 13 and 15, 1991. See also the editorial advocating pluralism in *Salam,* February 19, 1991.

167. *Salam* editorial, March 17, 1991.

168. *Ettela'at,* November 20, 1980 and January 28, 1989; *Salam,* July 8, 1992, and December 12, 1991; *Jahan-e Islam,* July 18, 1992; *Kar va Kargar,* July 19, 1992. For a longer speech on the topic, see Khatami's commemoration of Motahari on the anniversary of his death, *Salam,* May 8, 1993.

169. *Salam,* May 2, 1992.

170. *Ettela'at,* November 2, 1991.

171. *Ettela'at,* October 24, 1996.

172. A *Salam* editorial opines that what the regime gives to women is tantamount to charity *(sadaqeh)* (July 5, 1993).

173. *Asr-e Ma,* October 2, 1996.

174. Khatami won the presidency because of the youth votes he received and his emphasis that the regime must attend to the needs of the new generation in Iran. See, for example, his pre-election speeches in *Salam,* May 20–22, 1997.

175. *Asr-e Ma,* July 10, 1996.

176. *Asr-e Ma,* November 30, 1994, and August 7, 1996.

177. *Asr-e Ma,* June 26, 1996.

178. *Asr-e Ma,* July 24, 1996.

179. *Bayan,* no. 2 (July–August 1991): 24.

180. *Asr-e Ma,* April 3, 1995.

181. *Nazm-e Novin-e Jahani* (The New World Order), 7–9.

182. *Asr-e Ma,* April 20, 1995.

183. *Salam,* April 5, 1995.

184. *Resalat,* December 29, 1990.

185. *Asr-e Ma,* November 18, 1997. Mohtashami was speaking on the anniversary of the US embassy takeover.

186. *Asr-e Ma,* June 11, 1995.

187. *Asr-e Ma,* January 25, 1995.

188. *Asr-e Ma,* January 25, 1995.

189. *Salam,* October 14, 1995.

190. *Bahar,* March 7, 1996. In a brief piece on the Organization for Propagation of Islamic Culture, *Bahar* noted that the head of the Africa and Arab section of this organization is Ali Taskhiri, his brother Mehdi is the head of the Middle East section, and his other brother is in charge of legal affairs. Interestingly enough, the Taskhiris lived in Iraq and hardly speak Farsi.

191. *Salam,* April 5, 1992.

192. Skocpol (1979, 4–5).

193. Ibid., 161.

194. *Ettela'at,* October 5, 1979.

195. See the comments of Mohammad Salamati in *Asr-e Ma,* October 5 and 19, 1994.

196. The members were Ismail Shushtari, minister of justice; Ayatollah Mohajerani, the president's legal adviser; Mohsen Nurbaksh, head of Iran's central bank; Mohammad Hashemi, Rafsanjani's brother and his executive director; Mohammad Ali Najafi, minister of education; Morteza Mohammad-Khan, minister of economics; I'sa Kalantari, minister of agriculture; Mohammad Gharazi, minister of Post Telegraph and Phone; Bijan Namdar Zanganeh, minister of energy; Reza Amorllahi, head of atomic energy; Gholam Reza Foruzesh, minister of the construction crusade; Mohammad Reza Ne'mat-Zadeh, minister of industry; Mostafa Hashemi-

Taba, minister of physical education; Gholam Reza Shafe'i, minister of cooperatives; and Gholam Hossein Karbaschi, mayor of Teheran *(Hamshahri,* January 20, 1996).

197. *Hamshahri,* March 5–6, 1996.

198. *Hamshahri,* February 27, 1996.

199. Interview with Badamchian in *Abrar,* December 19, 1995.

200. *Asr-e Ma,* January 26, 1995.

201. Rafsanjani (1997, 108).

202. Ibid., 109–13.

203. Ibid., 214.

204. Ibid., 134.

205. Ibid., 271.

206. Ibid., 131.

207. Ibid., 240.

208. Ibid., 249.

209. Ibid., 248.

210. *Hamshahri,* March 5–6, 1996.

211. Interview with Mohsen Nurbaksh in *Iran,* January 24, 1996, and February 19, 1996.

212. *Hamshahri,* February 10, 1996.

213. *Iran,* January 9–10, 1996.

214. *Hamshahri,* March 3–4, 1996.

215. *Hamshahri,* March 3–4, 1996.

216. Interview with Mostafa Mohaqqeq-Damad in *Hamshahri,* March 16–17, 1996.

217. *Iran,* 23–24, 1996.

218. *Bahman* editorial, February 3, 1996.

219. *Hamshahri,* February 13, 1996.

220. *Hamshahri,* June 26–27 and 29, 1996.

221. *Bahman* editorial, February 24, 1996.

222. *Iran,* January 23, 1997.

223. Editorials in *Hamshahri,* February 19 and 22, 1996; *Iran,* March 7, 1996.

224. *Bahman* editorial, February 24, 1996.

225. *Bahman,* February 3, 1996.

226. *Iran,* April 21, 1996.

227. *Iran,* June 10–13, 1996.

228. See the two-part article by Mohsen Kadivar in *Bahman,* March 16 and April 6, 1996.

229. *Iran,* April 17, 1996.

230. *Resalat,* November 29, 1994.

231. *Sobh* editorial, March 6, 1995; *Neyestan* editorial, October–November 1995.

232. *Keyhan* editorials of April 1989.

233. *Ettela'at,* April 14, 1992.

234. *Sobh,* March 6, 1996.

235. *Ettela'at,* October 23, 1995.

236. *Shalamcheh,* September–October 1997.

237. *Neyestan,* first and second issues of September–October and October–November 1995.

238. "What Is to Be Done," *Neyestan,* July 1996.

239. *Sobh,* July–August 1996.

240. *Sobh,* January 16, 1996.

241. *Sobh,* April 10, 1995.

242. *Sobh,* August 12, 1995.

243. *Sobh,* April 18, 1995.

244. *Neyestan,* June–July, 1996.

245. *Akbar,* April 7, 1996.

246. *Sobh,* June 18, 1995.

247. "Survey on Iran," *Economist,* January 18, 1997.

248. *Shalamcheh,* December–January 1997.

249. *Akbar,* May 2 and 6, 1996.

250. *Neyestan,* November 23, 1995.

251. *Keyhan,* October 7, 1995; *Ettela'at,* January 8, 1996.

252. *Salam,* May 10, 1996; *Resalat,* October 26, 1995.

253. *Sobh,* May 23, 1995.

254. *Salam,* May 9, 1996; *Keyhan,* May 21, 1996.

255. *Resalat,* December 7, 1996.

256. *Resalat,* July 14, 1996.

257. *Sobh,* March 6, 1995.

258. *Akhbar,* April 28, 1996.

259. *Resalat,* May 18, 1996.

260. *Ettela'at,* April 25, 1996.

261. *Resalat,* October 31, 1995.

262. *Resalat,* May 20, 1996.

263. *Akhbar,* June 9, 1996.

264. *Resalat,* June 20, 1996.

265. *Akhbar,* October 26, 1995.

266. *Salam,* October 25, 1995.

Chapter 4. The Ascension of Rafsanjani, the Alliance of the Two Rights, and the Demise of the Left, 1989–92

1. *Keyhan-Havai,* November 14, 1990.

2. *Ettela'at,* November 30, 1991.

3. *Ettela'at,* December 1, 1991. Prior to the publication of the two newspapers associated

with the modern right faction *(Hamshahri* in 1991 and *Iran* in 1995), Mohajerani's editorials in *Ettela'at* reflected and advanced Rafsanjani's views during this period. His most famous and controversial editorial was "Direct Negotiation" in May 1990 in which he suggested closer ties with the United States. In fact, *Ettela'at* became the forum for dissidents and intellectuals in Iran to carefully voice their opinion.

4. *Ettela'at,* December 5, 1990.

5. *Keyhan,* November 26, 1989.

6. The head of the judiciary, Ayatollah Mohammad Yazdi, for example, maintained, "We must act in a revolutionary manner but within the confines of the law" *(Keyhan,* November 16, 1989).

7. *Keyhan-Havai,* December 5, 1990.

8. Five days after the death of Khomeini, Rafsanjani elaborated on the new socioeconomic and political orientation of the reconstruction stage *(Ettela'at,* June 9, 1989).

9. Rafsanjani was elected as president on July 30, 1989, with 94.51 percent of the votes cast, which totaled 16,439,247 *(Keyhan,* August 1, 1989).

10. Ibid.

11. For an excellent study of the Iran's postrevolutionary economy, see Amuzegar (1995).

12. *Ettela'at,* August 10, 1991.

13. Ibid.

14. Ibid.

15. As early as 1982, Rafsanjani believed in the need to provide incentives so that the nearly a million Iranians educated abroad would return. See *Keyhan,* October 30, 1982.

16. *Keyhan-Havai,* November 14, 1990.

17. *Keyhan,* August 1, 1989.

18. Ibid.

19. Ibid.

20. Ibid.

21. *Keyhan-Havai,* December 5, 1990.

22. *Ettela'at,* December 5, 1990.

23. *Ettela'at,* December 27, 1990.

24. *Keyhan,* December 29, 1989.

25. *Keyhan,* November 23, 1989.

26. Teheran Radio, March 15, 1990.

27. Ibid.

28. *Keyhan,* August 31, 1989.

29. *Ettela'at,* March 6, 1991.

30. Teheran Radio, January 1, 1993. Prominent among the selected theologians were Mehdi Rouhani, Mohammed Qomi, Mahmud Hashemi Shahrudi, and Jannati.

31. Teheran Radio, December 1, 1993. He spoke on the occasion of Women's Week.

32. *Keyhan,* July 17, 1990.

33. *Ettela'at,* December 12, 1991.

34. *Iran Times,* June 17, 1994.

35. *Salam,* May 30, 1991.

36. *Salam,* June 1, 1991.

37. *Salam,* June 2, 1991.

38. *Keyhan,* October 24, 1989.

39. *Tahkim* proclamation in *Keyhan,* January 8, 1990.

40. *Keyhan,* January 30, 1990.

41. *Keyhan,* August 26, 1989.

42. *Bayan,* May-June 1990.

43. *Bayan,* June-July 1990.

44. The MP Abolhasan Haerizadeh announced in the Majlis that Azari-Qomi had been engaged in land speculation and illegally obtained a permit for his son's factory *(Parliamentary Debates,* April 10, 1991).

45. *Resalat* on November 25, 1989, printed Khomeini's following speech without the two words: "the nation that pursues the line of pure Mohammadi Islam and is against arrogance, greed, petrifaction and pretentious Holiness. . ." Also, *Resalat* dated December 12, 1989, published Imam's will where the following statement—"I will the respected clerical society, especially the esteemed *Maraje'* not to shun from society's matters especially presidential and parliamentary elections"—was printed as "I will the JRM especially. . . ," making it sound as if the JRM was considered by the Ayatollah to be the only important and sanctified clerical association or that the MRM should not take a major role in society's affairs.

46. *Keyhan,* December 7, 1989.

47. *Keyhan,* December 30, 1989.

48. See, for example, *Keyhan,* August 19, 1989.

49. Ahmad Nateq-Nuri (the brother of Akbar Nateq-Nuri) in *Parliamentary Debates,* November 14, 1990.

50. The speech before the Majlis of Ilias Hazrati in *Parliamentary Debates,* October 2, 1991, was typical of the views of the left in this regard.

51. See *Bayan,* July-August 1990.

52. Ibid.

53. See the announcement of the MRM in *Bayan,* September-October 1990; see also the Majlis speeches of Abbas Dozduzani of September 30, 1990, and Hadi Khamenehi on October 3, 1990.

54. Khalkhali in *Parliamentary Debates,* September 3, 1990.

55. Ibid.

56. Ibid.

57. *Parliamentary Debates,* October 3, 1990.

58. MP Mohammad Baqer Baqeri Nejhadianfar in *Parliamentary Debates,* September 3, 1990.

59. *Resalat,* October 2, 1990.

60. MP Ali Movahhedi-Saveji, the most vocal mouthpiece of the right in the Majlis during the third parliament in *Parliamentary Debates,* September 2, 1990.

61. See the pamphlet issued in Qom by various conservative associations published in *Resalat,* October 27, 1990.

62. *Resalat,* October 28, 1990.

63. Zamanian's speech resulted in verbal as well as physical clashes between members of the two camps. See *Parliamentary Debates,* October 1, 1990.

64. *Resalat,* December 10, 1990.

65. See *Ettela'at,* February 21 and 23, 1991.

66. *Keyhan,* October 7, 1990.

67. Speeches in the Majlis of MPs Alireza Farzad and Hamid Rouhani, quoted in *Bayan,* September-October 1990.

68. Khalkhali in *Parliamentary Debates,* September 30, 1990.

69. *Parliamentary Debates,* October 16, 1990.

70. *Keyhan,* April 14, 1992.

71. *Ettela'at,* July 28, 1990.

72. *Ettela'at,* February 8, 1992.

73. For the text of this bill, see *Parliamentary Debates,* October 2, 1990.

74. MP Ghorbanali Salehabadi in *Parliamentary Debates,* October 3, 1999.

75. *Resalat,* February 27, 1991.

76. *Resalat,* March 4, 1991.

77. *Resalat,* March 16, 1991.

78. MP Saleh-Abadi in *Parliamentary Debates,* July 16, 1990.

79. *Bayan,* May-June 1990, 30–36.

80. Mohammad Reza Bahonar in *Parliamentary Debates,* July 17, 1990.

81. See *Resalat* editorials, April 10–13, 23–25, 29, 1990.

82. The bill was approved by the Majlis on December 10, 1990, and by the Council of Guardian on December 16, 1990. For the text of this law, see *Majmu'eh-ye Qavanin-e Sevvomin Dowreh-ye Majlis-e Showra-ye Islami* (Collection of the Laws of the Third Islamic Consultative Assembly), 456–58; hereafter referred to as *Majmu'eh.*

83. See Karrubi's comments in *Resalat,* March 11, 1991, and the interview with Khoeiniha in *Salam,* May 13, 1991.

84. *Salam,* March 18, 1992.

85. *Salam* editorial, March 18, 1993.

86. *Salam,* March 5, 1992.

87. *Salam,* May 28, 1992.

88. Ibid.

89. *Resalat,* November 18, 1990.

90. *Keyhan* editorial, May 16, 1992.

91. *Parliamentary Debates,* December 16, 1990.

92. *Parliamentary Debates,* November 13, 1990.

93. *Majmu'eh,* 261–320.

94. Ibid., 276.

95. See ibid., 227–80; interview with Morteza Alviri, the head of the Majlis Budget Committee in *Keyhan,* August 10, 1989.

96. Interview in *Ettela'at,* September 7, 1991.

97. For an informative assessment of government expectations of the reaction of the bazaaris to the FFYP, see Hossein Azimi *"Siyasatha-ye Tasbit"* (Structural Adjustment Policies) in *Salam,* February 15, 1996. See also MP Hossein Harati's comments in *Parliamentary Debates,* March 11, 1990.

98. See the declarations of JRM, the Friday prayer imams of the provinces, and the Islamic Propagatory Organization *(Sazman-e Tabliqat-e Islami)* in *Keyhan,* December 30, 1989.

99. *Resalat* editorial, August 23, 1990.

100. Speech in the Majlis by MP Hossein Shahrudi in *Parliamentary Debates,* October 29, 1991.

101. See the article *"Siasat-ha-ye Iqtesadi-ye Jari va Modafe'-in va Montaqedin-ne Anha"* (Current Economic Policies: Supporters and Opponents), in the daily *Salam,* June 9, 1991.

102. Budget debate in the Majlis, *Parliamentary Debates,* March 11, 1990.

103. *Bayan,* June–July 1990, 37–41.

104. *Parliamentary Debates,* March 11, 1990.

105. Budget Minister Masud Roghani Zanjani hoped that taxes would contribute nearly 26 percent of government revenues (interview with *Keyhan,* August 20, 1989).

106. Interview with Abbas Abdi in *Akhbar,* February 13, 1996.

107. On this point and on how the open-door economic policy created a quick-cash mentality, see Ezatollah Sahabi's *"Iqtesade Bazzari ba'-daz Jang"* (The Bazaari Economy after the War): 18–22.

108. See Rafsanjani's Friday prayer sermon of May 29, 1991. In May 1991, during a trip to New York, Mohsen Nurbaksh encouraged Iranian industrialists living in the United States to invest in the new phase of economic reconstruction of the country *(Keyhan-Havai,* May 15, 1991).

109. Prior to his death, Khomeini said, "If we lose [the war] in the cultural sphere, victory in the political and military realms becomes meaningless" *(Ettela'at,* June 23, 1988).

110. *Majmu'eh,* 276 and 279.

111. *Ettela'at,* July 29, 1991.

112. *Majmu'eh-ye Mosavvabat-e Showraye Inqelab-e Farhangi 1368–1372* (Collection of Laws of the High Council of Cultural Revolution 1988/1989–92/93); hereafter referred to as *Mosavvabat.* At its inception, the vague duties of the HCCR were, for instance, the spread of Islamic culture; purification of the scientific and academic environment from materialistic and Westernized influences; and direction setting of the cultural, educational, and scientific policies of the Islamic Republic. See the introduction.

113. Chief among them were permitted curriculum taught in classes and how to "filter" those employed by the higher education establishment.

114. *Mosavvabat,* 237.

115. Ibid., 238.

116. Ibid., 242.

117. Ibid., 244–45.

118. Ibid., 245–47.

119. *Ettela'at,* September 18, 1991.

120. *Ettela'at,* December 22, 1990.

121. *Ettela'at,* November 6, 1991.

122. *Salam,* June 23, 1993; speaking on the occasion of the week of PVPV.

123. See the numerous editorials in May 1992 in *Keyhan.*

124. *Ettela'at,* December 3, 1991.

125. Hadi Ghaffari, for example, accused Hashemi of advancing the interests of one faction (right) against others (left) through screening and manipulation of TV programs.

126. *Salam,* March 17, 1991.

127. *Ettela'at,* November 2, 1991.

128. *Ettela'at,* July 31, 1991.

129. Speech at a seminar on the press in Iran, *Ettela'at,* February 26, 1991.

130. *Asr-e Ma,* May 16, 1995.

131. *Keyhan-Havai,* May 8, 1991.

132. *Ettela'at,* February 26, 1991; *Salam,* November 24, 1992.

133. *Ettela'at,* February 7, 1991.

134. The main complaint was that by showing Western movies and thus Western lifestyles, Iranian TV was depicting Western societies as more democratic than the Islamic Republic and promoting liberal culture in the country *(Keyhan* editorials, April 22–25, 1992).

135. *Keyhan,* October 30, 1990. For the neo-fundamentalists, even government suggestions regarding the need to promote tourism in Iran were judged antirevolutionary because tourism brings Westerners who spread secular culture into Islamic Iran *(Keyhan-Havai* editorial, November 14, 1990).

136. Many newspapers and journals were either physically attacked by the Hizbollahis or were forced to close down under their pressure. *Gardun* was temporarily closed in October of 1991, *Donya-ye sokhan* was bombed by Hizbollahis in May of 1991, and *Farad* was closed in April 1992 after it published a drawing that resembled Khomeini.

137. *Payam-e Inqelab* (monthly journal of IRGC), September–October 1990.

138. *Keyhan-Havai,* November 14, 1990.

139. *Keyhan,* December 9, 1989.

140. *Resalat,* December 7, 1990.

141. *Resalat,* June 12, 1991.

142. *Resalat,* March 9, 1991.

143. *Keyhan,* May 9, 1992.

144. *Keyhan,* January 13, 1990.

145. *Resalat,* March 16, 1991.

146. *Keyhan,* April 19, 1992.

147. *JAM,* no. 41:82, 1992.

148. See *Salam,* February 26, 27, and 28, 1992, where Khatami describes his views on the cultural policies of the Islamic Republic.

149. For a brief but useful assessment on the views of Islam and the conservative establishment in Iran on women, see the journal of the Iranian Bar Association *(Majalleh-ye Kanun-e Vokala)* 67, 1992–93: 77–104.

150. Teheran Radio, July 5, 1990.

151. *Ettela 'at,* July 27 and August 1, 1991.

152. *Ettela 'at,* December 29, 1991.

153. *Ettela 'at,* January 20, 1991; for similar comments, see *Hamshahri,* February 26, 1996, and *Ettela 'at,* February 29, 1992.

154. *Ettela 'at,* December 26, 1991.

155. *Ettela 'at,* December 28, 1991.

156. In June 1991, Iran became a member of the UN Human Rights Commission, thus allowing the United Nations to monitor political, social, cultural, and economic development in the Islamic Republic (Teheran Radio, June 3, 1991). Addressing the International Conference for Understanding Basic Human Rights in September 1991, Rafsanjani remarked, "Human rights were among the most important jurisprudential/historical issues inspired by the verses of Holy Qoran" (Teheran Radio, September 11, 1991).

157. On foreign policy of Iran after Khomeini, see R. K. Ramazani (1992) and Hunter (1992).

158. Teheran Radio, July 20, 1990; speaking to Iran's ambassadors.

159. In July 1990, for instance, Rafsanjani opened the Center for Strategic Studies in Teheran and appointed Khoeiniha as its director. The president announced that the goals of the center should be to "fully observe free and objective thinking in its research pursuits" (Teheran Radio, July 18, 1990).

160. Sa'id Rajai-Khorasani speaking in the Majlis on May 15–16, 1990.

161. *Ettela 'at,* April 26, 1990.

162. *Jomhuri-ye Islami,* April 28, 1990.

163. *Keyhan,* April 29, 1990.

164. *Keyhan-Havai,* May 15, 1991.

165. *Resalat,* May 2, 1990. Even before Ayatollah Khomeini's death, influential members of the conservative right emphasized the need to enter into a new era in foreign policy with the outside world. Mohammad Javad Larijani, for instance, said, "We should begin a new strategy with regards to our relations with the West, one that includes expansion and closeness. This strategy will surely benefit Iran in the future" *(Keyhan,* May 28, 1988).

166. *Ettela'at,* May 7, 1991.

167. *Ettela'at,* August 21, 1989.

168. *Keyhan,* August 21, 1989.

169. *Keyhan,* August 24, 1989.

170. *Ettela'at,* May 7, 1991.

171. *Ettela'at,* January 19, 1991.

172. *Ettela'at,* January 20, 1991.

173. *Ettela'at,* February 3, 1991.

174. Sadeq Khalkhali speaking in the Majlis, *Parliamentary Debates,* December 19, 1991.

175. See the announcement of JRM in *Ettela'at,* February 27, 1991.

176. Arjomand (1991).

177. The fatwa was issued by Khomeini on January 31, 1988.

178. *Keyhan,* February 14, 1990.

179. *Keyhan,* February 15, 1990.

180. *Keyhan,* February 17, 1990.

Chapter 5. The Split of the Two Rights and the Alliance of the Left with the Modern Right

1. *Salam,* February 24, 1992.

2. *Salam,* March 10, 1992.

3. *Salam,* March 18, 1992.

4. Ibid.

5. *Ettela'at,* March 31, 1992.

6. *Ettela'at,* April 1, 1992.

7. *Ettela'at,* March 28, 1992.

8. *Keyhan,* April 5, 1992.

9. *Salam,* April 5, 1992.

10. *Salam,* April 4, 1992; *Keyhan,* April 5, 1992.

11. *Keyhan,* April 6, 1992.

12. *Keyhan,* April 5, 1992.

13. *Salam,* April 31, 1992. In the same vein, the coalition issued another memorandum where *Towse-'eh* and its capitalist managers were criticized *(Salam,* April 3, 1992).

14. *Salam,* February 13, 1992.

15. *Resalat,* March 29, 1992.

16. *Keyhan,* April 9, 1992.

17. *Resalat,* April 6, 1992.

18. *Keyhan,* April 7, 1992.

19. *Resalat,* March 29, 1992.

20. *Ettela'at,* March 31, 1992.

21. *Ettela'at,* April 7, 1992.

22. *Ettela'at,* April 8, 1992.

23. *Keyhan,* April 5, 1992.

24. *Ettela'at,* April 8, 1992.

25. *Keyhan,* April 18, 1992.

26. *Ettela'at,* April 5, 1992.

27. *Resalat,* May 3, 1992.

28. *Salam,* May 15, 1992.

29. For example, according to the MRM, many of its candidates such as Hashem Hejazi and Mohtashami were barred from speaking in the mosques *(Salam,* April 4, 1992). The Organization for Mosque Affairs was headed by the conservative Mo'ezzi.

30. *Salam,* March 12, 1992.

31. *Salam,* April 15, 1992.

32. *Salam,* April 12, 1992.

33. For the complete list of the MPs of the fourth Majlis, see *Parliamentary Debates,* May 28, 1992.

34. *Salam,* May 31, 1992.

35. *Salam,* June 4, 1992.

36. *Salam,* May 30, 1992.

37. *Parliamentary Debates,* May 28, 1992.

38. For a brief but concise look at the overall goals and achievements of the first FYP, see Sa'id Leila, "Nazari bar Amalkard-e Iqtesadi-ye Jomhuri-ye Islami" (A Look at the Economic Performance of the Islamic Republic).

39. Ibid.

40. Amuzegar (1995, 51).

41. *Keyhan,* September 26, 1993.

42. *Salnameh-ye Amari-ye Keshvar* (Iran's Statistical Yearbook: March 1995–March 1996), 571–73; hereafter referred to as *Amar.*

43. Amuzegar (1995, 56).

44. *Amar,* 286–89.

45. *Amar,* 571–77.

46. *Ettela'at,* May 5, 1992.

47. The figures were given in a speech in the Majlis *(Parliamentary Debates,* October 27, 1992).

48. *Resalat,* July 12, 1992.

49. *Resalat,* November 18, 1992, and February 1, 1993.

50. *Ettela'at,* January 16, 1993. For similar comments by Morteza Alviri on the effect of cash liquidity on the economy, see *Salam,* October 14, 1992.

51. Hossien Azimi, *"Iqtesad-e Iran: Bohranha va Cheshmandazha"* (The Iranian Economy: Crisis and Prospects).

52. *Keyhan-Havai,* April 24, 1992.

53. *Resalat,* July 1, 1992.

54. *Resalat,* December 31, 1992, and January 18, 1993.

55. MP Mahmud Astaneh in *Parliamentary Debates,* May 22, 1994.

56. According to Mohammad Mohammad-Khan, cited in *Keyhan-Havai,* January 19, 1994.

57. *Payam-e Imruz,* fall 1994.

58. Nurbaksh's interview with *Salam,* June 2, 1996.

59. *Salam,* October 5, 1992.

60. *Ettela'at,* August 25, 1991.

61. *Keyhan-Havai,* October 30, 1992.

62. *Resalat,* September 14, 1992.

63. Comments made by Mohammad Reza Ne'matzadeh (minister of industry) in *Salam,* June 1 and by Nurbaksh in *Salam,* May 30, 1992.

64. *Keyhan,* June 15, 1992.

65. *Payam-e Imruz,* spring 1994, 88–89.

66. For the text of the bill, see *Majmu'eh-ye Qavanin-e Sevvomin Dowreh-ye Majlis-e Showra-ye Islami* (The Collection of the Laws of the Third Majlis), 790–805; hereafter referred to as *Majmu'eh.*

67. *Parliamentary Debates,* October 27, 1992.

68. Amuzegar (1995, 59).

69. *Majmu'eh,* 191–94. The bill was passed on August 18, 1989.

70. *Ettela'at,* April 3, 1991.

71. See Rafsanjani's comments on the need to have a more coordinated armed forces in *Ettela'at,* January 18, 1992.

72. The law passed the Majlis on June 12, 1990. For the text of the law, see *Majmu'eh,* 400–404.

73. *Ettela'at,* May 4, 1994.

74. See the interview with Musavi-Saraji (a member of MRM), the director of the KII, in *Komiteh* (monthly journal of the KII), March–April 1989.

75. The editorial in *Komiteh,* November–December 1989, proposed that instead of the merger, the KII should remain independent and be called the Guardian of the Islamic Revolution.

76. *Komiteh* editorial, December–January 1989–90.

77. *Komiteh,* June–July 1990.

78. *Parliamentary Debates,* May 30, 1990.

79. Ibid.

80. *Parliamentary Debates,* June 19, 1990.

81. As examples, see the speech of Ali Movahhedi-Saveji in *Parliamentary Debates,* June 10, 1990, and of Morteza Nabavi on June 19, 1990.

82. *Ettela'at,* October 2, 1991.

83. *Ettela'at,* January 11, 1992.

84. *Ettela'at,* April 18, 1992.

85. *Keyhan-Havai,* April 6, 1994.

86. *Parliamentary Debates,* August 26, 1989.

87. Ibid.

88. *Ettela'at,* August 8 and 9, 1993, for the list of Rafsanjani's second cabinet.

89. *Keyhan,* August 10, 1989.

90. *Keyhan,* August 28, 1989.

91. Personal interview with Mr. Mohammad Taqi Banki, Musavi's head of the MBO; Oxford, August 1997.

92. *Iran-e Farda,* spring 1993: 23.

93. *Parliamentary Debates,* May 30, 1992.

94. *Parliamentary Debates,* June 16, 1992.

95. *Parliamentary Debates,* July 1, 1992.

96. *JIM,* July–August 1992.

97. *Parliamentary Debates,* September 1, 1992.

98. *Parliamentary Debates,* August 4, 1992.

99. *Parliamentary Debates,* October 7, 1992.

100. *JIM,* September–October 1992.

101. *Parliamentary Debates,* July 1, 1992.

102. *Parliamentary Debates,* October 20, 1992. The same views were held by other conservative MPs such as Hossein Sobhaninia *(Parliamentary Debates,* August 4, 1992) and Hasan Aminlu *(Parliamentary Debates,* July 25, 1992).

103. *Parliamentary Debates,* September 27, 1992.

104. *Parliamentary Debates,* December 15, 1992.

105. For Nurbaksh's comments, see *Salam,* February 15, 1992; Adeli is quoted in *Salam,* April 28, 1993.

106. M. Tanha, *"San'at-e Melli: Qorbani-ye Siasat-e Jadid-e Puli"* (The National Economy: The Victim of New Fiscal Policies). Along with many other observers, the writer believed that given the quick return of investment in the bazaar, it was unlikely that people would put money in the industrial sector.

107. Nurbaksh, *Salam,* February 15, 1992

108. *Parliamentary Debates,* January 24, 1993.

109. Ibid.

110. Ibid.

111. Ibid.

112. Ibid.

113. Ibid.

114. *Parliamentary Debates,* January 30, 1993.

115. *Parliamentary Debates,* November 29, 1992.

116. *Ettela'at,* October 20, 1992.

117. *Ettela'at,* October 22, 1992.

118. *Ettela'at,* November 26, 1993.

119. *Salam,* June 21, 1992.

120. *Resalat,* March 27, 1994.

121. *Ettela'at,* June 2, 1994.

122. *Resalat,* May 24, 1994.

123. *Keyhan,* November 18, 1992.

124. *Resalat,* April 24, 1993.

125. *Resalat,* October 11, 1993.

126. *Ettela'at,* June 7, 1993.

127. *Ettela'at,* June 8, 1993.

128. *Parliamentary Debates,* May 3, 1993.

129. *Ettela'at,* June 13, 1993.

130. *Salam,* June 14, 1993.

131. *Parliamentary Debates,* June 15, 1992.

132. *Parliamentary Debates,* May 3, 1993. He also accused the conservatives of not telling the truth about economic achievements and manipulating public opinion, particularly of the unlettered masses.

133. The conservatives had privately proposed to Rafsanjani their preferred list of ministers, which included Mohammad Hadi Nezhad-Hosseinian for roads and transportation, Mohammad Reza Bahonar for state, Ali Abbas-Pour for higher education, and Ali Naqi Khamushi for commerce *(Salam,* July 21, 1993).

134. *Parliamentary Debates,* June 24, 1993.

135. *Salam,* July 29, 1993.

136. *Parliamentary Debates,* August 26, 1992.

137. *Parliamentary Debates,* August 12, 1992. The MP claimed that he had seen a war veteran who wanted to speak to the minister being harshly brushed aside by Nuri.

138. *Parliamentary Debates,* August 8, 1993.

139. *Parliamentary Debates,* August 15, 1993.

140. Ibid.

141. Ibid.

142. *Parliamentary Debates,* August 16, 1993.

143. *Parliamentary Debates,* October 6, 1993.

144. *Parliamentary Debates,* August 29, 1993.

145. *Maliy'at,* summer 1993.

146. *Resalat,* May 7, 1992.

147. *Salam,* September 6, 1993.

148. *Resalat,* May 4, 1992.

149. *Resalat,* September 23–25, 1993.

150. *Resalat,* October 4–5, 1993.

151. *Resalat,* September 29, 1993.

152. Comments made by Kazem Mirvalad, the speaker of the Budget Committee, in *Parliamentary Debates,* January 29, 1994.

153. *Parliamentary Debates,* January 25, 1994.

154. *Parliamentary Debates,* January 29, 1994.

155. Ibid.

156. Ibid.

157. *Parliamentary Debates,* January 31, 1994.

158. Ibid.

159. *Parliamentary Debates,* February 1, 1994.

160. *Parliamentary Debates,* January 30, 1994.

161. *Parliamentary Debates,* January 31, 1994.

162. *Parliamentary Debates,* March 9, 1994.

163. *Parliamentary Debates,* June 3, 1994.

164. See the report of Baqer Nurbakht, the committee's reporter, in *Parliamentary Debates,* August 8, 1994, and *Parliamentary Debates,* November 6, 1994.

165. *Parliamentary Debates,* August 10, 1994.

166. *Parliamentary Debates,* August 8, 1994.

167. *Parliamentary Debates,* November 13, 1994.

168. *Parliamentary Debates,* November 6–8, 1994.

169. *Resalat,* November 23, 1994.

170. *Salam,* April 2, 1994.

171. *Asr-e Ma,* April 5, 1995, 4.

172. *Resalat,* May 9, 1994.

173. *Resalat* editorial, May 11, 1994.

174. Ibid.

175. *Parliamentary Debates,* May 23, 1994.

176. *Resalat,* May 24, 1994.

177. *JI,* September 5, 1994.

178. *Ettela'at,* October 8, 1994.

179. *Keyhan-Havai,* November 9, 1994.

180. *Salam,* December 5, 1994.

181. Ibid.

182. *Payam-e Imruz,* autumn 1994: 11.

183. In the opening ceremony of the first *Refah* chain stores, Rafsanjani remarked, "If we open one store for every 100,000 people, the distribution and supply of goods will be fundamentally transformed" *(Iran,* March 4, 1995).

184. *Resalat,* May 28–29, 1994.

185. *Ettela'at,* October 15, 1995.

186. *Asr-e Ma,* December 28, 1994, 1.

187. *Resalat,* September 30, 1993.

188. *Resalat,* May 4, 1994.

189. *Salam,* December 5, 1994.

190. *Resalat,* May 30, 1994.

191. *Resalat,* May 31, 1994.

192. For various reports and figures issued by the SAO, see *JI,* April 29, 1995, and *Resalat,* April 22, 1995.

193. *Keyhan,* August 1 and 14, 1995.

194. *Iran,* August 22, 1995.

195. *Keyhan-Havai,* May 11, 1994, 24.

196. *Sobh* editorial, March 5, 1995.

197. "Mr. President, We Have Things to Say," *Sobh,* April 10, 1995.

198. Nurbaksh interview with *Iran,* January 24, 1995.

199. *Parliamentary Debates,* February 4, 1995.

200. *Parliamentary Debates,* February 20, 1995.

201. *Parliamentary Debates,* March 4, 1995.

202. *Resalat,* March 5, 1995.

203. *Parliamentary Debates,* July 15, 1992.

204. *Parliamentary Debates,* August 11, 1992.

205. Ibid.

206. *Resalat,* July 29, 1992.

207. *Ettela'at,* August 1, 1992.

208. *Ettela'at,* July 19, 1992.

209. See his speech in the Majlis on August 11, 1992.

210. Ibid.

211. Ibid.

212. Ibid.

213. Ibid.

214. *Ettela'at,* November 22, 1992.

215. *Ettela'at,* November 7, 1992.

216. *Ettela'at,* December 31, 1992.

217. *Ettela'at,* February 17, 1993.

218. *Keyhan,* April 12, 1993.

219. *Ettela'at,* September 30, 1993.

220. *Ettela'at,* November 15, 1993.

221. *Resalat,* August 30, 1993; *Jahan-e Islam,* September 18, 1993.

222. *Ettela'at,* August 21, 1993.

223. *Ettela'at,* October 25, 1992.

224. *Ettela'at,* November 11, 1992.

225. *Keyhan,* October 19, 1993.

226. *Ettela'at,* June 24, 1993.

227. *Ettela'at,* July 16, 1993.

228. *Ettela'at,* June 8, 1993.

229. *Parliamentary Debates,* October 2, 1992. This issue also contains the text of the law.

230. Ibid.

231. *Ettela'at,* January 11, 1992.

232. See reports in *Salam,* June 20 and 24 and July 18, 1993.

233. *Salam,* July 2, 1993.

234. *Ettela'at,* November 26, 1992.

235. *Ettela'at,* December 17, 1992.

236. *Ettela'at,* September 2, 1993.

237. *Ettela'at,* March 11, 1992.

238. *Ettela'at,* October 17, 1992.

239. *Ettela'at,* June 26, 1993.

240. *Ettela'at,* August 26, 1993.

241. *Ettela'at,* July 21, 1993.

242. Rafsanjani speaking during *Basij* Week in *Ettela'at,* November 25, 1991. Note on Farsi: *Hizbollah* denotes a group and *Hizbollahi* is someone who believes in and practices the tenets of *Hizbollah.* Likewise, *Basij* is an organization and *Basiji* is someone who belongs to it.

243. *Ettela'at,* November 4, 1992.

244. *Keyhan,* April 29, 1992.

245. *Ettela'at,* October 29, 1992.

246. *Ettela'at,* November 5, 1992.

247. *Ettela'at,* November 17, 1992.

248. *Ettela'at,* November 22, 1992.

249. *Ettela'at,* February 16, 1994.

250. *Ettela'at,* October 4, 1993.

251. *Ettela'at,* September 15, 1993.

252. *Parliamentary Debates,* September 9, 1993.

253. For the full text of the report, see *Parliamentary Debates,* November 2–3, 1993.

254. *Parliamentary Debates,* November 14, 1993.

255. Ibid.

256. *Ettela'at,* December 1, 1993.

257. *Ettela'at,* December 7, 1993.

258. *Ettela'at,* February 16, 1993.

259. Based on personal interviews with seven high-ranking officials in the ministry of culture, June 1996.

260. For a brief profile of Mir-Salim, see *Keyhan,* February 22, 1994.

261. *Ettela'at,* April 4, 1994.

262. *Ettela'at,* August 17, 1994.

263. *Ettela'at,* January 23, 1995.

264. *Resalat,* February 23, 1994.

265. *Ettela'at,* February 22, 1994.

266. *Ettela'at,* September 1, 1994.

267. *Ettela'at,* October 24, 1996.

268. *Ettela'at,* December 6, 1994.

269. *Keyhan-Havai,* May 25, 1994.

270. *Ettela'at,* June 15, 1994.

271. *Asr-e Ma,* February 22, 1995.

272. *Jahan-e Islam,* February 9, 1995.

273. *Salam,* December 25, 1993, and January 12, 1994, for the story behind the arrest and imprisonment of Abdi.

274. *Hamshahri,* January 14, 1993; *Iran* June 25, 1996; *Resalat,* October 14, 1993.

275. *Salam,* May 3, 1993.

276. *Resalat,* April 21, 1993.

277. *Bahman,* February 6, 1996.

278. *Salam,* July 25, 1993.

279. *Salam,* April 6, 1994.

280. *Hamshahri,* November 12, 1995.

281. *Salam,* September 26, 1995.

282. *JI,* May 17, 1995.

283. *Ettela'at,* July 8, 1995.

284. *Ettela'at,* January 24, 1995.

285. *Keyhan,* July 1 and 6, 1995.

286. *Salam,* September 12, 1996.

287. *Ettela'at,* June 7, 1994.

288. *Payam-e Daneshju,* June 13, 1995.

289. *Parliamentary Debates,* October 19, 1993.

290. *Parliamentary Debates,* October 20, 1993.

291. *Ettela'at,* October 24, 1993.

292. *JI,* June 1, 1995.

293. *Keyhan,* June 10, 1995.

294. *Salam,* November 6 and 8, 1993.

295. *Parliamentary Debates,* December 28, 1994.

296. Ibid.

297. *Asr-e Ma,* May 31, 1995, 2.

298. *Asr-e Ma,* June 28, 1995.

299. See, for example, Abdi's editorial in *Salam,* June 23, 1993.

300. For the text of the proclamation, see *Asr-e Ma,* November 1995.

301. *Salam,* February 8, 1996.

302. *Kar va Kargar,* April 21, 1996.

303. *Jahan-e Islam,* June 11, 1994.

304. *Asr-e Ma,* December 13, 1995.

305. *Salam,* January 16, 1995.

306. *Iran,* April 10, 1995.

307. *Iran,* June 2 and 5, 1996.

308. *Hamshahri,* July 6, 1995.

309. *Resalat,* July 9, 1995.

310. *Resalat,* July 10, 1995. See also the editorial in *Resalat,* July 29, 1995.

311. *Asr-e Ma,* June 28, 1995.

312. *Salam,* July 24, 1995.

313. *Resalat,* November 4, 1995.

314. *Resalat,* October 22, 1995.

315. *Salam* editorial, November 8, 1995.

316. *Sobh,* July 25, 1995.

317. JRM Bulletin, October–November 1995, 82–88.

318. *Resalat,* June 30, 1995.

319. *Resalat,* July 1, 1995.

320. *Resalat,* July 2, 1995.

321. *Resalat,* July 3, 1995.

322. *Resalat,* July 4, 1995.

323. *Iran,* January 31, 1995.

324. *Keyhan,* October 1, 1995.

325. *Resalat,* November 6, 1995.

326. *Resalat,* February 6, 1996.

327. *Resalat,* February 6, 15, and 24, 1996.

328. *Resalat,* February 13, 1996. The term "the great civilization" was used by the shah to label the economic system in Iran. Thus, here, the *Ansar* were implicitly suggesting that the modern right was pursuing a similar Western-inspired path as the shah.

329. *Sobh,* April 18, 1995.

330. Ibid.

331. *Ettetla'at,* July 8, 1995.

332. *Hamshahri,* July 20, 1994.

333. *Asr-e Ma,* November 1, 1995.

334. *Parliamentary Debates,* July 16, 1995. For a brief but insightful piece on the ramifications of this bill, see *"Qanun-e Intekhabat Majlis va Hakemiyat-e Melli"* (The Election Law of the Majlis and Popular Sovereignty).

335. JRM's bulletin (October–November 1995): 46.

336. *Salam,* November 2, 1995. According to another MRM member, Asadollah Bayat,

"The new powers of the Guardian Council obliterate the legal and political rights of the people" *(Keyhan,* October 11, 1995).

337. *Asr-e Ma,* October 18, 1995, 8.

338. *Resalat,* February 19, 1996.

339. *Parliamentary Debates,* May 22, 1996.

340. *Akhbar,* February 1, 1996.

341. *Resalat,* January 27, 1996.

342. *Salam,* February 6, 1996.

343. *Parliamentary Debates,* May 23, 1996.

344. *Hamshahri,* February 14, 1996.

345. *Iran,* March 31, 1996.

346. *Iran,* April 2, 1996.

347. *Iran,* January 22, 1996.

348. *Hamshahri,* January 24, 1996.

349. *Hamshahri,* March 2, 1996.

350. *Hamshahri,* February 27, 1996. Similar suggestions were made in editorials in *Hamshahari* on February 29 and March 3, 1996.

351. *Salam,* February 12, 1996.

352. *Salam,* February 8, 1996.

353. *Salam,* February 10, 1996.

354. *Akhbar,* January 23, 1996.

355. *Akhbar,* January 8, 1996.

356. *Salam,* February 1, 1996.

357. *Hamshahri,* February 1, 1996.

358. *"Intekhabat va roushan shodan-e marzbandiha-ye siasi"* (The Election and the Clarification of Political Lines), *Asr-e Ma,* February 7, 1996.

359. *Akhbar,* April 11, 1996.

360. *Hamshahri,* February 21, 1996.

361. Ibid.; *Hamshahri,* February 25, 1996.

362. For the list of the candidates of *Arzeshha,* see *Resalat,* February 28, 1996.

363. *Salam,* February 14, 1996.

364. *Payam-e Imruz,* March–April 1996, 9–10.

365. Interview of Abolvahed Musavi-Lari in *Akhbar,* December 10, 1995.

366. *Hamshahri,* January 29, 1996. For similar remarks, see also *Hamshahri,* February 10, 1996.

367. *Keyhan,* April 17, 1996.

368. *Salam* reported that there were rumors that close aids of Khamenehi were present in the screening sessions of the Council of Guardian when he revealed his preferred choices (March 5, 1996).

369. *Hamshahri,* February 4, 1996.

370. *Resalat,* March 4, 1996.

371. *Salam,* February 7, 1996.

372. *Resalat,* February 7, 1996.

373. *Resalat,* February 14, 1996.

374. *Resalat,* February 27, 1996.

375. *Resalat,* February 5, 1996.

376. *Salam,* February 28, 1996.

377. Ibid.

378. Ibid.

379. *Salam,* March 2 and 6, 1996.

380. *Salam,* March 13, 1996; *Resalat,* March 10 and 13.

381. *Salam,* March 11, 1996.

382. *Salam,* March 18, 1996.

383. *Iran,* April 6, 1996.

384. *Resalat,* April 2, 1996.

385. *Iran,* June 5, 1996.

386. *Resalat,* June 1, 1996.

387. *Asr-e Ma,* July 10, 1996.

388. *Salam,* September 6, 1996; *Kar va Kargar,* September 16, 1996; and *Iran,* September 18, 1996.

389. In an interview with *Iran,* Abbas Abdi and Sa'id Hajjarian strongly supported Rafsanjani's economic policies and the president's accommodating foreign policy orientation *(Iran,* June 18, 1996).

390. *Salam,* September 21, 1996.

391. *Resalat,* September 19, 1996.

392. *Kar va Kargar,* September 16, 1996.

393. *Resalat,* October 13, 1996.

394. *Iran,* September 2, 1996.

395. *Iran,* September 25, 1996.

396. *Iran,* September 26, 1996. The term *aslah* was often used during the presidential race, particularly by the ulama, in support of the candidates. This language was an effort to appease the influential men in the country by stating that although one candidate is more suited for an office, all are qualified. Due to the conflict within the JMHEQ this term was particularly used by prominent ulama in the organization to minimize their political motivations for choosing candidates in the presidential election.

397. *Kar va Kargar,* August 6, 1996.

398. *Salam,* July 28, 1996.

399. *Keyhan,* September 24, 1995.

400. Ibid.

401. Ibid.

402. *Resalat,* July 29, 1996.

403. *Iran,* June 29, 1996.

404. Interview with Asadollah Badamchian, *Akhbar,* July 18, 1996.

405. *Iran,* October 9 and 10, 1996.

406. *Sobh,* November–December 1996.

407. *Akhbar,* November 16, 1996.

408. *Salam,* October 29, 1996. The same views were expressed by Bahonar in *Kar va Kargar,* October 22, 1996.

409. *Resalat,* November 27, 1996.

410. *Kar va Kargar,* November 9, 1996.

411. *Kar va Kargar,* August 6, 1996.

412. *Iran,* November 6, 1996.

413. *Iran,* May 10, 1997.

414. *Iran,* November 11, 1996.

415. *Kar va Kargar,* March 15, 1997.

416. For *JAM,* see comments of Morteza Nabavi and Hasan Ghafuri-Fad in *Resalat,* November 27, 1996; for *Hamsu,* see its declaration in *Resalat,* November 16 and 17, 1996; for *Mo'talefeh,* Asghar-Owladi in *Resalat,* April 19, 1997.

417. *Iran,* May 1, 1997.

418. *Salam,* April 21, 1997.

419. *Salam,* May 21, 1997. Mas'udi revealed that out of thirty members of the JMHEQ, only twenty-one were present for the discussion of candidates for the presidential election, and only fourteen voted for Nateq-Nuri. This was also confirmed by Ayatollah Reza Ostadi, who supported Nateq-Nuri *(Resalat,* November 2, 1996).

420. *Kar va Kargar,* November 2, 1996.

421. *Resalat,* January 6, 1997.

422. *Iran,* May 10, 1997. See also *Resalat,* April 19, 1997.

423. *Asr-e Ma,* March 6, 1997, 4.

424. *Iran,* October 15, 1996.

425. *Iran,* October 16, 1996.

426. Interview with Mohajerani, *Kar va Kargar,* October 15, 1996.

427. Ibid.

428. *Resalat,* December 4, 1996.

429. *Resalat,* November 19, 1996.

430. *Ettela'at,* December 22, 1996.

431. *Salam,* December 29, 1996.

432. *Salam,* October 27, 1996.

433. *JI,* November 6, 1996.

434. *Iran,* December 7, 1996.

435. *Asr-e Ma,* February 15, 1997.

436. *Salam,* February 27, 1997; *Asr-e Ma,* March 9 and April 8, 1997.

437. *Hamshahri,* March 17, 1997.

438. *Iran,* April 13, 1997.

439. Mohajerani's views in *Akhbar,* May 5, 1997, and Hossein Mar'ashi in *Kar va Kargar,* April 19, 1997.

440. *Salam,* April 8, 1997.

441. *Iran,* May 1, 1997.

442. *Salam,* April 8, 1997.

443. *Salam,* April 27, 1997.

444. Ibid.

445. *Salam,* April 8, 1997. For similar comments, see *Salam,* February 20, 1997, and *Iran,* February 22, 1997.

446. *Hamshahri,* March 13, 1997.

447. *Resalat,* November 6, 1996.

448. *Resalat,* November 15, 1996.

449. *Sobh,* November–December 1996.

450. *Resalat,* November 15, 1996.

451. *Iran,* May 20, 1997.

452. This is, for example, how Morteza Nabavi *(Iran,* October 16, 1996) and Mohammad Reza Bahonar *(Resalat,* October 22, 1996) designated a fit candidate.

453. *Mobin,* January 27, 1997.

454. *Resalat,* April 16, 1997.

455. *Salam,* April 17, 1997.

456. *Salam,* April 21, 1997.

457. *Hamshahri,* April 21, 1997.

458. *Salam,* April 22, 1997.

459. *Salam,* May 7, 1997.

460. *Akhbar,* January 21, 1997.

461. *Resalat,* May 4, 1997.

462. *Salam,* April 28, 1997.

463. *Resalat,* May 21, 1997.

464. *Iran,* May 18, 1997.

465. *Iran,* May 22, 1997.

Chapter 6. Factional Politics under Khatami: Civil Society vs. Guardianship Society

1. This is not to say that the aforementioned formed a coherent political base or functioned as a faction. Rather, they all supported the basic creed of the May Epic.

2. "Reflection on the May 23 Election," *Salam,* August 17, 1997.

3. Attempting to diminish the popularity of Khatami and the significance of the election,

both Ayatollahs Mohammad Yazdi and Mohammad Imami-Kashani claimed that the huge turnout at the polls was homage to the leader *(Resalat,* May 24 and 25, 1997).

4. An editorial in the daily *Iran* "enlightened those who have yet to grasp the essence of recent events" by claiming that "the basis of the regime's legitimacy in our regime has experienced a quintessential transformation" (August 9, 1997). A *Salam* editorial explicitly challenged the conservatives' reading of the May events and noted, "On May 23, people voted for Khatami and not for the leader or the policies of the regime" (August 14, 1997).

5. "The Election: Islam and the Revolution's Second Generation," *Asr-e Ma,* July 16, 1997.

6. These ideas were summarized by Khatami immediately after his election. See, for example, his interview with *Iran* three days after he was elected. See also his comments in *Resalat,* November 18, 1997. Similar comments were made by Abolvahed Musavi-Lari in *Salam,* December 13, 1997.

7. "Islam, the Society, and Politics," in *Asr-e Ma,* June 7 and 18, 1997. What the MII wished to debate was whether reliance on traditional *fiqh* would cause religious stagnation and prevent the regime from being able to answer contemporary questions.

8. The two men elaborated on this idea in *Salam.* To substantiate their notion of "religious pluralism," both argued that God had sent numerous prophets to spread his message in different communities, and thus the Islamic world has "religious pluralism" *(Salam,* January 1, 8, and 15, 1998). Similar views were expressed by Mohajerani *(Resalat,* November 12, 1997).

9. Khatami also spoke against a rigid reading of Islam, emphasized the dynamic nature of Shii *fiqh,* and noted, "The fundamentals of religion must be taken and appear as new forms based on [conditions of] the time and place to maintain their livelihood and dynamism" *(Ettela'at* May 3, 1998).

10. *Resalat,* August 6, 1997.

11. In his first press conference five days after the election, Khatami noted, "Our main goal is to institutionalize the rule of law and implement the constitution" *(Salam,* May 28, 1997). He reiterated these views in his inauguration speech *(Parliamentary Debates,* August 4, 1997).

12. *Salam,* November 28, 1997.

13. Ataollah Mohajerani also stressed that the first Islamic community formed by the Prophet was the first Islamic civil society. He said, "This tradition continued as freedom, democracy, and civic association became embedded in Islam" *(Resalat,* February 1, 1998).

14. Armin and Razzaghi (1999); for Kadivar's remark, see p. 166; for Abdi's, p. 140.

15. "Us, Civil Society, and Its Non-Modern Prescription," *Asr-e Ma,* August 29, 1997.

16. Behzad Nabavi predicted that the conservatives would use their institutional power to challenge the president *(Resalat,* December 30, 1997). He made similar remarks in an interview with *Arzesha,* December 15, 1997.

17. Kadivar (1998). Interestingly enough, Kadivar is highly laudatory of the views of Ayatollah Hossien Ali Montazeri, who construed a very limited role for the *faqih* and therefore fell from grace with Khomeini. In his footnote on page 381, Kadivar refers to Montazeri as "our venerable chieftain and teacher."

18. Khatami's inauguration speech in the Majlis, *Parliamentary Debates,* August 4, 1997.

19. *Resalat,* August 25, 1997, and November 18, 1997.

20. *Asr-e Ma,* November 19, 1997.

21. *Resalat,* November 23, 1997.

22. For example, see the comments of two high-ranking ayatollahs in Qom, Naser Makarem-Shirazi and Mohammad Fazel Lankarani, in support of Khamenehi and his rightful claim as a *vali-ye faqih* in *Salam,* November 23 and 25, 1997.

23. Abdollah Nuri (left-MR), interior; Kamal Kharrazi (left), foreign affairs; Bizhan Zanghaneh (left), oil; Ataollah Mohajerani (MR), culture and Islamic guidance; Gholamreza Shafei (left), industries; Morteza Haji (left), cooperatives; Mostafa Moin (left), higher education; Ali Shamkhani (center), defense; Qorban-Ali Dorri Najafabadi (center), intelligence; Ismail Shushtari (center), justice; Mohammad Shariatmadar (left), commerce; Mohammad Saidi-Kia (left), construction jihad; Ishaq Jahanghiri (MR), mines and metals; Mahmud Hojjati Najafabadi (left), roads and transport; Reza Aref (left), Post Telegraph and Telephone; Habibollah Bitaraf (left), energy; I'sa Kalantari (MR), agriculture; Mohammad Farhadi (MR), health; Ali Abdol'ali-Zadeh (left), housing and urban development; Hossein Mozaffar (left), education and training; Hossein Namazi (left), economic affairs/finance; Hossein Kamali (left), labor and social affairs.

24. Khatami's associates indirectly admitted to the president's partisan selection. Mohajerani said, "Those who did not vote for Khatami should not expect the president to fulfill their expectations" *(Ettela'at,* May 25, 1997). Khatami's choices for deputies were Abolvahed Musavi-Lari, judicial and parliamentary affairs; Mahmud Hashami, executive affairs; Mohammad Ali Najafi, planning and budget organization; Mostafa Hashemitaba, physical education organization; Mohammad Baqerian, administration organization; Masomeh Ebtekar (first woman in a cabinet), environmental affairs; Mostafa Tajzadeh, political and social affairs *(Salam,* August 24 and 31, 1997).

25. See the comments of the MP from Dezful Mehdi-Reza Darvishzadeh in *Parliamentary Debates,* August 3, 1997. One day before the voting, MP Ali Zadsar from Jiroft put the following explicit question to Mohajerani: "Will you kill Rushdie if you ever face him?"

26. Bahonar speaking in the Majlis, in *Parliamentary Debates,* August 18, 1997.

27. One day before the vote, Bahonar announced that the Majlis would give their vote of confidence to all but two or three candidates *(Parliamentary Debates,* August 19, 1997). Mohajerani, Nuri, and Kharrazi were presumed to be the ones who would not get votes.

28. *Parliamentary Debates,* August 20, 1997; Mohajerani 144 (for), 96 (against), 20 (abstained); and Nuri 153, 89, 21.

29. An editorial in *Asr-e Ma* accurately revealed of the conservatives' seeming majority in the parliament: "the Majlis is not the domain of one faction anymore and the rightists could at best count on the support of ninety MPs" (August 27, 1997).

30. Facing the prospect of being censured, and one day before the Majlis was to decide his fate, he courageously told conservative MPs, "I am one for social tolerance and cultural indulgence. I oppose the current methods employed by the ministry [of culture]. We must respect

writers and artists and create an atmosphere for them that allows them to flourish" *(Parliamentary Debates,* August 19, 1997).

31. *Salam,* October 22, 1997.

32. *Salam,* October 23, 1997.

33. *Asr-e Ma,* December 17, 1997.

34. *Salam,* October 2, 1992.

35. One year into Khatami's presidency, the ministry had issued 300 new publication permits *(Asr-e Ma,* June 18, 1998).

36. The strategy of Khatami's camp was to "pressure the conservatives from below and haggle for more freedom and power on the top," according to Sai'd Hajjarian (interview with *Rah-e No,* May 23, 1998).

37. For instance, Mohsen Kadivar continued his crusade against the principle of *velayat-e faqih.* In a two-part interview with *Rah-e No,* he claimed that the concept cannot be found in any Qoranic verses, nor is it religious or rational necessity (June 20 and August 14, 1998).

38. Speech of MP Mohammad Hosseini Vaez in *Parliamentary Debates,* February 21, 1998, and Morteza Nabavi in *Resalat,* February 28, 1998.

39. See the editorials in *Resalat,* May 26–27, 1997.

40. Interview with the daily *Azad,* September 30, 1997.

41. *Resalat,* November 20, 1997.

42. *Resalat,* November 25, 1997.

43. *Resalat,* December 2, 1997. With this editorial, the conservatives took the unassailability of the *faqih* to a new level when they suggested that the Assembly of Experts in fact "discovers" the rightful *faqih* and does not select him. They asserted that the *"faqih* is a holy appointee and if people withdraw their support from the leader, he does not lose his leadership." *Asr-e Ma,* on the other hand, rightfully responded to this reading of the *vali-e faqih* by noting that "the Imam in his January 1988 decree in fact boosted the power of the state [the central government] and not the domain of the *faqih.*" "Let us defend the *velayat-e faqih* properly," December 18, 1998.

44. *Ettela'at,* June 8, 1998.

45. See, for example, the declarations of the JMHEQ in *Resalat,* November 2 and 9, 1997. In fact, high-ranking conservative ulamas such as Mohammad Abbas Vaez-tabasi bluntly claimed, "Islam does not accept the modern democratic state, since Islam does not believe in the rule of the majority" (ibid).

46. *Shoma,* April 10, 1997.

47. See the words of their leader, Hossein Allah-Karam, in *Mobin,* December 21, 1998.

48. *Resalat,* February 5, 1998.

49. *Resalat,* July 24, 1998.

50. According to *Asr-e Ma's* article, "Problems and obstacles faced by Khatami are because his views are not the same as the officials in the judiciary [*yazdi*], National Radio and Television, and the Guardian Council." The article added, "If, according to the constitution, the president

does not enjoy vast powers in implementing his policies, in return he enjoys a tremendous reserve of social support in Iran" (September 24, 1997).

51. See the interview of Behzad Nabavi with *Salam,* September 1, 1997. He said, "Khatami was elected in a situation where the leader has control over the judiciary, the armed forces, radio and TV, revolutionary bodies. . ." Given these limits, he argued, people should not expect too much from Khatami.

52. Mehdi Karrubi, *Iran,* November 20, 1997. See also the comments of Ali Akbar Mohatashami in *Salam,* November 5, 1997.

53. He was accused of embezzling 14 billion rials, or about $90,000 *(Resalat,* April 2, 1998). To this list, illegal donations was later added when he was accused of supplying close to 250 million rials to the *Kargozaran* in the fifth Majlis election *(Jame'eh,* June 8, 1998).

54. *Resalat,* July 28, 1998.

55. *Salam,* December 26, 1998.

56. See the editorial in *Arzeshha,* August 4, 1998, a view shared by many in Iran.

57. According to *Jame'eh* (July 13, 1998), Karbaschi's trial was the most watched program since the revolution, with people staying up and cheering for him late into the night. Khatami called him "one of the most prominent administrators in the country" *(Tus,* July 27, 1998).

58. *Salam,* October 28, 1997.

59. Yazdi announced that the judiciary had independence to pursue the "prohibited: haram." He appeared to be fair when he said the wealthy and everyone else—even the big shots—are equal before the law *(Resalat,* August 27, 1997).

60. The conservative right entrapped Karbaschi with their customary attack on statism, emphasizing the need to keep a watchful eye on how officials in the government were spending public money. See comments made by Asghar Owladi and Morteza Nabavi in *Resalat,* July 26 and August 27, 1997.

61. In fact, it was he who implicitly gave the go-ahead when he called upon the judiciary to investigate and prosecute government officials who had amassed "effortless money" *(Resalat,* June 29 and July 17, 1998).

62. According to the conservative daily *Abrar,* in the first six months of Khatami's presidency, over one hundred interior ministry officials were replaced. MP Rasuli-Nezhad told the Majlis on October 19 that of nineteen new governors, ten are new and the rest have been reshuffled. "All decisions were factional," he complained (October 15, 1998).

63. He not only refused to dismiss "one of the most successful officials in the country" *(Resalat,* November 17, 1997), but he infuriated the conservatives (and arguably their leader) when he went to Karbaschi's house immediately after coming from his haj' trip and created "the Headquarters for the Defense and Support of Karbaschi" *(Resalat,* April 11 and 12, 1998).

64. During Montazeri's downfall, Nuri did not criticize him, showing implicit support for him and his ideas. After his dismissal, he openly supported Montazeri and his anti–*velayat-e faqih* views (interview with *Tus,* September 1, 1998).

65. *Jame'eh,* June 11, 1998. Bahonar went as far as saying that Nuri's actions could lead the country into a Lebanon-like situation *(Hamshari,* June 24, 1998).

66. *Jame'eh,* June 22, 1998.

67. See his fiery farewell speech to the students in *Jame'eh,* June 30, 1998.

68. Bahonar remarked that despite opposition to Khatami's second choice, the majority parliamentary fraction would approve Musavi-Lari, so it would not affect the government's administration of daily affairs a great deal *(Resalat,* July 23, 1998).

69. See the words of the editor of *Asr-e Ma,* Mohsen Armin, in the biweekly on May 2, 1998. I was in Iran at that time and was told by reliable sources in the regime that the conservatives had pledged to dethrone Khatami in six months.

70. People from the newly formed alliance attested to this: "If some people want to dilute *velayat-e faqih* and true revolutionary culture we will oppose them strongly" (Asghar Owladi and Badamchian in *Resalat,* November 21, 1997).

71. For example, see his Friday prayer sermon in *Salam,* November 28, 1998, and *Tus,* August 1, 1998.

72. Friday prayer sermon, *Resalat,* April 28, 1998.

73. *Keyhan,* November 15, 1997.

74. The former head of IRCG, Mohsen Rezai, was appointed as the Expediency Council's deputy.

75. *Jame'eh,* April 30, 1998.

76. Reacting to words of Savafi, Asghar Owladi noted, "According to the constitution, the IRGC is responsible for preserving the revolution and its tenets" *(Resalat,* May 5, 1998).

77. *Resalat,* June 13, 1998.

78. *Salam,* September 6, 1998.

79. *Jame'eh,* June 3, 1998.

80. *Salam,* September 6, 1998.

81. *Khordad,* June 1998.

82. *Salam,* September 19, 1998.

83. For Ijhei's comments, see *Salam,* September 20, 1998. D'Estaing told the paper that just before the revolution, all the Western powers thought they should maintain their support for the shah except the United States, who believed that the king's time was over *(Tus,* September 14, 1998). Two days earlier, *Tus* had published a caricature of a clergyman with swastika on his chest.

84. *Khordad,* February 4, 1999.

85. *Khordad,* January 26, 1999.

86. *Sobh-e Imruz,* January 5, 1999.

87. *Salam,* February 13, 1999.

88. For physical confrontation between *Basij*-Hizbollahi members and the university students, see *Salam,* December 1 and 2, 1998, and *Neshat,* March 8, 1999. One incident that generated a great deal of criticism occurred when the *Basijis* beat up young people on the street who came out to celebrate Iran's soccer victory in the Asian games *(Khordad,* December 22, 1998).

89. Nateq-Nuri said universities are witnessing the fight between Westernized intellectuals and the *Basij* *(Salam,* November 23, 1998). According to Khamenehi, "The faithful and *Basij* forces must become increasingly involved in the cultural debates" *(Salam,* November 24, 1998).

90. In a three-part interview with *Khordad* (February 14, 15, 16, 1999), he not only once again objected to the *Motlaqeh* reading of *velayat-e faqih,* but, like Montazeri, compared the authoritarian nature of the current regime with that of the shah. He also explicitly objected to the politicization of the clergy.

91. *Asr-e Ma,* January 12, 1999.

92. *Khordad,* March 4 and *Neshat,* May 19, 1999.

93. He chastised those who did not care about the vote of people and tried to impose their will on society *(Tus,* August 1 and 27, 1998).

94. *Khordad,* December 12, 1998.

95. *Salam,* November 23, 1998.

96. *Salam,* December 12 and 19, 1998.

97. *Salam* editorials, November 30, 1998, and December 13, 1998. The same tone was used by the MRM in *Salam,* December 8, 1998.

98. *Salam,* November 25, 1998.

99. *Salam,* December 12, 1998.

100. *Salam,* December 14, 1998.

101. *Keyhan,* for example, claimed that Forohar did not believe in Islamic laws and that is why no clergy had recited the death prayer for him (December 8, 1998). Similar comments were made by the deputy head of IRGC, Mohammad Baqer Zolqadr; see *Khordad,* December 17, 1998.

102. *Khordad,* December 15, 1998.

103. *Salam,* January 6, 1999.

104. For the text of the interview, see *Keyhan,* January 11, 1999.

105. *Salam,* January 17, 1999.

106. *Khordad,* February 10 and 25, 1998.

107. In April 1999, he warned that he would use his entire power to expose all those "who speak only the language of guns and bullets" *(Neshat,* April 19, 1999).

108. Interview with *Salam,* December 20, 1998.

Conclusion

1. For a brief but informative survey of the views of ulama in this regard, see Rahnema and Nomani (1990, 128–61).

2. *Keyhan,* February 6, 1979.

Glossary

ahkam-e avvaliyeh: primary ordinances based on the two pillars of Shii Islam (the Qoran and the *Sonna*)

ahkam-e sanaviyeh: secondary ordinances

Amr-e be ma'ruf va nah-ye az monkar: propagation of virtue and prohibition of vice

anjomanha-ye Islami: Islamic associations

aql: reason

Basiji: highly religious war veteran

caliph: a successor of Muhammad as temporal and spiritual head of Islam

chador: long veil worn by women to cover their bodies

Dadgah-he Vizheh-ye Rouhaniyat: Special Court for the Clergy, which prosecutes offenses committed by the clergy

dowlat: government, state

faqih (pl. *foqaha; fiqh-e sonnati*): traditional jurisprudence jurist, expert in Islamic laws; learned clergy

fatwa: religious edict issued by qualified *mojtahid*

fiqh: religious (Islamic) jurisprudence

fiqh-e puya: dynamic jurisprudence

Hadith: tradition of the Prophet, his words and deeds

haj': annual pilgrimage to Mecca

haq': right

haram: religiously forbidden

hejab: Islamic dress

Hizbollah: party of god

hojjatol-Islam: "proof of Islam," clerical rank below Ayatollah

Hojjatiyeh: a religious society opposed to the concept of *velayat-e faqih* which ended its public activities in the early 1980s.

hokumat: government, governance, regime

howzeh: theological seminary

ijma': consensus

ijtihad: use of independent judgment or original thinking in interpreting the Qoran and the *Sonna*

imam: spiritual leader, in Shii sect of Islam, one of the twelve infallible heirs to the Prophet descended from Ali

intesabi: appointed

jame'eh-ye velai: guardianship society

jihad: holy war

Kargozaran: servants; agents

khatt-e Imam: followers of Khomeini's beliefs and actions (literally meaning "the line of *imam*")

khlaq: the masses

Khobregan: abbreviation for *majlis-e khobregan* or the council of experts

khodi: related, familiar

khoms: one fifth of the surplus income of Muslims levied as a canonical tax

mahdi: guide, leader—the twelfth imam (the messiah) who the shi'is believe is in occultation and will appear at the end of the world and usher in a new order

Majam'-e Tashkhise Maslahat-e Nezam: Expediency Council, literately the assembly that determines what is in the best interests of the regime; an arbitration body that settles potential disputes over laws between the parliament and the Guardian Council

majlis: assembly, the Iranian parliament

Majlis-e Khobregan: Assembly of Experts, a clerical body which selects the leader

maktabis: followers of the Islamic school

marja' (pl. *maraje'*): source of emulation

marja'-e taqlid: source of emulation, role model

marja'iyat: emulating a *marja'*

maslahat: interest

mojtahid: a person qualified to undertake *ijtihad*

moabbah (pl. *monabbahat*): the admonishments

moqalled: imitator, emulator

mostazaf (pl. *mostazafin*): deprived, disinherited

Motlaqeh: absolutist

Ayatollah: "sign of God," a title given to leading mojtahid

Nehads: revolutionary bodies/foundation

ommat: community

Qoran: the holy book of Islam

rahbar: leader

Sazmanha-ye Aqidati-Siyasi: ideological-political organizations

shahid: martyr

shari'a: the canonical law of Islam

sherk: polytheism

Showra-ye Negahban: Guardian Council, made up of six clerics and six civilians who determine if laws are compatible with Islam.

Sonna: the prophet's words and deeds (his ways)

tahajom-e farhangi: [Western] cultural onslaught

taqlid: imitation

tojjar: merchants

Towse-'eh: political and economic development

ulama: religious scholars, clergy

vali-ye faqih: the guardian jurist

velayat: guardianship, agency, government

velayat-e faqih: guardianship of the jurist, Ayatollah Khomeini's doctrine of Islamic government

velayat-e motlaqeh-ye faqih: the absolute guardianship of the faqih

zakat: alms, canonical tax

Bibliography

In Persian

Books

Araqi, Mehdi. 1991. *Nagofteha*. Tehran: Rasa Publications.
Armin, Mohsen, and Hojjat Razzaghi, eds. 1999. *Bimha va Omidha*. Tehran: Hamshari Publication.
Asasnameh-ye Bonyad-e Mostazafin. 1979. Tehran: Bonyad Publication.
Asheni ba Majlis-e Showra-ye Islami-ye 1360. 1982. Tehran: Majlis Publication.
Azimi, Hossein. 1992. *"Iqtesad-e Iran: Bohranha va Cheshmandazha,"* in *Iran-e Farda*, winter.
Badamchian, Asadollah. 1995. *Shenakht-e Inqlab-e Islami va Risheha-ye an*. Tehran: Open University Press.
Baqi, Emaddoldin. 1983. *Dar Shenakht-e Hazb-e Qaedin-e Zaman: Mo'sum be Anjoman-e Hojjatieh*. Tehran: Nashr-e Danesh.
Barzeen, Saeed. 1995. *Zendeginameh-ye Siasi-ye Mohandes Mehdi Bazargan*. Tehran: Nashr Publisher.
Bazargan, Mehdi. 1984. *Inqelab-e Iran Dar do Harekat*. Tehran: Iran's Freedom Movement (Nehzat-e Azadi Publications).
———. 1995. *Intezar az din az Didgah-e Mohandes Bazargan*. Tehran: Center for Strategic Studies.
———. N.d. *Velayet-e Motlaqeh-ye Faqih*. Tehran: Nezahat-e Azadi Publications.
Farsi, Jalalodin. 1994. *Zavaya-ye Tarik*. Tehran: Azadeh Publications.
Ghaffari, Hadi. 1994. *Khaterat-e Hadi Ghaffari*. Tehran: Sazman-e Tablighat-e Islami.
Gilani, Momammad. 1995. *Imam-e Rahel va fiqh-e Iranian*. Tehran: Bonyad-e Farhang Iran. 3 volumes.
Kadivar, Mohsen. 1998. *Hokumat-e Velai*. Tehran: Ney Publication.

Kermani, Nazim–el Islam. 1967. *Tarikh-e Bidari-ye Sonnati.* Tehran: Amir Kabir Publication.

Khamenehi, Ali. *Ajwabul Estefsarat.* 1996. Beirut: Dara-l Haq' Publisher.

———. 1996. *Farhang va Tahajom-e Farhangi.* Tehran: Ministery of Islamic Culture and Guidance Publication.

Khomeini, Ruhollah. 1942. *Kashf-e Asrar.* Tehran: n.p.

———. 1978. *Velayat-e Faqih: Hokumat-e Islami.* Tehran: Amir Kabir Publication.

———. 1982. *Sahifeh-ye Nur.* 25 vols. Tehran: Government Publication.

Leilaz, Sa'id. 1993. "Nazari bar Amalkard-e Iqtesadi-ye Jomhuri-ye Islami," in *Iran-e Farda,* February–March.

Madani, Jalaloldin. 1995. *Hoquq-e Asasi va Nehadha-ye Siasi-ye Jomhuri-ye Islami-ye Iran.* Tehran: Hamrah Publication.

Malakzadeh, M. 1974. *Tarikh-e Inqlab-e Mashrut-e ye Iran.* Tehran: Elmi Publication. 7 vols.

Motahari, Morteza. N.d. *Piramun-e Inqelab-e Islami.* Tehran: Sadra Publication.

Nateq, Homa, and Adamiyat Fereydoun. 1977. *Afkar-e Ijtema'i va Iqtesadi der Asar-e Montashernashoday-e Dawran-e Qajar.* Tehran: Aqah Press.

"Qanun-e Intekhabat Majlis va Hakemiyat-e Melli." 1995. In *Iran-e Farda,* February–March.

Rafsanjani, Akbar. 1997. *Dowran-e Mobarezeh.* 2 vols. Tehran: Nashr-e Ma'aref-e Islami Publisher

Rouhani, H. 1982. *Nehzat-e Imam Khomeini.* Tehran: Uftst Publisher.

Sahabi, Ezatollah. 1992–93. "Iqtesade Bazzari ba'-daz Jang." In *Iran-e Farda,* no. 4, December/January.

Salnameh-ye Amari-ye Keshvar. 1997. Tehran: Islamic Republic of Iran's Plan and Budget Organisation.

Shariati, Ali. 1976. *Insan, Marksizm va Islam.* Qom: n.p.

———. N.d. *Islam shenasi.* Tehran: Hosseiniyeh Irshad Publication.

———. N.d. *Tashayo'-e Alavi va Tashayo'-e Safavi.* Tehran: Hosseiniyeh Irshad Publication.

Tanha, M. 1993. "San'at-e Melli: Qorbani-ye Siasat-e Jadid-e Puli." In *Iran-e Farda,* spring.

Ziba Kalam, Sadeq. 1993. *Moqaddam-e bar Inqlab-e Islami.* Tehran: Rozaneh Publisher.

Pamphlets, Occasional Papers, and Miscellaneous Works

Asasnameh va Maramnameh-ye Sazman-e Mojahedin-e Islami-ye Iran. 1992. Tehran: Mojahedin-e Inqlab-e Islami Publication.
Ashenai ba Mavaze'-e Sazman-e Mojahedin-e Inqelab-e Islami. 1980. Tehran: n.p.
Chahar Saal-e Dovvom 1989. Tehran: Ettela'at Publication.
Darabi, A. 1995. "Jame'eh-ye Rouhaniyat-e Mobarez." Ph.D. diss., University of Tehran.
Kadivar, Mohsen. 1997. "Nazariy-e Hay-e Dowlat Dar Fiqh-e Shi'a" (State Theories under Shii Jurisprudence). *Bahman,* no. 7: 1997.
Majmu'eh-ye Bayani-ye ha va Ittelai-e hay-e Sazman-e Mojahedin-e Inqlab-e Islami. 1979. 2 vols. Tehran: MII Publication.
Majmu'eh-ye Mosavvabat-e Showraye Inqelab-e Farhangi 1368–1372. 1994. Teheran: Majlis Publication.
Marja'iyat az Didgah-he Foqaha va Bozorgan. 1993. Qom: JMHEQ Publication.
Nazm-e Novin-e Jahani. 1991. Tehran: MII Publication.

Government Publications

"Ahkam-e Hokumeti va Maslahat." 1994. Tehran: Centre for Strategic Studies.
"Ashenai ba Majlis-e Showra-ye Islami 1360." 1982. Tehran: Majlis Publications.
Farhang va Tahajom-e Farhangi. 1996. Tehran: Ministry of Islamic Culture and Guidance Publication.
Khotut-e Kollei-ye Andisheha-ye Imam Khomeini. 1994. Tehran: Centre for Strategic Studies.
Khotbeha va Jom'eh-ha. 1981. Tehran: IRP Publication.
Majmu'eh-ye Mossavabat-e Showraye Inqelab-e Farhangi 1368–1372. 1994. Tehran: n.p.
Majmu'eh-ye Nazariyat-e Showra-ye Negahban; Dowreh-ye Avval 1359–1365. 1992. Tehran: Keyhan Publication. 3 vols.
Majmu'eh-ye Qavanin-e Sevvomin Dowreh-ye Majlis-e Showra-ye Islami. 1992. Majlis Publication.
Mashruh-e Mozakerat-e Majlis-e Showra-ye Islami 1990. Tehran: Majlis Publication.
Surat-e Mashruh-e Mozakerat-e Majlis-e Barresi-ye Nehai-ye Jomhuri-ye Islami-ye Iran 1982. 2 vols. Tehran: Majlis Publication.
Surat-e Mashruh-e Mozakerat-e Showra-ye Qanun-e Asasi-ye Jomhuri-ye Islami-e Iran. 1994. 4 vols. Tehran: Majlis Publication.

In English

Books

Abrahamian, Ervand. 1993. *Khomeinism.* Berkeley: Univ. of California Press.

Akhavi, Shahrough. 1980. *Religion and Politics in Contemporary Iran: Clergy-State Relations in the Pahlavi Period.* Albany: State Univ. of New York Press.

Algar, Hamid. 1969. *Religion and State in Iran, 1785–1906.* Berkeley: Univ. of California Press.

Aristotle. 1962. *The Politics.* Translated by T. A. Sinclair. Baltimore: Penguin.

Ayubi, Nazih. 1991. *Political Islam.* London: Routledge.

Bakhash, Shoul. 1984. *The Reign of Ayatollahs.* New York: Basic Books.

Baktiari, Bahman. 1996. *Parliamentary Politics in Revolutionary Iran: The Institutionalization of Factional Politics.* Gainesville: Univ. of Florida Press.

Banuazizi, Ali, and M. Weimer, eds. 1986. *The State, Religion, and Ethnic Politics: Afghanistan, Iran, and Pakistan.* Syracuse: Syracuse Univ. Press.

Brown, G. 1910. *The Persian Constitutional Revolution of 1905–1906.* Cambridge: Cambridge Univ. Press.

Directorate-General of International Agreements. 1995. *The Constitution of the Islamic Republic of Iran.* Tehran: Directorate-General of International Agreements Publication.

Ehteshami, Anoushirvan. 1995. *After Khomeini: Iran's Second Republic.* London: Routledge.

Gerth, H. H., and C. Wright Mills, eds. and trans. 1996. *From Max Weber: Essays in Sociology.* London: Routledge.

Hashim, A. 1995. *The Crisis of the Iranian State: Domestic, Foreign, and Security Policies in Post-Khomeini Iran.* Oxford: Oxford Univ. Press.

Heinz, H. 1991. *Shiism.* Edinburgh: Edinburgh Univ. Press.

Hunter, Shirin. 1992. *Iran After Khomeini.* New York: Praeger.

Keddie, Nikki. 1966. *Religion and Politics in Iran: The Tobacco Protest of 1891–1892.* London: Frank Cass.

———, ed. 1983. *Religion and Politics in Iran.* New Haven: Yale Univ. Press.

Keddie, Nikki, and Eric Hooglund, eds. 1986. *The Iranian Revolution and the Islamic Republic.* Syracuse: Syracuse Univ. Press.

Lambton, A. K. S. 1987. *Qajar Persia.* Austin: Univ. of Texas Press.

Mann, Michael. 1995. *The Sources of Social Power: The Rise of Classes and Nation States, 1760–1914.* Vol. 2. Cambridge: Cambridge Univ. Press.

Martin, Vanessa. 1989. *Islam and Modernism*. London: I. B. Tauris.

Marty, E., and R. Appley. 1990. *Fundamentalist Observed*. Chicago: Univ. of Chicago Press.

Menasheri, David. 1990. *Iran: A Decade of War and Revolution*. New York: Holmes and Meier.

Milani, Mohsen. 1988. *The Making of Iran's Islamic Revolution*. Boulder, Colo.: Westview Press.

Mohajerani, Masih. 1982. *Islamic Revolution and the Future Path of the Nations*. Tehran: Jihad-e Sazandegi Publication.

Momen, M. 1985. *An Introduction to Shi'i Islam: The History of Twelver Shiism*. New Haven: Yale Univ. Press.

Nozick, Robert. 1974. *Anarchy, State, and Utopia*. New York: Basic Books.

Pahlavi, Mohammad Reza. 1980. *Answer to History*. New York: n.p.

Parsa, Misagh. 1989. *Social Origins of the Iranian Revolutions*. New Brunswick, N.J.: Rutgers Univ. Press.

Pierson, Christopher. 1996. *The Modern State*. London: Routledge.

Poggi, Gianfranco. 1990. *The State: Its Nature, Development, and Prospects*. Cambridge: Polity.

Rabinowitch, A. 1968. *Prelude to Revolution: The Petrograd Bolsheviks and the July 1917 Uprising*. Bloomington: Indiana Univ. Press.

Rahnema, Ali, and Farhad Nomani. 1990. *The Secular Miracle*. London: Zed Press.

Schirazi, Asghar. 1997. *The Constitution of Iran: Politics and the State in the Islamic Republic*. London: I. B. Tauris.

Sheridan, J. 1975. *China in Disintegration: The Republican Era in Chinese History: 1912–1949*. New York: Free Press.

Skocpol, Theda. 1979. *States and Social Revolution: A Comparative Analysis of France, Russia, and China*. Cambridge: Cambridge Univ. Press.

Vincent, Andrew. 1987. *Theories of State*. London: Basil Blackwell.

Tucker, Robert. 1975. *The Lenin Anthology*. New York: Norton.

Zubaida, Sami. 1989. *Islam: The People and the State*. London: Routledge.

Articles

Akhavi, Shahrough. 1987 "Elite Factionalism in the Islamic Republic of Iran." *Middle East Journal*, 41, no. 2: 181–201.

Amanat, Abbas. 1988. "In Between the Madrasa and the Marketplace: The Designation of Clerical Leadership in Modern Shi'ism." In *Authority and Poltical Culture in Shi'ism,* edited by S. A. Arjmomand. Albany: SUNY Press.

Amirahmadi, Hooshang. 1990. "Economic Reconstruction of Iran: Costing the War Damage." *Third World Quarterly,* 12, no. 1: 26–47.

Arjomand, S. A. 1993. "Constitution of Islamic Republic," in *Encyclopedia Iranica.* Vol. 6, 1993.

———. 1991. "A Victory for the Pragmatics: The Islamic Fundamentalist Reaction in Iran." In *Islamic Fundamentalism and the Gulf Crisis,* edited by James Piscatori. Chicago: Univ. of Chicago Press.

Ashraf, Ahmad. 1981. "The Roots of Emerging Dual Class Structure in Nineteenth Century Iran." *Iranian Studies,* 14.

———. 1997. "The Bazaar Mosque Alliance: From the Tobacco Rebellion to the Islamic Revolution." Unpublished manuscript.

Bakhash, Shaoul. 1989. "The Politics of Land, Law, and Social Justice in Iran." *Middle East Journal,* 43, spring: 186–201.

Baktiari, Bahman. 1993. "Parliamentary Election in Iran." *Iranian Studies,* 26, no. 3–4.

Behrooz, M. 1991. "Factionalism in Iran under Khomeini." *Middle East Studies,* 27, no. 4: 597–614.

Enayet, Hamid. 1986. "Iran: Khomeini's Concept of Guardianship of Jurisconsult." In *Islam in a World of Nation States,* edited by James Piscatori. Cambridge: Cambridge Univ. Press.

Entessar, Nader. 1994. "Factional Politics in Post-Khomeini Iran: Domestic and Foreign Policy Implications." *Journal of South Asian and Middle Eastern Studies,* 17, no. 4.

Gilbar, G. 1977. "The Big Merchants and the Persian Constitutional Revolution of 1906." *Asian and Afrian Studies,* 2.

Hooglund, Eric. 1986. "Iran 1980–85: Political and Economic Trends." In *The Iranian Revolution and the Islamic Republic,* edited by Nikki Keddie and Eric Hooglund. Syracuse: Syracuse Univ. Press.

Huntington, Samuel P. 1993. "The Clash of Civilizations" *Foreign Affairs,* 72, no. 3.

Kazemi, Farhad. 1985. "State and Society in Ideology of Devotees of Islam." *State, Culture, and Society,* 1, no. 3.

Lambton, A. 1955. "Quis Catodiet Custodes? Some Reflection of the Persian Study of Government." *Studia Islamica,* no. 5.

Milani, Mohsen. 1992. "The Transformation of the Velayet-e faqih Institution: From Khomeini to Khomeini." *Muslim World,* 82, no. 3–4: 175–90.

Moslem, Mehdi. 1995. "The Iranian Constitutional Revolution of 1905–6: The Making of a Weak State." *CSD Perspectus,* Research Paper No 6. Center for the Study of Democracy. Univ. of Westminster, London.

Nathan, A. 1973. "A Factionalism Model for CCP Politics." *China Quarterly,* Jan–March.

Nettle, A. 1968. "The State as a Conceptual Variable." *World Politics,* 20, July.

Pesaran, Hashem. 1992. "The Iranian Foreign Exchange Policy and the Black Market for Dollars." *International Journal of Middle East Studies,* 24: 101–25.

Rahnema, Ali. 1997. "Islamic Jurisprudence and Public Policy." *International Review of Comparative Public Policy,* vol. 19, 118–19.

Ramazani, R. K. 1992. "Iran's Foreign Policy: Both North and South." *Middle East Journal,* 46: 393–412.

Sheikholeslami, A. Reza. 1986. "From Religious Accomodation to Religious Revolution." In *The State, Religion, and Ethnic Politics: Afghanistan, Iran, and Pakistan,* edited by A. Banuazzi and M. Weimer. Syracuse: Syracuse Univ. Press.

Siavoshi, Susan. 1992. "Factionalism and Iranian Politics: The Post-Khomeini Experience." *Iranian Studies,* 25, no. 3–4: 27–49.

Tabari, Azar. 1983. "Shii Clergy in Iranian Politics." In *Religion and Politics in Iran,* edited by Nikki Keddie. New Haven: Yale Univ. Press.

Tilly, Charles. 1975. "Reflections on the History of European State-Making," in *The Formation of National States in Western Europe,* edited by Charles Tilly. Princeton: Princeton Univ. Press.

Index

343